HANDICAPPING 101

FINDING THE RIGHT HORSES AND MAKING THE RIGHT BETS

BRAD FREE

DRF PRESS
New York

Published by
Daily Racing Form Press
100 Broadway, 7th Floor
New York, NY 10005

ISBN: 0-9726401-7-7
Library of Congress Control Number: 2003113644

Jacket designed by Chris Donofry
Text design by Neuwirth and Associates

Printed in the United States of America

All entries, results, charts and related information provided by

EQUIBASE
C O M P A N Y

821 Corporate Drive • Lexington, KY 40503-2794 Toll Free (800) 333-2211 or
(859) 224-2860; Fax (859) 224-2811 • Internet: www.equibase.com

The Thoroughbred Industry's Official Database for Racing Information

CONTENTS

ACKNOWLEDGMENTS

This text could not have been completed without help from a lot of good people, to whom I owe a huge debt of gratitude. It started one afternoon at Del Mar, when *Daily Racing Form* president Charlie Hayward outlined the idea for an introductory book on handicapping. But I had never gone a route of ground. Could a sprinter for a daily newspaper stretch out to two turns by writing a book?

Thanks to the generosity of colleagues, friends, and family, the answer is yes. Their charitable advice, honest critiques, and enthusiasm enabled this project to reach the finish line. For all those responsible for helping bring to life *Handicapping 101,* I am forever appreciative.

A sincere thank-you goes to many at *Daily Racing Form.* They include Charlie Hayward, who trusted this could be written; Steven Crist, who offered encouragement and guidance on the original manuscript; Robin Foster, whose meticulous copyediting smoothed out the bumps; and Chris Donofry and Dean Keppler.

It is my good fortune to consider as friends many of the country's top handicappers. I learned from them, and also leaned on them. They include premier handicapping teacher James Quinn, and pace expert Tom Brohamer. Quinn and Brohamer provided invaluable assistance throughout this project. Andrew Beyer and Barry Meadow, two of the country's most enthusiastic and opinionated horseplayers, donated time and provided direction.

Horsemen graciously offered knowledge and insight. They include jockey Jerry Bailey and trainers Jack Carava, Vladimir Cerin, and Craig Lewis. Others who assisted include racing officials Rick Hammerle and Mike Harlow; publicists Vince Bruun and Jack Disney; veterinarian Dr. Rick Arthur; Equibase's David O'Neill; The Jockey Club's John Cooney; clockers Gary Young and Larry Zap; and Tracy Gantz of Thoroughbred Owners of California.

The guy stuck next to me every day—Steve Andersen of *Daily Racing Form*—picked up my slack during completion of *Handicapping 101*. It could not have been finished without Andersen's relief help. In Southern California press boxes, I am fortunate to compete with—and learn from—leading newspaper handicappers Jerry Antonucci, Bob Ike, Jack Karlik, Bob Mieszerski, and Jeff Siegel.

Numerous horseplayers offered specific or general assistance, including Kurt Hoover, John Lies, Steve Nagler, and Lee Tomlinson. And this book could not have been completed without two early influences. It was *Pasadena Star-News* entertainment reporter Luaine Lee who opened the door to journalism, and *Star-News* sports editor Kevin Bronson who kicked me in the pants once I got inside. Thank you both.

My mom, Marcia Free-Munro, taught how to laugh at myself. My dad, Ed Free, used to carry me on his shoulders through the gates at Santa Anita. It's still my favorite racetrack, though I'd just as soon be home, where I am lucky enough to share love and laughter with my three kids—Laura, Sarah, and Michael. Their smiles make everything right.

Finally, this handicapping book was written mostly because of lasting support and trust from my best friend. That she happens to also be my wife is just an added bonus. Thank you, Maureen.

INTRODUCTION

All right, I confess. In the summer of 1986, when I was hired to be a handicapper for the *Pasadena Star-News,* a small daily newspaper in California, I did not know a lot about being a winning horseplayer. Chalk it up to being young and naïve.

Back then, of course, it did not matter much. Chasing dreams was less expensive on an entry-level sportswriter's salary. But I reasoned that as long as I did not blow my entire paycheck or my career, there was plenty of time to get horse racing all figured out. What I did not count on was that nearly 20 years later I would still be learning on the job. Good grief.

Once upon a time, I thought winning at the races required little more than good handicapping. All you need is to pick winners, right? Well, not quite. Today there are so many skilled handicappers out there that selection of winning horses can only be the first step. Believe it or not, a bettor also must know how to find losers. And, one needs to know how and when to wager. There are a lot of choices. To win consistently, a bettor frequently must separate himself from the crowd. That means knowing what the crowd is doing, and why. Betting on the favorite every race just won't get it done.

"You make your biggest gains . . . not by doing the accepted stuff better but by doing something totally innovative." While statistician Craig Wright was talking about baseball, the idea applies to racing. Logical, creative handicapping that dares to be different affords bettors a reasonable chance to win. Sometimes, being different means nothing more than being prepared. And the potential gains? They are both huge and attainable, so long as one recognizes the chief handicapping principles.

More than $15 billion was wagered on Thoroughbred races in the United States in 2002. It is big business. People just like you and I enjoy betting horse races, particularly when it is possible to generate consistent winnings. Funny thing is, racing prospers despite boundless contradictions. None is more curious than the resigned attitude of bettors who concede that gambling defeat is the cost of having fun. With a shoulder shrug, a large portion of racing's fan base simply accepts the notion that losing is part of the game. Losses are permitted, and usually expected. An occasional win? It must be accidental fortune, preparation not required.

Sure, it may be amusing to wager on a horse without considering details. Haven't we all bet on a stupid hunch? But there is an alternative to luck. Believe it. Racing is a game that can be won—through logic, examination, and discipline. Winning at the races is an elusive goal, for sure. Yet scores of successful horseplayers, rather than inviting fate, apply principles of handicapping, consider the element of chance, wager accordingly, and come out ahead. The notion that all horseplayers ultimately lose is just not true. Lose frequently, yes. Lose inevitably, no.

It is tempting to suggest this book will provide all horseplayers—from novices to longtime fans—with the ultimate keys to parimutuel success in the new millennium. But there can be no false assurances in the teeth of the parimutuel dilemma: Only about 80 cents of every dollar wagered is returned each race to winning bettors. The other 20 cents is raked for a variety of expenses including operating costs, purses, state parimutuel taxes, and breeders' fees. The gambling levy is steep. No kidding. Little wonder racing does not produce more winning bettors.

The upside to racing is that, unlike casino games, odds are not fixed. In racing, there is always a chance to make a score because the odds fluctuate based on bettors' determination of each horse's chances. The horse that attracts the most betting support is the favorite, and usually the most likely winner. Making the determination requires knowing which factors contribute to, or limit, a horse's chances. It's called handicapping, and is based on the premise that horse racing is quantifiable and predictable. Horses, like people, possess individual habits and various degrees of ability. Horseplayers able to recognize and interpret said characteristics discover that winnings are within reach.

Trouble is, not all horseplayers are equal, and the distinction is important. Beginning handicappers rarely win by jumping ahead of their skills. Doing so invites as much trouble as a novice downhill skier attempting to negotiate an expert run. Likewise, in racing, few rookie bettors are qualified to assess the chances of a longshot first-time starter. Before becoming an expert, every horseplayer was a novice. Of course, even novices get lucky sometimes. Often, luckier than they dreamed possible.

In early 1986, trying to finish college at California State University, Los Angeles, I was working part-time as an agate clerk in the sports department of the *Pasadena Star-News*. It was spring, and Snow Chief had burst forth as the 3-year-old star. A dark bay, almost black California-bred with a head-low-to-the-ground running style, Snow Chief swept to consecutive stakes wins at Santa Anita, Bay Meadows, and Gulfstream Park. Finally, a six-length romp in the Santa Anita Derby made Snow Chief the rightful favorite for the Kentucky Derby.

I was a brash, unsophisticated horseplayer with nothing more than confidence and a *Daily Racing Form* habit. It was Derby season, after all, the best time to stay informed and generate an opinion. Ferdinand did not finish close to Snow Chief in the Santa Anita Derby, but I thought his third-place effort was better than it looked, and that he might be an improving colt heading into May. After reading a Joe Hirsch "Derby Doings" report that chronicled Ferdinand's sensational workout at Churchill Downs in company with the brilliant filly Hidden Light, I climbed out on a limb.

Between important *Star-News* duties such as answering calls from high-school coaches and typing in game scores, I proclaimed all week that the 1986 Derby would be won by a longshot. I made a good-sized wager—win and place—through a local bookmaker, on Ferdinand, trained by Charlie Whittingham and ridden by Bill Shoemaker. A killer pace battle foiled Snow Chief, Shoemaker gave Ferdinand a legendary ride, and the chestnut won by 2¼ lengths. His $2 win-place payoffs were $37.40 and $16.20. I had him at full track odds, with bragging rights for all eternity.

The money, of course, is long spent. But the accurate Derby prediction so impressed the *Star-News* sports editor that two months later, when veteran public handicapper Ernie Mason retired, I was tabbed to replace him. It's a good thing such failed Derby predictions as Balto Star and Three Ring occurred later in my career.

If Ferdinand had lost, I might still be writing stories about high-school sports. But getting lucky on the right spring day in 1986 led to the biggest break of my career. Sometimes timing is everything. I was hired as a public handicapper. I admit, not a very good one at first. But with plenty of time to learn.

Most horseplayers, regardless of proficiency, fit a general description:

- Winning handicappers constantly seeking to improve their game.
- Break-even bettors that are almost winners, but not quite.
- Losing horseplayers just hoping to break even.
- Beginning handicappers wondering where to start.
- Sporting enthusiasts without regard for profit, so long as the betting is accompanied by good food and conversation.

So which description fits you? Be honest, no one is looking. Truth is, winning at the races is neither easy nor impossible. But first, one must know how to handicap, which is one reason for this text. Inside, new racing fans will find an introduction, while veteran handicappers may welcome the refresher. For both, the goal is the same—to win money by wagering logically on Thoroughbred races. Successful horseplayers everywhere do it every day, yet the notion of a regular guy winning consistently is an idea that rarely finds its way into racetrack advertising. Too bad, because the goal is attainable and familiar.

A few wise guys have always claimed to beat the game, including some that actually did. Pittsburgh Phil, a legendary turn-of-the-century gambler, reportedly made nearly $3 million wagering on horses before he died in 1905. He was in the minority then, but now it is clear that there was more to Pittsburgh Phil's success than luck. He uncovered an element of predictability to Thoroughbred racing. Horses that win races share distinct traits. Losers, too. Pittsburgh Phil dared to refer to handicapping as a science.

That was 100 years ago, yet even today casual sports fans see racing as a nut that cannot be cracked. They may not realize that both horses and horseplayers are creatures of habit. Using a little bit of common sense, one can perceive their inclinations. A reasonable person can view and comprehend a horse's race record, note current conditions, and arrive at a sensible determination of a horse's chances to win a race. An average person applying basic handicapping techniques can identify the most probable winner, most of the time. If you do not know how, you will soon.

Likewise, many old-school horseplayers remain as predictable as the sun, repeatedly applying the same ideas and making the same mistakes. Many adhere to unimaginative strategies, trading short-term gratification for long-term loss. Bet the favorite every race, and losses are guaranteed. You will see why. Beginning handicappers start with a clean slate, free from bad habits. Even novices can comprehend basics, recognize nuances, and be rewarded. The idea has been around for a while.

At the turn of the century, Pittsburgh Phil's triumphs were scarcely proclaimed. To gamblers, horse racing was merely a game of chance. The perception continued even after the 1930's, when the first in a series of handicapping books by Robert Saunders Dowst suggested otherwise. Few noticed. Betting horses was considered guesswork, gambling profit accidental. The progression of handicapping knowledge stalled.

As times changed, sophistication advanced. Soon, daring bettors began to challenge the notion that the odds were always stacked against the horseplayer. In 1966, author Tom Ainslie published *The Compleat Horseplayer,* in which he presented contemporary handicapping methods based on logic. It was a novel approach, followed by the 1968 handicapping benchmark *Ainslie's Complete Guide to Thoroughbred Racing.* Ainslie refused to believe that horseplayers are just a bunch of suckers. He saw then what is evident now—that capable handicappers can win money betting on horses. By applying logic, reason, and discipline to the facts, bettors can override the luck factor. Today, sensible fans from diverse backgrounds are able to mull the nuances of a horse race, arrive at a rational determination of the probable outcome, and wager accordingly. These are regular folks who generate unusual results—wagering profit.

I was four years old my first day at the races, during the 1963 winter meet at Santa Anita. I don't remember a thing, but my dad maintains it was a winning day. I believe him. It possibly is one reason I ended up as a handicapper for *Daily Racing Form*. Forty years ago, of course, parental instinct precluded my dad from suggesting that horse-race wagering could generate consistent profit, nor did he advise his son to consider handicapping as a profession. After all, betting horses was, and is, considered little more than recreation. So it was when I began wagering regularly as a teenager in the 1970's.

Early on, my main reason for betting horses was the sheer thrill of gambling. Whatever attempts I made at prudent handicapping decisions were based on only a few factors—mostly current form and class. Back then, I had never even heard of Dowst, Ainslie, or Andrew Beyer. The only speed figures I considered were the old-style speed ratings published in *Daily Racing Form*. Oh, how innocent.

At some point, probably because of an advertising barrage that promised winners, I started to believe horseplayers actually had a chance. Once, I paid $25 to a tout service that promised to reveal the winning daily double, and three exactas, at Santa Anita. The "exclusive release" produced a daily double that returned $14 for $2. The exactas ran out. I probably could have done as well myself and saved the fee. Or back then, maybe not.

I have purchased and experimented with mechanical systems. No shame admitting it now. Chalk it up to the education of a horseplayer. One of the most unique was "The Winning Formula," by L. D. Hurley. The system had promise. It measured "class" using guidelines based on purse earnings, with qualifications to determine current condition. Purchase of the formula included a betting scheme called the 5-for-5 Wagering Plan. For one long summer playing Del Mar, the system led to a good share of winners. My bankroll yo-yoed, and I wound up breaking even.

If "The Winning Formula" worked long-term, I would still use it. I suppose in a way I still do. The element of class remains an essential consideration. Yet what I have learned is that no factor stands alone. While there are means to evaluate class, the measure cannot be boiled into a digit. Handicapping is a layered, multidimensional process that requires consideration of multiple factors. That is what this book is about.

While there is a wealth of information available to modern horseplayers, there are also a greater number of educated handicappers to compete against. It's a tough game, with new ideas all the time. Old methods are overshadowed by advanced considerations. It can become confusing. Many longtime horseplayers have been left behind, not knowing where to look, or even what handicapping factors to consider.

Beyer's *Picking Winners* in 1975 created a revolution, calling for bettors to analyze and interpret exactly how fast horses ran, and how fast they might run again. Jim Quinn's *The Handicapper's Condition Book* in 1981 revamped the subject of class. The text provided guidelines to determine a horse's proper level of competition—majors, minors, or Little League? Then came pace experts Tom Brohamer and William Quirin, whose contributions required bettors to comprehend a horse's rate of speed, such as feet per second. It is enough to make one's head spin. Which factor to use? Where is it found? How does it apply?

A lazy gambler might just shrug off the details, and hide behind the idea that winning and losing at the races boils down mostly to good luck and bad luck. Except that it does not. Horse racing carries a high degree of built-in predictability—favorites win one out of every three races. Horses have habits, along with the people who train, ride, and wager on them. Despite a perceived glut of information, handicapping methods can be simplified and separated into manageable, understandable applications.

This text will not attempt to redefine handicapping theory. There is no reason to. Rather, it will offer an understandable approach to playing the races in the 21st century. It will sort and clarify ideas that might be considered complex. There is plenty to get caught up on. Nearly 40 years ago, Ainslie ushered in a new breed of horseplayer, one whose wagering decisions were based on deductive reasoning. As horseplayers became increasingly educated, the element of luck became less significant.

This book offers a contemporary explanation of basic handicapping truths—what works, and what does not. Winning at the races does not require a computer or a Ph.D., only that horseplayers possess a basic understanding of racing's mechanics. A sensible approach using proper tools.

Successful bettors do not need to know everything. No one does, anyway. *Handicapping 101* will separate the feasible from the impractical, reality from fantasy. I have chased enough pick-six carryovers, with little success, to recognize that there probably is no pick-six jackpot out there with my name on it. But I do know this: Educated bettors stand more than a fair chance wagering against uninformed racetrack gamblers, of which there are plenty.

Ideas employed by successful horseplayers will be detailed herein, with caution. Handicapping theory is universal, personal preference is not. What works for one horseplayer does not always work for another. This text, hopefully, will allow handicappers to discover an individual style of playing and winning at the races.

The approaches presented here are based on 30 years of betting on the races, and nearly 20 years as a public newspaper handicapper, the last 12 for *Daily Racing Form*. I still make mistakes. Who doesn't? They are part of the game, and if you can learn from them, you can live with them. Just don't make them again.

By now, you would think that all racing's precise nuances might be understood. Except for one thing—many subtleties have been exposed as utterly useless. Not to oversimplify, but good handicapping usually boils down to four related concerns. They are: current condition, which is a measure of a horse's present health and ability; class, the level of competition at which a horse is qualified or not; speed, the time required to complete a race; and pace, the rate of speed at which a horse travels during different parts of a race.

The interpretation and application of those four factors—condition, class, speed, and pace—constitute much of this book. Novices need not worry. Those primary elements, and others that are less critical, will be explained in understandable terms.

Readers should know that there are no quick and easy shortcuts to playing the races. It is too bad, because the initial chapter of a handicapping text might include enticing promises to unlock every secret. It might include simple instructions to uncover racing's riches. The delusion is as old as racing. It is one reason why most bettors wagering on horses still lose. Gamblers have long imagined the existence of clear-cut formulas that predetermine the outcome of a race. There has to be an easy way. Surely, handicapping can be simplified, quantified, and sanitized. Get rich quick.

Problem is, no handicapper or system can find every winner, though many try. In this game, you will be wrong a lot more often than you will be right. That is okay, because frequency is not the benchmark; success is measured only by the bottom line. Soon, you will see the flaw in old-fashioned rationale that suggests this game is about finding winners. It is true a handicapper must know how to pick winners, but it is more important to understand the reasons why winners are picked.

This text will explain legitimate handicapping, and why it requires room for interpretation, margin for error. The clues in these pages are merely logical applications. A reasonable person will grasp ideas that work, recognize their significance, and reach sensible conclusions most of the time. Good handicapping is only as complex as a bettor makes it. Usually, X plus Y equals Z. In these pages, you will learn to recognize situations in which it does not, and what to do about it, if anything.

You will acquire the ability to analyze a horse's past performances, focus on information that is relevant, and filter out what is not. Soon, you will recognize that there is an awful lot of superfluous information floating about, minor details that do little except bog down the handicapping process. For example, fast workouts or jockey changes. While this incidental trivia is sometimes meaningful, a great deal of it is largely irrelevant. Scrap it.

The challenge in becoming a successful horseplayer goes beyond applying someone else's ideas. Winning bettors do pattern methods after the success of others, but copycat techniques rarely hold up long-term. In a letter to *Daily Racing Form*, San Francisco horseplayer Sal Raguso expressed the handicapper's dilemma. "Finding the truth at the racetrack is no different than finding it outside the track. It must come from within ourselves. Someone else's truth about anything will never work for you. Each of us must find his own version of the truth."

The goal is to allow you to find your own way. This text will illustrate practical methods to select winners and avoid losers. It will explain where relevant factors are found in the past performances of each horse, how and when they apply, and how their significance can be gauged. Questions will be asked, and answered. How does one determine the chances of a first-time starter, a horse who has never raced? Is a drop in class good, or bad? How do you know? How can one determine if a horse is qualified for a raise in class, a jump to face stronger competition? Do jockeys and trainers make any difference? And the bottom-line query: What chance does a particular horse really have?

Wagering practice will be defined, and allow for personal resolution. A sensible wager for one bettor is not necessarily right for another. In this text, horseplayers will learn when and why to wager, and when merely to pass. You will not bet every race, because not every field of runners includes an overlay. Usually, the wagering public gets it right by "pricing" the odds to accurately reflect the true chances of the contenders. Bettors who insist on wagering on every race, without an advantage, are guaranteed to lose. You will see why.

You also will understand why it usually is unwise to make the same types of bets as the horseplayer seated next to you. A $2 bettor does not wager the same as a $100 bettor, though both players have like chances for parimutuel success.

A handicapper who has learned how to pick and bet on winners is not finished with the job. Handicapping is science, art, and a lot of continuing education. It evolves. Successful horseplayers grow and learn, challenge old ideas, and experiment with new ones. To win consistently, horseplayers must consider no truth impenetrable. There is no blueprint for playing the races. Bettors are urged to learn from others. In fact, collaborations are encouraged, so long as they are profitable. Then, it is time to move on. No hard feelings.

Interestingly, handicapping tools furnished by others can be massaged to personal preference. I found this out in the 1980's, before widespread publication of Beyer Speed Figures. Using the "performance ratings" of a California speed-figure service and applying my own interpretation, I picked more winners than any other public handicapper in Southern California in my first season as a full-time turf writer. Beginner's luck? You decide. The 1988 winter meet at Santa Anita was one of the few times in my wagering career when sheer volume of winners compensated for crude wagering practice. Inside this text, you will learn to find your own interpretations regarding speed figures and betting decisions. This book will not lead you by the hand. Its goal is to point you in the right direction.

While Southern California is home for me, handicapping fundamentals apply coast to coast—to maidens at Suffolk Downs, claiming routers at Churchill Downs, and first-time starters in New York. It is not that much different anywhere. Horses run fast; the handicapper determines which are likely to run fastest. *Handicapping 101* explains how Thoroughbreds run, and how they *will* run. It will clarify the questions, and provide tools for you to find your own answers. The questions change with every race.

My wagering philosophy promises no pots of gold. I rarely play the pick six. Less adventurous wagers make more sense, for reasons that will be made clear. For example, you will see how the pick four can be managed to a profitable return. You also will learn concrete strategies, and accompanying pitfalls, for other exotic wagers such as trifectas and superfectas.

There is purpose to the order of the chapters. We start with a description of handicapping, an explanation of past performances, and their intended use. Next, the handicapping chapters begin with the premise under which all other considerations must be interpreted. That is, current form, analyzing the health and current ability of a horse. The chapter on form precedes one on class, and asks the question, is this horse racing at the right level?

Speed and pace are next. The application of speed figures is not as tough as it sounds. It will be addressed accordingly, and this book will provide the necessary tools. Pace, rate of speed, will be explained. Gaining an understanding of how horses accelerate, and decelerate, allows a bettor to grasp the dynamics of an actual race.

Next we will address the "why" behind a horse's odds, and show that winning bettors do not have to agree with other horseplayers, so long as one understands how others arrive at their decisions. Parimutuel success does not require one to pick more winners, only to make a greater number of intelligent bets.

In *Handicapping 101*, you will find your best plan for winning at the races. It will show how to start from scratch, or polish skills you already have. It will reveal the spirit of the successful handicapper, and refute the idea that all horseplayers eventually lose.

Sure, a lot of good horseplayers still do not quite break even. This text may give them a push. And really, what is better than an afternoon of prepared gambling on horse races? Especially when it is possible to finish with more money than you started with.

CHAPTER 1

PAST
PERFORMANCES

An individual horseplayer never can know it all,
which is all right. Winning at the races does not require universal wisdom. Anyway, the numbers are too big. In 2002 in the
United States and Canada alone, 34,025 Thoroughbreds were
born, while 59,896 races were run. Try keeping track of every
horse and every race, and the only thing you get is dizzy.

Make no mistake. A handicapper does process a good deal of
relevant information. But trying to analyze and interpret too
many details can bog down a handicapper, just as excess computer files slow down a hard drive. It's okay to delete the stuff
you don't use. A good handicapper does not need to know everything. Really.

Horseplayers can keep it simple by first recognizing one of
racing's great truths. The betting favorite—the horse on which
the most money is wagered—wins one out of three races. The
trend holds year after year, from one racetrack to another. It's a
wonderful, reliable statistic. The ratio means that the horse perceived to have the best attributes wins a good portion of all
races. Talk about reassuring. A bettor stuck in a prolonged losing streak need not look far for help. Experts are everywhere—
the betting public picks the winner one-third of the time.

The 33 percent frequency affords comfort. Chicken soup for the horseplayer. It affirms that horse races are, in both theory and fact, relatively predictable. One only needs to know what to look for in the past performances, which are the racing records of the horses—what they mean, and how that information applies. In order to find the most likely winner of a horse race, all it usually takes is common sense.

The principles that affect the interpretation and application of a horse's race record—handicapping—have held true since records were first kept. Sure, racing has changed over the years. What hasn't? But the best, fastest horses still win most of the races. And when the newborn foals of spring 2004 begin to race in spring 2006, they will conform to most of the same handicapping tenets that affected their sires and dams.

This chapter introduces those principles, and the records—past performances—on which handicapping is based. Along the way, there will be some explanation of equine terms. You know most of them already.

Horses are foaled, or born, early in the year, mostly in February, March, and April. They typically weigh about 90 pounds, at times as much as 125 pounds, wobble to their feet within minutes of birth, and face a future that seems stacked against them.

Nearly one out of three Thoroughbreds will never start in a race, and almost half will never win. According to statistics compiled by The Jockey Club, 55 percent of the registered Thoroughbreds foaled in North America in the 10-year span from 1985 through 1994 retired from racing as "maidens"—horses who never won a race. Multiple winners were scarcer yet. Only one out of three foals (1985-1994) won more than once.

Beauty and grace aside, Thoroughbreds are far from perfect. Susceptible to injury and illness, many are structurally flawed and unable to withstand the rigors of training, much less competition. No matter how regally bred, some Thoroughbreds are simply not meant to be athletes.

By the time Thoroughbreds grow to full size, most weighing more than a half-ton, they have been through plenty. The initial hope is for a horse to have no glaring physical defects, so that he will be rugged enough to cope with the rigors of training. Many do not; some horses fall to pieces the first time they work three furlongs (three-eighths of a mile) at full speed. Others fall apart at five furlongs. Bear in mind this is only practice.

But miracles happen. Horses reveal enough ability during practice training sessions to justify competition, and they win races. It is in their blood. Thoroughbreds literally are born to run. Even as yearlings, horses that are one year old, they race against each other in open fields, as if the competition for which they were bred has already begun.

A lot happens before a horse runs in a race. Thoroughbreds typically begin preparation for a racing career before their second "birthday." January 1 is considered the universal birthday for Thoroughbreds, two to four months ahead of their "true" birthday. By the time horses turn 2, most have begun early training, and have experienced the weight of a rider on their backs. By early in their 2-year-old year, many have run full speed for an eighth of a mile, or a quarter-mile, at a racetrack or training center. Actual competition is right around the corner, at which time the horse begins to compile a racing record. For horseplayers, that is where the fun begins.

Horses typically begin to race as early as spring of their 2-year-old season, and about one-third of the crop will start at least once during the year. By the end of their second season as 3-year-olds, nearly 60 percent will have started at least once.

Thoroughbreds are sometimes considered fragile, but only because the demands placed on them are so great. Their careers typically last only two to three years. The average number of career starts, for horses who do start, is just 21. Dr. Rick Arthur, one of the country's most respected equine veterinarians, was asked why the careers are seemingly so brief.

"You could take these horses and turn them into riding horses and they'll last forever," he said. "But we ask them to perform at the very limit of their physical ability. We have bred these horses for 300 years to be competitive, and some horses will give you every ounce they have, and sometimes they will give you more than they have. Therein lies the problem. They try to exceed the limits of their own ability."

No wonder racehorses' careers are so short. They are asked to run full speed, time after time, and they do wear out. Racing is tough—on horses, owners, breeders, and trainers. As for handicappers, we have it relatively easy. All we have to do is analyze a horse and a race, one at a time. We may not like what happens after we place a bet, but we do not have to pay to feed the horses the next morning.

A Thoroughbred's inherent ability becomes increasingly clear once he commences full training. During full-speed exercise under a rider, horses begin to reveal distinct traits. In timed workouts, they may show they are quick, perhaps suited to sprint races of six furlongs, which is three-quarters of a mile, or less. Sprinters achieve full speed in the first quarter-mile of a race, then decelerate the rest of the way. Others distribute their energy gradually. They may utilize a steady-paced running style suited for longer races at one mile or more, in which stamina is important. Whereas sprinters are trained to race at top speed from the moment the starting gates open, distance horses, often called routers, may be trained to conserve energy in the early part of the race, and call on those reserves later. That is, go slow early and fast late.

The physical build of a racehorse is key to his future. A big, stocky, powerful horse with large hind muscles may be well suited to a sprint race in which a fast start and aggressive running style are essential. The horse would be built for speed. Conversely, long-distance specialists typically are leaner and longer. While not as quick as sprinters, route horses are able to carry their speed over longer distances.

As trainers become familiar with the idiosyncrasies of their young horses, and gain an idea of their level of ability, they face daily challenges. Craig Lewis trained Santa Anita Derby winner Larry the Legend and Hollywood Gold Cup winner Cutlass Reality. He describes the trials in training a half-ton Thoroughbred.

"When people go to work every morning, they put their car key in the ignition, and turn that key. Most of the time, that car starts. That's not true with a horse. Every single day is an adventure, there's always something that you don't want to see, or have happen. That's what makes this game so difficult, so demanding. You have to overcome things all the time."

Frequent setbacks include minor illnesses such as a cough or fever, or seemingly inconsequential injuries such as a bruised foot. These can throw a horse's entire schedule into disarray. Say, for example, the horse was scheduled for a workout on Tuesday to prepare for a race on Saturday. If the horse gets sick and the workout is canceled, his preparation for the race will be compromised. It happens often, sometimes at the worst possible time.

A bruised foot may have cost Empire Maker the 2003 Kentucky Derby. The bruise forced him to miss two crucial days of training less than a week before the Derby, and it showed in his performance. Instead of running right past Funny Cide as he had done in the Wood Memorial three weeks earlier, Empire Maker was flat for the stretch drive and finished a disappointing second behind the horse he had easily defeated in his previous start.

Another example of the uncertain nature of Thoroughbred health occurred during the summer of 2002. The Dubai-based stable Godolphin Racing Inc. sent more than three dozen expensive and well-bred 2-year-olds to the United States, with an eye on the summer's top races at Del Mar. The monetary value of the stable was staggering—20 of the runners had been purchased at auction for a total of $21.8 million, and another 17 were either bred by Godolphin or purchased privately. Expectations were high.

But when an illness swept through the Del Mar barns in July and August, it did not spare Godolphin. For nearly a month, from August 12 through September 6, not a single Godolphin 2-year-old started at Del Mar. The racing season there lasts just seven weeks, and ended without a Godolphin victory. By the time the stable's runners recovered, the summer season was lost. A year earlier, the Godolphin 2-year-old program accounted for the Breeders' Cup Juvenile Fillies with champion Tempera. She and graded stakes winner Essence of Dubai led the stable to a strong 2001 season during which it won 21 races and more than $1.7 million in purses. But in late 2002, the multimillion-dollar stable of 2-year-olds returned to Dubai, having earned only $285,580.

No matter how much money is spent, it is not an easy game. Illness aside, horses sustain a variety of injuries while training or racing. Though often not serious, the setbacks compromise schedules. Most of these minor injuries are related to horses' feet. Cracked hooves, bruised feet, and torn foot tissue, called grabbed quarters, are common maladies. Beyond these problems, a horse's level of ability soon becomes evident. Some horses run fast, others are relatively slow, others somewhere in between. Eventually, most horses gravitate to races in which they compete against runners of similar ability.

Handicappers and horses meet when the horse enters his first race. Here, expectations are fulfilled and surprises emerge. The most expensive yearling in 1998, Fusaichi Pegasus, was sold for $4 million and went on to win the 2000 Kentucky Derby. The most expensive horse ever was Seattle Dancer, sold in 1985 for a staggering $13.1 million long before he had ever raced. The colt was a half-brother to Triple Crown winner Seattle Slew, meaning that they had the same mother, but Seattle Dancer would never match his sibling's achievements. Seattle Dancer raced five times, won twice, and earned $164,728.

On the flip side are rags-to-riches stories. John Henry was a $1,700 yearling purchase and a $20,000 claiming horse before he developed into a two-time Horse of the Year. Funny Cide was an inexpensive gelding who in 2003 won the Kentucky Derby and the Preakness Stakes, the first two legs of racing's Triple Crown.

Thoroughbred owners, both those who breed their own runners and those who buy unraced yearlings and 2-year-olds, invest large sums of money without knowing for certain if a particular horse will pan out. In that regard, handicappers have it easy, even with first-time starters. By the time a horse reaches competition for the first time, his pedigree, trainer, and morning workouts often provide sufficient evidence on which to reasonably predict the horse's chance to win his first career start.

A horse's nuances emerge over several races, when it becomes clear just how fast a horse can run and the level of competition at which the horse performs best. Preferences regarding running style, distance, and surface also emerge. Over time, answers to obvious questions become clear. How good is this horse? How fast can he run? Under what conditions does he run best? When might he be compromised? Do the conditions of today's race compromise or enhance his chances?

Race Charts: The Box Score

Thoroughbred performances are recorded as they are for human athletes. A "race chart" is horse racing's version of a baseball box score. By showing where a horse was positioned during a race, and the margins between runners at specific points, a chart provides a vivid account of what transpired during the course of a race. A handicapper can view a race chart and envision how the race unfolded. There is little question that a race chart offers a greater precision than the box scores of other sports.

A baseball box score may show that a batter went 3 for 5 (three hits from five at-bats), which is a very good game. But the box score may not reveal those three hits were scratch singles that squirted off the end of the bat and trickled into the outfield. In the box score, the lucky hits are indistinguishable from a line drive that whizzed over the shortstop's head. Another hitter may go 0 for 5, but those outs may have been hard-hit shots nailed directly at an opposing fielder. In baseball, the entire story sometimes does not show up in a box score.

But there is no place to hide in a race chart. It gives you the who, what, where, when, and how of a race, exactly as it unfolded. In a chart, there is no denying a good performance, even one that did not result in victory. The performances are that clear. A race chart shows the speed at which a horse ran, and how hard he battled. A race chart distinguishes between a line drive and a scratch single. It shows whether a horse ran a good or bad race, and circumstances that may have affected the performance. The race chart is the foundation for most subsequent handicapping decisions.

Race charts are recorded initially by "chart callers," who narrate the racing action to a stenographer or tape recorder while the race is being run. The chart caller notes the position (first, second, etc.) of each horse at specific stages in the race, known as points of call. The caller also notes the margin between horses. For example, Horse A may lead by one length over Horse B, who leads Horse C by a half-length. Races are electronically timed, and the clocking is merged with the chart caller's narrative account. The information is input into a computer. Within minutes, a chart is produced by Equibase, the racing industry's official race-chart supplier.

The following page shows a race chart and its various elements.

Conditions

Medication and Equipment

Fractional Distances

Post Position

Last Race

Age

Running Positions + Lengths in Front of Next Horse

ELEVENTH RACE

Gulfstream

FEBRUARY 14, 2004

$1\frac{1}{16}$ MILES. (1.40[1]) 58TH RUNNING OF THE FOUNTAIN OF YOUTH. Grade II. Purse $250,000 FOR THREE YEAR OLDS. By subscription of $250 each which shall accompany the nomination, $2,000 to pass the entry box and $2,000 additional to start. Weight: 122 lbs. Non–winners of $75,000 once at a mile or over, allowed, 2 lbs.; $50,000 once at any distance or $30,000 at a mile or over, 4 lbs.; $30,000 at any distance or $24,000 twice at a mile or over, 6 lbs. Horses finishing first, second or third in the Fountain of Youth Stakes will automatically be nominated to the Florida Derby. Trophy to winning Owner. Closed Wednesday, February 4 2004 with (8) nominations. Early Bird Florida Derby Nominations Closed on Wednesday, November 12, 2003 with 160 nominations.

Value of Race: $250,000 Winner $150,000; second $50,000; third $27,500; fourth $15,000; fifth $7,500. Mutuel Pool $1,034,656.00 Exacta Pool $583,794.00 Trifecta Pool $484,686.00 Superfecta Pool $157,116.00

Last Raced	Horse	M/Eqt	A. Wt	PP	St	$\frac{1}{4}$	$\frac{1}{2}$	$\frac{3}{4}$	Str	Fin	Jockey	Odds $1
29Nov03 8Aqu1	Read the Footnotes	L	3 122	8	7	3$\frac{1}{2}$	3$\frac{1}{2}$	2²	2⁵	1nk	Bailey J D	2.10
17Jan04 10GP1	Second of June	L f	3 120	7	6	2¹	2$\frac{1}{2}$	1¹	1$\frac{1}{2}$	2$\frac{7}{2}$	Velasquez C	1.50
17Jan04 10GP2	Silver Wagon	L b	3 120	6	8	5hd	6³	6²	3²	3$\frac{5}{4}$	Santos J A	5.20
17Jan04 10GP4	El Prado Rob	L	3 120	3	3	7$\frac{1}{4}$	5hd	3$\frac{1}{2}$	4$\frac{1}{2}$	4$\frac{1}{2}$	Prado E S	19.90
15Nov03 10Crc1	Sir Oscar	b	3 122	1	1	4$\frac{1}{2}$	4$\frac{1}{2}$	4¹	5$\frac{1}{2}$	5nk	Garcia J A	5.20
1Jan04 9Crc2	Broadway View	L b	3 116	4	4	6$\frac{1}{2}$	7³	7⁶	7³	6$\frac{3}{4}$	Douglas R R	61.50
25Jan04 5GP1	Frisky Spider	L	3 116	2	2	1$\frac{1}{2}$	1$\frac{1}{2}$	5¹	6¹	7$\frac{1}{4}$	King E L Jr	14.70
25Jan04 5GP4	Hopefortheroses	L b	3 116	5	5	8	8	8	8	8	Aguilar M	75.30

Jockey

Odds

Weight Carried

OFF AT 5:44 Start Good. Won driving. Track fast.

Fractional Times

TIME :23⁴, :47³, 1:11¹, 1:36, 1:42³ (:23.97, :47.70, 1:11.21, 1:36.16, 1:42.71)

$2 Mutuel Prices:

8 – READ THE FOOTNOTES	6.20	3.20	2.20
7 – SECOND OF JUNE		2.60	2.20
6 – SILVER WAGON			2.60

$1 EXACTA 8–7 PAID $6.80 $1 TRIFECTA 8–7–6 PAID $17.10
$1 SUPERFECTA 8–7–6–3 PAID $79.10

B. c, (Apr), by Smoke Glacken – Baydon Belle, by Al Nasr–Fr. Trainer Violette Richard A Jr. Bred by Lawrence Goichman (NY).

READ THE FOOTNOTES stalked the pace three wide to the top of the stretch, then wore down SECOND OF JUNE in a long drive to be up at the wire. SECOND OF JUNE stalked the pace off the rail, moved to gain a slim lead outside FRISKY SPIDER leaving the backstretch, continued on gamely when challenged in the drive and just failed to last. SILVER WAGON reserved early, raced four wide on the far turn, angled in entering the stretch and closed to gain the show while unable to keep pace with the top ones. EL PRADO ROB was knocked into BROADWAY VIEW and steadied at the start, advanced off the rail to loom a threat on the far turn, then tired. SIR OSCAR tracked the pace three wide into the far turn and faltered. BROADWAY VIEW bumped at the start, saved ground and failed to be a factor. FRISKY SPIDER broke out and bumped with EL PRADO at the start, quickly moved to the fore, made the pace along the inside to nearing the far turn, then was fading when steadied inside SILVER WAGON leaving the far turn. HOPEFORTHEROSES trailed.

Owners– 1, Klaravich Stables Inc; 2, Cesare Barbara; 3, Buckram Oak Farm; 4, La Penta Robert V; 5, International Fair Play Inc; 6, Sacks Sidney; 7, Dender Carol R and Friedman Martin; 8, Rose Family Stable

Trainers– 1, Violette Richard A Jr; 2, Cesare William; 3, Ziadie Ralph; 4, Zito Nicholas P; 5, Azpurua Manuel J; 6, Procino Gerald M; 7, Durso Robert J; 8, Rose Barry R

Comments

Payoffs

Past Performances

Past performances are the accumulation of a horse's record, and are generated from race charts. Past performances are the recent racing history of a horse, and include his "running lines." The running line is transcribed from the chart, to the past performances. These are listed chronologically, with the horse's most recent effort at the top. Whereas a race chart shows what happened to every horse in a single race, past performances show every recent race of a single horse. They are what every horseplayer needs.

The legendary gambler Pittsburgh Phil described his handicapping strategy in 1905. "The secret of my betting is nothing more or less than an accurate study of past performances, present form, and a horse's willingness to run on the day of the race to the best that is in him." Nearly 100 hundred years later, little has changed.

Funny thing is, betting on horse races began long before charts were maintained. Imagine wagering on a sport in which the only records available were those a handicapper kept for himself. Think handicapping is difficult now? Try betting without knowing when, where, or how fast a horse had run.

London-born, Cleveland-raised newspaperman Frank Brunell left an indelible mark on horse racing around the turn of the 19th century. A sports editor of the *Chicago Tribune*, Brunell envisioned publication of race charts. Before 1894, there was no such thing. It was Brunell's idea that there was a market for documentation of a race. Brunell resigned from the *Tribune* to pursue his goal, and became the first publisher of *Daily Racing Form*.

The inaugural edition of *Daily Racing Form* was printed November 17, 1894. Soon, the significance of race charts was recognized. Horseplayers began to grasp the notion that a horse's future could be determined with reasonable probability by analyzing what he had done in the past. Professional gamblers such as Pittsburgh Phil had been doing it for years; the widespread publication of race charts allowed everyday folk to pick up the pastime by referring to charts when analyzing the chances of a horse.

Trouble was, it was a lot of work to thumb back through all the horse's charts. There had to be a more efficient way to display a horse's record. Brunell figured how. By transcribing the horse's individual running line from the race chart, and printing it in tabulated form on a separate sheet of paper, the horse's racing history could be displayed. It was the innovation on which most contemporary handicapping theory is based—past performances. The first past performances in *Daily Racing Form* were published June 27, 1905. No more thumbing through race charts. The history of a horse was right there on a single sheet of paper.

Past performances allow a handicapper to see the past. Analyzed properly, they allow one also to project the future. Past performances confirm that horses typically do what they have done. A horse may finish second in the first race of his career. When the horse runs again against similar competition, under similar circumstances, he is likely to run at least as well as the first time, and probably better. Horses sometimes are like kids. The first time a child tries something, he or she probably is not as good at it as the second time, right? It's the same with horses. Once they get the hang of it, and begin to understand what is expected, they improve.

Horses are creatures of habit. They do what they have done. By viewing and analyzing past performances, handicappers can figure what horses are likely to do again. That is, assuming one knows what information is important, where it is found, and when it applies.

Past performances are the most important tool for a handicapper, for they reveal most of the information required to make an intelligent prediction of what is likely to transpire in a race. That is what this book is about—viewing and interpreting a horse's past, and applying the information to arrive at a sensible determination of his probable future.

Beyond their utility for handicappers, past performances are used by a variety of racing-industry occupations. Horse traders, referred to as bloodstock agents, use past performances to buy and sell horses as they would any other commodity. Based on past performances, training regimens are modified and future matings are planned. Past performances typically are a reliable measure of current ability and allow a handicapper to forecast that horse's future with surprising accuracy. Remember—the betting public gets it right one out of three times.

There are four main factors that affect a horse's chances—current form, class, speed, and pace. Current form refers to the horse's physical condition. Class is the level of competition at which he has raced effectively. Speed is how fast the horse has run. Pace is the rate of speed at which the horse is most comfortable. Those fundamental handicapping issues—current form, class, speed, and pace—and how they relate to the race at hand, are the essentials. And they are not to be confused with incidental details such as jockey or post position. This chapter will show where the fundamentals are found. First up, a preview of the basics.

Current Form

Current form is the physical condition of the horse—now. It applies only to what a horse has done in the recent past, usually a good indicator of what a horse is capable of doing in the present. A race that occurred more than 45 days earlier might not be an indication of a horse's current form. Horses get sharp for limited periods of time, then often tail off. These patterns, or "form cycles," usually can be identified by a series of races.

The ups and downs of a racehorse's career are conspicuous. At times, a horse would rather do anything than race. Sometimes, they simply go through the motions, similar to humans. Have you ever had a bad day? Or a bad week? Horses do, too. There may or may not be anything inherently wrong. Sometimes, a horse simply needs a vacation. Who doesn't? Other times, declining performances suggest greater troubles. The form factor is addressed in detail in Chapter 2.

Class

Class is the level of competition at which a horse is suited. Not all horses are equal. Some, because they are relatively slow, may be valued as low as $2,500 and compete against horses of similar ability at minor racetracks such as Penn National in Pennsylvania, or Yavapai Downs in Arizona. Other horses may be Grade 1 caliber, racing in the most prestigious events in the country, such as the Kentucky Derby or Breeders' Cup races. Between the two extremes, there is a wide range of ability.

This diversity is why races are scheduled for various class levels. The idea is to bring together horses of similar ability. A horse able to run six furlongs in 1:09.50 at Santa Anita might be valued at $50,000 or more. That horse typically faces horses of comparable talent for prizes that may exceed $50,000. The winner of a race usually gets 60 percent of the purse.

Conversely, another horse might be able to run six furlongs at Santa Anita in only 1:10.50. That horse might be valued at $10,000 and compete for a purse of only $16,000. The faster a horse, the more money he can earn. Slow horses race against other slow horses to earn whatever they can.

From a wagering perspective, evenly matched races are most attractive. The idea is to create a balanced race with many potential outcomes, rather than a race with a standout at low odds. Not many bettors like to risk a lot to win a little. The preference is to risk a little to win a lot, and if the wagering action is spread across the entire field, winning bettors will be suitably rewarded. More on class in Chapter 3.

Speed

Speed is the measure of how fast a horse runs a particular distance. For example, six furlongs in 1:09. A horse's speed over a particular distance can be calculated into a "speed figure," which allows direct comparison of horses that raced dissimilar distances or over different racetracks. The reason is because not all the racing surfaces are the same. A horse that runs six furlongs in 1:09 at one track may run the same distance in 1:10 at a slower, deeper racetrack. Speed figures make sense of the difference.

Daily Racing Form publishes Beyer Speed Figures, and the less relevant speed ratings. Beyond enabling a handicapper to compare horses who raced at different tracks, Beyer Speed Figures allow him to compare a horse who raced six furlongs in 1:09 to another horse who raced seven furlongs in 1:22, and to determine who ran faster.

Speed figures are the most widely accepted measure of ability, and some horseplayers view them as the ultimate consideration. However, simpleminded handicapping strategy that relies primarily on speed will cause a bettor to make frequent withdrawals from the automated-teller machine. That is because a score of mitigating circumstances affect the speed at which a horse runs. No single factor stands alone, as will become evident. Chapter 4 addresses the subject of speed, and its contributing factor, pace.

Pace

There may be no greater influence on a dirt race than the rate of speed at which the race unfolds. Note the word *dirt*; grass races are altogether different. A dirt horse that typically runs to the lead might be compromised in a field with other similar front-runners. That is because the horse would be under pressure to run at a faster rate of speed to establish his customary position, and expend energy reserves long before the homestretch. Conversely, a front-runner who is able to clear his rivals without exertion often gets brave. Pace is indicated in past performances by where horses are positioned at specific points during the race, and how long it took to get there.

Late-runners do not win as often as front-runners on the main track, and often only win when a fast pace foils the speed. When the pace is slow, late-runners are compromised because the speed horses keep right on going. Many handicappers believe pace and class to be closely connected. The idea is that most horses can sustain a high rate of speed for a short distance; for example, a quarter-mile. But the higher the class, the more necessary it is to sustain rates of speed over longer distances. More on pace in Chapter 4.

The intertwined factors of form, class, speed, and pace form the basis of the handicapping "equation." Incidental factors that affect performance include peculiarities for surface and distance. Some horses prefer dirt; others prefer grass. Distance preferences also become evident. Some want to race as fast as they can start to finish, and are better suited to sprint. Others prefer longer races in which they conserve energy in the early stages. Some horses prefer racing alone, setting the pace. Others prefer to rally from behind. Golden Ticket provides a clear example of the fundamental element of class, and the incidental consideration of surface preference.

In his second career start at age 2, Golden Ticket scored an impressive maiden win. He won by 4½ lengths in fast time, and appeared to be a horse of much potential. But among traits that would become evident was Golden Ticket's deficiency in class. Following his November 12, 2000, win in a maiden race, Golden Ticket was thrown to the wolves in the Grade 1 Hollywood Futurity for 2-year-olds. The result was no surprise. Golden Ticket was trounced by Point Given, a top colt who, in his previous start, had finished second in the Breeders' Cup Juvenile. Golden Ticket's defeat in the Futurity was an early indication of his class deficiency.

Another characteristic became more pronounced. After the Futurity debacle, Golden Ticket's career floundered. He dropped lower and lower in class, finally into a $20,000 claiming race from which he was purchased by trainer Cliff Sise. Over time, Golden Ticket improved for Sise. He returned to peak form in fall 2002 and reeled off successive wins at Hollywood, moving quickly up the class ladder. When the circuit returned to Santa Anita for the winter, it was expected that Golden Ticket would maintain top form. He did not, and began another tailspin. Away from Hollywood, Golden Ticket was just another horse with a record of 1 for 9, but at Hollywood he was a monster whose record through spring 2003 was 4 for 7. These patterns are repeated time and time again.

Inasmuch as horses possess distinct inclinations, so do the men and women who train and ride them. *Daily Racing Form* past performances includes statistics for the trainers and jockeys of the horses. The jockey's record at the meet, and for the year, is listed next to his name. Trainer, too. The trainer's record in categories relevant to today's race is shown underneath the horse's workouts. These details will be examined later.

It sure does seem like a lot of stuff to consider. But the important fundamentals are form, class, speed, and pace. Handicappers should not worry about misinterpretation. Just be prepared to be wrong. Screw-ups happen. There are few right or wrong answers in handicapping. It's not a mathematical formula. What a winning horseplayer tries to do is identify the main contenders. Try to find good horses at good prices, logical horses at generous odds.

Bobby Frankel is one of the top trainers in the history of racing, with a career that includes induction into the Hall of Fame, five Eclipse Awards for outstanding trainer, six champions, and two Breeders' Cup winners. Frankel has a reputation for being brash and controversial, but he also is an astute handicapper with a dose of humility that occasionally surfaces.

One morning at Hollywood Park, Frankel was in an expansive mood when the conversation turned to training philosophy. Although Frankel has won scores of turf stakes, he rarely works his horses on turf. His horses often produce speed in races, but they rarely show speed in the morning. Frankel explained that high-speed, timed workouts are not the key to winning races. Nor does Frankel have any great secret other than common sense and keeping his horses healthy and happy. "Look, I'm not trying to outsmart the other guys," Frankel said. "I'm just trying to make fewer mistakes."

The premise applies to handicapping and wagering. While few horseplayers are able to pick more winners than the betting public, any sensible horseplayer can exploit the public's mistakes. When the crowd misinterprets a horse's chances, creative handicappers can tilt the odds in their favor. It often happens when the spotlight shines brightest. That is, big races can open the door for bettors able to adopt a daring, contradictory perspective.

For example, following an eight-month layoff, Bertrando reemerged during the 1993 winter meet at Santa Anita. He was a front-running terror with the potential to become one of the country's top handicap horses. Most bettors wagering on the Grade 1 Charles H. Strub Stakes in early February all but conceded the race to Bertrando. After all, he had demolished many of the same rivals three weeks earlier on a sloppy track, winning the Grade 2 San Fernando Stakes by nine lengths.

Though the track was labeled fast for the Strub, a repeat victory was expected. Bertrando's owners were similarly confident. Before the race, they made their way down from the box seats to watch from the rail, adjacent to the winner's circle. If he won, it would be a short walk. Bettors hammered Bertrando to odds of 3-10. In order to merely break even betting on 3-10 shots, a bettor must win 77 out of 100 wagers. Bertrando, however, had never raced a mile and a quarter, and he was running on different footing. It was a lot to ask.

The crowd had overestimated Bertrando, and underestimated Siberian Summer. Though he was unplaced at 6-1 in the sloppy-track San Fernando, he was sure to appreciate a return to a fast surface for the Strub. Siberian Summer did not figure to win, but he had a chance. An above-average chance, it turned out. Odds-on favorite Bertrando found the Strub's 1¼-mile distance too far, and Siberian Summer wore him down in deep stretch. He returned $34.40.

When a logical contender starts at inflated odds, a bold horse-player makes the bet and contradicts all those who consider any race a foregone conclusion.

It does not require decades of practice to learn to handicap, though racing stories in mainstream media often fall short in providing the type of objective analysis normally included in coverage of other sports.

A baseball story, for example, may refer to a pitcher's earned run average or a hitter's slugging percentage. A story about football might chronicle a running back's yards per carry or a team's turnover ratio. Even in basketball, free-throw and field-goal percentages are mainstays of the story. Everyone knows Shaquille O'Neill is a below-par free-throw shooter. But daily newspaper stories about racing frequently sidestep objective analysis.

Many newspaper accounts of horse races fail to inform the reader whether the race was particularly fast, or particularly slow. Whether the pace was fast or slow. Whether the field was strong or weak. Whether a jockey's screw-up was the reason for defeat. Racing stories often fail to evaluate, or refer to, the actual ability of the participants. They frequently do not reveal the technicalities on which racing is based.

Imagine reading a business story about a company with no reference to the price-to-earnings ratio of the company's stock. Or compare an article about racing to an article on baseball, which typically refers to the accomplishments of its participants. Not racing.

The void in analysis and reporting on the actual competition is unfortunate. It means many fans fail to understand the measurable aspects of the game they are betting on. The pieces in the puzzle are found in the past performances.

Perhaps there is a reason for underinformation. This game is not learned overnight. Yet by comprehending the "box scores" of racing—race charts and past performances—fans are provided the basis for lasting enjoyment, and learn to pick winners themselves. That is one reason you are here, in this book.

Let's look more closely at race charts, then past performances.

Sunday, December 29, 2002

FIRST RACE
Santa Anita
DECEMBER 29, 2002

5½ FURLONGS. (1.01³) CLAIMING. Purse $16,000 FOR THRE
Three-year-olds 122 lbs.; Older 123 lbs. Non-winners of two races sin
since then, 4 lbs. CLAIMING PRICE $10,000 (Maiden and claim
considered). (Clear. 62.)

Value of Race: $16,000 Winner $9,600; second $3,200; third $1,920; fourth $960; fifth $320. Mutu
127,172.00 Quinella Pool $14,492.00 Trifecta Pool $143,658.00

Last Raced	Horse	M/Eqt. A.Wt	PP St	¼	⅜	Str	Fin	Jockey	Cl'g Pr	Odds $1
Dec02 5Hol4	My Friend Lumpy	LBb 5 121	4 3	3½	3hd	22	1½	Pincay L Jr	10000	0.80
3Dec02 4LA1	Deal 'em Jack	LB 3 118	7 1	11	11	11	23	Baze T C	10000	17.80
6Aug00 8Sac1	Red Sky's	LB 6 119	2 4	6²½	6²	4¹	3no	Flores D R	10000	5.20
Dec02 3Hol7	Kinston	LBb 4 119	1 7	5hd	5½	3hd	46	Valenzuela P A	10000	2.80
9Nov02 9Hol3	Sonny Sal	LBb 5 119	3 6	7	7	6½	54	Rollins C J	10000	15.00
Dec02 9TuP4	Timeless End	LBbf 5 119	5 2	2hd	4¹½	7	65	Matias J	10000	68.10
Dec02 5Hol6	Able Hero-AU	LB 5 119	6 5	4¹	2¹	52	7	Sorenson D	10000	11.00

OFF AT 12:31 Start Good. Won driving. Track fast.
TIME :21⁴, :45, :57², 1:03⁴ (:21.91, :45.07, :57.46, 1:03.84)

$2 Mutuel Prices:	5—MY FRIEND LUMPY	3.60	2.60	2.40
	8—DEAL 'EM JACK		7.60	4.20
	2—RED SKY'S			3.20

$1 EXACTA 5-8 PAID $13.90 $2 QUINELLA 5-8 PAID $22.00 $1 TRIFECTA
5-8-2 PAID $65.70

Dk. b. or br. g, by Chaka–Cheserule, by Exclusive Encore. Trainer Spawr Bill. Bred by Jeffrey Mariani (Cal).
MY FRIEND LUMPY stalked between horses then off the rail on the backstretch, angled in for the turn, was in tight early on
he bend, came out in the stretch and rallied under urging to get up late. DEAL 'EM JACK bobbled at the start, sped to the lead
ff the rail, angled in for the turn, held on well through the drive but was worn down late. RED SKY'S bumped at the start,
hased between horses then outside a rival, drifted out on the turn, came three deep into the stretch and edged a rival late for
hird. KINSTON saved ground chasing the pace, came out into the stretch, split rivals in midstretch and lost the place late.
ONNY SAL broke in and bumped a rival, settled off the rail, drifted inward in the stretch and did not rally. TIMELESS END
talked the pace between horses, steadied in tight midway on the turn, angled to the inside into the stretch and weakened.
BLE HERO (AUS) was in a good position tracking the leader four wide on the backstretch and three deep on the turn, angled
some entering the stretch, gave way in the drive and returned bleeding from the nostrils.
Owners— 1, Giordano Mattias & Wineman; 2, Futrell Tom; 3, Heap & Ward; 4, Belmonte Gerson & Gould et al;
Mira Loma Thoroughbred Farm; 6, JP Racing Inc; 7, Loeb & Zanini
Trainers—1, Spawr Bill; 2, Aquino Angela M; 3, Ward Wesley A; 4, Mitchell Mike; 5, Lewis Craig A; 6, Parga Joe; 7, Treece Charles S
My Friend Lumpy was claimed by Harder Robert; trainer, Chew Matthew.,
Red Sky's was claimed by Fatman Stables; trainer, Monteleone Frank J.,
Kinston was claimed by Lake Forest Stable; trainer, Carava Jack.
Scratched— Smile Of Fortune (5May01 1HOL6)

The top portion of a race chart shows information regarding the specifics of the race before it is run. This includes:

- Racetrack, race number, and date
- Distance, track record, surface, conditions, class level
- Total purse, amount won by top finishers, and dollars wagered on race

The important facts above are those regarding distance and class level. That is, the length of the race, and the category of horses who contested it.

The next segment of the chart shows what happened. Horses are listed in the order they finished, and are accompanied by a "running line" that shows where the horse was positioned during the race. A wealth of information is included in the running line, which begins with the date, race and place, and finish position of the horse's previous start. Take a look at the winner, which is the first horse listed.

8Dec02 5Hol4: This means the horse's previous start was on December 8, 2002, in race 5 at Hollywood Park (Hol), where he finished fourth.

Next is the horse's name, followed by medication and equipment information.

My Friend Lumpy LBb: Horse's name, Lasix, Butazolidin, blinkers; also, front bandages, if worn (see Timeless End). Lasix is a medication to prevent lung hemorrhaging; Butazolidin, or "Bute," is an anti-inflammatory medication. Blinkers are head gear, eye cups attached to a hood, which keep a horse's attention focused on what is in front of him; front bandages are used for leg support.

Then, the age of a horse, and the weight carried:

5, 121: 5-year-old, carried 121 pounds.

Next comes a key part of the chart—the actual performance, which shows where a horse was at each stage of the race. In the case of My Friend Lumpy, the row of numbers shows the following:

"PP" is post position, the starting-gate stall from which he began the race. (People frequently refer to the past performances as PP's, but in this context, PP refers only to post position.) Next follows the start call, which is where the horse was positioned immediately after the gates opened, relative to the other horses. The "3" shows that My Friend Lumpy was third from the gate. (Look closer, and you will see that the horse who broke first was Deal 'em Jack; the horse who broke last of seven was Kinston.)

The next number indicates the horse's position at the first point of call (after a quarter-mile in sprints), accompanied by a superscript noting the margin in front of the next horse. The running line of My Friend Lumpy shows $3\frac{1}{2}$—he was in third position, a half-length in front of the horse in fourth. As the chart shows, Deal 'em Jack was in first place, one length in front of Timeless End, who was a head in front of My Friend Lumpy. Therefore, My Friend Lumpy was a length and a head behind the leader.

The same applies to the next point of call, which is after three-eights of a mile in this example. In a six-furlong sprint, this is after a half-mile. Here, My Friend Lumpy remains in third, a head in front of fourth, and two lengths behind the lead. (Deal 'em Jack remains one length in front, Able Hero is in second by a length; a total of two.)

Next comes the stretch call, the point in the race where only one-eighth of a mile remains. Finally, payday—the finish. My Friend Lumpy won by a half-length, ridden by Laffit Pincay, for a $10,000 claiming price, at win odds of .80-1 The odds are relative to $1; My Friend Lumpy's odds were 80 cents on the dollar. Claiming price means the horse could have been claimed, or purchased, from the race for that amount.

Farther down the chart is the time the race began ("OFF AT"); how well the field broke from the gate ("Start good" means no horse broke slowly; or "Start good for all but so-and-so"); the winner's level of exertion ("Won driving"); and finally, the condition of the racetrack ("fast," "muddy," etc.).

The running line of each horse will be translated into past performances. It's a lot of stuff, but don't fret. Not all of it must be memorized. Read on.

Next in the chart is "TIME." This reveals the time required for the leader to reach each stage of the race. The significance of fractions will be explained in Chapter 3. In the above example, the chart shows pacesetter Deal 'em Jack went the opening quarter-mile in 21⅘ seconds, a half-mile in 45, and five furlongs in 57⅖ en route to a final time of 1:03 ⅘. While the chart also shows these fractions in hundredths of seconds, they are shown in one-fifth increments in past performances. The fractions in hundredths show the first quarter in 21.91, followed by a half-mile in 45.07 and five furlongs in 57.46 en route to a final time of 1:03.84.

Then come the parimutuel results, showing $2 payoffs for win, place, and show wagers. Exotic bets specific to that race, such as exactas and trifectas, also are shown.

The next line is a description of the horse, including color, gender, pedigree, trainer, breeder, and the state where it was born. Below that is the trackman's (or chart caller's) descriptive paragraph of how the race was run. By reading the trackman's comments, one can recognize which horses may have been compromised by factors such as a slow start or traffic trouble.

At the bottom of the chart are the owners and trainers of the runners, in order of finish. A further notation shows which horses were claimed or scratched from the race. That's it—the official record of what happened in a race. There are more than 50,000 of these produced every year.

Based on what a horse did in the past—as shown in the race chart—a handicapper can arrive at a sensible determination on what a horse might do in the future.

It was Clinton B. Aves who wrote in 1930, "Ever since the chart system for tabulating records of past performances was devised, human ingenuity has been devoted to mathematically handicapping races—to giving every horse some kind of a basic figure or standing, from which to compute the chances of each horse in a given race by comparison with the record of each competing horse."

The essence of handicapping is that horses will repeat what they already have done. A horse such as My Friend Lumpy, who raced to the lead in past races, is likely to race to the lead again. A horse who raced six furlongs in 1:10 can be expected, under comparable conditions, to race the distance in about 1:10 again. Horses are athletes, similar to human track-and-field athletes or swimmers, whose competition is a race. And just like humans, horses have varying degrees of ability. Horses may look the same, but their degrees of performance are wide ranging.

Some horses run faster than others. Put a fast horse and a slow horse in the same race, and the outcome is predictable. Horses are classified by the distance, surface, and class levels in which they compete. Sprinters do not often race against horses that typically race longer distances of a mile or more. Think of the difference between a 100-meter track athlete and a Boston Marathon runner. They would never meet in the same event.

Fast horses and slow ones are easily distinguished most of the time. Horses generally race against horses of similar ability. For that reason, handicappers must consider more aspects than simply how fast a horse has run. Comparison of one horse's speed figures to another is only one feature of the big picture.

The preferences of a horse are revealed many ways. Beyond distance or surface, horses develop running styles that may be flattered or compromised by the situation—a front-runner in a field with other front-runners, for example. Some horses, regardless of their level of ability, are bulldogs. They appreciate a good fight against horses of similar ability. They look their rivals in the eye, and force them to surrender.

Watching You
Own:Hughes Bradley W
Orange/purple Quarters, Orange
ENS G L (78 15 11 10 .19) 2003:(78 15 .19)

Ch. f. 3 (Mar)
Sire: Coronado's Quest (Forty Niner) $75,000
Dam: Dodie Mae(Capote)
Br: B Wayne Hughes (Ky)
Tr: Stute Warren(17 1 4 4 .06) 2003:(15 1 .07)

L 114

Life	5	1	2	1	$120,590	90	D.Fst	5	1	2	1	$120,590	90
2003	2	0	1	1	$54,000	90	Wet(332)	0	0	0	0	$0	–
2002	3	1	1	0	$66,590	84	Turf(248)	0	0	0	0	$0	–
SA	3	1	1	1	$79,200	90	Dst(312)	0	0	0	0	$0	–

)3-7SA	fst	1	:241	:474	1:114	1:36	ⒻLas Virgnes-G1	90	4	31	2hd	21½	32	33¼	Solis A	LB 116	11.20	88-12	*Composure*120nk Elloluv1223 Watching You1168	Pressed pace,held 3rd	6
)3-3SA	fst	7f	:222	:451	1:10	1:23	ⒻSanta Ynez-G2	89	4	3	42	4¾	21	22½	Desormeaux K J	LB 116	3.60	88-11	Elloluv1212½ Watching You1168 Himalayan1162	5wd bid 3/8,2nd best	5
)2-4Hol	fst	1 1/16	:232	:47	1:112	1:424	ⒻHol Starlet-G1	78	1	41¼	41½	41½	34½	49	Desormeaux K J	LB 120	3.90	80-10	*Elloluv*1204 *Composur*1201½ SummrWindDncr1203½	Pulled,inside,wkened	7
)2-3Hol	fst	7f	:221	:451	1:09	1:214	ⒻMoccasin100k	84	3	2	11	2hd	2hd	22	Desormeaux K J	LB 116	2.80	88-12	PuxaSaco1192 WtchingYou1165½ *AtlnticOcen*1199	Speed,dueled,2nd best	5
)2-7SA	fst	6f	:211	:442	:573	1:101	ⒻMd Sp Wt 42k	80	6	10	87¾	75¼	21½	12½	Stevens G L	B 118	12.30	87-06	WtchingYou1182½ [D]*Rmisvst*1183 *DvousImpct*1181	Hopped strt,5wd rally	10

(S: Mar19 SA 5f fst :593 H *5/66* Mar13 SA 7f fst 1:262 H *2/4* Mar7 SA 4f fst :484 H *18/38* Mar1 SA 6f fst 1:132 H *15/47* Feb22 SA 4f fst :484 B *34/52* Feb16 SA 4f gd :49 B *37/74*
NER: Route/Sprint(9 .11 $0.69) 31-60Days(41 .15 $2.53) Dirt(129 .17 $2.02) Sprint(112 .18 $2.18) Stakes(14 .29 $5.10)

Buffythecenterfold
Own:Brian Allen A & Stronach Stables
Black, Black A On Red Emblem On Gold
NOZA V (309 33 36 44 .11) 2003:(281 29 .10)

B. f. 3 (Mar) KEESEP01 $40,000
Sire: Capote (Seattle Slew) $30,000
Dam: Augusta Springs(Nijinsky II)
Br: Overbrook Farm (Ky)
Tr: Stute Melvin F(35 2 1 4 .06) 2003:(34 2 .06)

L 121

Life	6	3	1	0	$222,160	90	D.Fst	5	3	1	0	$222,160	90
2002	6	3	1	0	$222,160	90	Wet(345)	1	0	0	0	$0	69
2001	0	M	0	0	$0	–	Turf(295)	0	0	0	0	$0	–
SA	1	0	1	0	$40,000	88	Dst(315)	1	1	0	0	$90,000	81

02-4AP	gd	1⅛	:461	1:101	1:354	1:493	ⒻB C Juv FillG1	69	7	53¼	43	52½	610	720	Garcia M S	L 119	24.70	80 –	Storm Flag Flying119½ Composure1199¾ *Santa Catarina*1192	6 wide, tired	10
02-6SA	fst	1 1/16	:231	:47	1:11	1:423	ⒻOak Leaf-G2	88	4	2hd	1½	1½	2hd	23	Garcia M S	LB 119	4.60	88-07	Composure1193 Buffythecenterfold1191½ Sea Jewel1193½	Dueled,2nd best	6
02-8Dmr	fst	7f	:221	:444	1:101	1:232	ⒻDmrDebutnte-G1	60	6	1	1hd	2hd	55	713	Garcia M S	LB 121	3.80	72-13	MissHoudini116nk SntCtrin1159½ IndyGroove115hd	Dueled btwn,weakened	8
02-8Dmr	fst	6½f	:214	:443	1:101	1:171	ⒻSorrento-G2	81	3	6	2hd	2hd	1½	1¾	Garcia M S	LB 121	*1.90	89-09	Bffythcntrfold121¾ TrcksHr1153 IndyGroov1173	Forced out early,game	8
02-6Hol	fst	6f	:22	:444	:572	1:102	ⒻLandaluce-G3	90	5	4	1½	1hd	1hd	11	Garcia M S	LB 116	6.90	88-17	*Bffythcntrfold*1161 TrcksHr115nk LttlBtASwss116nk	Dueled btwn,gamely	9
02-2Hol	fst	5f	:214	:451		:58	ⒻMd Sp Wt 43k	82	6	4	1hd	2½	2½	11	Garcia M S	B 119	10.20	92-12	*Buffythecenterfold*1191 TricksHer1194 SerfinPekkl1191	Dueled, gamely	8

KS: Mar18 SA 5f fst 1:012 H *34/56* Mar12 SA 4f fst :46 H *2/36* Mar6 SA 7f fst 1:261 H *2/5* Feb28 SA 5f fst 1:002 H *10/55* Feb20 SA 6f fst 1:124 H *6/17* Feb14 SA 5f my :593 H *2/15*
NER: 61-180Days(2 .00 $0.00) Route/Sprint(24 .04 $0.22) Dirt(224 .10 $1.86) Sprint(203 .10 $1.30) Stakes(21 .10 $0.72)

When the 3-year-old fillies Buffythecenterfold and Watching You met March 23, 2003, at Santa Anita, many believed Watching You held the advantage over Buffythecenterfold. Watching You had been racing regularly at the meet; Buffythecenterfold was racing for the first time in five months. Often, an inferior horse that is "racing fit" has an advantage over a better horse returning from a layoff. That was the story of the Santa Paula Stakes.

The race unfolded predictably, and when the fillies entered the homestretch, Watching You had gained a half-length advantage. Apparently, the race was over. Her rival was defeated. But wait. Watching You, whose only previous win was in her debut against maidens, did not finish the job. Instead of drawing off, Watching You raced alongside Buffythecenterfold. The latter, a multiple winner who began her career with three consecutive victories, re-rallied and won by a nose. Watching You's inability to put away her rival—in a race she had all but won—indicated she could never be trusted to win a fight. That is one means of illustrating class, as it relates to a minor stakes race.

The fundamentals of handicapping are codependent. Analysis of current form, class, speed, and pace cannot be done independently of one another. A horse in peak condition can only be expected to run well if he is spotted at a realistic class level. A horse at the proper class level can compete, typically, if his speed figures are appropriate to the level and the competition. A horse will earn credible speed figures if the pace is suitable. And pace, of course, is closely related to class. It's a circle.

Beginning handicappers can rest easy—not every detail in a past-performance record is absolutely relevant to accurate prediction of a horse's future performance. Before offering a complete definition of a horse's entire past-performance line, let's keep it simple. A reasonable person will find a wealth of information in just a few places. In many cases, it's enough to arrive at a proper analysis of a horse's chance to win a particular race. It is enough to identify the main contenders.

2 Ride And Shine
White **Own:Bisharat & Bisharat**
Green, Black B On Yellow Shell Emblem
DESORMEAUX K J (49 7 9 6 .14) 2002:(977 160 .16)

Ch. g. 6
Sire: High Brite (Best Turn) $5,000
Dam:Shining Ryder(Red Ryder)
Br: Souheil Bisharat & Raed Bisharat (Cal)
Tr: Stute Gary(3 1 0 0 .33) 2002:(39 8 .21)

L 121

Life	39	5	8	6	$241,529	101	D.Fst	34	5	8	5	$235,529	[illegible]
2003	1	0	0	0	$0	86	Wet(325)	0	0	0	0	$0	
2002	19	3	2	5	$181,029	101	Turf(220)	5	0	0	1	$6,000	
SA	6	1	0	3	$59,456	101	Dst(335)	14	1	1	2	$78,007	[illegible]

5Jan03-6SA	fm	*6½f Ⓣ	$:21^1$ $:43$ $1:05^3$ $1:11^4$	4↑	[S]SensatnlStrH108k	**86**	3	7	7^{11}	$7^{8\frac{3}{4}}$	$7^{5\frac{3}{4}}$	6^6	Puglisi I L	**LB 115**	21.70	92-02	Spinelessjellyfish119^{nk} Macwrd117^1 TurkishPrize118^1	Bit wide into lane
7Dec02-8Hol	fst	6f	$:22$ $:44^3$ $:56^3$ $1:09$	3↑	VOUnderwood-G3	**87**	7	2	$8^{6\frac{3}{4}}$	$8^{7\frac{1}{2}}$	$8^{5\frac{1}{2}}$	$6^{3\frac{1}{4}}$	Puglisi I L	**LB 120**	20.10	92-10	*DebonirJoe*$112^{\frac{1}{2}}$ FJ'sPce$116^{\frac{3}{4}}$ **AmericnSystem**116no	3wd into str,mild bid
21Nov02-3Hol	fst	6f	$:22^1$ $:44^3$ $:57$ $1:09^4$	3↑	OClm 62500N	**101**	1	6	6^8	$5^{5\frac{1}{2}}$	$5^{3\frac{3}{4}}$	$1^{\frac{1}{2}}$	Puglisi I L	**LB 120**	11.70	91-18	Ride And Shine$120^{\frac{1}{2}}$ Simony$118^{1\frac{1}{4}}$ Ex Federali118^3	3wd into str,up late
2Nov02-6SA	fst	6f	$:21^1$ $:43^3$ $:55^3$ $1:08^1$	3↑	[S]CalCpSprintH150k	**86**	8	1	8^{12}	6^{14}	6^{13}	$5^{7\frac{3}{4}}$	Puglisi I L	**LB 115**	12.70	89-04	UnlimitedVlue$115^{3\frac{1}{4}}$ TresuredNote117^1 ConQuixot116^1	Spill,swerved 5/16
12Oct02-4SA	fst	6½f	$:21^4$ $:44^2$ $1:09^1$ $1:15^2$	3↑	Alw 53910N1X	**96**	2	6	$6^{4\frac{3}{4}}$	6^6	$4^{1\frac{1}{2}}$	1^{hd}	Puglisi I L	**LB 122**	12.50	96-09	RideAndShine122^{hd} *OurNewRcruit*118^{hd} BigAppl$118^{2\frac{1}{2}}$	Came out 1/8,rallied
28Sep02-9Fpx	fst	$1\frac{1}{16}$	$:23^2$ $:47^1$ $1:12$ $1:43^1$	3↑	OClm 40000N	**92**	1	$5^{4\frac{1}{2}}$	6^5	6^4	$3^{1\frac{1}{2}}$	$2^{1\frac{3}{4}}$	Puglisi I L	**LB 122**	9.40	94-08	Dixie Law$122^{1\frac{3}{4}}$ *Ride And Shine*122^{nk} Further118^3	4-wide, up for 2nd
15Sep02-10Fpx	fst	6f	$:21^3$ $:44^3$ $:57$ $1:09^2$	3↑	OClm 40000N	**77**	4	6	6^8	6^7	$6^{5\frac{1}{2}}$	$4^{5\frac{1}{2}}$	Puglisi I L	**LB 122**	*1.80	94-06	BillsPid$120^{3\frac{3}{4}}$ TrmpusToo$122^{1\frac{1}{2}}$ ContinentlPrss118^{nk}	4wd into str,missed 3d
2Sep02-9Dmr	fst	1	$:22^3$ $:46$ $1:11^2$ $1:36^4$	3↑	Alw 63240N1X	**92**	1	$6^{4\frac{1}{4}}$	$6^{6\frac{3}{4}}$	$6^{3\frac{1}{2}}$	4^3	3^3	Baze T C	**LB 121**	6.00	88-07	HotelHll121^{no} InfiniteFith123^3 RideAndShin121^4	Lugged out,4w into str
18Aug02-2Dmr	fst	6½f	$:22^1$ $:44^4$ $1:10$ $1:16^3$	3↑	[S]Alw 56000N1X	**89**	5	4	$5^{1\frac{1}{4}}$	4^2	$4^{1\frac{1}{4}}$	1no	Desormeaux K J	**LB 121**	3.50	92-08	RideAndShine121^{no} BettorRoylty121^1 FullStrik$121^{\frac{1}{2}}$	4wd into str,up wire
2Aug02-1Dmr	fst	6f	$:22$ $:45^1$ $:57^3$ $1:10^1$	3↑	[S]Alw 53000N1X	**91**	4	9	9^9	$9^{5\frac{3}{4}}$	4^2	2^1	Desormeaux K J	**LB 121**	14.50	88-14	TresuredNote121^1 *RidAndShin*121^1 Aplch'sNtiv$121^{1\frac{1}{2}}$	Tight early,6wd bid
14Jly02-7Hol	fst	7f	$:22$ $:44^2$ $1:09^1$ $1:22^2$	3↑	[S]Alw 48000N1X	**81**	3	7	$8^{7\frac{3}{4}}$	8^{10}	7^{10}	$4^{8\frac{1}{2}}$	Puglisi I L	**LB 119**	10.20	78-15	*Stoney*121^2 Apalachee's Native119^4 Black Bart$114^{2\frac{1}{2}}$	4 wide into stretch
30Jun02-9Hol	fm	5½f Ⓣ	$:22^1$ $:44^2$ $:56^1$ $1:02^2$	4↑	Clm 50000 (50-45)	**80**	2	8	$9^{6\frac{3}{4}}$	$8^{6\frac{3}{4}}$	$7^{5\frac{1}{4}}$	$6^{3\frac{3}{4}}$	Puglisi I L	**LB 118**	21.70	88-06	JohnnyBGood118^{no} FtForAKng$122^{1\frac{1}{2}}$ SvnJllon118^1	Came out,imp position

WORKS: ● **Jan3 SA 3f fst :34 H** *1/18* **Dec29 SA 5f gd 1:02 H** *15/24* **Dec22 SA 5f fst** $:59^2$ **H** *9/35* **Dec15 SA 5f fst** $:59^2$ **H** *3/31* **Dec5 SA 3f fst** $:35^1$ **H** *2/23* **Nov29 SA 5f fst :59 H** *5/36*
TRAINER: 1-7Days(0 .00 $0.00) Turf/Dirt(2 .00 $0.00) Dirt(33 .21 $3.15) Sprint(31 .16 $2.62) Alw(15 .20 $4.09)

On initial inspection, only a few key parts of Ride and Shine's past performances are necessary. A horseplayer learns to handicap by first understanding four basic factors. This example reveals Ride and Shine's current form, current class, speed, and pace. It is enough to get started, by reducing the data to manageable pieces of information.

A lot of incidental data is not necessary at first, including post position, trainer, jockey, career record, current-year record, recent workouts, age, owner, breeder, pedigree, recent jockey, recent weight and equipment/medication, earlier starts, career-high speed figure, and previous speed ratings. You will hear people offer reasons for liking a horse that are little more than extraneous fluff. The horse has a good post, or a top jockey. Or, the horse has a bad post or a bad jockey. When a handicapper says the reason he likes a horse is because the horse is adding blinkers or changing riders, the best thing is to run and hide. It might mean the handicapper has not considered the fundamentals.

Incidental details are window dressing. Meaningful handicapping is based on concrete evidence and interpretation of the basic factors. In the past performances of Ride and Shine, the essential components are categorized into manageable segments. There is no comparison of horses, no measuring of Ride and Shine against other starters. Rather, Ride and Shine is analyzed merely against the backdrop of the type of race. The objective is to determine whether or not he is an appropriate runner in this race. Is he a contender? Comparison between runners occurs later. For now, note that Ride and Shine is racing in a six-furlong sprint for nonwinners of three-other-than/optional $100,000 claiming on January 12, 2003, at Santa Anita.

The four main handicapping components follow.

Current Form

The most recent running line is the factor most indicative of current form. It is shown by the following.

5Jan03-6SA: date, race number, and track of last race
fm (firm): course condition
*6½ f Ⓣ (approximately 6½ furlongs): distance and surface
Class level/conditions of last race.
Post, start call, running line.

If a horse raced within the last 45 days, his last start generally is an accurate indicator of current form. The running line shows the dates of the horse's races, and where the races were run. If the horse's most recent start was more than 45 days ago, other sources of information will reveal current form, including how the horse fared in a previous race when returning from a layoff.

The track at which the horse raced is key. Most horses will be racing at the same track as their last start, in which case the performance can be taken at face value. If the horse is a shipper from another track, it will be addressed accordingly.

The distance of the last start should be similar to the distance of the race today. If so, the horse's performance speaks to his form.

Class level is even more important. Assuming the horse is placed within one level of his last start, the performance speaks for itself. It is acceptable for a horse to remain at the same level, or move one level in either direction. When a horse is racing at a similar level and distance, his last-start performance is generally a good indicator of what to expect today. Within reason, of course.

For now, we will skip the horse's Beyer Speed Figure and move on to the post position, start call, and running line, which show how the horse ran. This is the most important piece of information published in the past performances because it shows what a horse did. The running line shows the post position the horse started from, where he was positioned soon after leaving the gate, followed by his running position throughout the race, and ends with his finish position. A horse is more likely to run similarly to his last start than any other race he has run. The running line shows the margin by which a horse is either leading the field, if he is the front-runner, or the total number of lengths behind the leader, if he is racing off the pace. (Note the difference between the past performances and the race chart, which shows only the margin between a horse and the one directly ahead of or behind him.) The last number before the jockey is finish position.

After the jockey's name and the information on medication, weight carried, and equipment, we see the odds of the horse's last start. These offer revealing insight. Odds higher than 10-1 suggest the horse may have been overmatched and racing in situations in which expectations were low. In these cases, current form is a trickier read. When expectations are low, an inferior performance might be expected. A horse whose odds have been high in recent races was possibly overmatched. If he is racing under similar conditions, he probably is overmatched again.

Conversely, if a horse's recent odds were relatively low, at 5-1 or under, it suggests the horse has been racing in appropriate situations. Expectations were relatively high. In this case, finish position generally speaks for itself regarding current form. The lower the odds, the better the horse should have run. If odds were high, a low finish position may be excusable. Of course, if the horse is racing under similar conditions, a low finish may be expected again.

Bypassing the next element in the past-performance line, the speed rating, we see the company a horse raced against—the one-two-three finishers (and the margins between them), followed by the trackman's comment. Finally, the line shows the number of horses in the race. A fourth-place finish in a five-horse field is nothing to brag about; a fourth-place finish in a 12-horse field may be acceptable.

That is the nutshell version of analyzing current form. There is more, much more, in Chapter 2.

Class

There is some redundancy in analyzing the fundamentals. Data used to analyze class may also be used to analyze form. Factors frequently overlap, and few stand alone in handicapping. One piece of information can be used to analyze several fundamentals. That includes the data regarding class, which also was used to gauge current form. The class level at which the horse has recently been competitive is key.

Look at the class level/conditions of the last race. If they are similar to those of today's event, a credible performance would indicate that the horse is an appropriate fit here. If he did not run well last time, he might not be expected to perform well today.

The running line, post, start call, and position at each call relative to the pacesetter show whether the horse ran well. If so, at a similar class level, then he fits on class.

Speed

The Beyer Speed Figure is the boldface number that is a measure of how fast a horse ran. Details of Beyer Speed Figures are addressed in Chapter 3. The figures should be looked at as a whole. For example, a horse who jumps up with one big figure might be treated skeptically unless there is evidence he can run as fast again. A big speed figure can be an indication of good current form, but in gauging speed, figures should be viewed in groups, rather than individually.

In the case of Ride and Shine, he is entering a three-other-than allowance/optional $100,000 claimer, which is typically won by a horse who earns a 101 Beyer. This is known as par, and refers to the figure that usually is required to win that type of race. Ride and Shine earned a 101 on November 21; a 96 on October 12. Based on speed figures, he would be considered a marginal contender for today's race.

Pace

The pace of the races in which a horse has run is indicated by the fractional times. These are noted in increments of one-fifth seconds, and show the time of the leader of the race. The horse's running line shows the margin by which he led the field, or trailed the pacesetter. By determining the horse's running style, and taking into account the running style of the other starters, a handicapper can reasonably determine if the pace scenario complements or compromises the horse. More on this in Chapter 4.

Based only on fundamentals, a sensible horseplayer can reach a reasonable determination of Ride and Shine's chance to win—without even considering the competition. For now, it is enough. In viewing past performances, the task is to reduce the information into manageable pieces. Consider first only what is utterly relevant. It is not hard to do, and usually leads to obvious identification of the contenders.

That is the initial step in handicapping—merely recognizing which horses are in form and in the right spot. Finding the horses that do have a chance. Simultaneously, a handicapper can reject the noncontenders. In most races, a number of runners either do not belong, or are not prepared for a winning race this time.

Now, let's walk through the entire past-performance line, with a short explanation of what each piece of data can mean.

Most of the information above the past performances is secondary. That does not mean it is unimportant, only that it is incidental. At the bottom of the past performances, the horse's workouts are listed, along with statistics related to the trainer's proficiency in certain areas. These useful tools are meant to complement the primary factors.

The most important part of the past performances are the recent running lines of the horses. The other incidental information will be discussed in Chapter 5, which explores secondary factors, and in the complete description of the overall past performances shown on page 27.

Here is a left-to-right look at the running line in the past performances.

Past Performance Explanation

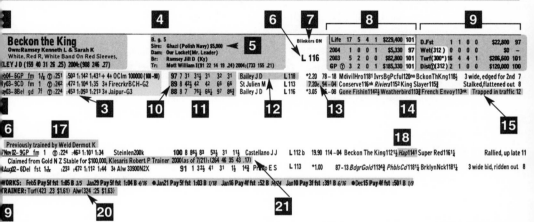

Note: Beckon the King's past performance was altered for illustrative purposes.

1 Betting Number, Horse, Country of origin (if foreign), Owner, Silks, Jockey with record at meet, record year to date

2 Date, Race number, Track, Track condition, Distance, Surface

3 Fractional times for horse in lead, Final time of winner, Age, Sex, Restrictions, Class of race, Purse, Claiming high/low range

4 Color, Sex, Age, Month of foaling, (2/3-year-olds); Where sold at auction, year, price; Sire (sire's sire), Dam (dam's sire); Breeder, State or country of foaling; Trainer with record at meet, record year to date

5 Stud Fee

6 Medication, Weight to be carried today; "L" in reverse type indicates first-time Lasix

7 Indicates blinker change from last start

8 Lifetime record in all races
Record for current year
Record for previous year
Record at today's track
Best Beyer categories

9 Lifetime record on fast track
Lifetime record on wet tracks,
Lifetime record in turf races,
Record at today's distance
Tomlinson Ratings

10 Beyer Speed Figure

11 Post position, Fractional calls with margins, Finish with margin First call margins in routes

12 Jockey, Medication, Weight, Equipment Apprentice allowance would follow after jockey's name

13 Odds to $1, (* indicates favorite, e indicates coupled entry, f indicates field) Speed rating, Track variant.

14 First three finishers, Weights, Margins

15 Comment line, Number of starters

16 Layoff line: single line indicates 45 days or more (double line indicates year or more)

17 Previous trainer line

18 Key race indicator Italics indicate horse finished first in his next start. Bold indicates prior meeting(s) between these horses

19 Workouts: date, track, distance, track condition, final time, comment, ranking

20 Trainer Form

21 Record of "claimed from" trainer

Date of last start. This can be an indicator of current form. The more recent the race, the more likely the horse is to run a similar race today.

Race number and racetrack. This shows where the horse ran, and what race he ran in. The racetrack is important for class distinction, the race number is used as primarily as reference to further research the horse's last start in race charts.

Track condition/surface and distance of race. This is important relative to today's race. To determine if the horse belongs, a handicapper finds the most recent race at a similar distance and surface.

Fractions and final time. This shows the fractions of the pacesetter; that is, how long it took him to reach a specific stage of the race. This is used for speed and pace analysis.

Class level, conditions. This is another factor that is important relative to today's race. To determine if the horse belongs, a handicapper finds the most recent race at similar class level and conditions.

Beyer Speed Figure. This measures how fast the horse ran. Beyer Speed Figures earned over different tracks and distances can be compared to one another, within reason.

Running line. This is the actual performance, and speaks to form, class, speed, and pace. The data includes the factors below.

- The first number shows what post position the horse broke from. A horse who breaks from the 12 post, the far outside, in a two-turn race that starts right before the first turn may find himself caught wide.
- The second number is the start call, which indicates where the horse is positioned immediately after the break, relative to the rest of the field. A horse that breaks last in a sprint probably is compromised.
- The next numbers are running positions. That is, where the horse is positioned in the field, and the margin between him and the leader. If the horse leads the field, the margin shows the distance between him and his closest pursuer. This shows how well the horse ran, and indicates his running style.
- Finally, finish position. This shows where the horse finished. It can reveal whether the horse is in good physical condition, and whether he fits on class.

Jockey. This shows who rode the horse.

Medication, equipment. The bold letters show whether the horse was treated with Butazolidin and/or Lasix; the light letters indicate blinkers and/or front bandages.

Weight. This shows how much weight the horse carried in his last start.

Odds last start. This shows how bettors regarded the horse in his last start. Previously mentioned.

Speed ratings, track variant. The first number shows how fast the horse ran relative to the track record for the distance. The second number is a calculated figure that theoretically reveals the speed of the track. Some days, the racing surface may produce fast times and the track variant is low. Other days, when the track is producing slower times, the track variant is high. More about this in Chapter 3.

Other finishers. Also referred to as the company line, these are the names of the horses who finished one-two-three, and the distances between each. A runner whose name is italicized won his next start. Horses whose names are in boldface are entered in today's race. Distance between runners can be revealing also.

Trackman comment. A brief description of what the horse did in the race, based on what the chart caller saw. If the horse had trouble, it would be duly recorded.

Finally, number of starters. This provides a greater understanding of whether a particular finish position was good or not. Fourth in a five-horse field is not so good, fourth in a 12-horse field would be just fine.

That's about it for a running line. It's not so tough. The information is what horseplayers have looked at for decades in their pursuit of winners. But inasmuch as aged-tested handicapping ideas are familiar, the application of the handicapping process is never too old that it cannot be tweaked. In this game, there is always something new, always a unique spin on the fundamental applications of form, class, speed, and pace.

The purpose of this text is to help you learn to find good horses at good prices. The hope is for a bettor to gain the confidence necessary when the moment of parimutuel truth arrives. If you are fortunate, you will have more than one such moment. These are the times when you are on your own—when the principles you have learned, the theories you have digested, the rules you have followed are relegated to the background. It's when you face a cold, hard dilemma at the betting window or computer screen. When everything lines up just right, and you are positioned for a major score. That is, if you play it the right way.

The 1999 Del Mar meet opened on a Thursday, a day later than the traditional Wednesday opener. For a handicapper, who also is a creature of habit, the day-late start was akin to a horse breaking a step slow. It was a good excuse anyway, and I was desperate for an alibi. The late opening threw me off stride, and the first three weeks of the meet nearly ruined the entire summer. For 17 consecutive days, three racing weeks in all, I lost money. My return on investment was 33 cents on the dollar. Bet $1 and get back 33 cents. At that rate, I would be out of action soon.

Del Mar, however, is no place to raise the white flag after only three weeks. The season was not half finished; there was plenty of time to recover. And I still had two key elements in my favor—wagering capital and confidence, however shaken that confidence might be. Eventually, good things happen when one bets the overlays. Trouble is, they do not always happen in a timely manner. The meet began July 22. As of August 11, I still had not experienced one winning day.

Losing streaks are never much fun, but the parimutuel torture felt less painful this time. I was making all the right plays, mostly pick threes and trifectas, and coming close. Just not close enough. Sooner or later, my luck would have to change. It needed to be sooner. My summer bankroll was on life support.

Happyanunoit (NZ)
Own: Amerman Racing Stables LLC

Dk. b or b. f. 4 (Oct)
Sire: Yachtie*Aus (Broad Reach*NZ)
Dam: Easter Queen*Aus (Rajah*Aus)
Br: J. D. Corcoran (NZ)
Tr: Frankel Robert J(0 0 0 0 .00) 2003:(411 114 .28)

Happyanunoit arrived months earlier, from New Zealand, with lofty expectations. She had defeated males in a Group 1 in New Zealand, and placed in a similar Group 1 in Australia, before being purchased by California owner John Amerman. The filly was supposed to be a superstar, but after four starts in the U.S. for trainer Bobby Frankel, she was stuck in neutral. Or was she?

Happyanunoit's most recent start—a wide-trip fourth in which she closed nearly six lengths in the final quarter-mile—suggested she was coming around. Frankel certainly had not given up on the filly, and added blinkers for the Grade 3 Palomar Handicap. Horses typically produce more speed when equipped with blinkers for the first time. And since the Palomar field had little speed, the slow pace figured to complement Happyanunoit. She was a Frankel trainee at long odds (13-1), stepping up in class following a good effort. A bet had to be made, even by a handicapper who had lost for 17 straight days.

The only thing that Happyanunoit really figured to do was outrun her odds. And she did. Happyanunoit pressed the slow pace, collared the leader in the middle of the stretch, and inched clear. She paid $28.80, anchored a pick three that returned $322.60, and ended one of the most frustrating losing streaks of my career. By the end of the meet, I was in the black.

Any sensible handicapper could have found Happyanunoit. She was a good horse, physically fit, well trained by Bobby Frankel, entered in the right race. Happyanunoit was no lock. She might not have been good enough. But that summer day, she was—a good horse at a great price.

There are lots of horses just like Happyanunoit out there. Middle-priced contenders who can make your meet, along with logical, sensible winners at lower prices. This text will allow horseplayers a means to find them. It is an entry into the wonderful world of handicapping and betting horse races. So let's get started with the meat and potatoes.

We begin in Chapter 2, by looking at current form.

2

FORM

It was the first truly painful handicapping mistake of my wagering career. It would not be the last. But this one hurt because it resulted from sheer ignorance. Or maybe it was arrogance.

It was June 1991, and I had been a public newspaper handicapper all of five years. Long enough for a know-it-all to cop a cheeky attitude. One spring afternoon, speed was holding on the Hollywood Park main track. Marquetry, the only front-runner in the Hollywood Gold Cup and carrying 12 pounds less than 7-5 favorite Farma Way, raced gate to wire and returned a fat win mutuel of $56.80. I had him. Sort of.

Marquetry was a "single" on a pick-three wager, the only Gold Cup starter on the ticket. To cash, I needed to win the next two races. I had multiple horses in each, including another longshot, 26-1 Saber Six, who won the next race by a nose. Two races down, one to go. With three horses on my ticket in the final leg of the pick three, I was positioned for a jackpot equal to one-fifth my annual salary.

What a genius I was. This game that I learned from my dad was easy. It was my dad who taught me the importance of current form. He said physical condition of racehorses fluctuates. Dad's

old-school "form handicapping" concerned analyzing and interpreting the state of a horse's health. Was the horse improving? Or
regressing? Sometimes, a racehorse just doesn't fire; other times,
he delivers at maximum potential. It was Dad—he started handicapping and betting in the 1950's—who emphasized that one of
the most important considerations was current form.

Form handicapping would be a one-step process if horses were
machines. A handicapper would only need to view the past performances of the horse's most recent start, and compare the race
with the last race of the other horses using basic measurements of
class, speed, and pace. But the truth is, horses do change. Trainer
Craig Lewis sees it daily.

"People labor under misconceptions. They say, look at that big,
strong animal—he's healthy. Well, nothing is further from the truth.
There is always something wrong—always. There is a misconception about the saying 'You're as healthy as a horse.' If your doctor
ever tells you that, I suggest you immediately check into the hospi-
tal and demand a thorough evaluation of your health situation.

"It's not that different from a human. There might be a nice-
looking, handsome guy. But he could have cancer, he could have
heart disease, he could have a lung infection. There are all kinds
of things. It's the same with a horse. That is why betting on
horses, you have a much greater chance of [financial] success
than owning horses."

Twilight Agenda
MOYGLARE STUD FARM LTD

B. h. 18 (Mar)
Sire: Devil's Bag (Halo) $10,000
Dam: Grenzen (Grenfall)
Br: Moyglare Stud Farm, Ltd. (Ky)
Tr: Lukas D. W(62 0 7 3 .00) 2004:(84 4 .05)

91–7Hol fm $1\frac{1}{16}$ ① :23 :45⁴ 1:09² 1:39³	4↑ ⑱JohnnysImag62k	– 1 $1\frac{1}{2}$ $1\frac{1}{2}$ 11 $2\frac{1}{2}$ 22¼	Flores D R	LB113 b	14.60	– –	Super May121²¼ *Twilight Agenda*113ⁿᵏ Laxey Bay118²	Bore out, held place 8
91–8SA sly $6\frac{1}{2}$f :21⁴ :44¹ 1:15¹	4↑ Alw 55000Nc	– 1 6 $3\frac{1}{2}$ $3\frac{1}{2}$ 3³ 35½	Santos J A	B114 fb	7.00	– –	TankerPort115¹ LurensQuest114⁴¼ TwilightAgend114¹¼	Stlk pace; empty 6
90♦Leopardstwn (Ire)	7f ⑦	Stk 23100	88	Kinane MJ	0	–	Takwim Home Truth Heroes Sash	0
90♦Phoenix Park (Ire)	7f ⑦	Stk 23100	2	Kinane MJ	0	–	*Norwich* Twilight Agenda Just Three	0
90♦Leopardstwn (Ire)	7f ⑦	Stk 23100	4	Kinane MJ	0	–	*Norwich* Takwim Kyra	0
90♦Ascot (GB)	gd 1 ⑦	3↑ Hcp 82700	87½	Kinane MJ	131	–	Pontenuovo105ⁿᵏ Curtain Call118¹ Pride of Araby131½	32
90♦Phoenix Park (Ire)	7f ⑦	Alw 6200	1	Kinane MJ	0	–	Twilight Agenda Gilt Throne Puissance	0
89♦Leopardstwn (Ire)	7f ⑦	Stk 22800	1	Kinane MJ	0	–	*Twilight Agenda* Closette Run to Jenny	0
89♦Leopardstwn (Ire)	7f ⑦	Hcp 4600	1	Kinane MJ	0	–	*Twilight Agenda* He's a Flyer No Dreaming	0

Of course, on June 29, 1991—Hollywood Gold Cup Day—I
was thinking less about current form and more about how to

spend the pick-three jackpot I was about to win. With three horses in the final leg of the sequence, I was a lock. The one contender I dismissed was a former European that trainer D. Wayne Lukas was wheeling back just eight days after a fierce comeback effort. I knew enough about current form to expect the horse to regress. You may have heard the expression—Twilight Agenda was going to "bounce." It was a modern concept, and I thought I was a modern handicapper. Certainly I was smarter than Lukas. Figuring as much, and ignoring the fact that Twilight Agenda's comeback race was super, I predicted he would not reproduce his last start. Lukas had not given him enough time to recharge.

Twilight Agenda, of course, performed to Lukas's expectations, not mine. In a minor stakes race, the bay front-runner shot to the lead, set a fast pace, and raced wire to wire. He never looked like a loser. I felt like an idiot, which was quite a change from my self-congratulatory mood minutes earlier. It hurt. Twilight Agenda, who would blossom into one of the country's top handicap runners, reminded me that a smug handicapping novice is asking for trouble when he leaps to premature conclusions. Good trainers know their horses, and what races they belong in. Lukas knew his horse.

I had attempted to make an analysis I was not qualified to make. Handicappers do it all the time. With Twilight Agenda, I had leaped past the fundamentals, to an advanced handicapping concept about which I was underinformed. I expected the horse would bounce even though at the time the only thing I really knew about a bounce was what I had read. Dad was right—current form usually is a matter of logic. Lukas had one reason for pushing Twilight Agenda back just eight days after his comeback. The horse was in good form. He was ready.

The Beginning

The handicapping process always starts with the horse. Some are sharp and healthy, others are dull and disinterested. A sharp horse is "in form," and generally can be relied on to produce an effort that corresponds to previous top efforts. His recent races are strong, his workout pattern is solid, the class level at which he is racing is sensible. A horse that is "off form" has tailed off, or is in the process of tailing off. His recent races are subpar, or his speed figures declining; his workout pattern may be flawed, or the class level at which he is racing unusual. Because of sub-standard current form, the horse is likely to fall short of prior accomplishments.

Without form, it may not matter that a horse routinely earns faster speed figures than his rivals. Without current condition, pace is less relevant. In the absence of form, class hardly matters. Make no mistake—speed, pace, and class are key, but only in the context of current condition.

The chief premise of handicapping is that horses are likely to do what they have done. But their condition does change, and catches unwary bettors by surprise. Horseplayers often expect horses to remain the same, even when obvious change is imminent. Form fluctuates. The dilemma is determining the direction—up, down, or sideways.

A blatant example of how horses change—how quickly they can go sour—occurred December 29, 1994, at the start of the 1994-95 winter meet at Santa Anita.

It was only six weeks after Saratoga Gambler had scored a three-length win in the $100,000 Ancient Title Handicap, and trainer Bill Spawr entered him in a $32,000 claiming race. The horse was for sale, and relatively cheap. Something was amiss. Graded stakes winners are not offered up in low-level claiming races without reason. Expectations had been lowered. In a *Daily Racing Form* story the day of the race, Spawr was quizzed about the maneuver. One did not need to be an expert to read between the lines. The first question was, why run Saratoga Gambler cheap, in a claiming race?

"He's for sale," Spawr said.

Then he must not be as good as he was six weeks earlier.

"No, he's not," Spawr said.

How do you think he will run?

"I think he'll win," Spawr said.

What about his physical condition?

"He's not going to break down," Spawr said.

So how good is he?

"Well, he's not as good as he was, but where do you draw the line?" Spawr said.

Where, indeed? Saratoga Gambler's form was going downhill, as evidenced by Spawr's reduced expectations. Nevertheless, bettors hammered him to odds of 6-5. He was the worst kind of favorite—a good horse going bad. Saratoga Gambler finished eighth, was claimed (purchased by another owner) for $32,000, and never raced again.

Current-condition flaws usually are in black and white in the past performances, and call only for simple interpretation and rational thinking. It is the essence of handicapping—common sense. Anyone could see Saratoga Gambler was dropping in class. But it was an illogical class drop, and usually that means a horse's form is declining.

To find winners, handicappers need to understand why a horse is entered in a particular race. And when possible, project improvement or regression. To bet winners and make money, the change must be projected before it becomes obvious to everyone. That is, while it still has parimutuel value. A trainer's intentions and expectations provide a key determinant in a handicapper's analysis of current form.

Despite Saratoga Gambler's obvious flaw, he started at depressed odds, showing there is hope for skeptical handicappers. Current form refers to the state of a horse's health, and here is one golden rule related to it. Never bet on a horse—at low odds—whose health is declining. Never bet on horses like Saratoga Gambler, or Young Husband.

Trainer Peter Eurton claimed Young Husband for $20,000 in January 1999, waited a month, and ran him back for half the claiming price—$10,000. The horse bore out (horses who drift out often are ailing), and scored an ugly win. Yes, he won. Horses going downhill do win. The example still applies. Young Husband ran twice more, and never ran again. The message was clear. In dropping Young Husband to $10,000, after claiming him for $20,000, Eurton revealed lowered expectations. Take note. No one knows a horse like a trainer. To determine if a horse is in form, the first look should be at the class level at which the horse is placed.

There are enough uncertainties in racing to deal with already; the last thing a bettor needs is to guess about the state of a horse's physical well-being. So do not worry about class, speed, or pace until after considering current form. The good, healthy horses on which you will wager come in different shapes and sizes. Most look obvious.

Different Types

Horses typically fall into one of three categories: those racing regularly, comebackers, and first-time starters. Horses racing regularly comprise the majority of starters. Current form of comebackers (horses returning from layoffs of more than 45 days) and first-time starters (horses who have never raced) is based largely on workout patterns and trainers. Analyzing their form will be the focus later in this chapter. With all three groups, the class level at which a trainer places the horse often answers the issue of condition. Is this horse ready? Is he entered in a race in which he is expected to perform well? How is the horse feeling?

Trainer Vladimir Cerin developed Early Pioneer from a horse he claimed for $62,500 into a Grade 1 winner of the Hollywood Gold Cup. Cerin describes sharp current form.

"You'll hear trainers talk about how a horse is tearing down the barn. They mean that literally as well as figuratively. Because a horse feels so good, he's not really crazy about being confined . . . once he gets done with his exercise in the morning and goes back in his stall, he'll roll, he'll jump up, he'll buck and kick, and sometimes kick the walls just because he feels so good. He wants to go out there into combat. That would be an example of a horse tearing down the barn, of a horse jumping out of his skin."

Horseplayers may not see exactly how a horse behaves at his backstretch stable. But when a horse is feeling that good, it usually is clear from his sharp recent races and the class level at which the trainer places him. If a handicapper can figure out why a horse has been placed in a particular spot, he usually can determine the horse's form. The common-sense approach generally corresponds to the horse's recent races.

A horse that is "in form" typically races at a level corresponding to one he raced well at recently. A class drop below a level of recent success is reason for concern. Typically, a horse that is in form will have produced a competitive effort, or efforts, under circumstances similar to today's race. When a veteran horse is feeling good, a top trainer finds a spot to run him.

"You might as well strike while the iron is hot," explains Jack Carava, consistently one of the leading claiming trainers in Southern California. "These old, sore claiming horses, so many of them do good for such a short period of time, that if you find a little window of opportunity where a horse gives you a sign he's doing well, you try to find any race where they could be halfway competitive. I look at works. If a horse works in 1:03, 1:03, 1:03 . . . then all of a sudden he works in :59 with his neck bowed, I kind of surmise that maybe the horse is doing a bit better than he was before."

An in-form horse usually has raced in the past month. If his last race was more than a month ago, the horse usually will show a workout pattern in the interim. While less important than the actual pattern of works, the workout clocking sometimes can be revealing, particularly if it was extraordinarily fast or slow. This is indicated by the ranking of the workout as shown below. Typically, a horse works out within two weeks of his most recent race. If he does not, there may be reason for concern.

Nine Chimes worked five furlongs on October 11, 2003, which was 15 days after his most recent start. Close enough. The bullet in front of the date of the October 11 work indicates it was the fastest work of the day at that distance. The "$\frac{1}{22}$" designation after the time of the work means it was the fastest of 22 works that day at that distance. His previous work on September 17 was "$\frac{9}{15}$." The work was ninth-fastest of 15 at the distance.

An in-form horse often will have finished in the money or within three lengths of the winner at a class level similar to today's race. When an in-form horse has won his last race, he usually will move up in class. An in-form horse that lost his last start will typically remain at the same level, or drop one level.

Trainers

A great deal of faith can be placed in good trainers, particularly when evaluating the class level at which they place their horses.

Why? Because win percentage has become a paramount concern for trainers. Today, horsemen believe that client-owners are increasingly reliant on win percentage as a means of choosing a trainer. For this reason, trainers are reluctant to waste starts by running horses in spots where they do not belong. So long as horsemen remain concerned about maintaining credible win percentages, handicappers can rely that top horsemen, most of the time, will run their horses in races they can win.

A horse that is in undeniably good form usually has a competent trainer and jockey who win at an acceptable rate, typically above 10 percent. A trainer who wins with less than 10 percent of his starters, or a jockey that wins with less than 10 percent of his mounts, is producing fewer wins than average. The preceding guidelines are purposely liberal, and low. Obviously, a trainer who wins with 15 percent of his starters is more reliable about sending them into the right races. The higher a trainer's win percentage, the more likely his starters are in peak current form and running well. Pretty simple, don't you think?

Finish Position

The definition of "running well" can be wide ranging. For example, if the horse has finished in the top one-third of the field in recent races, it is likely that he is in form. Specifically, the horse should have done so under conditions similar to today's race. If a horse finished in the lower half of the field, without having been competitive at any stage of the race, it probably was a bad race and the horse is likely to be off form. This precludes extenuating circumstances such as traffic trouble or unusual track condition.

Likewise, low finish position can be excused if the horse is a front-runner. He may be in form even if he finished far behind the winner. Front-runners typically race to the point of exhaustion. That is, they race as fast as they can for as far as they can. When a front-runner's energy is spent, he often stops to a virtual walk. Therefore, final finish position may not be an accurate gauge of form. The horse may have been passed late in the race by others who did nothing more than pick up the pieces.

Flying Soldier
Own: Hopkins David, Peters, Todd and Robb,

B. c. 3 (Mar) BARMAR01 $40,000
Sire: Lost Soldier (Danzig) $7,500
Dam: Wing It Baby (Alysheba)
Br: John Franks (Fla)
Tr: Perez Ricardo(0 0 0 0 .00) 2003:(55 3 .05)

18Sep02–6Fpx fst 7f	:21³ :44⁴ 1:10¹1:23⁴	3↑ Md 20000	52 9 5	2ʰᵈ 21½ 34½ 76¾	Almeida G F	LB 115	4.00	87– 08	Mamone115¹¾ Apollicee115½ Foxy Johnny120²		Vied,stalked,wke
4Sep02–8Dmr fst 6f	:22 :45¹ :58¹1:11³	3↑ Md 25000(25-22.5)	26 3 5	21 4³ 69½ 8¹6½	Almeida G F	LB 119 b	4.90	65– 15	FightforFreedom123¹½ FabDo123³ ARealKing119¹½		Stalked inside,wke
24Aug02–2Dmr fst 6f	:22 :45 :57²1:10⁴	3↑ Md 50000(50-45)	57 5 1	31½ 22½ 46½ 5¹0½	Almeida G F	LB 119 b	12.50	75– 15	OrngeEm119²½ TriblTrick119½ AlohGoodbye119¹½		Lunged bit strt,wke
4Nov01–6SA fst 6½f	:21⁴ :44³ 1:09³1:16¹	Md Sp Wt 40k	44 6 3	105½ 11⁸ 11¹⁴ 12¹⁹	Enriquez I D	LB 118 b	93.60	68– 14	BringemJung118²½ AcdemySpy118ⁿᵒ VnRouge118²		Angled in turn,no
30Sep01–3SA fst 5½f	:21⁴ :44³ :56⁴1:03¹	Md Sp Wt 38k	46 6 4	43½ 47½ 59½ 5¹8	Solis A	LB 118 b	14.40	74– 14	AmericnSystem118¹½ Rqusto118²½ BringmJung118⁴½		Angled in, weake

Running Style

A speed horse that has been fading, such as Flying Soldier, often only needs slightly softer foes in order to win. Handicappers can be more forgiving when looking at the finish position of a front-runner. If a speed horse has contended for the lead at the pace call, he is probably in form. The pace call is the next-to-last point of call, before the stretch call and the finish position. By the time horses arrive at the pace call, most of their energy has been expended. A horse able to stay in contention to that late stage of the race is generally considered to be in form. Flying Soldier dropped into a $20,000 maiden claiming race, the lowest class level in Southern California, and won by 1¼ lengths in his second start at the level.

Workouts

Regarding a horse's training pattern, his final workout before a race should have been within seven days of the race. A horse with an irregular workout pattern—one who does not have a timed workout in the last week—may be in dubious form, regardless of recent starts. While actual race performance provides most of the information a handicapper requires, there are times when a sketchy workout pattern sends up a warning flag.

Below is an example of a horse with a questionable workout pattern. Hot Weekend was a 2-year-old filly perceived as a standout in the $75,000 Cinderella Stakes on June 8, 2003, at Hollywood Park. View the work pattern that followed her winning debut, and try to spot the flaw.

6 **Hot Weekend**
Black Own:Soares Michael & Suarez Pablo
Royal Blue, Red/yellow Superman
VALENZUELA P A (172 33 28 32 .19) 2003:(637 125 .20)

Dk. b or br f. 2 (Mar) BARMAR03 $50,000
Sire: Summer Squall (Storm Bird) $50,000
Dam:Burning Season(Crafty Prospector)
Br: Winsong Farm (Ky)
Tr: O'Neill Doug(98 22 13 13 .22) 2003:(263 52 .20)

	Life	1 1 0 0	$26,400	84	D.Fst	1 1 0 0	$26,
	2003	1 1 0 0	$26,400	84	Wet(330)	0 0 0 0	
L 116	2002	0 M 0 0	$0	–	Turf(285)	0 0 0 0	
	Hol	1 1 0 0	$26,400	84	Dst(320)	0 0 0 0	

15May03–2Hol fst 4½f	:21⁴ :45¹	:51¹	⑥Md Sp Wt 45k	84 1 1 1¹	12½ 1³	Valenzuela P A	LB 119	*1.40	99 –09	HotWeekend119³ CherishDestiny119²½ HieklSunris119½	Bit off rail

WORKS: Jun3 Hol 4f fst :53³ H 17/17 May4 Hol 5f fst :59⁴ H 4/12 ●Apr26 Hol 4f fst :46³ H 1/41 Apr19 Hol 3f fst :37¹ H 11/26 Apr12 Hol 2f fst :24² H 3/9 Apr6 Hol 1f fst :12⁴ H 6/13
TRAINER: 2ndStart(56 .20 $3.18) 2YO(70 .16 $1.70) Dirt(515 .20 $1.88) Sprint(442 .21 $2.10) Stakes(41 .24 $2.17)

Hot Weekend's winning Beyer Speed Figure was 10 points higher than her nearest foe's, which made me think she might be able to win the Cinderella despite her work pattern. Truthfully, I thought she would. I was wrong. Hot Weekend had only one slow workout in the 24 days since she had raced; her condition had to be considered dubious, especially at low odds of 3-2. Note the dissimilarity in workouts before her winning debut, and before the Cinderella. Hot Weekend surrendered at the top of the stretch and finished a weary sixth in the stakes.

A lot goes on behind the scenes to prepare a horse for a race. In order to compete effectively, horses endure rigorous exercise that usually includes a full-speed workout once a week, in addition to standard daily exercise. On a normal day, horses typically gallop a mile and a half to two miles. Although extended gallops provide some benefit, full-speed workouts are what fully activate the aerobic system and simulate the demands that will be placed on a horse during a race. As the Hot Weekend example shows, horses with a workout deficit often come up short.

m A To Z	B. c. 3 (Apr) OBSMAR01 $47,000		Life	2 M 0 0	$3,820 80	D.Fst	2 0 0 0	$3,820 80
Kruse David R & Linda	Sire: Alphabet Soup (Cozzene) $30,000							
iing Pink, Green Golf Emblem On Back	Dam: E.Cherie(Go Step)		2002	1 M 0 0	$2,880 74	Wet(279)	0 0 0 0	$0 –
	Br: Brereton C Jones (Ky)	L 120	2001	1 M 0 0	$940 80	Turf(267)	0 0 0 0	$0 –
NSON P (20 1 3 0 .05) 2002:(20 2 .10)	Tr: Jackson Bruce L(14 1 1 1 .07) 2002:(13 1 .08)		SA	1 0 0 0	$2,880 74	Dist	0 0 0 0	$0 –

02- 4SA fst 6½f :21³ :44⁴ 1:10 1:16⁴ Md Sp Wt 48k   74 3 5 2ʰᵈ 1ʰᵈ 3² 44½ Atkinson P   LB 120 18.40 84-12 Regiment120¹ DoWhtsRight120³½ DoublOption120ʰᵈ   Dueled btwn,lost 3rd 12
01- 4Dmr fst 5½f :22 :44⁴ :56⁴ 1:03 Md Sp Wt 47k   80 7 2 2¹½ 54½ 55½ 57½ Atkinson P   LB 118 36.60 89-07 Sunray Spirit118² Requesto118² Timely Action118²½   Early speed, tired 9
KS: Apr2 SA 3f fst :37² H 7/8 Mar26 SA 3f fst :35⁴ H 5/11 Mar10 SA 6f fst 1:13³ H 4/17 Mar4 SA 7f fst 1:26 H 1/1 Feb25 SA 6f fst 1:14³ H 18/23 Feb19 SA 6f fst 1:13 H 2/31
NER: Dirt(40 .18 $4.37) Sprint(26 .15 $5.68) MdnSpWt(14 .07 $1.57)

Racing Performance

The horse's most recent start—his last running line—provides the greatest indication regarding current form. Horses who are in form typically will have challenged for the lead at a late stage of the race. Regardless of where the horse finished, an in-form horse will have challenged at either the pace call (usually the point in the race with a quarter-mile remaining), or the stretch call (the final call before the finish). The above example of From A to Z shows a horse whose last start meets the criteria. He would be considered to be in form. In his next start on April 6, he won a maiden race and paid $58.40.

In referring to the last running line, the issue is determining what it means to "challenge for the lead" or "loom a threat." Some handicappers use fixed rules that mandate eliminating horses that were not within three lengths of the lead at the stretch call in sprint races, or within five lengths of the lead at the stretch call in route races. By those standards, horses not within the guidelines are considered to be off form.

The drawback to specific rules is that they discourage handicappers from thinking for themselves. A horse that was positioned within a reasonable margin of the leader at the pace call can be considered to be in form. A reasonable margin can be within three lengths of the lead at the pace call in a sprint. But what if the horse was within 3½ lengths, then what? Use common sense. The guidelines are not meant to be precise. In routes, the "reasonable margin" guideline might be extended to four lengths at the pace call. Basically, if a horse was relatively competitive deep into the race, then he might be considered to be in form. These general guidelines refer mostly to horses with speed. Come-from-behind types rarely challenge for the lead until the final furlong, when the front-runners are spent. Determining current form of come-from-behinders is more difficult because they often are dependent on a collapse of the pacesetters in order to be competitive.

Late-Runners and Turf Horses

It probably is overly simplistic to abandon late-runners altogether, though in dirt races they do not win their fair share. Dirt racing favors horses with speed. There are times, of course, when a handicapper can anticipate a pace meltdown and seek an opportunistic late-runner to pick up the spoils. An in-form late-runner typically will have finished in the top half of the field in his last start, or a recent start under comparable conditions.

Similar guidelines apply when analyzing the current form of a turf horse. A turf horse whose style is to race close to the lead should have been competitive at the pace call, or stretch call. A turf horse that rallies from behind should have finished in the top half of the field, or within a reasonable margin of the winner.

There are differences in analyzing the current form of a Grade 1 stakes horse and a $10,000 claiming horse. Current form is considered in light of the class of the horse. Grade 1 horses typically reproduce top form regardless of the 45-day parameter. A Grade 1 horse with a steady work pattern and top trainer can be expected to run well in a Grade 1 even if he has not raced in two months, or longer.

The same is not true with a low-level claiming horse. Cheaper horses should have raced recently if their most recent start is to provide indication of form. Otherwise, the horse might be considered a layoff horse and evaluated accordingly. Claiming horses typically do not go more than a month between starts.

While the issue of current form is the first and foremost consideration for a handicapper, one must use care. This is only the initial stage, after all. Some discretion is required in eliminating horses. There are few worse feelings for a handicapper than prematurely throwing out the ensuing winner without evaluating class, speed, or pace. Consideration of current form is purposely broad, and intended primarily to cast doubt on otherwise logical contenders, or give reason for a closer look at borderline entrants.

The class-level placement of horses works in both directions. A horse dropping in class following a good race may be deteriorating. Conversely, a horse moving up in class after a seemingly nondescript race might be worth extra consideration, particularly if a winning stable is the one employing the raise.

A handicapper places himself in the position of the trainer by asking, what is the reason for this horse to enter this particular race? When an in-form horse is raised in class by a competent trainer, it means expectations have been raised. The horse is moving ahead to face stronger competition, and race for higher purse money, because the trainer believes the horse can handle tougher company. There are few reasons for a top trainer to raise a horse in class if the horse is not up to the challenge. Especially these days, when horsemen are increasingly concerned with win percentage. Strike while the iron is hot.

Heightened expectations of a trainer still produce generous payoff potential. This is such a basic concept that sometimes it can be employed without extensive consideration of speed or pace.

Form and class, however, are closely intertwined, and change radically in short periods. A horse that struggles to hit the board in a $10,000 claiming race may be winning regularly at the $20,000 claiming level or higher only a few weeks later. Horses "get good" for bursts of time, and during those periods, they frequently offer the best bets in racing. When a horse is sharp and getting sharper, the sky is the limit. A hot horse going up the ladder, into virgin class territory, often offers unlimited possibilities.

Early in his career, Bluesthestandard was a $10,000 claiming horse who shifted from one barn to another and raced well for everyone. But he had a fair share of infirmities, which precluded an aggressive workout regimen that could have led to improved performances against better competition. Instead, trainers Susan Weston, Scott Hansen, Mark Glatt, and Ahmad Salih all trained Bluesthestandard delicately, and appropriately. His physical problems were properly managed, and the gelding responded by winning races for every trainer who cared for him.

Then, over time, Bluesthestandard's imperfections waned. The horse began to feel better, and was able to withstand more rigorous training. His racing performances improved along with the stepped-up workout pattern and he gradually rose in class. By the time that Ted H. West claimed him for $50,000 on December 31, 2002, Bluesthestandard had never been better. Up the ladder he continued, responding to aggressive workouts, and winning graded stakes in the spring of his 5-year-old season.

While Bluesthestandard's ascent was gradual, improvement that is sudden occurs each spring with 3-year-olds. During the 2003 Santa Anita meet, Jeff Mullins was the hottest trainer in California, winning at a sizzling 35 percent rate (20 percent is considered very good). Mullins entered horses in the proper races, and they consistently delivered. Still, horseplayers are reluctant to back a horse based on nonquantifiable factors. Rather than attribute improvement to simple improved form, they credit it to other factors, such as change of surface or distance. That is what happened with the 3-year-old gelding Buddy Gil, a Mullins-trained longshot in the Grade 2 San Felipe Stakes on March 16.

Buddy Gil
Own: Desperado St & McFadden & Merrill St
Black, Gold Compass Rose On Back
NS G L (65 11 8 9 .17) 2003:(65 11 .17)

B. g. 3 (Feb)
Sire: Eastern Echo (Damascus) $3,000
Dam: Really Rising (For Really)
Br: Billingsley Creek Ranch (Ky)
Tr: Mullins Jeff (65 20 21 7 .31) 2003:(64 20 .31)

L 119

Life	7	3	1	1	$129,455	106	D.Fst	4	2	1	1	$58,850	95
2003	2	1	0	0	$68,730	106	Wet(355)	2	0	0	0	$1,875	78
2002	5	2	1	1	$60,725	95	Turf(260*)	1	1	0	0	$68,730	106
SA	0	0	0	0	$0	–	Dst(300)	1	0	0	0	$0	78

8SA	fm	*6½f	Ⓣ	:214	:432	1:062	1:122	Baldwin-G3	**106**	8	2	53½	52¾	22½	12	Stevens G L	**LB** 117	26.70	95-11	BuddyGil1172 KingRobyn1164 **FlirtWithFortun**1161	5wd into lane,rallied 11
iously trained by Jenda Charles J.																					
8GG	my	1 1/16		:221	:452	1:103	1:433	GldnGate DbyG3	**78**	2	44½	45½	42	43½	74½	Krigger K	**LB** 120	7.70	80-17	Standard Setter120nk Ozzie Cat1201 Pine ForJava120¾	Bid rail, weakened 10
8GG	sly	1		:222	:452	1:104	1:381	Gold Rush81k	**65**	6	1hd	2hd	1hd	44	511	Figueroa O	**LB** 117 f	1.50	68-22	Spensive115hd AlwysRemembr1152½ NturlBlnc1172	Dueled outside, stppd 6
2GG	fst	6f		:22	:45	:572	1:103	Golden Bear65k	**95**	4	2	3½	2½	13	17½	Figueroa O	**LB** 115	7.30	84-21	BuddyGil1157½ NturlBlnce1172 BsesAreLodd116hd	Bid 3w,drew clear drvg 5
6BM	fst	1		:231	:47	1:111	1:363	Md Sp Wt 31k	**75**	3	21	2½	2hd	1hd	11¼	Lumpkins J	**LB** 118	*1.40	87-10	*Buddy Gil*1181¼ Onebigbag118½ *Winning Stripes*113½	Dueled 2w, drvng 8
1BM	fst	6f		:221	:443	:564	1:094	Md Sp Wt 29k	**74**	6	4	2hd	2hd	2hd	21¼	Lumpkins J	**LB** 118	2.00	89-11	Quietly Quick1181¼ *Buddy Gil*1185½ Thanks Dr. G.118½	Hustled, outrun late 7
5BM	fst	5½f		:211	:441	:564	1:032	Md Sp Wt 28k	**64**	2	3	44	45½	34½	33½	Lumpkins J	**LB** 118	4.60	87-15	Endemaj118½ *Attack Force*1133 Buddy Gil1186	Svd grnd, gaining 7

: ●Mar11 SA 5f fst :574 H *1/25* ●Mar5 SA 5f fst :582 H *1/12* Feb15 SA 5f gd 1:043 H *61/68* Feb5 SA Ⓣ 5f fm 1:013 H (d) *2/3* ●Jan29 SA 4f fst :461 H *1/33* Dec24 GG 4f fst :511 H *69/90*
:R: Turf/Dirt(18 .22 $2.50) Sprint/Route(29 .14 $1.23) Dirt(201 .23 $2.29) Routes(91 .19 $2.10) GrdStk(10 .20 $8.60)

Buddy Gil had raced three weeks earlier in a turf sprint, his first start since being transferred to Mullins, and woke up with a 26-1 upset. The victory earned him a career-high speed figure. Improved speed figures are a sure indication of improved form. But handicappers still questioned why Buddy Gil had woken up. Conventional reasoning was the surface switch to grass, or the distance switch to sprint. Possibly both. But form analysts offered an alternative. Perhaps, after transferring into Mullins's barn, Buddy Gil had simply become a better, faster racehorse. That is yet another sign of pending form improvement—a transfer into a winning barn.

A brilliant work pattern following the turf sprint indicated Buddy Gil remained in peak form going into the San Felipe. Buddy Gil was a sharp horse moving up in class. If the reason for his improvement was surface or distance, he would be exposed. However, if the reason was simple improved form, then 9-1 odds were fat. Buddy Gil, razor sharp, won the San Felipe by a nose and returned $21.60 for $2.

Buddy Gil's example illustrates a number of signs of imminent form improvement. These include:

- Improved finish position
- Improved speed figures
- Faster workouts
- Transfer to winning barn

Considering all of the above, the only real surprise would have been if Buddy Gil had not run well in the San Felipe.

Charismatic
Own: Lewis Robert B. and Beverly J

Ch. h. 8 (Mar)
Sire: Summer Squall (Storm Bird) $50,000
Dam: Bali Babe (Drone)
Br: Parrish Hill Farm & W. S. Farish (Ky)
Tr: Lukas D. W(18 0 1 1 .00) 2003:(663 71 .11)

Life	17	5	2	4	$2,038,064	108	D.Fst	15	5	2	4	$2,035,93
1999	10	4	2	1	$2,007,404	108	Wet(317)	1	0	0	0	$2,13
1998	7	1	0	3	$30,660	85	Turf(275)	1	0	0	0	$
Sa	7	1	1	2	$96,610	94	Dst(356)	1	0	0	0	$45,00

5Jun99-9Bel	fst	$1\frac{1}{2}$	$:47^3$	1:12	$2:01^4$	$2:27^4$	Belmont-G1	**107**	4	2^{hd}	$2\frac{1}{2}$	1^{hd}	$2\frac{1}{2}$	$3^{1\frac{1}{2}}$	Antley C W	L126	*1.60	103-06	LmonDropKid126hd VisionndVrs126 1½ Chrismtic126 4¾	Drifted, vanned
15May99-10Pim	fst	$1\frac{3}{16}$	$:45^1$	$1:10^1$	$1:35^1$	$1:55^1$	Preaknss-G1	**107**	6	10^6	$10^{7\frac{3}{4}}$	$8^{3\frac{3}{4}}$	1^3	$1^{1\frac{1}{2}}$	Antley C W	L126	8.40	89-09	Charismatic126 1½ Menifee126hd *Badge*126 2½	5wd mv,drftd 3/16,d
1May99-8CD	fst	$1\frac{1}{4}$	$:47^4$	$1:12^2$	$1:37^2$	$2:03^1$	KyDerby-G1	**108**	16	$7^{3\frac{1}{2}}$	$7^{2\frac{3}{4}}$	$3^{1\frac{1}{2}}$	$2\frac{1}{2}$	1^{nk}	Antley C W	L126	31.30	89-14	*Charismatic*126nk Menifee126¾ Cat Thief126 1¼	5-wide trip,driv
18Apr99-8Kee	fst	$1\frac{1}{16}$	$:23^1$	$:46^4$	$1:10^3$	1:41	ClmrLex-G2	**108**	5	6^5	$4^{2\frac{1}{2}}$	$3^{1\frac{1}{2}}$	2^{hd}	$1^{2\frac{1}{2}}$	Bailey J D	L115	12.10	103-07	*Charismatic*115 2½ YnkeeVictor115¾ FindersGold115 2	3 wide 2nd turn,drv
3Apr99-5SA	fst	$1\frac{1}{8}$	$:47^1$	$1:11^2$	$1:36^1$	$1:48^4$	SADerby-G1	**94**	8	$6^{3\frac{1}{2}}$	$6^{3\frac{3}{4}}$	6^4	5^7	$4^{8\frac{1}{4}}$	Pincay L Jr	LB120	44.30	83-13	GenrlChllng120 3½ PrimTimbr120 3½ DsrtHro120 1¼	Improved position so
6Mar99-7BM	fst	$1\frac{1}{16}$	$:22^4$	:46	1:10	$1:43^1$	ElCamRlD-G3	**95**	2	$6^{7\frac{1}{2}}$	$6^{7\frac{1}{2}}$	$6^{4\frac{3}{4}}$	$3^{3\frac{1}{2}}$	2^{hd}	Warren R J Jr	LB115	10.60	83-24	Cliquot115hd Charismatic115 3½ No Cal Bread117¾	Angled out, rall
19Feb99-6SA	fst	7f	$:21^4$	$:43^4$	$1:08^1$	$1:21^2$	Alw 50000N$Y	**94**	2	4	$5^{9\frac{1}{2}}$	5^9	$3^{6\frac{1}{2}}$	2^5	Pincay L Jr	LB117	17.20	93-08	Apremont119 5 Charismatic117 2 *Forestry*119 7	Finished willin
11Feb99-6SA	fst	$6\frac{1}{2}$f	$:21^4$	$:44^2$	$1:10^2$	$1:17^1$	Clm 62500(62.5-55)	**80**	8	7	$8^{6\frac{1}{4}}$	6^5	5^4	2^{nk}	McCarron C J	LB117	2.70	82-17	[D]What Say You110nk Charismatic117nk ValleyDon117 1	Bothered near
Placed first through disqualification																				
31Jan99-8SA	gd	$1\frac{1}{16}$	$:23^4$	$:47^3$	1:12	$1:42^4$	StCtlina-G2	**71**	2	$5^{2\frac{1}{2}}$	$5^{4\frac{1}{4}}$	5^5	$5^{7\frac{1}{2}}$	$5^{13\frac{1}{2}}$	Pincay L Jr	LB117	30.10	75-15	GeneralChallenge117 3 BuckTrout120 1 Brillintly115 3½	Bit tight 7/8,wker
16Jan99-5SA	fst	$1\frac{1}{16}$	$:23^3$	$:47^2$	$1:11^4$	1:44	Alw 54000N$Y	**78**	8	$7^{3\frac{1}{4}}$	$7^{5\frac{3}{4}}$	$7^{3\frac{1}{2}}$	$7^{3\frac{1}{4}}$	5^4	Pincay L Jr	LB117	17.90	79-16	Mr. Broad Blade116hd Brilliantly116 1 Outstanding Hero116 2	Bit tight

Sudden improved form frequently can be accepted at face value, particularly with 3-year-olds early in the season. Form interpretation allows handicappers to delay applications of speed and pace. Instead, it allows one to wager with confidence. After all, what limits are there on improving horses?

When a horse's last start is better than the one before, there is a pretty good chance the horse is getting better. This is common-sense stuff. Charismatic was on the road to nowhere in winter 1999, producing a series of stale, noncompetitive performances. For those reasons, trainer D. Wayne Lukas and owners Bob and Beverly Lewis lowered expectations and dropped the chestnut into a $62,500 claiming race.

Illustrating the meteoric improvement that frequently occurs in spring, Charismatic got good. He crossed the wire second in the claiming race (placed first via disqualification), and was on his way. Runner-up in an allowance race, and again in a Bay Meadows stakes, he followed with a modest fourth in the Santa Anita Derby. Two weeks later, his form bloomed further, as Lukas hinted by where he placed the horse. Raising expectations, Lukas flew Charismatic to Kentucky, where he uncorked a smashing performance in the Lexington Stakes at Keeneland, winning clear and earning a huge speed figure. Charismatic's form was going through the roof.

Two weeks afterward, and less than three months after needing a disqualification to win a claiming race, Charismatic won the Kentucky Derby. His rapid ascension shows how quickly horses can progress, and when a winning horseman reveals heightened expectations, the ride can be thrilling from every perspective. When he won the Derby, Charismatic paid $64.60.

The same thing happens in claiming races, all the time. Trainer Craig Dollase claimed Roncesvalles on January 20, 2000, for

$32,000. He ran poorly, finishing last. But three weeks later, new trainer Dollase brought Roncesvalles back at a higher class level. The message? Roncesvalles had improved. Expectations had been raised. Roncesvalles paid $18.

The patterns repeat year after year. In winter 2002, Dollase scored a maiden sprint victory with a filly making her second start. The final time was moderate, but one month later Dollase brought the filly back in the Grade 1 Hollywood Starlet, facing odds-on favorite Composure. Elloluv broke on top, and raced gate to wire. She paid $63.60. Dollase, high percentage throughout his career, does not waste starts. When a good trainer pushes a horse up in class, look out.

OW
ooper M & Est of C Straub–Rubens

B. c. 3 (Mar)
Sire: Cee's Tizzy (Relaunch) $5,000
Dam: Cee's Song(Seattle Song)
Br: Cecilia Straub Rubens (Cal)
Tr: Robbins Jay M (—) 2000:(60 9 .15)

Life	9	5	3	0	$3,445,950	119	D.Fst	9	5	3	0	$3,445,950 119
2000	9	5	3	0	$3,445,950	119	Wet(345)	0	0	0	0	$0 –
1999	0	M	0	0	$0	–	Turf(160)	0	0	0	0	$0 –
CSC	0	0	0	0	$0	–	Dist	0	0	0	0	$0 –

40CD	fst	1¼	:472	1:12	1:36	2:003	3↑ BC Classic-G1	116	12	1hd	1hd	1hd	1hd	1nk	McCarron C J	L 122	9.20	107 –	Tiznow122nk Gint'sCusewy1223¼ CptinSteve122hd	Duel,headed,gamely,drv	13
-7SA	fst	1⅛	:47	1:104	1:35	1:471	3↑ GoodwoodBCH-G2	119	7	11½	11	1½	1hd	1½	McCarron C J	LB 116	*1.20	99–13	Tiznow116½ Captain Steve1171½ Euchre1154	Rated, repulsed rival	7
-6LaD	fst	1¼	:471	1:102	1:351	1:594	Super Derby-G1	114	4	1hd	1½	11	13	16	McCarron C J	L 124	*.80	103–05	Tiznow1246 Commendable1241 Mass Market1249	Restrained, ridden out	6
-8Dmr	fst	1¼	:452	1:094	1:35	2:011	3↑ PacificClsc-G1	115	4	32	33½	21½	22½	22	McCarron C J	LB 117	4.00	93–14	Skimming1242 Tiznow1171¼ Ecton Park124½	Chased,bid, 2nd best	7
-6Hol	fst	1⅛	:464	1:103	1:352	1:48	Swaps-G1	107	1	41½	42	41	21½	22½	Espinoza V	LB 118 b	2.90	86–11	Captain Steve1202½ Tiznow1181 Spacelink1182	Pulld,trapped rail 3/8	6
-8Hol	fst	1 1/16	:231	:46	1:101	1:421	Affirmed H-G3	103	3	42	31	3½	2hd	1nk	Espinoza V	LB 111 b	10.80	89–18	Tiznow111nk Dixie Union1222 Millencolin1172	Tight rail 7-1/2 & 3/8	6
-4Hol	fst	1 1/16	:233	:462	1:104	1:424	3↑ Md Sp Wt 52k	95	5	2½	2hd	12	14½	18½	Solis A	LB 115 b	*1.30	86–21	Tiznow1158½ ColdwterCnyon1163½ FctulEvidenc115hd	Drew off, ridden out	9
-6Hol	fst	1 1/16	:232	:47	1:12	1:431	3↑ Md Sp Wt 47k	99	3	73½	41¼	42	21	2nk	Solis A	LB 115 b	*2.20	84–15	SpicyStuff115nk Tiznow1154 ColdwterCnyon116½	Crowded strt,waitd 1/4	9
-7SA	fst	6f	:212	:441	:563	1:10	Md Sp Wt 47k	82	8	5	63¾	810	78¼	63	Solis A	B 122 bn	13.80	86–13	Mr.Wondrfl1222½ ProgrmmdAppl122no CocontWlly122hd	Steadied near 3/8	10

Want to understand current form? Watch where good horsemen place their horses. In summer 2000, an unknown California-bred won a maiden race by open lengths. He was entered next in a Grade 3 stakes, an enterprising move by conservative trainer Jay Robbins. Expectations were clear. Robbins said before the race that Tiznow—winner of a single maiden race—was one of the best horses he had trained in more than 30 years at the track.

Handicappers could surmise Robbins's intent simply by viewing the past performances. They showed a recent maiden winner in a graded stakes. Tiznow won the Affirmed Handicap, and paid $23.60. He went on to win the Super Derby, Goodwood, Breeders' Cup Classic, and be named Horse of the Year. For some bettors, Tiznow already was the play of the summer.

This does not mean a handicapper should automatically embrace every horse moving up in class. There must be reasons in the horse's improving performances to support the maneuver. But when the class raise is employed by a good trainer, and the horse's last start was good, a bettor can confidently infer that the horse is improving.

Negative Drops

Opposite heightened expectations shown by class raises, curious class drops reveal lowered expectations. Wagering on horses whose connections are surrendering is a losing angle, as Saratoga Gambler showed earlier. Illogical class drops are reason to be wary; they send up a red flag regarding current form. The warning signs do not always lead to winning wagers, but they help avoid losing ones.

```
6     Chalet Chanteuse                                        Ch. f. 2 (Mar)                                              |Life  6 2 1 0 $52,500 71| D.Fst      6 2 1 0  $52,
      Own: A & R Stable LLC or Class Racing Stab              Sire: Swiss Yodeler (Eastern Echo) $4,000                   2003  6 2 1 0 $52,500 71 | Wet(413)   0 0 0 0
Black Blue, Red And White A/r In White              $25,000   Dam: Peggy Do (Sharp Victor)                          L 118 2002  0 M 0 0      $0  - | Turf(241*) 0 0 0 0
ESPINOZA V (63 11 7 10 .17) 2003: (1076 161 .15)              Br:  Carol A Turner & Heinz Steinmann (Cal)                 SA    0 0 0 0      $0  - | Dst(351)   0 0 0 0
                                                              Tr:  Hines N J(6 0 0 1 .00) 2003:(131 19 .15)

18Aug03-1Dmr fst 5½f  :22  :451 :58  1:05   (F)Clm c-(40-35)       71 4 2 11   11½ 11½ 12    Espinoza V  LB118 fb  3.30 90-09 ChaletChnteuse1182 FreesLilLss1207 BongoKitty1181  Inside, held g
   Claimed from Steinmann Heinz for $40,000, Harrington Mike Trainer 2003(as of 8/18): (152 16 20 18 0.11)
9Jly03-1Hol  fst 5½f  :214 :452 :582 1:06   (F)Clm 55000(62.5-55)  53 4 1 1hd  11  2hd 22½   Espinoza V  LB114 b   2.30 75-17 FstSplsh1162½ ChletChnteuse1143½ ConclthDl1206½  4wd,angled in,2n
8Jun03-7Hol  fst 5½f  :213 :444 :572 1:042  (F)Cinderella84k      30 4 4 52½  76  810 818½  Solis A O   LB116 b  33.90 67-15 YogisPolrBr1133 SmokBrk1162 OutrgousOystr1162½  Pulled,steadie
26May03-1Hol fst 5f   :22  :46       :584   (F)Md 40000(40-35)     68 1 2 12½  13  12  13    Espinoza V  LB119 b   4.00 90-11 ChltChntus1193 ChmpsRockt1194½ Girlsnthoffc1191  Rail,strong har
15May03-8Hol fst 4½f  :22  :461      :522   (F)Md 40000(40-35)     50 9 8 77¼      65¼ 43¼   Espinoza V  LB119    10.00 90-09 ConceltheDel1191¼ PpsPickpockt1191 TwistdHumor1191  Late bid o
1May03-8Hol  fst 4½f  :22  :461      :524   (F)Md 40000(40-35)     29 7 7 56½      64  67    Espinoza V  LB119     5.00 84-10 OkieDokiKooki1192 HiddnImg1191 ChmpsRockt1192½  Steadied 1/8,
WORKS: Oct11 Hol 5f fst 1:021 H 30/42 Oct4 Hol 5f fst 1:053 H 39/39 Sep19 Hol 3f fst :374 H 2/6 Sep9 Dmr 3f fst :361 H 5/11 Sep4 Dmr 4f fst :501 H 30/33 Aug14 Dmr 3f fst :361 H 7/24
TRAINER: 1stClaim(39 .05 $0.26) 61-180Days(27 .11 $0.92) 2YO(6 .00 $0.00) 31-60Days(121 .11 $1.01) Dirt(236 .12 $1.20) Sprint(175 .11 $1.13)
```

A good example occurred during the 2003 fall Oak Tree meet at Santa Anita. Chalet Chanteuse was returning from a two-month layoff for a new trainer. Nick Hines had claimed the filly for $40,000—she won the race—but then she did not resurface for two months. And when she did, she was entered for a claiming price of only $25,000. Her new connections were willing to take a loss of $15,000.

Chalet Chanteuse was hammered to even money, and finished a dreadful third in a slow race. The performance was hardly surprising. The filly's current condition was in a state of decline, as shown by the class level at which she was entered.

Avoiding mistakes such as low-odds losers is part of winning. Every horseplayer occasionally goofs. Sometimes, you are just plain wrong. Low-odds horses may attract most of the attention, but to win at the races, a bettor must be cold and shrewd. At the very least, bettors must ask, is this horse worth wagering on at low odds? What is he doing in this race, anyway? Horses who have moved from a winning barn into a losing barn also should be treated with skepticism.

Avoid the mistake of betting low-odds runners who have conspicuous flaws, and you will find yourself ahead of horseplayers banging their heads against the wall trying to make sense of something that does not make sense. The current form of horses that have been racing regularly is usually obvious. When their recent races are strong and their form is improving, they usually go up in class. When their form is regressing, they usually are lowered in class, beneath levels of past success. Many times, the only thing a handicapper can surmise is that the horse will run similarly to how he ran last out.

When a low-odds horse is off form, the options are to wager on another horse, or skip the race entirely. Winning often is a matter of not losing—that is, limiting the number of mistakes to as few as possible. The inevitable screw-ups will only kill you if you let them. The idea is to fail fewer times than other bettors. No handicapper is right every single time.

Comebackers and first-time starters offer unique challenges, and a familiar theory applies, particularly with comebackers. The class level at which they return speaks volumes about their current form. Comebackers are horses who have not raced in more than 45 days.

Storm Flag Flying
Own:Phipps Ogden Mills
Black, Cherry Cap
.AZQUEZ J R (37 14 4 3 .38) 2003:(372 86 .23)

Dk. b or br f. 3 (Apr)
Sire: Storm Cat (Storm Bird) $500,000
Dam: My Flag(Easy Goer)
Br: Phipps Stable (Ky)
Tr: McGaughey Claude III(10 2 1 0 .20) 2003:(64 18 .28)

L 122

Life	4	4	0	0	$967,000	102	D.Fst	2	2	0	0	$327,000	98
2002	4	4	0	0	$967,000	102	Wet(345)	2	2	0	0	$640,000	102
2001	0	M	0	0	$0	–	Turf(330)	0	0	0	0	$0	–
Aqu	0	0	0	0	$0	–	Dst(330)	1	1	0	0	$120,000	94

:t02-4AP	gd	1⅛	:46^{1} 1:10^{1} 1:35^{4} 1:49^{3}	ⒻB C Juv FillG1	102	3	2^{2}	3^{2}	2^{1}	2^{hd}	1½	Velazquez J R	L 119	*.80	100	—	StormFlagFlying119½ Composure1199¾ *SntCtrin*119^{2}	Headed, very game	10
:t02-6Bel	fst	1$\frac{1}{16}$	:23^{3} :47^{2} 1:12^{1} 1:44^{1}	ⒻFrizette-G1	98	3	3^{1}	2½	2½	1½	1^{2}	Velazquez J R	L 120	*.60	79	22	*StrmFlgFln*120^{2} SntCtrn120^{11} ApplbGrdns120^{3}	When asked, shown whip	7
:p02-6Bel	gd	1	:22^{2} :46 1:12^{2} 1:38^{2}	ⒻMatron-G1	94	2	3^{1}½	3^{2}	2^{hd}	1^{3}	1^{12}¾	Velazquez J R	L 119	*1.40	77	22	*Storm Flag Flying*119^{12} Wild Snitch119^{1} Fircroft1195¼	Greenly, kept busy	7
:g02-6Sar	fst	6f	:22^{1} :45^{3} :58 1:11	ⒻMd Sp Wt 45k	86	3	6	5^{6}½	4^{2}	2^{1}½	1^{1}	Velazquez J R	L 119	3.65	87	13	*StrmFlgFlyng*119^{1} SmthngSlvr119^{5} OrNncyL1194½	4 wide move, greenly	9

RKS: Apr13 Bel 5f fst 1:01^{3} B *4/7* Apr6 Bel 4f fst :47^{1} B *3/19* Mar31 GP 5f fst 1:02^{4} B *6/17* Mar25 GP 4f fst :50^{1} B *12/20* Mar19 GP 5f fst 1:02 B *8/21* Mar13 GP 4f fst :50^{1} B *37/59*
INER: 61-180Days(36 .22 $1.79) Dirt(290 .20 $1.31) GrdStk(52 .17 $1.43)

Comebackers

It had been nearly six months since Storm Flag Flying capped her unbeaten 2-year-old campaign with a stirring triumph in the Breeders' Cup Juvenile Fillies. That autumn day at Arlington, seemingly defeated in midstretch, Storm Flag Flying battled back. She re-rallied when it appeared hope was lost and won by a half-length, delivering one of the most impressive championship performances of the 2002 Breeders' Cup.

But now it was spring, and Storm Flag Flying was returning to battle on April 18. The winter racing season had come and gone, and trainer Shug McGaughey was behind schedule. The season's premier race for 3-year-old fillies, the Kentucky Oaks, was only three weeks away, and Storm Flag Flying was just now getting back into action. She returned in the Grade 3 Comely at Aqueduct.

The situation was not ideal, but Storm Flag Flying's spring training pattern had been delayed. With the Kentucky Oaks—the main goal—bearing down, time was running out for a prep race. Despite a six-month hiatus and a formidable rival—Cyber Secret, who was coming off a Grade 3 win—bettors hammered Storm Flag Flying to odds of .25-1.00, even though her ultimate objectives were the more prestigious races ahead on the calendar.

To break even at those odds, a bettor must win four of every five wagers. No handicapper is that good. Storm Flag Flying was the best filly in the Comely, but so what? The facts were clear. She was returning from a six-month layoff, and aiming for a bigger race ahead. For most bettors, the Comely was a mistake, and Cyber Secret, going up in class off a sharp win, rolled home to the tune of a $9 mutuel.

Bettors who wager on low-odds runners with drawbacks such as Storm Flag Flying's are practically guaranteed to lose over the long haul. Perhaps Storm Flag Flying could have won the Comely despite her layoff and long-range plans. But at depressed odds, the expectations were unreasonable.

When a horse enters a race that is not the main goal, be assured that victory is less important than pure exercise. McGaughey had not prepared Storm Flag Flying for an all-out effort to win a Grade 3. It was only a comeback race.

It happened again May 9, 2003, at Belmont, when Breeders' Cup Classic winner Volponi returned in an allowance race, his first start in six months. He was the best horse in the race, but the intentions of trainer P. G. Johnson went beyond a mere $56,000 allowance. The rich spring-summer racing season was ahead, and it made little sense for Johnson to have trained

Volponi up to a smasher in his first start back. Which is not to say Volponi could not have won. He could have. At odds of 2-5, he made a serious bid, then flattened out and finished second. Bettors who expected him to reproduce his Classic victory following a six-month layoff were foiled. He was 2-5, but lacked current form. How tough is it to wager against horses like that? Or at the very least, to pass the race?

Wagering on low-odds runners who may not be geared up is a road to parimutuel failure. The issue of current form—or lack of current form, regarding Storm Flag Flying and Volponi—must always be a paramount consideration. When the warning signs are out and the odds are low, these horses are to be avoided.

These examples illustrate the pitfalls in backing short-priced top-class comebackers. Horses are laid off for a variety of reasons. They get hurt, tired or sour, or have changed locales and require time to acclimate. Horses need vacations, just like people. When they return, they often do so with a fresh attitude, fresh legs, and renewed purpose. But the negative reasons, including injury and form decline, do not lead to high expectations when the horse returns. There are a sufficient number of uncertainties facing bettors anyway, and no reason to compound them by backing layoff horses who may or may not be ready to fire.

Make no mistake, low-odds comebackers do win races. But so what? No bettor is required to wager against them, or on them. When indecision prevails in a race with a low-odds comebacker, there is nothing wrong with simply passing the race. Do not fret. Another wagering opportunity is only minutes away.

Comebackers cover all levels, from maiden claiming to Grade 1. All face the same question—is the horse ready? When a significant period of time has passed since a horse's last race, how can a handicapper know if the horse is primed to deliver a top effort, or if he needs a race or two before returning to form?

Consideration of the class level is first. Does it make sense? When a stakes horse returns in an allowance, the answer is no. There is rarely good reason for a top-caliber horse to deliver maximum effort in a comeback race that is designed solely as a prep. Likewise, when a claiming horse returns in an allowance, the intention is clear. The horse is in a race he is not qualified to win. The purpose is to provide exercise. Following the comeback prep, the horse may be lowered in class into a race where he belongs.

When a comebacker returns at a logical level for a competent trainer, with a credible workout pattern, bettors can feel confident the horse is in form. However, a return above the class level at which he has been competitive in the past suggests the horse is not in the race to win. Rather, he is out for exercise. For example, a $16,000 claiming horse who returns from a layoff in a $25,000 claiming race is probably only in for a prep. The purpose in racing the horse at a level above his true value is to protect him from being claimed. Conversely, horses that return from layoffs below their established class level may have lost value since their last start.

Toga Mania
Own: Ward Wesley A
Ch. m. 5
Sire: Saratoga Six (Alydar) $3,500
Dam: Rainbank(Water Bank)
Br: Petrosian Brothers Racing Stables (Ky)
Tr: Ward Wesley A (—) 2001:(46 13 .28)

Life	7	2	2	1	$72,520	91	D.Fst	5	2	1	1	$61,600
2001	1	0	0	0	$0	43	Wet(375)	1	0	1	0	$10,000
1999	6	2	2	1	$72,520	91	Turf(245)	1	0	0	0	$920
CSC	0	0	0	0	$0	-	Dist	3	2	0	0	$45,600

30May01-1Hol fst 6f :22 :452 :574 1:112 4↑ ⒻClm c-(10-9) 43 2 7 33½ 22 43½ 79¼ Rodriguez M5 LB 113 fn *.70 74-13 BocDrem1181½ NineEst118nk OcenOfStorms1181½ Stalked pace, weakene
Claimed from Fan Stables & Rikmar Stables for $10,000, Sise Clifford Jr Trainer 2001(as of 05/30): (69 10 11 12 0.14) Previously trained by Dollase Craig
1Aug99-8Dmr fst 6f :213 :443 :571 1:102 3↑ ⒻAlw 52250N1X 91 5 1 42¾ 2hd 12½ 12 Nakatani C S LB 116 *1.30 88-12 Toga Mania1162 Maria Alana1182 Valdastar1233 Bid,cleared,drivin
19Jun99-1Hol fm 5½f Ⓣ :221 :442 :562 1:023 3↑ ⒻAlw 55200N1X 68 1 5 1hd 1½ 2½ 54½ Nakatani C S LB 117 *.90 86-09 DustyHthr116½ *MonyInThSht*122½ BtThDvil1192 Inside duel,wkend lat
20May99-7Hol fst 7f :22 :441 1:084 1:213 3↑ ⒻAlw 51000N1X 89 6 2 32½ 22½ 22 24½ Gomez G K LB 115 4.20 89-14 *PennyMarie*1164½ TogaMania1153 KalooknBby1203 Chased, second bes
25Apr99-8Hol fst 6½f :214 :444 1:094 1:162 ⒻAlw 57500N1X 82 3 5 31½ 32 31½ 31½ McCarron C J LB 117 *2.00 87-13 Becoming120½ *Miss Chips*1171 Toga Mania1172 Split horses into lan
7Apr99-7SA my 6½f ⊗ :222 :452 1:094 1:161 ⒻAlw 51500N1X 88 5 2 2½ 2½ 2½ 22 Gomez G K LB 118 1.90 85-14 Dianehill1202 Toga Mania1187 Memoranda12210 Dueled, second bes
3Mar99-2SA fst 6f :221 :452 :573 1:102 ⒻMd 50000 (50-45) 88 1 5 31½ 2hd 12½ 112 Nakatani C S LB 120 *.60 88-12 Toga Mania12012 Lake Princess1205 Diane G1205 Broke inward, handily
WORKS: May21 Hol 6f fst 1:134 H *8/19* May15 Hol 6f fst 1:144 H *6/14* May9 Hol 5f fst 1:02 H *22/29* May3 Hol 5f fst 1:02 H *23/32* Apr27 Hol 4f fst :49 H *8/19* Apr15 Hol 4f fst :491 H *20/33*

Comebackers who return below the level of previous wins can signal trouble, as Toga Mania did at Hollywood Park on May 30, 2001. Toga Mania had been off nearly two years when trainer Cliff Sise brought her back at the lowest level—$10,000 claiming. The message was clear—Sise's expectations were much lower when Toga Mania returned than when she left. You can see what happened. She finished off the board at 3-5, lost once more, and never raced again.

Common sense is the guideline. If a return at a particular level does not make sense—say, the horse returns at two or more levels higher than before, or two or more levels lower—his current condition has to remain suspect.

4 Guiding Force
Own: Beckett Family Trust
Yellow Powder Blue, Dark Blue V-sash, Powder
PEDROZA M A (73 7 8 11 .10) 2003:(376 49 .13)
$16,000
Dk. b or br g. 6
Sire: Hollywood Brat (Cannonade) $500
Dam: Eddies Angel(Mo Bay)
Br: James L Beckett (Cal)
Tr: Sadler John W(37 8 5 6 .22) 2003:(136 25 .18)
L 118

Life	11	3	2	0	$133,125	99	D.Fst	10	3	2	0	$133,125
2002	3	1	1	0	$42,000	99	Wet(289)	0	0	0	0	$0
2001	6	1	1	0	$53,950	96	Turf(225*)	1	0	0	0	$0
Hol	4	1	2	0	$65,380	96	Dst(270)	6	1	2	0	$67,605

11May02-4Hol fst 6f :221 :443 :564 1:094 3↑ Alw 50880N1X 96 4 3 3½ 2½ 22 21½ Krigger K5 LB 118 b 7.60 89-14 *HevenlySerch*1211½ GuidingForce1181 Primeric1211 Stalked,bid,held 2
10Apr02-4SA fst 6½f :213 :441 1:084 1:153 4↑ Clm 40000 (40-35) 99 3 4 1hd 1½ 1hd 11 Espinoza V LB 118 b 5.00 95-12 GuidingForce1181 *Wallahtchie*1181 SingBecuse1173½ Bit off rail, gam
9Feb02-7SA fst 6½f :212 :434 1:094 1:162 4↑ Alw 59000N1X 76 3 6 1hd 21 34 68 Espinoza V LB 123 b 4.50 83-16 *Warm April*1231 *Bingo Card*1201½ Wild Roar1201½ Inside duel, weaken
3Jun01-4Hol fst 6f :22 :444 :563 1:09 3↑ Alw 53000N1X 96 3 2 1hd 11 2½ 21¼ Espinoza V LB 123 bn 4.70 94-10 Mr Freckles1171¼ Guiding Force1233½ Mandola117no Inside lane,2nd be
12May01-9Hol fst 6f :22 :444 :57 1:094 3↑ Alw 50900N1X 86 1 5 1½ 11 11½ 42½ Espinoza V LB 123 bn 8.50 88-08 RiyadhCity123½ LytleCreek123½ AmericnPstime1171½ Inside,wkened la
25Mar01-4SA fm *6½f Ⓣ :222 :443 1:073 1:132 4↑ Alw 55120N1X 69 6 1 1hd 2hd 51¾ 77¾ Baze T C LB 122 bn 3.10 85-06 Riverside1201¼ Solarino122nk *Ira S*118¾ Veered out 1/4, tir
3Mar01-8SA fst 6f :214 :443 :57 1:101 4↑ Alw 89850N1X 85 5 2 11 1hd 2hd 43½ Baze T C LB 122 n 12.30 84-16 FierceHert1221½ Greenbypcker122hd *Significnt*1222 Inside,dueled,wken
28Jan01-5SA fst 6f :212 :44 :562 1:094 4↑ ⓈOClm 40000N 89 1 2 1½ 12½ 14½ 1hd Baze T C LB 118 n 21.70 90-12 GuidingForce118hd RetiredHbit1183½ *WrmApril*1193 Inside,clear,just he
7Jan01-8SA fst 7f :22 :443 1:094 1:224 4↑ ⓈOClm 40000N 29 8 2 11 31 1217 1229¾ Baze T C LB 118 n 7.30 61-14 *FierceHeart*1191¼ It'sAReality119no WrmApril1192¾ Speed,dueled,gave wa
30Apr00-7Hol fst 6½f :22 :443 1:094 1:161 3↑ ⓈMerial60k 96 8 2 11 11 11½ 1½ Chavez J F LB 116 n 6.00 90-11 GuidingForc116½ *KnowSumthn*1162½ IrshMuldoon1232 Kicked clear,he
9Apr00-4SA fst 6f :211 :443 :571 1:101 3↑ Md Sp Wt 54k 84 7 6 58½ 55 55 55¼ Garcia M S LB 116 n 11.10 83-21 *Matriculate*124nk Sure Man1243 *Martel*1161½ Wide early,rail tu
WORKS: May17 Hol 5f fst 1:003 H *8/28* ●May11 Hol 6f fst 1:131 H *1/9* May5 Hol 6f fst 1:152 H *21/22* Apr29 Hol 5f fst 1:02 H *14/20* Apr23 SA 5f fst :593 H *4/31* Apr17 SA 5f fst 1:003 H *4/40*
TRAINER: +180Days(31 .19 $2.68) Dirt(395 .17 $1.65) Sprint(327 .16 $1.64) Claim(157 .18 $1.72)

Good trainers are motivated by fiscal responsibility. When a good trainer drops a horse in class for his comeback, the message is that the horse is not what he once was. Sometimes, he wins anyway. Guiding Force dropped into a $16,000 claiming race on May 24, 2003, for his first start following a one-year layoff. His class-drop placement suggested he was not the same horse. He won by 3½ lengths and paid $5.20. Droppers often start at low odds. A bettor who believes it is possible to generate consistent wagering profit by backing layoff horses at 8-5 is only kidding himself.

Most modern-day trainers are skilled at preparing horses for top races in their first start back. The greater number of horses a trainer has in his barn, the more likely the horses will be ready in their comeback. High-volume trainers typically send out "live" starters. Most top horsemen train horses to deliver a peak effort in their comeback. The exceptions are previously listed. Even when one is handicapping an unfamiliar circuit, the trainer statistics at the bottom of the past performances provide insight to a trainer's specialties and/or weaknesses. The trainer's record with comebackers is directly related to the horse's current form.

A trainer who typically wins with at least 15 percent of his overall starters can be considered "live" in most of the appropriate spots, including comeback races. The past-performance lines also include subcategories of trainer records that can be used to complement the issue of current form.

For example, the June 7, 2002, past performances of Revello show that trainer Richard Mandella had won with 13 percent of his most recent 31 starters who were away 180 days or more. The win rate was average; the $1.48 return on investment suggests they were frequently overbet.

```
Thady Quill                    Ch. c. 4 TATHOUS8 $757,777          Life  7  4  0  1  $124,800 101   D.Fst    0  0  0  0
Own: Seidler Gary              Sire: Nureyev (Northern Dancer) $125,000                                2001  2  2  0  0  $74,400 101   Wet(315) 0  0  0  0
Dark Green, Green/beige Diagonal  Dam: Alleged Devotion(Alleged)                                                                       Turf(365) 7  4  0  1  $124,80
                               Br: Orpendale & Barronstown Stud (Ky)      115    2000  2  0  0  0   $5,695 85   Turf(365) 7  4  0  1  $124,8
DELAHOUSSAYE E (21 1 7 4 .05) 2001:(493 71 .14)  Tr: Frankel Robert(7 2 1 1 .29) 2001:(207 46 .22)        Dmr ① 0  0  0  0     $0  –   Dist①    3  2  0  0   $80,05
28Jan01–6SA  gd  1  ①:222 :46 1:11³ 1:35³ 44 OClm 88000N          101  4  5⁹  5⁹½  4¹½  1½  1ʰᵈ  Delahoussaye E LB 119    2.80  89–17 Thady Quill119ʰᵈ Entorchado119²½ Duke Of Green117²   Split foes 1/4,
6Jan01–7SA  fm  1  ①:224 :45 1:09³ 1:33⁴ 44 Alw 60360N2x           100  4  78½ 71²  64¼  3²  1¹  Delahoussaye E LB 117    9.30  90–13 ThadyQuill117¹ GoodJourney123¼ OneForHrry119¹¼  Split foes 1/8,ra
  Previously trained by Byrne Patrick B
5May00–8CD  fm  1¼  ①:23² :46⁴ 1:11 1:41¹  CrwnRylAmTf–G3         —  1  1ʰᵈ 4¹  11¹⁵ 11²⁵  —   Albarado R J    L 123    8.70  — 02 King Cugat123²¼ Lendell Ray116³¼ Go Lib Go123³¼   Dueled, gave way,ea
7Apr00–8Kee fm  1  ①:224 :46 1:10³ 1:35  Transylvania113k          85  8  5⁵  6⁶  5⁴  44  45  Sellers S J     L 116    3.40  92–09 Field Cat116¹½ Lendell Ray116² Go Lib Go123¹¼   Bobbled start,no ʳ
  Previously trained by O'Brien Aidan P
5Nov99–4GP  gd *1½  ①  1:14 1:40 1:51⁴+ Prized200k                84  7  2ʰᵈ 1ʰᵈ 1ʰᵈ 2¹½ 33   O'Donoghue C    L 110   *2.70  74–20 KngCugt112¹½ FourOnThFloor120¹½ ThdyQill110¹¼  Dueled,weakened,st
8Jly99♦ Newmarket(GB)  gd 7f ① Str 1:25⁴  Superlative Stakes (Listed)        1ⁿᵒ   Kinane M J     123   *1.00       Thady Quill123ⁿᵒ Full Flow126²Launfal126¹¼
  Timeform rating: 93            Stk 28200                                                                   Rank tracking leader,led over 1f out,drifted right,c
13Jun99♦ Gowran Park(Ire)  gd 7f ① RH 1:24¹  Chill Chainnigh EBF Maiden      15½  Kinane M J     128    *.45       Thady Quill128⁵½ It Happens Now128² Ezra128⁵
  Timeform rating: 98+          Maiden 7900                                                                   Trckd in 4th,rallied to lead over 1-1/2f out,clear 1f out,h
WORKS:  Jly21 Dmr 6f fst 1:15¹ H 24/28  Jly15 Hol 6f fst 1:15² H 5/9  Jly7 Hol 6f fst 1:14³ H 13/21  Jly1 Hol 6f fst 1:14² H 10/18  Jun23 SA 5f fst 1:01 H 26/54  Jun17 SA 5f fst 1:01 H 22/34
TRAINER: 61–180Days(84 .20 $1.92) Turf(417 .25 $2.06) Stakes(43 .35 $2.71)
```

Here is an example with a horse trained by Bobby Frankel.
Thady Quill had not raced in six months when he returned July
27, 2002, in a minor stakes race at Del Mar. Frankel's record
with horses off more than 180 days showed 20 percent winners
from his last 84 runners. The win rate was above average; the
$1.92 return on investment also was well above average.

When a horse is laid off following a victory, it often suggests
something has gone amiss. When a horse is good, the horse stays
in competition. There is little reason to give a horse an extended
layoff when he or she has achieved top form. When a horse runs
well, look for him to run again soon. If he does not, be suspi-
cious. What is "soon"? You decide what makes sense. For the
sake of simplicity, we are using the 45-day layoff line. There are,
of course, exceptions. Thady Quill was laid off following a victory, but he returned in a stakes race—high expectations—for a
leading barn.

The length of layoff is a consideration. Horses who have been
away more than a year do not win their fair share. Horses that
have been away that long generally have endured extraordinary
setbacks. Eliminate them from consideration, and if they beat
you at a short price, what difference does it make? Good handicapping sometimes means nothing more than turning one's back
on damaged goods, and daring them to beat you.

The distance and surface at which a comebacker runs are
prime considerations, and the "does it make sense?" standard
applies. When a horse returns at an unfamiliar distance, it is less
likely he will deliver a top race—for example, when a two-turn
specialist returns from a layoff in a six-furlong sprint. Surface
also is a consideration. When a horse has not run well previously
on the surface of today's race, there is less reason to expect him
to do so first start back. A dirt horse returning in a grass race is

generally not expected to win. Why would a trainer bother racing a dirt horse in a grass race? It could be the grass race is the only race available. The horse needs a prep. He is not expected to win. So why not run him there?

Several criteria should be met to determine if a comebacker is in form. The class, surface, and distance at which he returns should be commensurate with past success. Also, a trainer's statistics reveal how well he does with layoff horses. It is an added benefit if the horse has won previously following layoffs, but not mandatory. The horse's workout pattern should be steady, and increasingly longer in distance. Usually, a horse returning from a layoff will have a short workout as his initial timed work on the comeback trail. The pattern will include perhaps two works at three furlongs, two more at four furlongs, two more at five furlongs, and gradually up.

A sprinter typically has at least two workouts at distances within a furlong of the distance of today's race. For example, a horse returning in a six-furlong sprint should have at least two five-furlong works in order for a handicapper to consider the horse fit enough to deliver first start back.

It is slightly different with route horses. Modern training methods are such that a horse who returns in a mile race does not necessarily require a timed workout at the distance. Thady Quill was returning in a mile race, yet his longest work was six furlongs. He had several of them, of course, so it was logical to believe he was physically fit. It is easier for a comebacker to win a two-turn turf race than a two-turn dirt race, due to the unlike dynamics of the two races. The bottom line: If the workout pattern is consistent, and distances gradually longer, the horse may be physically fit. Workouts as a secondary factor are examined further in Chapter 5.

First-Time Starters

Handicappers who are accustomed to viewing past performances of seasoned veterans may be confused by horses without a racing history. They have no speed figures, cannot be analyzed on pace, and are virtually impossible to evaluate on class. A beginning handicapper might look at horses with no history and admit to utter confusion.

And yet, they are really not so difficult. Despite individual histories that are mere blank pages, first-time starters can be analyzed with as much confidence as veteran campaigners. First and foremost is the question of whether the horse is in form. Rather than base current-form decisions on past performances, one looks to other sources of information. Those include workout pattern, trainer tendency, pedigree, sales price, and where the horse was bred.

A first-time starter can be deemed to be in form if his work pattern is steady, his trainer typically does well with first-time starters, and if his pedigree and sales price make it sensible for him to win this race. The information is available in the past performances.

The primary question is, does the workout pattern imply readiness for a top effort? A positive work pattern with a first-time starter is similar to that of a well-prepared combacker—consistently spaced, and increasingly longer in distance. The actual times of the workouts are less important than their uniformity. Some trainers—Bob Baffert, for example—always work horses fast. Others work them slow. Familiarization with trainers is helpful.

More important than the workout times is that the pattern be regular. If a horse works every five days, he should stay on that five-day pattern. Whatever the pattern is, the horse should adhere to it, be it every six days, or seven days. It is beneficial, though hardly mandatory, for a horse to have a short workout as his final prerace drill. When a trainer conditions a horse up to a big effort first time out, the trainer often sharpens the horse's speed in his final workout before the race. It should be noted that most winning first-time starters are in sprints. Few trainers prepare a horse for a winning debut in a two-turn race. The subject of workout speed will be further examined in the chapter on secondary factors. For now, the idea is to identify a first-time starter who is in form.

As important as workouts are to determine current form, they are considered in the context of the trainer. There may be no trainer-preference category that is as specialized as with first-time starters. The trainer categories at the bottom of the past performances often provide a good indication of whether a first-time starter is in form. A trainer who wins with less than 10 percent of his first-time starters is below par. A trainer who wins with 15 percent is doing well. Anything above 20 percent, and a handicapper has to take notice every time.

The fact that a trainer does well with first-time starters does not mean the horse is necessarily in form. It only increases the likelihood that he is. Trainers whose records show they are inclined to start well-prepared first-timers tend to repeat those inclinations time and time again.

More Warning Signs

It was January 10, 1999, at Santa Anita, and Silver Charm was making the 20th start in a global career. He had won the Kentucky Derby, Preakness, and Dubai World Cup, always with a distinct running style. Silver Charm was continually on the attack. He was the most lethal kind of a front-runner, because he could also finish.

ver Charm
Lewis Robert B. and Beverly J

Gr/ro. h. 5 (Feb)
Sire: Silver Buck (Buckpasser) $7,500
Dam: Bonnie's Poker (Poker)
Br: Mary Lou Wootton (Fla)
Tr: Baffert Bob(23 5 3 1 .22) 2003:(674 127 .19)

Life	24	12	7	2	$6,944,369	123	D.Fst	23	11	7	2	$6,644,369	123
1999	5	1	0	2	$431,363	118	Wet(310)	1	1	0	0	$300,000	113
1998	9	6	2	0	$4,696,506	123	Turf(235)	0	0	0	0	$0	-
Sa	9	5	3	1	$1,234,720	118	Dst(312)	8	4	2	1	$1,383,339	123

99-9CD	fst	1⅛	$:46^4$ 1:11 $1:35^2$ $1:47^1$	3↑SFosterH-G2	**104**	3	$4^{2½}$	$4^{4½}$	$4^{2½}$	4^4	$4^{8½}$	Antley C W	L123	1.40	98-03	*VictoryGllop*120^5 *NiteDremr*$110^{¾}$ Littlbitlivly$115^{2¾}$	Hopped start,weakened	7
eviously trained by Baffert Bob																		
99♦Nad al Sheba (UAE)	fst	*1¼	$2:00^3$	4↑Dubai World Cup-G1 Stk 5000000							$6^{14¼}$	Stevens G	126	-		Almutawakel$126^{¾}$ Malek$126^{¾}$ *Victory Gallop*$126^{1½}$	*Tracked in 5th,weakened over 2f out.Daylami 5th,Running Stag 7th*	8
meform rating: 101																		
eviously trained by Baffert Bob																		
99-5SA	fst	1¼	$:47^2$ $1:11^2$ $1:35^2$ $2:00^3$	4↑SAH-G1	**118**	1	$3^{1½}$	$4^{1¼}$	$4^{2¼}$	$4^{1½}$	3^1	Stevens G L	LB124	*1.00	97-11	FreeHouse$123^{½}$ EventoftheYer$119^{½}$ SilvrChrm124^3	Came back on outside	6
99-10GP	fst	1⅛	$:46^3$ $1:10^2$ $1:35^3$ $1:48^1$	3↑DonnH-G1	**106**	12	$9^{9½}$	$9^{9¼}$	$7^{6¾}$	$6^{3½}$	$3^{5¼}$	Stevens G L	L126	*.80	91-14	Puerto Madero$120^{2¾}$ *Behrens*$113^{2½}$ Silver Charm126^{nk}	Mild wide rally	12
99-8SA	fst	1 1/16	$:24^2$ $:47^2$ $1:10^4$ $1:41^3$	4↑SnPsqalH-G2	**109**	3	3^3	$3^{8½}$	3^6	3^1	$1^{1¼}$	Stevens G L	LB125	*.30	95-10	Silver Charm$125^{1¼}$ Malek$119^{3½}$ Crafty Friend118^2	Rallied,good handling	5
98-11CD	fst	1⅛	$:47^2$ $1:11^2$ $1:36^1$ 1:49	3↑ClarkH-G2	**113**	2	1^{hd}	1^{hd}	2^{hd}	$2^{½}$	1^{hd}	Stevens G L	L124	*.30	99-14	*SilverChrm*124^{hd} Littlebitlively113^1 WildRush$117^{½}$	Dueled, headed, gamely	8
98-10CD	fst	1¼	$:47^3$ 1:12 $1:37^1$ 2:02	3↑BCClasic-G1	**115**	8	$5^{2¼}$	4^1	$2^{½}$	1^{hd}	$2^{¾}$	Stevens G L	L126	2.50	94-07	Awesome Again$126^{¾}$ *Silver Charm*126^{nk} Swain126^{no}	Led, drifted late	10
98-8SA	fst	1⅛	$:46^4$ $1:10^1$ $1:34^3$ $1:47^1$	3↑GdwdBCH-G2	**111**	5	$3^{4½}$	$3^{1½}$	$3^{½}$	1^{hd}	$1^{2½}$	Stevens G L	LB124	*.50	100-07	Silver Charm$124^{2½}$ *Free House*$124^{2½}$ Score Quick115^6	Bid 3 wide, driving	6
98-10TP	fst	1⅛	$:46^2$ 1:10 $1:34^3$ $1:47^2$	3↑KyCpClH-G3	**123**	1	3^2	3^1	2^{hd}	2^{hd}	1^{17}	♦Stevens G L	L123	*.50	100-14	DH *SilverCharm*123 DH WildRush117^{17} Acceptable117^5	Long drive, brushed	5
98-8Dmr	fst	1 1/16	:23 $:46^4$ $1:10^2$ 1:41	3↑SnDiegoH-G3	**63**	4	$2^{1½}$	2^1	3^1	5^{10}	5^{27}	Stevens G L	LB125	*.30	72-09	Mud Route117^6 Hal's Pal$113^{5½}$ Benchmark$117^{5½}$	Stalked,gave way	5

But that winter day at Santa Anita, running in the San Pasqual, Silver Charm failed to produce his customary speed. He dropped more than eight lengths off the pace, farther behind than ever. It was as if he had lost interest. The second half of the race, of course, was a different story. Silver Charm blasted home, and won going away. But a skeptical handicapper may have suggested something was not right about Silver Charm's newfangled style. He was losing his speed.

Perhaps Silver Charm was wearing down. He had done something different, and it was not good. Three weeks after the Santa Anita race, Silver Charm was favored at 4-5 in the Donn Handicap at Gulfstream Park. Once again he fell back early, and lost by more than five lengths. He was defeated three more times at low odds, and was retired.

Silver Charm's loss of speed in one race was reason to question the form of a 20-start veteran. Loss of speed often signals the downside of a form cycle. It did for Silver Charm.

A handicapper who saw the San Pasqual as a signal of potential form regression need not have bothered with other handicapping fundamentals related to Silver Charm when he ran in the Donn. High speed figures and proven Grade 1 class carry less relevance when a horse is losing his form. When a good horse goes bad, there is no way to predict how far he will fall.

Handicappers must take note when a horse does anything different. Successful bettors are able to project form changes before they become obvious. Positive and negative form patterns must be exploited while they still carry parimutuel value. To make money gambling on horses, it is a handicapper's cold-hearted responsibility to identify situations in which low-odds runners are compromised. It happens many ways. Kona Gold went downhill more gradually than Silver Charm. The slide began before Kona Gold's effort in the 2001 Frank J. De Francis Handicap at Laurel.

Kona Gold
Own: Headley B & Molasky Irwin & Andrew

B. g. 8
Sire: Java Gold (Key to the Mint)
Dam: Double Sunrise(Slew o' Gold)
Br: Perez Carlos (Ky)
Tr: Headley Bruce (—) 2001:(120 21 .18)

Life	23	12	7	1	$2,069,364	123
2001	6	3	1	0	$392,420	119
2000	6	5	1	0	$1,042,630	119
CSC	0	0	0	0	$0	-

D.Fst	22	12	6	1	$2,037,054	1:
Wet(320)	1	0	1	0	$32,310	1
Turf(270)	0	0	0	0	$0	
Dist	0	0	0	0	$0	

17Nov01-9Lrl	fst	6f	:21^{2}	:44^{1}	:56^{2}	1:09	3↑ DeFrancsMem-G1	**106**	7	3	4^{6}	3^{6½}	4^{3}	4^{4}	Solis A	L 125	*2.10	90-19	DelawareTownship125^{3} ErlyFlyer115^{¾} *XtrHet*117^{nk}	4wd trip, no response
27Oct01-6Bel	fst	6f	:22^{2}	:44^{3}	:56^{1}	1:08^{2}	3↑ B C Sprint-G1	**108**	4	5	11^{6¾}	13^{7½}	8^{6}	7^{4}	Solis A	L 126	*3.50	92-03	Squirtle Squirt124^{½} Xtra Heat121^{nk} Caller One126^{nk}	Inside trip, no rally
6Oct01-8SA	fst	6f	:21^{1}	:43^{2}	:55^{3}	1:07^{3}	3↑ AncntTtlBCH-G1	**115**	6	1	4^{3½}	4^{5}	2^{1}	2^{2½}	Solis A	LB 127	*.60	98-12	SweptOverbord116^{2½} KonGold127^{3} *ILoveSilvr*116^{1}	Led past 1/8,2nd best
22Jly01-8Dmr	fst	6f	:22	:44^{1}	:55^{4}	1:08^{1}	3↑ BngCrsbyBCH-G2	**119**	4	2	2^{5}	2^{1½}	2^{1½}	1^{¾}	Solis A	LB 126	*.90	99-07	KonGold126^{¾} CllerOne124^{½} SweptOvrbord115^{5}	Wore down rival,gamely
1Apr01-7SA	fst	6½f	:21^{1}	:44	1:08^{2}	1:15	4↑ PotrGrndBCH-G2	**112**	2	2	3^{4½}	3^{2}	2^{hd}	1^{nk}	Solis A	LB 126	*.30	93-12	*Kona Gold*126^{nk} [DH]Hollycombe114 [DH]Explicit116^{4}	3wd bid,gamely
4Mar01-7SA	fst	7f	:22^{1}	:44^{4}	1:08^{4}	1:21^{1}	4↑ SanCarlos H-G1	**112**	7	3	4^{1¼}	3^{1}	1^{1}	1^{2}	Solis A	LB 125	*.30e	99-12	*KonGold*125^{2} *BldeProspector*113^{2} GreyMmo115^{hd}	4wd,cut inside,cleared

Kona Gold's descending Beyer figures were one reason to question his form. Going into the De Francis, his figures had rapidly declined—119 at Del Mar, 115 at Santa Anita, 108 at Belmont. He also had begun to lose his speed, and was falling farther off the pace than early in his career. He did blaze through a pair of blistering three-furlong blowouts November 6 and 12 at Santa Anita, but performance in competition speaks far louder than the quiet of a fast morning workout.

Kona Gold finished fourth as the 2-1 favorite in the De Francis. He won only two of his last eight starts, and was the beaten favorite in six of his last 10. Even the popular old warriors like Kona Gold eventually wear down.

Everything starts with form. Lacking current condition, there is less reason to consider a horse as a likely winner. Handicapping is a tiered process, replete with stipulations. Once current form is satisfied, other considerations such as class, speed, and pace can be regarded.

To determine a horse's current form, a few basic questions might be asked:

- Does the horse's presence in this race make sense?
- Does the class level suggest improvement, regression, or neither?
- Has the horse achieved success in a similar race?
- Has the horse recently been competitive under similar conditions, or not?
- Are the horse's recent performances good, bad, or indifferent?
- Are the horse's speed figures improving, declining, or static?
- Is the horse's workout pattern appropriate?

A handicapper cannot always answer every question with unequivocal resolve. One cannot always say for certain a particular horse is in form, or not in form. That's okay. When the issue of form is unclear, simply move on. Handicapping is a process of elimination. If a horse cannot be eliminated on form, do not force it.

Yet because current form is the factor on which everything is contingent, it makes sense that it be the first consideration, even if it is not the ultimate consideration.

A handicapper is asking for trouble by attempting to make an analysis he is not qualified to make. For example, projecting that a horse will "bounce." The theory is valid, and says that when a horse delivers a maximum performance, frequently in his first start following a layoff, the horse needs sufficient time to recover before he runs again. However, the theory applies more to cheap horses and less to top horses. We'll get to that later.

Too bad I misunderstood current form, and the influence of the trainer, way back in summer 1991. That is when I dismissed the chances of razor-sharp Twilight Agenda. I can still see him carrying jockey Corey Nakatani, black and red silks, loose on the lead, strong to the wire. The mistake cost me several thousand dollars. Good horses do not bounce. Twilight Agenda had form.

Did he have sufficient class? That is the subject of Chapter 3.

3

CLASS

It was a sleepy Monday afternoon at Suffolk Downs. The policeman and I stood together along the rail, adjacent to the eighth pole. He was tolerant, even though the original itinerary— we were on vacation from California—did not include betting horses at a minor-league track. Besides, cops and horseplayers typically have little in common.

But this was different. The policeman's daughter had married a horseplayer. Go figure. So on a quiet spring day outside Boston, the officer listened politely while I tried to explain one of the basics of class handicapping. Specifically, reasons why a mare who had lost her first 10 starts, and had not raced in six months, was a standout in a $3,500 maiden claiming sprint.

It was the eighth race at Suffolk on May 26, 1986. Waterford Hills, who had been facing maiden special weight foes at Aqueduct and Belmont, sped to the front, opened a three-length lead on the turn, led comfortably into the stretch, and coasted home. The outcome was never in doubt. A $2 win ticket on Waterford Hills was worth a big, fat $11.60. The payoff was not enough to turn a policeman into a horseplayer, but that spring day, he learned that an intelligent handicapper stands a real chance to win. Maybe it was all right after all, that his daughter had married a horseplayer.

There is more to class handicapping than finding New York droppers entered in cheap maiden claimers in Boston, of course, yet that may be the essence of class handicapping—determining if a horse is facing opposition that he has a legitimate chance to beat. Is he racing at the proper class level?

Waterford Hills certainly was. She had shown just enough speed against better company to suggest all she needed was an easier assignment. But class handicapping also addresses whether a horse can handle a class raise, or whether he should simply stay at the same level and try again. The subject of class is slippery, yet manageable.

What is class? How does it apply? Why is it important? How do you tell? Where is class found in the past performances? And how do you know if a horse is suited to the particular demands of the class level?

The handicapping basics of class and current condition are so closely intertwined that the terms are used interchangeably. The "class" of runners in a race often is referred to as the "form" of the race. In his 1984 book *Thoroughbred Handicapping: State of the Art,* William Quirin wrote that "Class and form cannot be separated . . . a horse's 'class' is measured by its performances when fit and capable of doing its best." That is, determining the class level at which a horse is expected to perform well when at the top of his game. Or, put another way, what's he doing in this race, anyway?

ething Supreme
am Valor Stables Karlik, Spero, et

Ch. g. 7 (Mar)
Sire: Something Lucky (Somethingfabulous) $1,500
Dam: Mean Colleen (Gaelic Dancer)
Br: Old English Rancho (Cal)
Tr: Fierce Fordell(0 0 0 0 .00) 2003:(0 0 .00)

Life	7	5	1	0	$79,675	104	D.Fst	7	5	1	0	$79,675	104
1997	1	0	1	0	$6,800	104	Wet(318)	0	0	0	0	$0	-
1996	2	2	0	0	$23,375	103	Turf(294)	0	0	0	0	$0	-
Sa	3	2	0	0	$34,100	93	Dst(347)	0	0	0	0	$0	-

6GG	fst	6f	:213	:44	:56	1:083	4↑OClm 80000	104	3	3	31½	2hd	2½	2½	Carr D	LB119 f	2.90	95-	13	RisingPowr119½ SomthingSuprm1194½ JzzmninDvl1195	Bid 3w, no impact	7
usly trained by Gregson Edwin																						
7Hol	fst	6½f	:214	:44	1:081	1:141	4↑Clm 40000(40-35)	103	7	1	2½	1½	12	13	Black C A	LB116	2.30	-	-	SomthngSuprm1163 FuMnSlw1162½ PolrRot1163½	Rapid pace, much best	7
2Hol	fst	6½f	:212	:44	1:084	1:154	4↑[S]Clm 10000(10-9)	93	4	2	23½	2½	15	110	Black C A	LB116	*1.30	-	-	*SomthngSuprm*11610 LongGonJls116½ *JstLCrson*1162½	Drew off, much best	9
usly trained by Fierce Fordell																						
8BM	fst	6f	:221	:45	:571	1:093	3↑Alw 28000N$Y	93	1	6	11	11	12½	15½	Baze R A	LB117	*.70	-	-	*SomthngSprm*1175½ BdgttsHonor1173½ DvlsStr1172	Step slow start, drvng	6
usly trained by Gregson Edwin																						
3SA	fst	6½f	:213	:44	1:092	1:16	3↑Alw 40000c	64	1	6	2½	2hd	31	613	Pincay L Jr	LB117	*1.30	-	-	Juiceberry117hd SummerAtSrtog1152½ OcenOrbit1171½	Step slow, rushed	7
7SA	fst	6½f	:213	:441	1:083	1:151	4↑[S]Alw 42000c	93	5	2	2hd	12½	15	15	Solis A	LB118 f	2.50	-	-	SomthingSuprm1185 *DncingTorch*1213 KolbsGold1187	Quick gain, handily	6
9SA	fst	6f	:213	:444	:571	1:103	4↑[S]Md c-32000	83	6	7	41¾	21	2hd	1nk	Solis A	LB120	*1.30	-	-	*SomethingSuprm*120nk AnothrEcho1206 BMovi1181¼	Step slow, long drive	10
ed from Betty E W & Judy Johnston for $32,000, Warren Donald Trainer 1995(as of 3/1): (-)																						

I wondered as much in 1995, when I owned a very small percentage of a California-bred gelding named Something Supreme. He was a good-looking chestnut splashed with white markings, with raw talent exceeded only by his aches and pains. More than once, trainer Eddie Gregson said Something Supreme was the best sprinter he had trained, but the horse's physical problems included chronic soreness and cracked hooves. He once reared in the paddock, smashed his head against the wall, and was believed to have fractured his skull. It turned out he was fine, and back racing only a few months later.

After Something Supreme dusted a Bay Meadows allowance field by 5½ lengths—his third win from four starts—we had visions of stakes races. But the horse's wheels were coming off. He could barely withstand training, and was forced to the sidelines. Something Supreme's physical condition was deteriorating; Gregson believed the horse might be able to race only two or three more times before he would need to be retired. Racing is hard on a horse. Something Supreme could not take much more. It was time to drop him to the lowest class level so that he would not have to run particularly fast. Make it as easy as possible. Something Supreme was entered in a $10,000 claiming race April 28, 1996, at Hollywood Park. It was an unusual spot for a comeback, considering he had won a fast allowance in his most recent start. We wondered if anyone would claim him.

Something Supreme was co-owned by California handicappers Jeff Siegel (Team Valor) and Jack Karlik, and Michael Spero. None of us bet a dollar because we honestly did not know what to expect. Something Supreme could either win, or finish last. It would be no surprise either way. The horse went out and did what a real racehorse does when he is feeling good. Something Supreme won by 10 lengths, geared down. Suddenly, he was back. His aches were gone. His condition improved. Something Supreme was feeling better, and Gregson was able to train him again. Back up the ladder. When he started June 21 at Hollywood Park, Something Supreme jumped five levels to $40,000 claiming. We wagered on him that day, at odds of 2-1, because we knew he was healthy. He ran to his figures, and buried the field. It was his fifth win from six starts.

Finally, it all caught up with him. Something Supreme did not race again for nine months. He ran once more, then ultimately could not withstand the rigors of training. He was retired to a second career as a show jumper. Something Supreme's racing career illustrates the ebbs and flows of class, and what happens when a good horse starts feeling good.

A horse's class is the level at which he is competitive. Simple enough. A horse that has established himself as a $10,000 claimer typically is competitive against other $10,000 claimers. Run him at a higher level, and he might get creamed. Likewise, a Grade 1 runner typically is competitive against other Grade 1 runners, and would be expected to pummel lower-class horses. Handicapping would be that easy if class were a fixed measurement. But class fluctuates, particularly at the bottom level. Claiming horses do not spend their entire careers competing against the same caliber of claiming horses. Rather, horses move up and down the class ladder relative to their physical condition. A horse whose physical imperfections render him ineffective at former levels can drop into an easier spot and find horses he can beat. Something Supreme did that. And he went up the ladder. Horses do that, too.

Wait Till Monday was a former European stakes runner, imported to the U.S. with expectations that he failed to live up to. He had a bad back and a chronic bleeding problem (tiny blood vessels in his lungs sometimes ruptured during competition, which is a common malady and often preventable with medication). Trainer Ron McAnally gradually lowered Wait Till Monday in class, trying to find a spot—any spot—where he could be competitive. He finally landed at the $10,000 claiming level in summer 1988 at Del Mar. Wait Till Monday woke up that day and finished second.

Trainer Victor Garcia and owner Geoffrey Power took a chance and claimed the former European stakes runner from his next start. "I thought it was one hell of a deal [for $10,000]," Power explained. "He had run six times in Ireland before coming to the U.S. He was second in a Group 2 race and third in a Group 1, and was never out of the money . . . he was a champion overseas." Well, almost.

Wait Till Monday won the race from which he was claimed, and soon began to perk up. By autumn, Wait Till Monday was as good as ever. He scored a 50-1 upset in an allowance race, followed by a 23-1 upset in the H. P. Russell Handicap. You see, Wait Till Monday was not a typical claimer. His stakes credentials were established two years earlier in Europe. Intrinsically, he already was a stakes horse. The only reason he raced in a $10,000 claimer was because his imperfections had caught up with him. But for one brief autumn season, Wait Till Monday went back up the ladder, culminating with a 28-1 upset in the Grade 2 Bay Meadows Handicap. Over a four-race span covering two months for his new owners, Wait Till Monday earned more than $200,000. Up, down, up, down. You bet that class changes.

Class fluctuations are evident in the past performances, which show the levels at which a horse is competitive, and barriers at which a horse is typically foiled. The handicapper's job is to identify the levels, to find the right races for the right horses. The athletic ability of horses varies wildly. It seems odd, relative to a sport such as major-league baseball. When a ballplayer reports to spring training, his ability is expected to be similar to the previous season. Not horses. They change monthly, weekly, even daily. Their ability is elastic, as is the fleeting measure of class.

A horse's class depends largely on his physical condition, particularly with claiming horses. In class handicapping, yesterday's hero is tomorrow's goat. And vice versa. Horseplayers need not fret about mistaken analyses. They happen. But there are guiding principles that allow a reasonable answer to the main question: Is this horse racing against horses he can beat?

The hierarchy of Thoroughbreds goes from the lowest of lows—maidens that have never won a race, to the highest of highs—Grade 1 winners that repeatedly prove they are the best of the breed. Between the low and the high, there are class levels for all different types of horses. Below is the class structure in Southern California, from highest to lowest. The class parallels indicate that a N3X allowance horse (nonwinners of three races other than maiden or claiming) is roughly equivalent to an $80,000 claiming horse.

Southern California class structure

Grade 1

Grade 2

Grade 3

Nongraded stakes

Classified allowance

N3X .... $80,000 claiming

N2X .... $62,500 claiming

N1X .... $40,000 claiming

$32,000 claiming

$20,000-25,000 claiming

$12,500-16,000 claiming .... Maiden special weight

$8,000-12,500 claiming .... $32,000-50,000 maiden claiming

$25,000 maiden claiming

Racing secretaries, employed by racetracks, are responsible for bringing together horses of similar ability in appropriate races. Every two to three weeks, racing secretaries publish a schedule of upcoming races in a paper pamphlet called a condition book. The book details the types of races that will be run each day during the designated period, and includes races for a variety of class levels, at different distances, over dirt and turf. The condition book is to a trainer what a restaurant menu is to a diner.

Santa Anita Park

EIGHTEENTH DAY -- Saturday, January 17, 2004
(Entries Close on Thursday, January 15, 2004)
(Scratch Time 9:30 AM Friday, January 16)

1 | **FIRST RACE** CLAIMING
Purse $29,000. For Fillies Four Years Old.
Weight . . . . 121 lbs.
Non-winners Of Two Races Since November 11 . . . . 2 lbs.
A race since then . . . . .4 lbs.
CLAIMING PRICE $25,000, if for $22,500, allowed . . . . 2 lbs.
(Races Where Entered For $20,000 Or Less Not Considered)
SIX AND ONE HALF FURLONGS

2 | **SECOND RACE** MAIDEN CLAIMING
Purse $18,000. For Maidens, Fillies And Mares Four Years Old and Upward.
Four Year Olds . . . . 122 lbs. Older . . . . 123 lbs.
CLAIMING PRICE $25,000, if for $22,500, allowed . . . . 2 lbs.
ONE MILE AND ONE SIXTEENTH

3 | **THIRD RACE** MAIDEN CLAIMING
Purse $30,000. For Maidens, Fillies And Mares Four Years Old and Upward.
Four Year Olds . . . . 122 lbs. Older . . . . 123 lbs.
CLAIMING PRICE $50,000, For Each $2,500 To $45,000 . . . . 2 lbs.
ONE MILE AND ONE SIXTEENTH

4 | **FOURTH RACE** MAIDEN SPECIAL WEIGHT
Purse $47,000. (Plus up to $14,100 to Cal-Breds) For Maidens, Fillies Three Years Old.
Weight . . . . 120 lbs.
(Non-starters For A Claiming Price Of $32,000 Or Less In The Last 3 Starts Preferred)
ABOUT SIX AND ONE HALF FURLONGS((Turf))

5 | **FIFTH RACE** CLAIMING
Purse $39,000. (Plus up to $4,680 to Cal-Bred Winners from the CBOIF) For Four Year Olds and Upward.
Four Year Olds . . . . 122 lbs. Older . . . . 123 lbs.
Non-winners Of Two Races Since November 11 . . . . 2 lbs.
A race since then . . . . .4 lbs.
CLAIMING PRICE $40,000, For Each $2,000 To $2,500 . . . . 2 lbs.
(Races Where Entered For $32,000 Or Less Not Considered)
SIX AND ONE HALF FURLONGS

The racing secretary's objective is to supply suitable races for the local horse population. When the condition book is published, trainers match their horses to the appropriate race. For example, the trainer of a horse who recently finished second in a $10,000 claiming sprint will look for another $10,000 claiming sprint. Sometimes the conditions of the available race are not ideal.

Take, for example, a $10,000 claiming horse that is effective up to six furlongs. When the condition book is released, the choices may be a $12,500 claiming race at six furlongs, or a $10,000 claimer at seven furlongs. Put yourself in the trainer's shoes. Do you race at the right distance against the wrong (higher) class? Or, do you race at the wrong distance (too far) at the right class? Or, do you wait another three weeks for the perfect race in the next condition book, and not run at all? This means earning no purse money while expenses mount, along with the ever-present possibility of injury.

Whether they are racing regularly or not, horses continue to incur expenses. At major racetracks in California, the monthly cost to keep a horse in training is more than $3,000. Horses must earn their keep.

This is why horses are occasionally entered in races that do not suit them. It may be the only race available. Trainers and owners may be compelled to run. Handicappers, however, have an easier time. We are not compelled to wager on a horse at the wrong level, or wrong distance. We can sit out the race or, better yet, find another horse suited to the situation—a horse that fits the conditions of the race.

Class hierarchies reflect the economic principles of a free market. The better the horse, the more money he can earn. It's all fine and dandy to race for the sport of it, but there is a profit motive. Horse owners pursue the richest races in which their horses have a real chance to win. Faster horses race for more money. Although horses sometimes run in races they have little chance to win, they usually are entered in races where they do have a chance.

Conversely, owners could enter a good horse in an easy, low-purse race. But it would be a waste, akin to sending a major-league all-star to play in the minor leagues. Good horses race for good money against other good horses. Modest horses race for modest money. Low-level horses race for low money. Economic logic keeps horses of diverse ability apart, while bringing horses of similar ability together.

A horse's class changes throughout his career, and all horses start out as untested prospects. They begin their careers in races for maidens—that is, horses that have not won. After "graduating," their subsequent racing campaign depends primarily on how fast they ran in their maiden-race victory. After winning a maiden race, a horse typically goes in one of two directions—into conditioned allowance races, or onto a path that leads to claiming races.

The best horses proceed into allowance races with higher purses than claiming races. The initial allowance level is for horses that have won only a maiden or a claiming race. This is called a one-other-than (N1X) allowance. The tiered "conditions" extend to N2X, N3X, or N4X. After using up their eligibility conditions, horses may proceed into classified allowance races that restrict horses based on the date of their most recent win, or into stakes races, or drop into claiming races. As a horse moves up the allowance ladder, the competition intensifies, and the purses increase, at each subsequent level.

Shining Strike B. f. 4 (May) KEESEP00 $100,000
Own: Robert B & Beverly J Lewis Sire: Smart Strike (Mr. Prospector) $20,000
Green, Yellow Hoops And Sleeves, Yellow Dam: Raj Dancer (Rahy)
Br: Dr Charles S Giles (Ky)
ZUELA P A (14 4 1 4 .29) 2003: (1314 264 .20) Tr: Baffert Bob(14 2 1 2 .14) 2003:(609 116 .19)

L 121	Life	6	2	0	1	$58,680	96
	2003	5	2	0	1	$58,680	96
	2001	1	M	0	0	$0	46
	Hol	1	0	0	0	$960	74

D.Fst	4	1	0	0	$23,160	96
Wet(424)	2	1	0	1	$35,520	83
Turf(320)	0	0	0	0	$0	-
Dst(435)	3	2	0	0	$51,960	96

1Dmr	fst	6½f	:23	:454	1:093	1:154	3↑ⒻClm 32000(32-28)	96	6	2	1hd	1hd	12½	17	Valenzuela P A	LB119 fb	*2.40	96-07	ShiningStrik1197 Ohforcrftsks1194 ShyRutilnt1192½	Drew off, ridden out	7
7Hol	fst	6½f	:213	:44	1:09	1:153	3↑ⒻAlw 50880N1x	74	1	6	1hd	1hd	32	57¼	Nakatani C S	LB121 b	11.80	88-11	Styler1211½ Bold Roberta1232 Siphon Honey1213½	Inside duel,weakened	6
3SA	fst	1	:232	:47	1:114	1:38	4↑ⒻOClm 40000N	37	1	66	64¼	78½	715	727½	Flores D R	LB118 b	*1.40	53-26	TropclBlossom1183 MssGts1183½ TwoFrDncr1182½	Pulled,inside,gave way	7
8SA	gd	1	:231	:463	1:11	1:374	4↑ⒻAlw 59360N1x	83	6	43	43	31	31½	35	Bailey J D	LB118 b	2.40	77-19	CunningPlay1181 Jenna'sJoy1184 ShiningStrike1184	Bid 3deep, weakened	8
9SA	gd	6½f	:22	:45	1:103	1:173	4↑ⒻMd Sp Wt 48k	77	1	7	1hd	1½	11½	11	Flores D R	LB122 b	9.80	85-13	ShiningStrike1221 Sophisticatedbluff122½ *Styler*1223½	Inside, very gamely	9
4Dmr	fst	5½f	:214	:452	:58	1:043	ⒻMd Sp Wt 47k	46	6	7	51¾	31	34	610	Espinoza V	LB118 b	*1.50	79-09	*Tlisluckybusride*1182½ Devlish1181½ *Shzsummrbrz*1181	Bid 3w, flattened out	8

: Nov16 SA 5f fst 1:022 H *27/40* ●Nov11 SA 5f fst :582 H *1/38* Nov2 SA 5f fst :573 H *2/48* Oct26 SA 5f fst :583 H *2/41* Oct18 SA 4f fst :502 H *48/55* Oct7 SA 4f fst :481 H *14/42*
ER: 61-180Days(76 .21 $1.30) 2Off45-180(117 .18 $0.98) Dirt(1089 .20 $1.44) Sprint(827 .19 $1.50) Alw(314 .18 $1.51)

Sooner or later, most horses reach a level that is simply too tough. They just aren't good enough to win at that class level, so they drop into the claiming ranks, searching for the level at which they are competitive. That is the essence of class. After three starts against allowance company it was clear that Shining Strike was not going to pan out, so trainer Bob Baffert dropped her into the claiming ranks. She found her level.

In contrast to impressive maiden winners that advance into allowance races are those whose final times were slow, or whose maiden victories came at the expense of weak competition. For these maiden winners, a career in the claiming ranks may be their destiny. A horse that runs in a claiming race can be claimed (purchased) for the designated amount.

In a $10,000 claiming race, any starter can be claimed for $10,000. The horse becomes the property of the new owner as soon as the starting gate opens, though any purse money the horse earns in that race goes to the previous owner. Horses typically are placed at the highest level at which they can be competitive, because purses correspond to higher claiming prices. Likewise, horses usually do not race below their level of ability, even though they could. But it would be like giving away money.

Say a horse wins a $16,000 claiming race. The owners could run the horse in a $10,000 claiming race next time, and be virtually assured victory because the horse would simply be the best in the race. However, other owners could then claim the horse for the $10,000 price, return the horse to its previously established (higher) class level, and earn money the previous owners left behind. Conversely, the owner of a $16,000 claiming horse usually would not enter him in a $32,000 claiming race. The horse would be overmatched, and have less chance of earning anything. When these horses show up in a race—and they do—they often can be eliminated from consideration, but not always. Sometimes, horses' recent improved performances suggest the class hike is feasible. Nearly half of all races in the U.S. are claiming races for winners, and often are referred to as the bread and butter of the racing menu.

The task for handicappers is to determine whether a horse is racing at an appropriate level. Does he "fit on class"? Is it logical for this horse to be in this race, and how do you know? Further, is it reasonable to expect a competitive performance? If it makes sense that the horse belongs in the race, and his previous performances indicate he is up to the demands of the race, then he fits on class.

Class analysis can include incorporating speed figures. This chapter will introduce the concept of speed figures, and how they are used as a measure of class. For example, if a horse wins a $10,000 claiming race by two lengths, what chance does he have next time out against $12,500 claimers? The answer may depend on how fast the horse ran.

It makes sense. If a handicapper knows the speed figure earned by a typical winner at a particular class level, he can determine which horses belong at that level. For example, the Beyer Speed Figure par for first-condition allowance races in Southern California is 97. It means that most N1X allowance winners win by racing fast enough to earn a 97 Beyer. A horse that won a maiden race with an 87 Beyer will have a tough time winning the allowance race in which a 97 is likely to be required. Conversely, a horse that wins a maiden race with a 100 Beyer could be the rightful allowance-race favorite even while moving up in class to face tougher company.

Another factor in analyzing class is evaluating current form, as we saw in Chapter 2. In this regard, supposedly "classy" horses can often be eliminated because of unsatisfactory current condition. In handicapping, it is as important to identify losers, and avoid them, as it is to find winners.

ral Challenge
den Eagle Farm

Ch. g. 7 (Mar)
Sire: General Meeting (Seattle Slew) $40,000
Dam: Excellent Lady (Smarten)
Br: Mr. & Mrs. John C. Mabee (Cal)
Tr: Baffert Bob(2) 5 3 1 .22) 2003:(674 127 .19)

	Life	21	9	3	1	$2,877,178	119	D.Fst	18	6	3	1	$2,193,478	119
	2003	3	0	0	0	$1,160	94	Wet(339)	3	3	0	0	$683,700	117
	2000	6	2	1	1	$1,198,118	117	Turf(327)	0	0	0	0	$0	–
	Sa	8	5	1	1	$1,642,018	118	Dst(376)	6	3	2	1	$1,029,098	118

5Hol fst 1⅛ :23² :46³ 1:10 1:41 4+ Alw 76880c 63 2 7⁴¹ 5²¹ 8⁷¹ 8¹⁵ 8²⁹ Flores D R LB118 b 5.80 70–01 SkyJck118² LegendryWeve118¹¹ Romnceishop118⁷ Off bit slow,gave way 8

7Hol fst 1⅛ :23 :45⁴ 1:09³1:41¹ 4+ OClm 100000N 94 1 68¹ 61¹¹ 68¹ 56 59¹ Nakatani C S LB118 b 4.10 88–02 Candy Ride118³ Primerica120³ Bonus Pay118²¹ Off bit slow,no threat 6

8Hol 7¾f :22² :44⁴ 1:09²1:28 4+[S]Tiznow150k 60 9 3 2ʰᵈ 2ʰᵈ 9¹⁰ 9²⁰¹ Nakatani C S LB120 b *1.80e 77–07 JoeyFranco122¹ BonusPyDy120¹ CommndersFlg120² 3wd,gave way,eased 9

3Dmr fst 1¼ :45²1:09⁴ 1:35 2:01¹ 3+ PacifcCl-G1 112 2 67¹ 53 33¹ 33¹ 43¹ Pincay L Jr LB124 b *.90 91–14 Skimming124² Tiznow117¹¹ Ecton Park124¹ Split foes,no late bid 7

5Hol fst 1¼ :46²1:10 1:34⁴2:01² 3+ HolGldCp-G1 111 7 3² 3¹ 2¹ 1¹ 2¹ Nakatani C S LB124 b *1.40 87–12 EarlyPioneer124¹ GeneralChllenge124¹¹ Dvid124¹¹ 3wd,bid,led,outkicked 9

8SA fst 1⅛ :47¹:111 1:36 1:49 4+ SnBrdnoH-G2 108 4 59¹ 51² 51⁰ 45¹ 32¹ Nakatani C S LB123 b *.20 87–18 EarlyPioneer113ⁿᵈ David113²¹ GeneralChllenge123² Lagged,along for 3rd 5

5SA gd 1¼ :47²1:12 1:36³2:01² 4+ SAH-G1 117 2 76¹ 75² 3¹ 1¹ 1¹¹ Nakatani C S LB121 b *2.00 94–13 GenerlChllenge121¹ Budroyl122¹ PurtoMdro118¹ 4wd move,led,driving 8

8SA fst 1⅛ :46 1:10²1:35⁴1:48⁴ Strub-G2 112 1 45 49 45 13¹ 19¹ Nakatani C S LB123 b *.60 91–09 GenerlChllenge123⁹¹ Luftikus117³ SintsHonor121¹ Bold move 4wd,rid out 4

8SA fst 1⅛ :22³ :46²1:101¹:41⁴ SnFndoBC-G2 100 5 55¹ 52¹ 54¹ 53¹ 42¹ McCarron C J LB122 b 1.80 91–06 SaintsHonor117¹ CatThief122ⁿᵈ MrBroadBlde118¹ Bumped,steadied 3/8 7

8Hol fst 1⅛ :47²1:112 1:36²1:49 3+ NtvDivrH-G3 109 6 43¹ 32¹ 41¹ 31¹ 1ⁿᵏ McCarron C J LB123 b *.50 81–19 GenerlChllenge123ⁿᵏ MooresFlt117⁴¹ Koslnin113¹ 3wd bid,wore down foe 6

General Challenge had been injured and sidelined 2½ years when he returned to training in early 2003. A Grade 1 winner, General Challenge's so-called class was ancient history. When he returned in a stakes race at Hollywood Park in April, many bettors discounted the extended layoff and assumed General Challenge would pick up where he left off. Talk about a leap of faith. Older, likely weaker, and returning from a severe injury, General Challenge was a shadow of his former self. In his comeback, General Challenge finished last. He fared little better in two subsequent starts, and was retired. Class and current condition are undeniably inseparable.

SIXTH RACE
Gulfstream
JANUARY 3, 2004

1¹⁄₁₆ MILES. (1.40¹) ALLOWANCE . Purse $34,000 FOR THREE YEAR OLDS WHICH HAVE NEVER WON A RACE OTHER THAN MAIDEN, CLAIMING OR STARTER OR WHICH HAVE NEVER WON TWO RACES. Weight, 122 lbs. Non–winners Of A Race Other Than Claiming At A Mile Or Over Since December 1 Allowed 2 lbs. Such A Race Since November 1 Allowed 4 lbs.

Value of Race: $34,000 Winner $20,400; second $6,120; third $3,400; fourth $1,360; fifth $340; sixth $340; seventh $340; eighth $340; ninth $340; tenth $340; eleventh $340; twelfth $340. Mutuel Pool $421,819.00 Exacta Pool $364,784.00 Trifecta Pool $251,824.00 Superfecta Pool $60,054.00

The initial step in class handicapping is identifying the type of race you are looking at. For example, an N1X allowance is shown above. Here are the basic class levels.

Maiden claiming. These are races for maidens (horses who have never won), in which all the entrants are eligible to be claimed.

Nearly 16 percent of the races in the U.S. in 2001 were for maiden claimers, which represent the lowest class level at every racing circuit. These are the slowest horses on the grounds. The levels of maiden claiming races vary. Thistledown in Ohio runs races for $3,500 maiden claimers. Del Mar and other higher-class tracks offer maiden claiming races from $25,000 to $62,500 and above.

Maiden special weight. These are maiden races in which none of the runners can be claimed. Maiden special weight races comprised about 10 percent of all races in the U.S. in 2001. These races sometimes carry restrictions regarding the state where the horses were bred. A maiden race limited to state-breds would be weaker than a maiden race open to all comers. When a restriction excludes a portion of the horse population, it weakens the race. It means fewer horses are eligible. This applies across all class levels, not just to maidens. More than one of four U.S. races in 2001 were for maidens (including maiden claimers). Put another way, in one of every four races, a horse is winning for the first time.

Claiming. This is the heart and soul of racing. These are races for horses that have won, and whose contestants are eligible to be claimed for anywhere from $2,000 to $100,000 or more. Claiming-race fields include a wide array—from former allowance horses down to lower-quality horses that never were good enough to compete in allowance company. Claiming races, and starter allowance races (restricted to horses who have started for a particular claiming price), made up more than half of the nation's races in 2001. Most claiming races are for horses valued at less than $20,000.

Allowance. Allowance races carry staggered eligibility conditions, starting with "one other than" (N1X). The phrasing is "nonwinners of a race other than maiden, claiming, or starter." Basically, it means a horse is eligible if he has not previously won an allowance race. Allowance races comprised 14 percent of the country's races in 2001.

Stakes. Finally, at the top of the class ladder are stakes races, which account for only 4 percent of the races but nearly one-quarter of the purses, and most of the media attention. These are the ones you read about in *Daily Racing Form* and the sports pages of daily newspapers.

Those categories—maiden claiming, maiden special, claiming, allowance, and stakes—comprise the bulk of class levels in U.S. racing. The type of race is shown in the conditions at the top of the past performances for each race. This boldface type holds the key. Based on the conditions of a race, a handicapper can determine which of the runners are appropriate contenders.

When the conditions identify the race as a $16,000 claiming sprint at six furlongs, handicappers identify the logical contenders based on the parameters for a typical $16,000 claiming sprint. The contenders may include a horse dropping one level after pressing the pace and tiring against $20,000 claimers, another horse moving up after winning a $12,500 claimer, and yet another who finished second for $16,000 last time out. They would all "fit."

A horse that finishes second or third typically returns at the same level. He may be "sitting on a win"—ready to win his next start. A horse that finished fourth or lower may drop at least one level, assuming good sense by the owner and trainer. A horse that wins will usually be raised one level.

Class does change over time, though typically not in a rapid manner. It is true that a horse that was a $10,000 claimer three months ago may be a legitimate $25,000 claimer today, but rarely will a horse make such a leap in one swoop. In fact, the class changes in older horses (3-year-olds and up) are deliberate. Horses move up in class a notch at a time. It is like a ladder. The climb is steep, but one rung at a time gets the job done. The question is whether the class change makes sense. Has the horse shown enough ability, or potential ability, to indicate he can handle a raise? What are the demands of this level, anyway?

The "does it make sense?" examination applies at all levels. It is usually acceptable for a horse that finished in the money in a Grade 2 to move to a Grade 1. But class analysis also can be used in reverse, as a means to eliminate losers. If a horse does not fit on class, his chances plummet. Say, for example, a horse finishes fourth in a $10,000 claiming race without being competitive at any stage. Next, the horse is entered for $16,000. Does it make sense? Hardly.

8 Van Rouge
Pink
Own: Mr & Mrs J S Moss
Green, Pink Hoop And Bar On Sleeves
FLORES D R (62 9 8 7 .15) 2003: (882 136 .15)

Gr/ro. c. 4 (Apr)
Sire: Red Ransom (Roberto)
Dam: Tarte Aux Pommes*Fr (Noblequest*Fr)
Br: Mr & Mrs J S Moss (Ky)
Tr: Shirreffs John(11 1 1 2 .09) 2003:(122 25 .20)

L 113

Life	13	3	0	5	$159,280	102	D.Fst	4	0	0	2	$
2003	6	1	0	2	$54,120	98	Wet(301)	0	0	0	0	
2002	5	2	0	2	$98,080	102	Turf(299)	9	3	0	3	$14
SA Ⓣ	5	1	0	3	$52,380	97	DstⓉ(301)	2	1	0	1	$

2Aug03-5Dmr	fm	1	Ⓣ :212	:444		1:321	3↑ Ⓡ WickerrH76k	91	6	810	512	65¼	98¾	96¼	Smith M E	LB116	9.80	96-06	*Touch of theBlues*122no Inesperado121½ Suances1201	4wd into lar
28Jun03-6Hol	fm	1	Ⓣ :232	:464	1:10	1:333	4↑ Alw 55000N2x	98	4	31½	21½	21	2½	1hd	Valenzuela P A	LB118	4.50	96-13	VanRouge118hd GoldenArrow1181 MrshllRooster1182	Stalked,bid
1Jun03-5Hol	fm	1 1/16	Ⓣ :233	:47	1:103	1:41	3↑ OClm 80000N	90	6	78	66	42½	42½	42¼	Espinoza V	LB119	4.80	89-13	Soud1211½ Speedy Pick119½ Albatros119nk	4wd into lane
18Apr03-8SA	fm	1	Ⓣ :231	:461	1:11	1:343	4↑ OClm 80000N	94	7	12	17	14	2½	42¾	Lopez C C	LB118	4.10	86-15	*Denied*1181 Marine118nk Meteor Storm1201½	Speed,inside,
27Mar03-7SA	fm	1	Ⓣ :23	:461	1:093	1:333	4↑ OClm 80000N	96	2	21	2½	2½	11	32¼	Stevens G L	LB118	*1.00	92-06	GoldenDragon1182 MrshllRooster120nk VnRouge1182	Stalked,led,
6Mar03-7SA	fm	*6½f	Ⓣ :214	:434	1:06	1:114	4↑ OClm 80000N	97	1	5	33½	31½	33	31½	Stevens G L	LB118	3.20	96-02	**ThunderBullet**120½ DevilsHorn1181 VanRouge1184½	Came out str,t
12May02-3BM	fm	1 1/16	Ⓣ :231	:462	1:11	1:413	AscotH-G3	102	2	1hd	13	12	13	14½	Lumpkins J	LB114	2.40	98-09	Van Rouge1144½ *Doc Holiday*118¾ Hecandigit1122	Met bid 2d trn
19Apr02-4SA	fm	*6½f	Ⓣ :221	:443	1:07	1:124	3↑ Md Sp Wt 48k	96	9	3	31½	2½	11	13½	Delahoussaye E	LB117	3.10	93-07	*VnRouge*1173½ GretWhiteFther1242½ MyorMurphy1172	Bid btwn,l
24Mar02-2SA	fst	1	:221	:452	1:103	1:363	Md Sp Wt 50k	83	4	2hd	1hd	1hd	3½	45¼	Delahoussaye E	LB120	3.20	83-12	*Like a Hero*120nk Hecandigit1202 *Sugar Babe*1203	Inside duel,we
24Feb02-1SA	fm	1⅛	Ⓣ :47	1:111	1:354	1:474	Md Sp Wt 48k	77	2	11½	12½	11	11	3¾	Delahoussaye E	LB120	*.90	89-10	*Johar*120nk February Storm120½ Van Rouge1205½	Inside,game,ou
21Jan02-7SA	fst	7f	:222	:452	1:102	1:23	Md Sp Wt 46k	79	9	5	52½	52½	32½	34½	Delahoussaye E	LB120	3.50	85-10	*Sunday Break*1204½ *Relentless Seller*120no Van Rouge1206	3wd,mis
4Nov01-6SA	fst	6½f	:214	:443	1:093	1:161	Md Sp Wt 40k	83	3	10	61¾	3½	2½	32½	Delahoussaye E	LB118	4.50	84-14	BringemJung1182½ AcdemySpy118no VnRouge1182	Rail bid,nippe

WORKS: Oct12 **Hol 5f fst 1:012 H** *6/26* Oct5 **Hol 5f fst 1:014 H** *12/26* Sep27 **Hol 5f fst 1:024 H** *27/33* Sep17 **Hol 5f fst 1:052 H** *34/35* Sep4 **Dmr 4f fst :482 H** *13/33* Jly29 **SA 4f fst :482 B** *4/14*
TRAINER: 61-180Days(35 .23 $3.61) Route/Sprint(16 .19 $1.40) Turf(103 .14 $2.16) Sprint(99 .16 $1.38) GrdStk(34 .21 $1.33)

Sometimes a sharp horse attempts a class hike that he is simply unequipped to make. Van Rouge was razor sharp, with speed figures that compared well to his rivals, when he attempted to jump from a two-other-than allowance into the Wickerr Handicap, annually one of the toughest nongraded turf stakes on the California calendar. The climb was too steep. Van Rouge was attempting a three-level jump (he won a N2X, and was jumping past N3X and classified allowance, all the way to a nongraded stakes). A successful leap past that many levels is improbable, and Van Rouge predictably was thwarted.

Mere victory is not necessary for a horse to move up in class, as horseplayers are reminded year after year. Horses that have established themselves as genuine Grade 1 runners can move up successfully despite defeats at lower class levels. Denon, for example, won the Grade 1 Hollywood Derby in 2001, lost two Grade 2 races early in 2002, but went up in class anyway. He subsequently won two Grade 1 races, and placed in two others.

Unbridled won the 1990 Kentucky Derby, lost his next four graded stakes, then won the Breeders' Cup Classic. Guided Tour, a Grade 2 winner in early 2001, lost a Grade 2 at Hawthorne before his 15-1 upset in the prestigious Grade 2 Stephen Foster at Churchill Downs. The point is, horses that have established credentials at the current level are considered suitable on class, notwithstanding losses against easier company in their most recent starts.

The measure of class, of course, is general. Class is similar to every other handicapping dynamic—it is one of many factors that will point a reasonable horseplayer in the right direction. There are plenty of longshot winners out there that make sense. Backing illogical horses in races when they are outclassed, however, will send a bettor to the poorhouse.

Let's look more closely at the main class levels—maiden claiming, maiden special weight, claiming, allowance, and stakes. Distinctions between the groups are clear. The traits of maiden claiming race winners are similar, and repeated often. The same applies to maiden special weight races, claiming races, and allowance and stakes. Different parameters apply. The past performances of a maiden claiming winner look decidedly different from the past performances of a Grade 1 winner. Let's start at the bottom, with the slowest horses on any circuit—maiden claiming.

Maiden Claiming

There is not much "class" at the bottom level. These are horses that have not won a race, and are eligible to be claimed. Many at this level will never win because they are simply too slow. Form reversals in the maiden claiming ranks are typically confined to lightly raced (two starts or less) horses, and droppers from maiden special weight races.

Due to limited ability, maiden claimers are easily evaluated. Slow horses are slow horses. They are proven losers, and they rarely just pop up and win. The genuine contenders are usually limited to just a handful of starters.

Most maiden claiming winners have shown a semblance of ability during competition, and typically fit one of four general categories.

- Droppers from higher maiden class levels.
- Previously finished in the money at the level of today's race.
- Have displayed early speed.
- First-time starters with steady works, and a trainer and jockey who win at least 12 percent of their starts/mounts.

That's it. Most maiden claiming winners fall into one of those four groups, and are listed according to preference.

A high percentage of maiden claiming winners are dropping from maiden special weight races, or higher-class maiden claiming races. The drop from maiden special into maiden claiming is one of the steepest class drops in racing.

Maiden special weight races often include future stakes horses whose careers are just getting started. A drop into a maiden claiming race is huge. These races are filled with talent-deficient runners with little chance of amounting to anything. Therefore, a bettor can support droppers out of maiden special weight races without regard to where they finished, providing they showed a little something. That is, they were positioned near the lead during the race, or outfinished at least half the field.

6 Unleash The Law — Own:Stony Oak Farm — Black — Silver, Hunter Green Sleeves, Silver Cap — $30,000
GUIDRY M (177 30 21 23 .17) 2003:(636 101 .16)
Dk. b or br c. 3 (Mar) KEEOCT01 $47,000
Sire: Unbridled (Fappiano)
Dam: Li Law(Known Fact)
Br: Newbyth Stud (Ky)
Tr: Barnett Bobby C(47 6 3 6 .13) 2003:(173 18 .10)
L 116

Life	3	M	0	0	$0	38	D.Fst	2	0	0	0		
2003	3	M	0	0	$0	38	Wet(385)	0	0	0	0		
2002	0	M	0	0	$0	–	Turf(280)	1	0	0	0		
CD	1	0	0	0	$0	26	Dst(350)	0	0	0	0		

22May03-6CD fm 1 Ⓣ :22^4 :45^4 1:10^4 1:36 3↑ Md Sp Wt 35k 38 9 5^7 5^{11} 7^{14} 9^{14} 9^{22¾} Albarado R J L 115 b 20.40 69–11 G P Fleet115^3 B. A. Way115^{6¼} Deputy Jack115^{1¼} 5w

27Apr03-5CD fst 6f :21^3 :46^1 :58^3 1:10^3 3↑ Md Sp Wt 39k 26 6 4 3^{½} 2^{hd} 5^{5½} 9^{20¼} Borel C H L 114 b 17.70 65–14 *Clock Stopper*114^{9¾} Stoker114^{¾} Galena Summit116^{½} Forced pace

23Mar03-5FG fst 6f :22^1 :45^2 :57^3 1:09^4 Md Sp Wt 26k 35 6 5 2^{½} 5^4 6^9 7^{22¾} Borel C H L 119 6.20 68–13 ClosToRno119^1 *ScoutsEmblm*119^{6¾} Ct'sCrft119^{2¾} Bore out, dropped

WORKS: ●Jun20 CDT 3f fst :36^2 B *1/6* ●Jun13 CDT 4f sly :48^3 B *1/12* Jun6 CDT 3f fst :36 B *2/8* May7 CD 7f sly 1:28^2 B *1/1* Apr19 CD 4f fst :48^3 B *14/62* Apr11 CD 4f fst :48^1 B *3/40*

TRAINER: Turf/Dirt(48 .08 $0.74) Route/Sprint(58 .02 $0.17) 31-60Days(111 .09 $0.71) Dirt(350 .11 $1.29) Sprint(192 .06 $0.92) MdnClm(127 .13 $1.48)

2 Favorite Magic — Own:Joseph Lacombe Stable — White — Dark Blue, Tan Diamond, Tan Chevrons — $30,000
VELASQUEZ C (279 43 46 40 .15) 2003:(921 146 .16)
B. c. 3 (Jan)
Sire: Favorite Trick (Phone Trick) $15,000
Dam: Magic Feeling*Ire(Magical Wonder)
Br: R C Durr & George Budig (Ky)
Tr: Kenneally Eddie(12 2 1 0 .17) 2003:(34 8 .24)
L 116

Life	4	M	0	0	$2,472	58	D.Fst	2	0	0	0	
2002	4	M	0	0	$2,472	58	Wet(140*)	1	0	0	0	$1,3
2001	0	M	0	0	$0	–	Turf(288*)	1	0	0	0	$1
CD	1	0	0	0	$990	57	Dst(230*)	0	0	0	0	

22Dec02-10FG fst 1$\frac{1}{16}$:23^3 :48^1 1:13^2 1:45^3 Md Sp Wt 28k 55 11 9^{9¾} 10^{7¼} 10^{8½} 9^{13} 9^{16} Martin E M Jr L 119 52.30 66–17 *SettleHoofer*119^{½} GurnteedSwp119^{½} *Commndr'sAffir*119^1 Showed
Previously trained by Moyer Steven L

22Nov02-10CD fst 1$\frac{1}{16}$:23^3 :47^1 1:13 1:46 Md Sp Wt 40k 57 10 4^3 4^4 3^2 5^{6¾} 5^{12¾} Meche L J L 120 32.40 65–22 CaptainFantastic120^{½} DocRobbins120^{3½} SintWki120^4 4-5w,flattene

10Oct02-4Kee sly 1$\frac{1}{16}$:22^4 :47 1:13^1 1:48^3 Md Sp Wt 50k 58 11 5^{5¾} 6^{3¾} 4^1 5^{3¾} 5^8 Meche L J L 118 f 29.90 54–30 ⒹSirCherokee118^{½} CherokeePrinc118^{3¾} CubbyBr118^{3½} 6w trip,empty

2Sep02-8EIP fm 1 Ⓣ :23^2 :46^1 1:10^3 1:35^3 Md Sp Wt 20k 55 5 12^{10} 11^{11} 11^{6½} 9^7 8^6 Meche L J L 121 53.60 79–09 Swdust121^2 SlutThCount121^{hd} WwConquistdor121^{no} Bmp start,no t

WORKS: Jun16 CD 5f fst 1:04^3 B *27/29* May31 Kee 3f fst :37^3 B *6/18*

TRAINER: +180Days(3 .00 $0.00) Route/Sprint(11 .18 $1.22) Dirt(110 .18 $1.96) Sprint(52 .15 $1.83) MdnClm(34 .09 $0.59)

The fifth race at Churchill Downs on June 25, 2003, was a $30,000 maiden claiming sprint with 11 starters. Seven already had lost at the level, and two others had run in maiden special weight races on lesser circuits and been soundly beaten. That left two main contenders—Favorite Magic and Unleash The Law, dropping into a maiden claimer for the first time. Unleash The Law showed speed and quit. But not Favorite Magic. He tucked behind the speed, angled three-wide into the lane, and shot clear to win by 2¼ lengths. Trained by Eddie Kenneally, who was 24 percent on the year to that point, and ridden by Churchill leading rider Cornelio Velasquez, Favorite Magic paid $14.80. Maiden droppers are still a favorite play, nearly 20 years after Waterford Hills at Suffolk Downs.

The pace call in a horse's past performances is a leading indicator of where he might fit on class. It is the third-to-last number in the horse's running line, typically with a quarter-mile remaining in the race. By then, every horse in the field has expended most of its energy. A horse able to be in contention at that late stage of the race—even if he faded in the stretch—may require only a drop in class to win.

When a dropper from a maiden special weight finished in the top half of the field, or beat half the field to the pace call, he may be a rock-solid choice to win a maiden claimer.

An experienced maiden that has not lost at the level of today's race must be treated as a potential contender. That includes horses dropping from $50,000 maiden claiming to $25,000 maiden claiming. A horse that has not been defeated at the level—has not proven to be a bust—will be considered a contender.

A horse that finished in the money (first, second, or third) in a maiden claiming race fits on class. Likewise, a horse that vied for the lead to a late stage of the race also fits, irrespective of finish position. That is, the horse was positioned first, second, or third at the pace call. At the lowest class levels, any early speed is a clear indicator of ability. Even cheap speed horses that have compiled 0-for-10 records sometimes win. A bettor does not have to "like" them, particularly at low odds, but they cannot be eliminated. They have shown just enough ability that eventually they may find a field they can beat.

Elimination of maiden claimers can be bold and cold-hearted. If a horse has not finished in the money, or at least shown speed by pressing the pace in his last start, he can be eliminated. This emphasizes the most recent running line, for good reason. Maiden claimers are "class-less" horses whose past achievements are minimal. If they have not done anything in their last two starts, forget them.

Second-time starters are an easy read when returning at the same level. A good performance—within three lengths at the pace call, or outfinished half the field—is followed usually by an improved effort. While some handicappers will excuse a horse's poor finish position if he encountered traffic problems, it is asking for trouble with maiden claimers. Because their ability is limited, they have a tendency to find trouble. They are less agile, and often wind up in compromising situations simply because of their clumsiness. It is poor practice to forgive a maiden claimer because of a bad trip.

Similarly, some handicappers are willing to excuse a first-time starter that was well-bet and did not fire. The approach is unnecessarily forgiving. First-time starters are well-bet because of morning workouts. It's a lot different in the afternoon. A maiden claimer who runs poorly should be considered a bust until he shows something in the heat of actual battle. Workouts only count for so much, and are not to be confused with ability. Once a maiden claimer has raced, workouts are used only to gauge fitness, not how fast he can run.

First-time starters do win maiden claiming races. Usually, they are no big surprise. They often are well-bet, debut with a credible workout pattern, and have an established stable with a proven record of winning first time out. During the 2002-03 Santa Anita winter meet, 13 percent of the maiden claiming winners were first-time starters, and more than half of the debut winners paid $8 or less. In a race that lacks a credible dropper, a first-time starter can be supported

In every maiden claiming race, a host of horses are proven losers with only a smidgen of ability. Unless they finished in the money last time, or had speed and challenged for the lead at the pace call last time, forget them.

Imagination is encouraged in handicapping, but there is no sense reaching for something that is not there. A slow horse is a slow horse. Once he has established his lack of ability at the level, eliminate him from consideration. Longshot winners in maiden claiming races can be found, and typically fit a familiar description. River Adventure, a wacky upsetter at Del Mar, had shown speed against better, dropped in class, and paid $126.60.

Speed figures are less applicable in maiden claiming races. The preferred selection in a maiden-claiming race is a dropper from a maiden special weight. That horse is not likely to have earned a respectable speed figure, because he most likely will have been drilled against the better company. Frequently, a horse that has earned a speed figure equal to the maiden claiming par will have done so while having lost the race. In other words, he is a proven loser. Speed-figure pars are a major part of handicapping higher-class races, but less relevant with maiden claimers.

These are guidelines a handicapper can look for in maiden claiming races, in order of preference:

- Droppers from maiden special weight races that have shown speed.

- Droppers from maiden special weight races that have defeated half the field.
- Droppers from maiden special weight races regardless of performance.
- Droppers from higher-class maiden claiming races that have shown speed.

(From this point down, the horses become slow and unreliable. Some handicappers consider a maiden claiming race unplayable unless it includes a starter from one of the above categories. Yet the oversupply of maiden claiming races means that bettors who play serial-race wagers such as the pick three find them a necessary evil. So we continue, embarrassingly.)

- Has displayed contending speed, at any level.
- First-time starters with a trainer and jockey that win at least 10 percent.
- A maiden claimer that has exhibited ability by finishing in the money.

If you get down this far on the list without finding a contender, it is probably time to pass the bet entirely.

On to the next class level, as we move up.

Maiden Special Weight

This is where the good horses get started. A top horse wins in his first two or three starts. Those unable to win after three starts typically need a drop into a maiden claiming race to win. It's an important point, because maiden special weight races are filled with career maidens who pile up endless defeats. A maiden that has made three starts (some handicappers insist on only two starts) without hitting the board or earning a speed figure normally required to win at this level is a horse to avoid.

One reason that maiden special weight sprints do not lend themselves to victory by career losers is because maiden special weight races usually are strong. At the best circuits in the country—California, New York, Kentucky, and Florida—wave after wave of promising horses begin their careers in maiden special weight races. Invariably, there is a fresh face—a potential star—

arriving on the scene.

The most probable winner of a maiden special weight race is a second-time starter who ran a winning race in his debut. A winning race is a performance that earned a Beyer Speed Figure reasonably close (three points) to par for that track. Speed figures provide keen insight into maiden races.

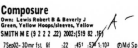

6 During
Own: McIngvale James
Blue, White Stars, Red Chevrons On White
ESPINOZA V (150 16 20 25 .11) 2002:(1143 188 .16)

Dk. b or br c. 3 (Feb) KEESEP01 $350,000
Sire: Cherokee Run (Runaway Groom) $20,000
Dam: Blading Saddle(Blade)
Br: Gulf States Racing Stables II (Ky)
Tr: Baffert Bob(74 11 14 11 .15) 2002:(686 133 .19)

Blinkers ON | Life 1 M 0 0 $960 77 | D.Fst 1 0 0 0 $S
2003 1 M 0 0 $960 77 | Wet(415) 0 0 0 0
L 120 2002 0 M 0 0 $0 – | Turf(205) 0 0 0 0
SA 1 0 0 0 $960 77 | Dst(340) 0 0 0 0

4Jan03– 6SA fst 6f :21² :44² :57 1:10¹ Md Sp Wt 48k 77 6 5 31½ 4² 4² 53½ Bailey J D LB 120 5.00e 83–11 Atswhtmtlknbot120½ BckIndMnr120½ MchImg120¹ Angled in, weak
WORKS: Jan26 Hol 5f fst 1:01¹ H 4/15 Jan19 Hol 5f fst 1:02 H 1/9 Dec30 Hol 5f fst :59⁴ H 2/14 ●Dec23 Hol 5f fst 1:00¹ Hg 1/9 Dec15 Hol 5f fst :58⁴ Hg 2/38
TRAINER: 2ndStart(97 .20 $1.20) 1stBlink(107 .15 $1.34) Dirt(644 .19 $1.46) Sprint(498 .18 $1.40) MdnSpWt(211 .18 $1.43)

At the Santa Anita winter meet, for example, the par for maiden 3-year-old colts is 88. A horse that finished second in his debut and earned a Beyer reasonably close to par (within 10 points with a first-time starter) would be a contender second time out. There is a distinction between a probable winner and a mere contender. A maiden who ran within three points of par would be difficult to beat; a horse that ran within 10 points of par would only be considered a contender. After earning a 77 Beyer Speed Figure in his debut, During was a contender second time out. He added blinkers and won like the good colt he would become—a graded stakes winner on both coasts. During paid $14.80 when he won the maiden race.

Any maiden who exceeds the Beyer par is difficult to oppose, providing the performance occurred in his first or second start. Here is an example of a third-time starter who got her act together second time out, and followed with a maiden win.

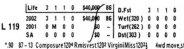

Composure
Own: Lewis Robert B & Beverly J
Green, Yellow Hoops/sleeves, Yellow
SMITH M E (9 2 2 2 .22) 2002:(519 82 .16)

B. f. 2 (Apr) KEESEP01 $470,000
Sire: Touch Gold (Deputy Minister) $40,000
Dam: Party Cited(Alleged)
Br: Rancho San Peasea S A (Ky)
Tr: Baffert Bob(6 0 1 3 .00) 2002:(511 106 .21)

97-103
to-85

Life 3 1 1 0 $40,000 86 | D.Fst 3 1 1 0 $40,0
2002 3 1 1 0 $40,000 86 | Wet(320) 0 0 0 0
L 119 2001 0 M 0 0 $0 – | Turf(262) 0 0 0 0
SA 0 0 0 0 $0 – | Dst(303) 0 0 0 0

7Sep02– 3Dmr fst 6f :22 :45¹ :57 1:10³ ⑩Md Sp Wt 50k 86 7 3 4² 2½ 11½ 14 Smith M E LB 120 *.90 87–13 Composure120⁴ Rmisvest120² VirginiMiss120¾ 4wd move,stdy hand
18Aug02– 4Dmr fst 5½f :21⁴ :45¹ :58¹ 1:05¹ ⑩Md Sp Wt 50k 68 6 5 31½ 3¹ 2½ 2½ Flores D R LB 119 1.30 84–08 Ain'tJtSweep119¹½ Composure119¼ PointCler119² Stalked btwn,held
28Jly02– 7Dmr fst 5f :21 :45½ :58¹ ⑩Md Sp Wt 47k 31 10 10 8⁹ 7⁷ 8¹⁰ 10¹⁷¾ Flores D R LB 118 b .60e 79–12 SeaJewel118⁴ Ain'tJtSweep118² RousingAgain118½ Hesitated,off sl
WORKS: ●Sep30 SA 4f fst 1:11² H 1/28 Sep24 SA 1 fst 1:37⁴ H 1/3 ●Sep18 SA 5f fst :58² H 1/30 Sep1 Dmr 5f fst :58² H 1/55 Aug26 Dmr 5f fst :59² H 7/49 Aug13 Dmr 5f fst :58³ H 2/46
TRAINER: 2YO(243 .25 $2.06) Sprint/Route(130 .24 $1.96) Dirt(994 .22 $1.65) Routes(404 .21 $1.68) GrdStk(143 .23 $1.81)

(—)X

The illustration occurs in the summer of Composure's 2-year-old campaign, but it applies. It shows a filly whose Beyer figure improved 37 points over her debut. It was reasonable to expect she would improve further in her third career start, which she did.

Before handicapping a maiden race, it is necessary to know the speed-figure par. What does it take to win? Only then can one recognize when a race is more likely to be won by a first-time starter. In a maiden race in which none of the experienced runners has approached par, a handicapper can expect the race to be won by a new face.

In the absence of an experienced maiden who has exceeded par, or run within three points of par, the maiden race is likely to be won by a first-time starter. The horse would have responsible connections (a trainer who wins at least 10 percent) and a pedigree that suggests early-career wins (sire statistics show which stallions produce offspring that win at least 10 percent first time out). Also, a sensible workout pattern should accompany the horse into the race.

These are guidelines a handicapper can look for in maiden special weight, in order of preference.

MDSPWT

- Second-time starters who ran within three points of the Beyer Speed Figure par first out.
- Third-time starters who showed improved ability second time out, and ran within three points of par.
- First-time starters with good connections, debuting against modest foes.
- From here on down the pickings are slim. Career losers should be eliminated, unless the race is restricted to older (4-year-olds and up, female routers, or state-breds). Horses who have lost any maiden claiming race rarely win maiden special weight races.

lazareen
wn: Moss Mr & Mrs Jerome S
reen Pink Hoop/bar On Sleeves
ZA V (109 15 17 18 .14) 2003:(896 131 .15)

Gr. f. 4 (Feb)
Sire: Holy Bull (Great Above) $25,000
Dam: Zoonaqua(Silver Hawk)
Br: Mr. & Mrs. J. S. Moss (Ky)
Tr: Sadler John W(30 7 4 4 .23) 2003:(227 44 .19)

Blinkers OFF — L 123

Life	7	M	3	2	$39,640	83	D.Fst	6	0	3	1	$34,240	83
2003	3	M	1	0	$10,080	67	Wet(325)	0	0	0	0	$0	–
2002	4	M	2	2	$29,560	83	Turf(290)	1	0	0	1	$5,400	70
Dmr	2	0	1	0	$9,800	76	Dst(310)	2	0	2	0	$19,000	76

6Dmr fst	1	$:22^1$	$:45^2$	$1{:}10^4$	$1{:}37^3$	3↑ ⒻMd Sp Wt 51k	**28**	4	$4^{2\frac{1}{2}}$	5^5	9^{10}	9^{14}	$9^{27\frac{1}{4}}$	Espinoza V	LB 123 b	*3.30	59-16	Lf'sPlsurs117^5 **SntlyPrsson**117^2 UnlmtdFth117^{nk}	Chased btwn,gave way	9
1Hol fst	$1\frac{1}{16}$	$:23^3$	$:47^1$	$1{:}11^3$	$1{:}45^1$	3↑ ⒻMd Sp Wt 55k	**67**	5	3^{nk}	2^{hd}	2^{hd}	$2^{\frac{1}{2}}$	$2^{\frac{1}{2}}$	Espinoza V	LB 123 b	4.10	77-17	Abby'sNotNorml116½ Nzreen123½ *Lif'sPlsurs*117^1	Vied btwn,led,caught	7
3Hol fst	6f	$:22^2$	$:45^2$	$:58^2$	$1{:}11$	3↑ ⒻMd Sp Wt 44k	**63**	6	4	5^4	$5^{4\frac{1}{2}}$	$5^{4\frac{1}{2}}$	$5^{4\frac{1}{2}}$	Smith M E	LB 123	1.10e	80-12	Cat Fighter117^1 American Saga117^1 Playgirl117½	Off rail, no rally	7
3Dmr fst	$1\frac{1}{16}$	$:23^2$	$:47^3$	$1{:}13^1$	$1{:}45^2$	3↑ ⒻMd Sp Wt 49k	**76**	1	$5^{2\frac{1}{2}}$	$6^{3\frac{1}{2}}$	$7^{2\frac{1}{2}}$	3^1	$2^{3\frac{1}{2}}$	Smith M E	LB 117	1.80e	72-20	Smart Lacy117$^{3\frac{1}{2}}$ Nazareen117^4 Que Bonita117½	Came out,2nd best	8
1Hol fm	$1\frac{1}{16}$ Ⓣ	$:23^4$	$:47$	$1{:}11^3$	$1{:}43^1$	3↑ ⒻMd Sp Wt 45k	**70**	7	5^5	$5^{4\frac{1}{2}}$	$5^{4\frac{1}{4}}$	3^5	3^6	Lumpkins J	LB 116	*.60	73-21	ViwFromThTop116$^{2\frac{1}{2}}$ JunprSprngs123$^{3\frac{1}{2}}$ Nzrn116^{no}	3wd move,just held 3rd	7
8Hol fst	$6\frac{1}{2}$f	$:22$	$:44^3$	$1{:}09^3$	$1{:}16$	3↑ ⒻMd Sp Wt 43k	**83**	8	3	9^6	8^7	$6^{9\frac{1}{2}}$	2^7	Smith M E	LB 117	4.20	84-14	ReineDesNeiges117^7 Nzren117^{hd} DimondEmblm118$^{3\frac{1}{2}}$	Swung out,late 2nd	9
1SA fst	6f	$:21^2$	$:44$	$:57$	$1{:}10^1$	ⒻMd Sp Wt 48k	**82**	8	8	$5^{3\frac{1}{2}}$	5^3	5^4	$3^{3\frac{1}{4}}$	Espinoza V	LB 120	18.80	84-10	MinisterThtcher120^{nk} *MissTropics*120^3 Nzreen120^1	4wd,3wd,bested rest	11

Aug11 Dmr 5f fst $1{:}01^2$ **H** *42/62* **Aug5 Dmr 4f fst** $:49^1$ **H** *26/43* Jly22 **Dmr 6f fst** $1{:}13^3$ **H** *8/14* Jly16 **Hol 5f fst** $:59^4$ **H** *2/34* Jly10 **Hol 5f fst** 1:02 **H** *19/34* Jly3 **Hol 5f fst** $1{:}01^4$ **H** *18/33*
R: BlinkOff(9 .11 $0.82) Dirt(466 .18 $1.82) Routes(204 .18 $1.79) MdnSpWt(88 .11 $0.83)

Although career maidens (three or more losses) usually need a drop to win, they do not always drop because they were expensive and/or well-bred. Despite these horses' limited ability, their connections often are reluctant to drop them into a maiden claimer. There is always a remote chance that horses will turn it around. Usually, they do not. The dilemma is recurrent with fillies and mares. When the filly Nazareen ran July 28, 2003, at Del Mar, she already had finished in the money five times from six starts, with a descending pattern of Beyer figures. Yet some handicappers were fooled based on a flashy recent workout. Workouts are not to be mistaken for ability. Nazareen ran poorly, typical for a career maiden.

A well-bred filly that lacks sufficient ability to win a maiden special weight retains value as a future broodmare. Many of these career maidens could win if dropped to a maiden claimer. They do not drop because their residual value is higher than the $50,000 claiming price they should race for. Instead, they toil in maiden races, sometimes running just well enough to tease bettors into believing a win is forthcoming. They are sucker horses, best avoided.

When a "career loser" finally does win, extenuating circumstances often play a role. Maiden races for 4-year-olds and up typically are weak. Horses who have not won by then are often hopeless. And yet, even older career maidens sometimes find weak foes they can defeat. In that regard, older maidens are similar to maiden claimers. An older maiden with only a smidge of ability can win in a weak enough spot. But they remain poor wagering propositions, and are never to be confused with lightly raced maidens who still have potential.

We move on to the next class level, for winners.

Claiming

Want to buy a horse? Here's where you go. Claiming horses are established racehorses whose ability is clear. They run about every three weeks, and are at the heart of a track's racing schedule. A claiming horse is entered for his perceived value. It is the handicapper's job to view the horse's history and determine if he has enough ability—class—for the task at hand.

Bill Spawr is one of the leading trainers on the Southern California circuit. He says the health of a claiming horse—its "soundness"—is the tell-all.

"The question with a cheap horse, like a $10,000 or $12,500 [claimer] is, where does he belong? It's all soundness—90 percent of them are not going to be sound. There is going to be something wrong. Well, what is it that is wrong? What does it mean? What is he worth because of it? Does he have a knee with a chip?

Maybe it's old, and maybe he can get along with it. Does he have a bowed tendon that's soft and mushy and sore? Does he have a suspensory? You have to evaluate, where does he belong with this problem? What can he take?"

Heat of the Moment	Ch. f. 3 (Apr)		Life	11	5	1	1	$89,340	83	D.Fst	11	5	1	1	$89,340	83
Own: Ivan C Baker	Sire: Unusual Heat (Nureyev) $2,500		2003	10	5	1	1	$89,340	83	Wet(263)	0	0	0	0	$0	–
White, Red Stripes, White Stars On Blue	Dam: Flying Blonde (Mehmet)	L 117	2002	1	M	0	0	$0	25	Turf(268)	0	0	0	0	$0	–
J M (18 1 5 2 .06) 2003: (501 68 .14)	Br: Barry Abrams (Cal) Tr: Sherman Art(13 4 4 1 .31) 2003:(335 73 .22)		BM	0	0	0	0	$0	–	Dst(332)	4	3	1	0	$54,000	83

1Dmr fst 6f	:22 :45 :57 2 1:10 4	©Clm c-(32–28)	79 6 3	2 hd	1 1	12 1	1 1	Berrio O A	LB 118 b	*1.80	87– 14 HtofthMomnt118 1 Hgrstown118 1 Blusrobnsggs116 2 1 Clear,angled in,held 9
d from Auerbach, Houston and Team Green for $32,000, Spawr William Trainer 2003(as of 8/13): (184 41 34 13 0.22)											
1Hol fst 6f	:22 :44 2 :56 3 1:09 4	©Clm 20000(20–18)	83 1 5	2 1	1 2	15	15 1	Berrio O A	LB 118 b	3.00	91– 10 HtofthMomnt118 5 1 Hgrstown118 1 1 CompnyfMry118 1 1 Inside,in hand late 7
11Hol fst 6f	:22 1 :44 4 :57 2 1:11 1	©Clm 16000(16–14)	72 10 2	1 1	11 1	1 4	11 1	Valenzuela P A	LB 118 b	*2.30	84– 10 HetoftheMomnt118 1 1 LughingSunris118 2 ThCstl120 1 1 Dueled,clear,driving 10
1Hol fst 6f	:22 1 :44 4 :57 3 1:10 3	©Clm c-(16–14)	63 3 4	2 1	1 hd	1 1	22 1	Lovato A J	LB 120 b	3.80	84– 08 The Castle118 2 1 Heat of the Moment120 1 Cortina118 1 Dueled,held 2nd 6
d from Xitco, John and Sobel, Steven for $16,000, Abrams Barry Trainer 2003(as of 3/29): (138 13 17 16 0.09)											
1SA fst 6 1 f	:21 4 :44 4 1:11 1 1:18 4	©Clm 25000(25–22.5)	49 5 5	4 1 1	3 nk	3 3	47 1	Garcia M S	LB 118 b	1.90	71– 19 EndurngFrdom118 2 Honyofscor120 1 1 JoysWorld118 4 4wd bid turn,wkened 5
1SA fst 6 1 f	:21 3 :44 2 1:10 1:17	©Clm 45000(50–45)	67 3 4	4 2	31 1	32 1	38 1	Garcia M S	LB 114 b	8.40	79– 16 Forthlfofm118 2 1 AkronAvn118 6 HtofthMomnt114 3 Angled in,bested rest 5
1SA fst 6 1 f	:22 :45 4 :58 4 1:05 4	©Clm c-(32–28)	60 3 5	3 1	3 nk	12 1	1 2	Martinez F F	LB 118 b	3.20	82– 10 HetoftheMoment118 2 Honyofscor120 nk Cortin118 2 3w bid,angled in,clear 6
d from Abrams, Diane and David and Litt, Jason R. for $20,000, Glatt Mark Trainer 2003(as of 3/29): (77 13 12 7 0.17)											
1SA fst 6 1 f	:22 :45 1:10 4 1:17 4	©Alw 40000s	52 3 8	8 2	2 hd	32 1	71 1 1	Martinez F F	LB 120 b	33.60	73– 13 Thgrlfrmstrd120 3 NncsMgcBrsh120 4 1 LttlMsGnrl118 2 1 5wd,3wd,weakened 9
1SA fst 6 1 f	:22 :45 1 1:10 3 1:17 1	©Clm c-(32–28)	57 2 8	4 1 1	4 1 1	54	59 1	Garcia M S	LB 118 b	3.00	77– 12 MyHoneyBunny118 no AlpinSingr118 4 MgicSmok118 5 Stalked rail,wkened 8
d from Abrams, Barry Trainer 2003(as of 1/31): (311 39 40 36 0.13)											
1SA fst 6 1 f	:22 :45 4 :58 4 1:05 4	©Md 32000(32–28)	59 3 8	52 1	4 2	2 hd	1 2	Garcia M S	LB 120 b	2.90	83– 16 HtofthMomnt120 2 LckyLos120 2 ShlbystooSmrt120 no Stdied start,rallied 8

Aug31 BM 3f fst :36 3 H 7/22 Aug7 Dmr 4f fst :51 1 H 57/62 Aug1 Dmr 4f fst :50 3 H 33/36 Jly7 SA 6f fst 1:15 2 H 14/16 Jly1 SA 5f fst 1:02 4 H 32/32 Jun21 SA 5f fst 1:03 3 H 39/46
: 1stClaim(38 .21 $1.70) Dirt(749 .20 $1.87) Sprint(541 .21 $2.03) Alw(91 .20 $2.33) Wet(117 .19 $2.21)

Spawr claimed Heat of the Moment on April 30, 2003, for $16,000. "When I got her, she was definitely 'off' in the right knee. I X-rayed it and there was no bone damage, but you knew there was something going on there—probably soft tissue, or cartilage, or something. So I put her on some medication to see if it would help. And we did some other things with her, she was very nervous and upset, [then] she improved so much, and the knee kind of went away.

"She was a digger"—a nervous horse who paws holes in the ground inside her stall—"and she was just scared of everything. We put her in a little half-stall so she couldn't do anything. And she was right next to my office, and I just made her my pet. I'd go by every once in a while and give her carrots. All day long, just pet her. And when she got her confidence back, she started putting weight on.

"I ran her back for the same price [$16,000] and she won, then her knee got better again, and then the way she won last time [$20,000 claiming] . . . I don't know what she's worth now because her body has changed, and her knee's okay now. She's a different filly.

"Now I have to decide, what is she worth? I've been evaluating her habits—she eats good now, and she's not nervous. She used to stall-walk. And she looks like a different horse. She must have gained 80 pounds, all muscle, and her temperament is different now. She won easy the other day, so I have to evaluate . . . how much has she improved? I think she's worth $40,000."

The first week of the 2003 Del Mar meet, Heat of the Moment looked a picture in her outside pen at Spawr's barn. She had filled out, her chestnut coat shined, her eyes looked half-asleep, and one of her rear legs was lifted slightly off the ground—a sign of passive bliss. For the filly Heat of the Moment, all was right with the world. Spawr pondered where to run her next.

"I'm looking at a Cal-bred allowance going six and a half. What I'm waiting to see when the next book comes out is if there's a 40 [$40,000 claiming race]. I'd rather run her there, against straight 3-year-olds, and it could be as much money as the Cal-bred allowance. If somebody wants to give me 40 . . . well, they're not going to give me 40 for her. I don't think so."

In the case of Heat of the Moment, it was suggested that $40,000 might be the maximum she would ever be worth. "Yeah, maybe the knee starts bugging her again. Then she comes back down. My job is to evaluate, 24 hours a day, their habits, their physical problems, and put it all together, and see what they're worth. I could take the bandage off one morning and it's got a bowed tendon. So each day they're worth something different. Each day they're worth a different number.

"With claimers, it's who's good right then? Who's good now? Horses dropping, if they get two or three bad races in a row, it's a bad sign. You could throw one race out, maybe, but not three. When I claim a horse, I don't want a project where I have to spend three months and $7,500 in training bills . . . to do what? Get back to [the original price]? But if I think [it will take] a month, I'll do it. There has to be something there, enough substance."

Claiming-race principles apply everywhere. Few race meets are filled with as much quality as the annual spring meet at Keeneland. Held in April in Lexington, Kentucky, the 16-day festival features top-echelon racing every day it runs, and includes two of the country's premier races for 3-year-olds—the Blue Grass Stakes for Kentucky Derby hopefuls, and the Ashland Stakes for fillies aiming toward the Kentucky Oaks.

But not every race includes a future star. Keeneland offers a fair share of claiming races, and for a horseplayer able to negotiate the minefield, claiming races provide abundant opportunity.

t Charm
eck Edward L. and Rowena

B. f. 4 (May) KEEAPR01 $40,000
Sire: Quiet American (Fappiano) $35,000
Dam: Bright Majesty (Majestic Light)
Br: Donald & R. Mary Zuckerman, as Tenants by the Entireti (Ky)
Tr: Beck Edward L(0 0 0 0 .00) 2003:(1 0 .00)

-1Kee	my	6½f	:22^2 :45^3 1:12^3 1:19^2	4↑ⒻClm c-10000	**60**	9	1	4^3	4^7	3^{3½}	1^{1½}	Stortz M^7	L109 f	*3.20	76- 15	*Quiet Charm*109^{1½} Celestial Sea116^1 *Wolf Girl*116^{nk}	7w lane,driving,clear	9
ned from Full O Run Racing Team for $10,000, Cain Joe Trainer 2003(as of 4/10): (40 11 4 3 0.28)																		
-7TP	fst	6f	:21^4 :45^1 :58 1:11^1	3↑ⒻAlw 5000s	**54**	2	4	6^{4¾}	6^{8½}	4^{7½}	4^6	Peck B D	L116	3.20	80- 14	*Aat Falt*122^{3¾} All Quacked Up116^{1¼} Lady Chelsea116^1	4 wide mid turn	6
-3TP	fst	6f	:22^1 :45^4 :59 1:12^3	3↑ⒻClm 7500(7.5-6.5)	**58**	9	8	4^{5½}	5^7	4^{5½}	1^½	Peck B D	L119	3.70	79- 18	Quiet Charm119½ Broad Breadth116¾ Makes a Fist114^{5½}	5 wide, up in time	10
-3TP	fst	6½f	:23^1 :47^2 1:13^4 1:20^4	4↑ⒻClm 7500N3L	**58**	9	3	2^2	2^{hd}	1^3	1^½	Lumpkins J	L119	*1.90	73- 29	*Quiet Charm*119½ Roberto's Victory116^{5¾} Smart Doll116^{no}	Lasted late	9
-2TP	fst	6f	:22 :46 :59^2 1:13^2	4↑ⒻClm 7500N3L	**50**	4	4	3^5	3^{2½}	3^{1½}	5^{3¾}	Woods C R Jr	L122	7.40	71- 25	AirStorm116^{1¼} ChmpgneAlley116¾ ReflectionBy116^{nk}	3 wide, nothing left	11
-3TP	my	6½f	:23^2 :47^3 1:14^2 1:21^2	3↑ⒻClm 7500N2L	**61**	11	4	5^{1¼}	4^{nk}	1^3	1^3	Butler D P	L115	*1.40	70- 29	Quiet Charm115^3 R P's Lady115½ *Take Me Home Lady*108^{4½}	5 wide, driving	12
-2Hoo	gd	6f	:23^2 :48^2 1:01 1:13^4	3↑ⒻClm 5000N2L	**59**	8	2	6^{2½}	2^{hd}	1^½	2^{nk}	Thompson T J	LB116	*1.80	75- 25	ClerDenil116^{nk} *QuitChrm*116^{8¾} AnglofShrcco119^{hd}	4wd bid,dueled,missed	10
-2Hoo	sly	6f	:23 :48^1 1:01^1 1:14^3	3↑ⒻClm 5000N2L	**46**	1	7	7^{5¼}	6^5	4^{6½}	3^{5¾}	Noll C S	LB116	*2.60	65- 30	Isle of Tunes116^2 Twin Stripes119^{3¾} Quiet Charm116¾	Angle out, no gain	10
-7EIP	fst	6f	:22^3 :46^3 :59^3 1:12^4	3↑ⒻClm 7500(7.5-6.5)N2L	**41**	4	6	11^{9¾}	11^{13}	9^{8¼}	6^{9¾}	Lopez J	L112	4.10	72- 15	Princess Iris114^{3¾} Hers Funny116^{3½} Sassy Six107½	Minor gain	12
-8EIP	fst	1	:23^2 :47^1 1:13 1:39^3	3↑ⒻClm 15000(15-13.5)N2L	**42**	3	5^3	6^{6½}	6^{8½}	7^{11}	6^{13¾}	Nagle V^7	L107	5.20	68- 20	*Skorch*113^{2¼} French Reign117^{4¼} Spirits Girl114^{no}	Tired	9
40EIP	fst	6f	:22^2 :45^4 :58^2 1:11^2	3↑ⒻClm 30000(30-25)N2L	**52**	4	4	6^7	6^{9½}	7^{11}	6^{11¾}	Martinez J R Jr	L112	16.00	77- 13	Nerissa111^{5¾} *KatesPistol*112^{1¾} ChampgneAlley116^{hd}	Unruly at gate,empty	11

The handicapping problem is determining the appropriate claiming level at Keeneland for a horse shipping from another track, a question that accompanied the 4-year-old filly Quiet Charm in the first race on April 10, 2003. Quiet Charm had been racing through winter and spring at Turfway Park, a "lower-class" track than Keeneland.

Keeneland's high purse structure means it attracts better allowance horses than Turfway, and also better claiming horses. And claiming horses do ship from the minors to the majors. Quiet Charm had been running in claiming races at Turfway Park, where she had won three of her last five. She was entered in a $10,000 claiming race at Keeneland, having won her race before last for $7,500. A handicapper might wonder if she could handle the bump up in class.

In fact, Quiet Charm was hardly being raised at all. Keeneland offers only four claiming levels in the spring: $10,000, $15,000, $25,000, and $50,000. Quiet Charm had entered a $10,000 claiming race, the lowest level on the Keeneland claiming-class ladder. She had already progressed beyond the bottom claiming level at Turfway, and therefore was expected to fit at the bottom level at Keeneland—$10,000 claiming.

Quiet Charm won and paid $8.40, hardly a surprise. She was racing at a low class level—the bottom—where she had proven to be competitive.

You see, the bottom level at many racetracks includes horses that are so slow they should be racing at an even lower level. But once a horse is already racing at the bottom, there is nowhere else to drop. Another example of comparative class occurred in a tougher claiming race at Keeneland. Take a look at the past performances of Prince Consort, as they looked going into April 10.

Prince Consort
Own: Michael James A

Ch. c. 4 (May) OBSFEB01 $75,000
Sire: Gilded Time (Timeless Moment) $17,500
Dam: Dubiously (Jolie Jo)
Br: Mark Johnston Racing, Ltd (Ky)
Tr: Maker Michael J(0 0 0 0 .00) 2003:(114 14 .12)

```
10Apr03-4Kee my 6f      :21^2 :45   :57^3 1:11    4↑Clm 50000          84 5 4 3^3½ 3^2½ 2½ 1^no Borel C H     L116fb *2.70 84-15 PrinceConsort116^no DnceMusic116^no MiBrujo116½ Hop start,gamely,
13Mar03-9FG sly 6f      :22^2 :46   :57^4 1:10^4  4↑OClm 40000N        82 5 1 1½ 1^hd 2^hd 3^2½ Borel C H       L118fb *.80  83-10 Halo's Tiger118^1¾ Jarret'sOdyssey118¾ PrinceConsort118^3½ Weakened
4Mar03-7FG fst 5½f ⊗:22 :45^2 :57^4 1:04^3  4↑OClm 40000N        89 5 4 4^2 3^2 2½ 2^1 Borel C H          L118fb 4.40  92-14 KristysExcellent118^1 PrinceConsort118^1 Guapzo118½ Loomed, no m
2Feb03-9FG fst 6f       :22   :46   :58^1 1:10^4  4↑OClm 40000N        86 6 1 2½ 2^hd 1^hd 4^2¼ Borel C H      L122fb 11.90 84-15 Big Team Spirit118^no Guapazo120^2 Explosive Count118^nk Weakened
3Jan03-7FG fm *5½f Ⓣ:21^4 :46  :58^1 1:05    4↑Alw 30000N1x       85 2 4 2^1 2^1 1½ 1¾ Theriot H J II      L118b  6.90  91-09 PrinceConsort118¾ FrAwyBell118^1¼ OpenChronicl118^hd Bid, edge, al
20Dec02-7FG fst 5½f ⊗:22^3 :45^3 :57^2 1:03^4 3↑Alw 30000N1x     92 2 2 1^hd 1^1 1^hd 2^2¼ Meche L J        L116fb 6.80  95-17 Guapazo120^2¼ Prince Consort116^3¾ Bully Bully118^1½ Exchanges bru
6Jly02-5CD fst 6f       :21^2 :45   :57^1 1:10      Clm 50000(50-40)   61 7 1 3^4½ 3^3 5^7 8^10 Borel C H    L116fb *2.60 78-09 Bold Prospect116^1 Lunar Bounty120^1½ Piston120^1½ Stalked,4w,flatte
21Jun02-3CD fst 6f      :21^4 :45^1 :57^2 1:10^1    Clm c-(40-30)      77 2 5 2^1½ 2^hd 2^hd 3^2¼ Court J K  L118fb *2.00 85-14 DelrsSupris122^1½ ByontChrg120¾ PrincConsort118¾ Hop start,empty
  Claimed from Social Circle Stable for $40,000, Bemiss James H Trainer 2002(as of 6/21): (8 2 2 2 0.25)
5Jun02-8CD sly 6f       :21^3 :45^2 :57^3 1:10^4    Clm 30000(30-20)   83 1 2 1^1½ 1^1½ 1^2½ 1^4¼ Court J K  L115fb 9.00  84-20 PrinceConsort115^4¼ DelersSupris121¾ ByontChrg119^1½ Pace, steady
```

Where should he run at Keeneland—$10,000, $15,000, $25,000, or $50,000? Prince Consort had finished in the money for a $40,000 tag at Fair Grounds in Louisiana. But what did that mean? Was he already racing at the highest claiming level? Or, was he in the middle? To evaluate a claiming horse, a handicapper must be familiar with the claiming hierarchy of the originating track. So the question again—what was a $40,000 claiming race at Fair Grounds? It ranked right near the top.

The highest Fair Grounds claiming levels were $50,000 to $75,000 during the 2003 meet. The next grouping down was $35,000 to $49,000. Below are the claiming class levels, with Beyer Speed Figure pars, of Fair Grounds, and Keeneland.

Fair Grounds	
$50,000 to $75,000	93
$35,000 to $49,000	91
$21,000 to $34,000	89
$15,000 to $20,000	87
$10,000 to $14,900	82
$7,900 to $8,900	79
$6,000 to $7,400	78
$5,000 to $5,900	77

Keeneland	
$50,000	99
$25,000	90
$15,000	84
$10,000	79

As the chart shows, a $40,000 claimer at Fair Grounds was near the top of the claiming-class ladder. Prince Consort, having established himself near the top level at Fair Grounds, figured to run well at a similar level at Keeneland. And he did so even though his recent Beyer Speed Figures indicated he might be in tough. In fact, the figures implied he fit at $25,000 claiming, an unreasonable suggestion considering he had established himself as a genuine $40,000 competitor at Fair Grounds. A perfect fit for $50,000 at Keeneland, Prince Consort won by a nose and paid $7.40. He was racing at a level at which he was qualified. Sometimes, a handicapper does look beyond speed figures and employ simple common sense.

In order to know the level at which a horse fits, a handicapper must know what the class levels are, and the Beyer pars for those levels. They vary from track to track. (As this was written, plans were in the works for Beyer Speed Figure pars to be introduced in *Daily Racing Form* past performances. They are also available in *DRF Simulcast Weekly*.)

Here is a final example from Keeneland. Knotty Knows had won her most recent start at Turfway Park by 14½ lengths, racing for a $15,000 claiming tag. Viewing her past performances, where should she have been placed at Keeneland?

There were three choices. She could run for a $15,000 claiming tag again. But she had just won for that price, by the length of the grandstand. It was unreasonable to expect that her connections would risk her again for the same claiming price. It made sense she would be raised to a higher claiming level.

But how far? Trainer Jim Walsh took the logical approach and bumped Knotty Knows up one level to $25,000 claiming, a sensible move. A perfect fit on class, in excellent form, Knotty Knows raced to the lead and never looked back. Proving that longshots in sharp current form, racing at the appropriate class level, do win, Knotty Knows paid $31.60.

While spring at Keeneland is a highlight of the Kentucky racing season, summer at Del Mar offers the best racing on the year-round Southern California calendar. Del Mar offers higher purses than Santa Anita and Hollywood, making it a natural attraction for owners. Beyond the financial ramifications, there is an element of prestige attached to Del Mar. At the seven-week seaside meet, which runs late July through early September, everyone wants to win a race.

Beyond the prestigious reputation of Del Mar, standard class applications apply in claiming races. It helps to know what types of horses win what types of races. During the 2002 summer meet at Del Mar, there were 12 sprint races for $10,000 claimers, 4-year-olds and up—the bottom level for winners. Though only two favorites won, most winners fit on class. Jack's Ole' is an example.

Jack's Ole'
Own: Hollendorfer Jerry

B. h. 6 (Mar)
Sire: Ole' (Danzig) $2,500
Dam: Someday Jack*Mex (Dr. Blum)
Br: Granja Mexico (Cal)
Tr: Hollendorfer Jerry(0 0 0 0 .00) 2003:(1216 282 .23)

8Aug02- 3Dmr	fst	6f	:22^1 :45^2 :57^3 1:10^2	3↑ [S]Clm 10000(10-9)	**84**	4	7	4^2	3$^{1\frac{1}{2}}$	3^2	1^{hd}	Baze T C	**LB**119 fb	7.10	88- 12	Jack's Ole'119^{hd} Guadalupes Tailor119^3 *Mr. Reed*117^2	Rallied,up at w
21Jly02- 1Hol	fst	6½f	:22^1 :44^4 1:10^1 1:16^4	4↑ Clm 9000(10-9)	**85**	7	6	7$^{6\frac{1}{2}}$	6$^{3\frac{3}{4}}$	3^2	3$^{\frac{3}{4}}$	Escalona G S	**LB**118 fb	10.70	86- 12	*BigShakespeare*120no Itsallinthehert120$^{\frac{3}{4}}$ *JcksOle*118^5	4wd into lane,willi
16Jun02- 6Hol	fst	6½f	:22^1 :44^4 1:09^3 1:16	4↑ Clm c-(10-9)	**68**	10	8	5$^{2\frac{1}{2}}$	6$^{3\frac{1}{2}}$	5$^{5\frac{1}{2}}$	6$^{10\frac{3}{4}}$	Pincay L Jr	**LB**118 fb	*2.30	80- 14	ValintVision118^{nk} HevensTret118$^{2\frac{1}{2}}$ Sideburn118^3	Chased btwn,stdied
Claimed from Brewer, Haagsma and Haagsma, et al for $10,000, Hines N J Trainer 2002(as of 6/16): (78 6 13 14 0.08)																	
22May02- 8Hol	fst	7f	:21^3 :44^2 1:10^2 1:24	4↑ [S]Clm 10000(10-9)	**83**	9	10	8$^{8\frac{1}{4}}$	6$^{8\frac{1}{2}}$	4^3	2^{nk}	Pincay L Jr	**LB**118 fb	3.70	79- 16	Pennysenyen115^{nk} JcksOle118^{hd} Sunnybgood118$^{\frac{1}{2}}$	Stmbld start,lugged
1May02- 3Hol	fst	6f	:22^2 :44^4 :57^1 1:09^4	4↑ [S]Clm 10000(10-9)	**82**	7	7	4$^{4\frac{1}{2}}$	3$^{2\frac{1}{2}}$	3$^{2\frac{1}{2}}$	2$^{\frac{1}{2}}$	Pincay L Jr	**LB**118 fb	3.10	90- 08	Scoop of Ice118$^{\frac{1}{2}}$ Jack's Ole'118^3 Mr. Reed118$^{5\frac{1}{2}}$	Off slow,ralli
11Apr02- 6SA	fst	6½f	:21^3 :44^4 1:10^4 1:17^4	Clm 10000	**71**	3	9	8$^{8\frac{3}{4}}$	8$^{8\frac{1}{4}}$	6$^{4\frac{1}{4}}$	4$^{1\frac{1}{2}}$	Pincay L Jr	**LB**117 fb	3.80	82- 08	InstntKrm119$^{\frac{1}{2}}$ LtUpthKnght119^{hd} TndrLvnJns117^1	Off bit slw,stdied
31Mar02- 9SA	fst	6f	:21^3 :44^2 :56^2 1:08^4	4↑ Clm 10000	**75**	8	9	7^4	5^5	5^4	5$^{7\frac{1}{2}}$	Pincay L Jr	**LB**118 fb	4.10	86- 12	*Aggressive*118^1 Wagul118$^{2\frac{1}{2}}$ Joe Holiday118^3	Steadied ea
15Feb02- 4SA	fst	1	:22^2 :46 1:11^1 1:37^2	Clm c-(20-18)	**80**	10	6$^{6\frac{1}{2}}$	6$^{4\frac{1}{2}}$	5^3	5$^{4\frac{3}{4}}$	5^4	Pincay L Jr	**LB**117 b	9.30	80- 14	[D]BrronH117^{no} Ivgtndrmyskn117^{hd} *FnEntrtnmnt*117^{nk}	4 wide into stret
Claimed from Manoogian Jay for $20,000, Mitchell Mike Trainer 2002(as of 2/15): (246 45 44 29 0.18)																	
2Feb02- 1SA	fst	6f	:22 :44^3 :56^4 1:09^2	4↑ Alw 40000s	**86**	4	5	4$^{2\frac{3}{4}}$	3$^{4\frac{1}{2}}$	4$^{3\frac{1}{2}}$	3$^{6\frac{1}{2}}$	Pincay L Jr	**LB**120 b	7.10	84- 09	As ItUsedtoBe122^4 *PeakAtYou*122$^{2\frac{1}{2}}$ Jack'sOle'120no	Btwn to turn,late 3
Previously trained by Hess R B Jr																	
9Jan02- 5SA	fst	6½f	:22^1 :45 1:09^3 1:16	4↑ Alw 40000s	**82**	3	10	5$^{2\frac{1}{4}}$	5$^{2\frac{1}{4}}$	4^3	3^4	Pincay L Jr	**LB**122 b	12.00	89- 15	[D]Workum115^3 Para Alquilar122^1 Jack's Ole'122^1	Off bit slow,best re
Awarded second purse money																	
30Nov01- 4Hol	fst	6f	:22 :45 :57^2 1:10^3	3↑ [S]Md 32000(32-28)	**75**	4	10	7$^{4\frac{3}{4}}$	3$^{5\frac{1}{2}}$	3$^{1\frac{1}{2}}$	1^2	Pincay L Jr	**LB**120 b	3.90	87- 11	JcksOle120^2 Bringdownthehous122$^{1\frac{1}{2}}$ ShrdViw120^{hd}	Off bit slw,stdied7,
25Feb01- 9SA	sly	6½f	:22 :45^2 1:11^4 1:18^4	[S]Md 40000(40-35)	**60**	4	6	6^{11}	6$^{7\frac{1}{2}}$	5$^{4\frac{1}{4}}$	3^3	Desormeaux K J	**LB**120 b	*1.40	71- 19	Spacey120^{hd} *Golden Bonus*120^3 *Jack's Ole'*120$^{1\frac{1}{4}}$	Off bit slow,wide t
15Jan01- 4SA	fst	6½f	:22^1 :46 1:11^2 1:17^4	[S]Md c-(40-35)	**76**	5	9	5$^{2\frac{1}{4}}$	6$^{3\frac{1}{4}}$	4^{nk}	3$^{\frac{3}{4}}$	Espinoza V	**LB**120 b	3.20	78- 15	NobleKinsman120$^{\frac{3}{4}}$ ThatCoolCat120^{hd} Jack'sOle120^5	5wd into lane,ralli
Claimed from Granja Mexico and Palma for $40,000, Palma Hector O Trainer 2001(as of 1/15): (57 8 7 7 0.14)																	
3Nov00- 4SA	fst	1	:22^4 :47^1 1:11^3 1:37^4	Md 50000(50-45)	**59**	3	7^5	7^5	7$^{7\frac{1}{2}}$	7$^{9\frac{3}{4}}$	6^{10}	Sorenson D	**LB**120 b	*2.00	72- 15	*BnkStreet*120^1 Jgurmnspssion120$^{3\frac{1}{2}}$ GoldnLightning120^{hd}	3wd 1/2, no ra
11Oct00- 8SA	fst	5½f	:21^4 :45^1 :57^4 1:04^2	Md 45000(50-45)	**73**	9	8	4^3	3^4	3^3	3$^{1\frac{1}{4}}$	Sorenson D	**LB**118 b	4.30	85- 14	Tkhmtothlmt120$^{1\frac{1}{4}}$ Upsnddowns115^{no} JcksOl118$^{1\frac{1}{2}}$	Stmbld strt,5wd to t
27Sep00- 7Fpx	fst	6f	:22^2 :46^2 :59^3 1:12^2	[S]Md Sp Wt 30k	**65**	2	2	7^7	4$^{1\frac{1}{2}}$	3^1	2$^{1\frac{3}{4}}$	Sorenson D	**LB**118 b	3.90	83- 13	BrazenFlstff118$^{1\frac{3}{4}}$ JcksOle118$^{1\frac{1}{4}}$ MysteriousCt118$^{2\frac{1}{2}}$	No room rail 2nd tu
15Sep00- 3Fpx	fst	6f	:22^3 :46^4 :59^4 1:12^1	[S]Md Sp Wt 29k	**61**	4	6	4$^{2\frac{1}{2}}$	4$^{1\frac{1}{4}}$	2^2	2^2	Sorenson D	**LB**118 b	5.50	84- 10	ProperMotion113^2 JcksOle118^2 KingGorgsWy118^{12}	Came out,bumpd

The $16.20 win by Jack's Ole' was typical. Of the 12 horses that won $10,000 claiming sprints, seven had acceptable current form at low class levels. Four were dropping from higher levels, or returning from layoffs. This small sampling hardly covers the entire array of claiming races, but the patterns of the winners repeat continually.

Most bottom-level claiming winners are racing regularly. It is more difficult to train a low-level horse up to a winning race than it is to train a top horse to a winning race. Preference in claiming races goes to horses currently racing. In fact, though Del Mar is a meet for which California horsemen plan months in advance, most claiming-race winners at Del Mar just happen to be "doing well" when the meet starts. No fewer than 27 of the 34 Del Mar claiming sprints in 2002 were won by horses that had raced within the last 45 days. The other seven were comebackers that had not raced in more than 45 days.

Claiming-race winners generally have run well recently at or above the level of today's race. And they have done so within their last three starts. If a horse is dropping in class after being defeated by tougher, typically the dropper will have defeated half the field, or been within striking range at the pace call in that race. It is perfectly fine to back a dropper if his last performance was acceptable.

Layoff horses in claiming races are to be treated with caution. When a claiming horse is laid off, it is usually because of a negative reason. Either an infirmity has flared up, or the horse has gone sour. There is little guarantee a horse will fire first start back. In all likelihood, his value has diminished. However, a layoff of less than two months, heading into a top meet such as Del Mar, may only mean that the trainer has freshened the horse for a winning effort early in the meet.

er Magic Gr/ro m. 5
gden & Sanger Sire: Petersburg (Danzig) $1,500
een Horizontal Stripes, Blue Dam: Wild Ignition(Conquistador Cielo)
Br: Mr & Mrs Guy C Roberts (Wash)
C (105 10 18 5 .10) 2002:(547 46 .08) Tr: Sadler John W(51 11 6 7 .22) 2002:(251 42 .17)

L 121

Life	21	4	2	4	$95,445	83	D.Fst	11	3	2	2	$72,160 83
2002	6	2	1	2	$51,080	83	Wet(400)	2	1	0	0	$10,800 66
2001	14	2	1	2	$43,625	80	Turf(255*)	8	0	0	2	$12,485 80
Dmr	1	1	0	0	$24,600	82	Dst(340)	8	2	2	2	$47,560 83

-1Dmr fst 6f :214 :451 :574 1:11 3↑ ⒻClm 35000(40-35) 82 4 3 32 21 1½ 11¼ Baze T C LB 117 b *2.20 85-19 Silver Magic117 1¼ Sister Patricia119no Farah Love1191½ Stalked,bid,clear 6
-1Hol fst 6½f · :22 :443 1:093 1:161 4↑ ⒻClm 20000(20-18) 83 7 1 1½ 11 11½ 15 Baze T C LB 118 b 3.80 90-11 *SilverMgic*1185 ShezJzzySlw1182 StormySpirit1183 Dueled,clear,driving 7
-3Hol fst 6½f :22 :442 1:101 1:164 4↑ ⒻClm c-(20-18) 66 4 7 42½ 42½ 43½ 36½ Pedroza M A LB 118 b 2.20 80-13 CfeDelMr1202½ MidnightMngo1184 *SilvrMgic*118no Squeezed strt,late 3rd 7
med from Mevorach Samuel for $20,000, Carava Jack Trainer 2002(as of 05/05): (140 18 24 23 0.13)
-6SA fst 6f :212 :442 :571 1:102 4↑ ⒻClm 32000(32-28) 67 1 5 44 45½ 65 66¾ Desormeaux K J LB 118 b 4.00 79-12 *Svea Dahl*118nk Boca Dream1182½ Dare Bunny1162 Saved ground,no rally 7
-5SA fst 6½f :213 :443 1:101 1:171 4↑ ⒻClm 25000(25-22.5) 79 2 4 31½ 31 21 21 Valenzuela P A LB 119 b 7.60 86-18 Boca Dream1191 Silver Magic1191 Lurefan1191 3wd into lane,held 2nd 8
-3SA fst 6½f :22 :45 1:102 1:17 4↑ ⒻClm c-(20-18) 72 4 1 3½ 1hd 1hd 32 Valenzuela P A LB 117 b 17.20 86-16 Zodiaque1191 Lurefan1141 Silver Magic1172½ Btwn foes,stdied 1/16 8
med from Harris Arnold & McCurley Clifton for $18,000, Bacorn Herbert L Trainer 2002(as of 02/08): (41 3 4 4 0.07)
-1SA fst 6½f :222 :453 1:111 1:174 3↑ ⒻClm 20000(20-18) 55 4 7 3½ 32 63¾ 58 Baze T C LB 119 b 7.40 71-12 Catfit1213½ Silver Del Sol119hd Native Gold Digger1191 3 wide, weakened 9
-6Hol gd 5½f Ⓣ :222 :453 :58 1:042 3↑ ⒻClm 50000(50-45) 71 6 9 107¼ 1010 108¾ 76½ Baze T C LB 118 b 44.00 75-19 *Lady Cadet*118hd *Isit Class*1182½ Dandy Night1181 Pulled,shuffled,no bid 10
-5Hol fm 5½f Ⓣ :222 :444 :571 1:032 3↑ ⒻAlw 46020N1X 70 7 3 53¾ 54 42½ 75 Pincay L Jr LB 120 b 13.80 82-13 *ExcessivelyHot*122hd PrincssTi1221 SyingGrc1201½ 3wd,angled in,wkened 8
-3SA fst 6f :213 :442 :564 1:094 3↑ ⒻOClm 40000N 62 5 2 41½ 35 36 69 Baze T C LB 118 b 25.10 81-13 ParadeOfGold1202 FortLauderdale117no *SveaDhl*1183½ Chased, weakened 7
-2Hol fm 5½f Ⓣ :22 :443 :563 1:024 4↑ ⒻClm 40000(40-35) 74 3 7 42½ 42 61¾ 62¾ Delahoussaye E LB 118 b 6.70 87-07 Courtesan118hd SndsAglow118nk BestLidPlns118nk Trapped rail,outkicked 7
-5Hol fm 5½f Ⓣ :214 :444 :563 1:023 3↑ ⒻAlw 46500N1X 77 1 7 74¾ 43½ 42¼ 33 Baze T C LB 119 b 9.80 88-07 Sylvan Girl1163 Go Ruby Go115no Silver Magic1191½ Lacked room 1/4-3/16 9
: Sep2 Dmr 5f fst 1:004 H *21/58* Aug27 Dmr 6f fst 1:142 H *6/8* Aug21 Dmr 5f fst 1:014 H *24/35* Aug15 Dmr 4f fst :472 H *7/51* Jly28 Dmr 4f fst :473 H *8/46* Jly22 Hol 6f fst 1:134 H *3/5*
ER: 31-60Days(197 .17 $2.22) Dirt(494 .16 $2.06) Sprint(410 .16 $2.15) Alw(125 .15 $2.34)

Silver Magic earned a career-high Beyer on June 19, her first start for trainer John Sadler. At age 5, she had gained a new lease on life. Sadler could have wheeled her right back, but instead took his time and gave the mare nearly two months off. Her training pattern—a sharp work every six to seven days—revealed her readiness when Sadler jumped her three levels for her comeback. Off a career-best performance, and raised in class by a high-percentage trainer (Sadler was 17 percent for the year), Silver Magic earned a similar Beyer and won again.

All seven layoff sprinters that won claiming races at Del Mar in 2002 had solid workout patterns. Six of the seven had a recent work at the distance of their comeback, nearly all had top trainers, and every horse was proven at or above the level at which he was returning.

Most claiming-race winners:

- are proven at the class level, recently finished in the money at the level, or have beaten half the field in a higher-class race;
- are in solid form, racing regularly, or with a strong workout pattern;
- are racing at a level that makes sense.

Turf racing is different, because the dynamics of the race are almost the opposite of those on dirt. On turf, early speed is hardly meaningful. Instead, the most important part of a turf race is either the final quarter-mile or the last three furlongs. The dilemma will be further examined in the next chapter, on pace and speed. Since we are still talking about class, an important factor to consider is that the claiming hierarchy on turf is elevated from dirt. That is, the bottom class level for a turf claimer is higher than on the main track.

In Southern California, for example, the bottom level for turf runners is typically $40,000 claiming. The various class levels go from $40,000 to $50,000 to $62,500 to $80,000. With only four levels from which to choose, class analysis might seem relatively easy in turf claiming races. It is.

What you see is what you get. The winners of claiming races on turf are established, proven veterans. Many have exhausted their eligibility to allowance races, and are not quite good enough to compete in stakes. So they compete in claiming races. Some are former stakes horses that have slowed over the years and now face softer competition.

With few exceptions, claiming-race winners on turf are no secret. At Del Mar in 2002, 12 of the 14 races were won by a horse that had finished first or second at the level, or above. Turf claimers are won by fit, established horses. Before backing a layoff horse in a turf route, one should insist the horse be facing easier company.

A general summary is in order regarding claiming horses. When a claiming horse finishes second or third, his next start can be in any class direction without handicapping concern.

Class is like a ladder. It is ascended and descended one rung at a time. Class does fluctuate, but changes generally are deliberate. Class can change radically, over a three-month period, but the change is less drastic from one race to the next. Horses jumping more than a single class level often find it difficult to win.

Conversely, horses may drop more than a single level to win. Again, picture a ladder. It is difficult to skip a rung on the way up. But with a tight grip, it is possible to ease down more than a single rung. Horses sometimes need a severe drop to get back to form. It is a lot easier to go down than it is to go up.

Claiming horses sometimes are the allowance horses of yesterday. Which brings us to the next level of class.

Allowance

After a horse wins a maiden special weight race, what next? As with many things in racing, it depends. A horse that wins an ordinary maiden claiming race will soon be racing against other claiming horses. But a horse that wins a maiden race in inordinately fast time will move into the allowance ranks. A top horse will proceed right through his conditions.

The first allowance condition is "nonwinners of a race other than maiden or claiming." This is for horses that have done nothing more than win a maiden race—or, in some cases, sharp claiming horses trying allowance company. The shorthand designation is N1X. The term "nonwinners . . . maiden or claiming" means a horse that wins that allowance condition is ineligible to run in that race again.

A typical first-condition allowance winner is lightly raced, typically having started no more than five times. The first-condition allowance winner will have earned a good speed figure against similar allowance company, or in his maiden victory. While maiden winners often move into allowance races regardless of how fast they ran, speed figures provide an easy tool of elimination.

A horse coming off a maiden-race win is considered a contender in an allowance if the speed figure he earned in the maiden race approaches the allowance par. Even then, the faster pace that the horse usually must face means many maiden winners may be up against it when they meet allowance foes for the first time. Horses ascend the class ladder in deliberate fashion, even future stars. Perhaps the most difficult barrier in racing is the jump from a maiden race into an allowance race.

Rather than progress rapidly through the allowance conditions, most horses are thwarted along the way, even while they continue to improve. Fact is, they usually do not win the first time they tackle tougher competition. But they are competitive. A first-condition allowance winner usually will have earned a Beyer Speed Figure within three or four points of par, frequently having earned the figure in a similar allowance race.

These were the first-condition allowance pars for older males at various tracks in 2003.

Santa Anita	97
Aqueduct	91
Fair Grounds	88
Gulfstream	85
Hawthorne	81
Turf Paradise	72

When few, or none, of the entrants have approached par, it may be time to shop for a claiming horse in an allowance race. These are professional racehorses who may lack brilliance, but give it their best every start.

It gets tougher at the second condition. That is, "nonwinners twice other than maiden or claiming." Horses are eligible to the N2X condition if they have won only one allowance race. They have not won twice in allowance company and are referred to as "nonwinners twice." Only a small percentage of horses make it to the second condition. Many are future stakes horses, powering through their conditions while gaining mental and physical seasoning.

Next is N3X, or "nonwinners three times other than maiden or claiming." The higher the restrictions, the tougher the race gets. The N3X condition is open to horses that have not won three allowances or stakes. A horse eligible to an easier condition (N2X, for example) could race "above his conditions," but there would be little point. Why face tougher, anyway? The purse money is not that much better from one allowance condition to the next, yet the demands are much greater.

After a horse wins a conditioned allowance race, proving his superiority at that particular level, he cannot race under those conditions again. Otherwise, a horse could stay at the same allowance level, and continue to pummel the same horses. They don't. There are richer races ahead. Future stakes horses usually progress through allowance races before they become stars.

:ee Gentleman
ygod Mr. and Mrs. Martin J

B. h. 5 (Apr)
Sire: Storm Cat (Storm Bird) $500,000
Dam: Key Phrase (Flying Paster)
Br: Mr. & Mrs. Martin J. Wygod (Ky)
Tr: Shirreffs John A(0 0 0 0 .00) 2003:(163 33 .20)

Life	10	4	1	0	$202,547	117	D.Fst	8	3	0	0	$164,947 117
2003	4	2	0	0	$129,247	117	Wet(410)	1	1	0	0	$27,600 98
2002	6	2	1	0	$73,300	98	Turf(336)	1	0	1	0	$10,000 90
Bel	3	1	0	0	$44,100	98	Dst(415)	3	1	0	0	$93,847 117

5SA	fst	6f	:21 :43^{1} :55 1:07^{4}	3↑BCSprint-G1	107	12	3	$5^{1\frac{3}{4}}$	3^{1}	$4^{3\frac{1}{2}}$	5^{5}	Valenzuela P A	LB126	10.80	94-05	*CajunBeat*$123^{2\frac{1}{4}}$ Bluesthestndrd126^{2} ShkeYouDown$126^{\frac{1}{2}}$	Chased five wide	13
7SA	fst	6f	:21^{2} :43^{2} :55^{2} 1:08	3↑AnTIJBCH-G1	99	1	6	$5^{4\frac{3}{4}}$	5^{3}	4^{2}	4^{3}	Krone J A	LB114	*1.20	95-06	Avnzdo$116^{1\frac{1}{2}}$ CptinSquire117^{hd} Blusthstndrd$115^{1\frac{1}{2}}$	4wd into lane,outkickd	6
4Dmr	fst	6f	:21^{4} :44^{1} :56 1:07^{4}	3↑Ⓡ PirtsBntyH77k	117	5	6	3^{3}	$3^{1\frac{1}{2}}$	$1^{1\frac{1}{2}}$	1^{5}	Krone J A	LB114	2.50	102-09	YankeeGentleman114^{5} *Avnzdo*120^{hd} RushintoAltr118^{1}	3wd bid,ridden out	8
7Dmr	fst	$6\frac{1}{2}$f	:22 :44^{2} 1:09 1:15^{4}	3↑OClm 62500N	102	1	6	$2^{\frac{1}{2}}$	1^{hd}	$1^{1\frac{1}{2}}$	$1^{3\frac{1}{2}}$	Valenzuela P A	LB119	*1.30	96-11	*YnkeeGentlemn*$119^{3\frac{1}{2}}$ HurricneSmok$119^{1\frac{1}{2}}$ Plirrojo119^{8}	Off bit slow,pulled	6
ously trained by Mott William I																		
0Sar	sf	1 Ⓣ	:24^{2} :48^{1} 1:12^{2} 1:36^{4}	3↑Alw 50000N2X	90	9	3^{4}	$3^{2\frac{1}{2}}$	$3^{1\frac{1}{2}}$	$2^{1\frac{1}{2}}$	$2^{3\frac{1}{2}}$	Bailey J D	L117	*1.40	80-16	*RivrRush*$121^{3\frac{1}{2}}$ *YnkGntlmn*$117^{1\frac{3}{4}}$ FbruryStorm117^{no}	Stayed on well stretch	9
8Bel	fst	$1\frac{1}{16}$	:23^{3} :47 1:10^{3} 1:42^{2}	Dwyer-G2	82	1	3^{5}	$2^{\frac{1}{2}}$	$2^{\frac{1}{2}}$	2^{6}	$5^{8\frac{1}{2}}$	Bailey J D	L115	1.55	79-13	*Gygistar*$121^{\frac{1}{2}}$ Nothing Flat117^{5} American Style115^{3}	Hit gate, ducked in	6
8Bel	fst	7f	:22 :44 1:09^{1} 1:22^{3}	RvaRdgBC-G2	92	9	2	3^{1}	$1^{\frac{1}{2}}$	2^{1}	$4^{5\frac{1}{2}}$	Bailey J D	L115	*1.35	84-10	*Gygistar*$119^{4\frac{1}{2}}$ Draw Play$115^{\frac{1}{2}}$ *True Direction*$119^{\frac{1}{2}}$	3 wide move, tired	9
7Bel	gd	$1\frac{1}{16}$	:22^{3} :45^{1} 1:10 1:43^{4}	3↑Alw 46000N1X	98	1	$1^{\frac{1}{2}}$	$1^{1\frac{1}{2}}$	$1^{1\frac{1}{2}}$	1^{6}	1^{5}	Bailey J D	L115	*.40	81-25	YnkeeGentlemn115^{5} DputyDsh$115^{5\frac{1}{2}}$ InugurlAddrss115^{nk}	Cruised in hand	10
4Aqu	fst	7f	:23 :46 1:09^{4} 1:22^{2}	3↑Alw 43000N1X	–	3	8	-	-	-	-	Bailey J D	L114	*.20	- 12	PersonblePete$119^{4\frac{3}{4}}$ LordOfthThundr112^{no} Gico$115^{\frac{1}{2}}$	Stumbled, lost rider	8
9GP	fst	7f	:22^{1} :45 1:09^{3} 1:22^{2}	Md Sp Wt 32k	98	3	5	2^{hd}	1^{1}	$1^{4\frac{1}{2}}$	1^{11}	Bailey J D	122	5.00	95-07	Yankee Gentleman122^{11} Tell J$122^{\frac{1}{2}}$ HudsonStreet122^{2}	Inside, kept to task	10

●Nov16 Hol 5f fst :58 H *1/33* Nov8 SA 4f fst :49^{1} B *21/31* Oct21 SA 3f fst :36^{1} B *3/19* Oct15 SA 5f fst :58^{1} H *2/38*

Yankee Gentleman is a perfect example. His runaway maiden win was followed two starts later by a runaway allowance win. Two starts in Grade 2 races proved futile, and he was laid up after dropping back into a second-condition allowance. Yankee Gentleman resumed his career in summer 2003 at Del Mar.

Most of the examples apply to older horses. With 2-year-olds and lightly raced 3-year-olds, improvement is anything but deliberate. In fact, it can be explosive. In 2-year-old races, it is not uncommon for a maiden winner to jump directly into a graded stakes. It happens every year. In fall 2002, Composure made the successful leap from a maiden sprint win at Del Mar to a Grade 2 route during the fall Oak Tree meet at Santa Anita.

The volatile improvement in 2-year-olds is not always a surprise. Young horses do not automatically gain stakes credentials merely by winning a maiden race. But when they are moving up following powerful maiden wins, are well-bred, and trained by horsemen with a history of 2-year-old success, the sky is the limit. While speed figures can be a rough estimate of the power of a 2-year-old win, the radical improvement of 2-year-olds means a handicapper often must project further advancement. Given a good pedigree and a top trainer, they usually do improve.

8 Congaree
Own:Stoneriside Stable
White, Green Chevron, Green/white
ESPINOZA V (1 0 0 0 .00) 2001:(461 60 .13)

Ch. c. 3 (Apr)
Sire: Arazi (Blushing Groom*Fr)
Dam: Mari's Sheba(Mari's Book)
Br: Stonerside Stable Ltd (Ky)
Tr: Baffert Bob(3 0 1 0 .00) 2001:(205 45 .22)

L 126

Life	4	3	0	0	$512,400	108	D.Fst	3	2	0	0	$483,60
2001	3	3	0	0	$512,400	108	Wet(326)	1	1	0	0	$28,80
2000	1	M	0	0	$0	81	Turf(430*)	0	0	0	0	$
CD	0	0	0	0	$0	–	Dist	0	0	0	0	$

14Apr01-10Aqu	fst	1⅛	:46	1:10	1:35	1:474	Wood Mem-G2	108	5	2 2½	2hd	1hd	15	12¾	Espinoza V	L 123 b	1.70	97-14	Congaree1232¾ Monrchos1237 RichlyBlended1234	Steady left hand w
17Mar01- 2SA	fst	1 1/16	:231	:463	1:104	1:42	Alw 56000N1X	102	5	2½	21	11	14	18	Espinoza V	LB 120 b	*.50	94-13	*Congaree*1208 Sudden Glory1181 Bills Paid1181½	Stlkd, clerd, ridn
28Feb01- 4SA	wf	1 ⊗	:222	:452	1:091	1:341	Md Sp Wt 48k	100	1	41½	11½	12	12½	15	Espinoza V	LB 120 b	1.80	100-02	*Congaree*1205 IrishMinstrel1208 Hadrin'sWll1205	Rail, strong hand
10Sep00- 7Dmr	fst	6f	:214	:452	:58	1:11	Md Sp Wt 47k	81	11	2	63¾	21	42	63¼	Baze T C5	LB 113 b	*2.10	82-17	Chinook Cat118¾ Mo Mon118½ *Matta*1181	4 wide,no late

WORKS: ●Apr30 CD 5f fst :581 B *1/29* Apr24 CD 4f gd :474 B *2/34* ●Apr9 SA 6f fst 1:112 H *1/14* ●Apr3 SA 6f fst 1:113 H *1/5* Mar28 SA 5f fst :59 B *3/46* Mar13 SA 5f fst 1:004 B *4/12*
TRAINER: Dirt(729 .22 $1.50) Routes(343 .22 $1.42) GrdStk(127 .22 $1.36)

The following year, 3-year-olds burst onto the scene. Though their improvement is only slightly less meteoric than that of 2-year-olds, they do surprise. Particularly with lightly raced 3-year-olds, improvement is often swift. It is not uncommon for a fast allowance winner to move directly into a graded stakes. In measuring the "class" of improving 2- and 3-year-olds, we must put our faith in the trainer. Congaree ran a fast time winning a Santa Anita allowance race, and was trained by Bob Baffert. In the Wood Memorial, he upset Monarchos, who turned the tables next time in the Kentucky Derby.

Let's switch back to older horses, and move up the ladder. After conditioned allowance races (N3X is as high as they go in Southern California; Eastern tracks offer N4X) come the classified allowances. These are races with restrictions on the date of a horse's most recent allowance or stakes win. For example, "nonwinners of $35,000 or more since July 23." A horse is eligible if he has not won a $35,000 first-place prize since the designated date. Classified allowance races typically include stakes horses that have not won in some time or are returning from layoffs, or improving allowance horses that have gone through their conditions (N1X, N2X, N3X).

Next come restricted or minor stakes, with purses ranging from $50,000 to $100,000. Usually, these are won by sharp allowance horses or runners that are not quite good enough to win a graded stakes, though they may have tried.

Stakes

Finally, the elite of the racing population—the stakes. You wouldn't know it by the volume of publicity, but stakes races comprise only 4 percent of racing programs in the U.S. Even within this category, there is a higher subset: graded stakes.

There are three levels of graded stakes. Grade 1 races are the pinnacle of the sport. They attract the best horses in training, and typically offer the highest purses. A horse that wins a Grade 1 stakes becomes more valuable—for breeding purposes—at the end of its career.

For handicappers, the primary concern is cashing a bet. Well-known handicapping author James Quinn has adopted a straightforward approach to handicapping Grade 1 races for older horses. He says, simply, "Except by accident, Grade 1 races are won by Grade 1 horses."

The maxim applies to older horses, not lightly raced 2- and 3-year-olds. Young horses often move up seemingly overnight, producing explosive improvement that can carry them to victory even while jumping up radically in class.

Yet with older horses, the Grade 1 class guideline generally holds true. And even then, horseplayers sometimes outwit themselves by making a case for an outclassed longshot in a Grade 1. There may be nothing wrong with taking a shot at a price, but handicapping logic was blatantly sidestepped during the 2003 summer meet at Hollywood Park. It occurred in the Grade 1 Hollywood Gold Cup.

The Hollywood Gold Cup featured three Grade 1 winners—Congaree, Harlan's Holiday, and Kudos. Congaree and Harlan's Holiday were multiple Grade 1 winners, just the type of horse that typically dominates Grade 1 races. In *Daily Racing Form,* I tried to make a case for Piensa Sonando, a South American import whose closing style had netted him a Grade 3 win, a Grade 2 second, and scattered fourth-place finishes against top company. He was a tease, nothing more than a counterfeit at the Grade 1 level. But he was the pick because Congaree was rightfully perceived to be vulnerable at a mile and a quarter; Harlan's Holiday might still be feeling the effects of a trip to Dubai; and Kudos had won only a single Grade 1 and was not nearly as sharp as the previous year.

But in fact, those three horses—perhaps only the first two—were the only three qualified to win the Grade 1. Congaree and Harlan's Holiday were multiple Grade 1 winners; Kudos had only won a single Grade 1. It was standard, nuts-and-bolts class handicapping, and unfortunately overlooked in the biggest handicap race of summer. What happened in the Gold Cup is what happens in most Grade 1 races—the best horses dominated. Congaree won by three lengths; Harlan's Holiday finished second, two lengths in front of third-place Kudos. Piensa Sonando was nowhere to be found.

The point is, the best races—the Grade 1's—are won by the best horses. Quinn is right. Upsets happen only by accident. During the 2002 racing season, there were 60 Grade 1 races for older horses in the United States. The results speak for themselves. Which is to say, predictability reigned. No less than 63 percent were won by one of the first two betting choices; the median payoff for a $2 win bet was $6.80.

A horseplayer need not be overly clever in analyzing a Grade 1. Identify the best horses in the race, and go from there. In Grade 1's for older runners, the best horse will already have won at least one Grade 1, preferably two; he will be consistent; and he will reliably earn Beyer figures well above 110. If the odds are too short, simply do not bet. Congaree paid $4.40 when he won the Gold Cup. Perhaps the price was too short. But it probably was ill-advised to support a horse such as Piensa Sonando. It's true—outclassed horses win Grade 1 races only by accident.

Grade 2's and Grade 3's are for up-and-comers, or horses slightly inferior to Grade 1 runners. A Grade 2 race can be won by a Grade 1 horse, so long as the horse is not merely prepping for an upcoming Grade 1. Similar to Grade 1 horses, a Grade 2 horse will already have won multiple races at the level, and be capable of earning Beyers in the 105 range and above.

Grade 3 races are a notch below, yet the gap is much wider than the gap between Grade 1 and Grade 2. A Grade 3 race is child's play for top-class Grade 1 and Grade 2 runners. Top horses rarely even bother with Grade 3 races. Nowadays, many trainers prefer to train horses directly up to Grade 1's and Grade 2's, without a prep race. A Grade 3 race is similar to a classified allowance. It can be won by a horse that has flirted with success against lesser company.

Piensa Sonando (Chi)
Own: Hunt Nelson B

Dk. b or b. h. 5 (Oct)
Sire: Gallantsky (Nijinsky II)
Dam: Asi No Mas (Mocito Guapo)
Br: Haras Santa Olga (Chi)
Tr: McAnally Ronald L(0 0 0 0 .00) 2004:(44 6 .14)

13Jly03-9Hol	fst	1¼	$:45^3$	$1:09^2$	$1:34^1$	$2:00^2$	3↑HolGldCp-G1	**107**	7	7^{16}	7^{13}	$5^{6\frac{1}{2}}$	5^6	4^6	Stevens G L	**LB**124 b	5.70	99- 07	$Congaree124^3$ $Harlan's Holiday124^2$ $Kudos124^1$	3 wide, r
14Jun03-8Hol	fst	1⅛	$:46^3$	$1:10^3$	1:35	$1:47^4$	3↑Calfrnin-G2	**107**	4	7^8	5^4	3^1	3^{nk}	$2^{\frac{1}{2}}$	Stevens G L	**LB**118 b	5.20e	94- 04	$Kudos116^{\frac{1}{2}}$ $Piensa Sonando118^{1\frac{1}{2}}$ $Reba's Gold118^{1\frac{1}{2}}$	4wd,3wd
10May03-8Hol	fst	$1\frac{1}{16}$	:23	$:45^3$	$1:09^2$	$1:40^4$	3↑MrvnLRyH-G2	**99**	5	8^{15}	8^{16}	8^{12}	8^9	3^6	Solis A	**LB**115	6.40	94- 04	$TotlImpct114^2$ $FleetstreetDncer114^4$ $PiensSonndo115^1$	Came out
5Apr03-10SA	fst	1⅛	$:46^2$	$1:10^2$	$1:35^1$	$1:48^2$	4↑SnBrdnoH-G3	**106**	7	8^{12}	8^{15}	8^{11}	6^6	$4^{3\frac{3}{4}}$	Flores D R	**LB**116	4.40	88- 14	$WesternPride116^{nk}$ *$TotlImpct113^1$* $FleetstrtDncr112^{2\frac{1}{2}}$	Improved
1Mar03-9SA	fst	1¼	$:46^3$	$1:11^1$	$1:35^2$	$1:59^4$	4↑SAH-G1	**105**	2	$5^{2\frac{1}{2}}$	$5^{3\frac{1}{2}}$	4^2	$5^{3\frac{3}{4}}$	5^7	Stevens G L	**LB**116	30.40	99- 05	*$Milwaukee Brew119^{hd}$* *$Congaree124^{4\frac{1}{2}}$* $Kudos117^{1\frac{1}{2}}$	Split foes 5/
2Feb03-8SA	fst	1⅛	$:46^2$	$1:10^1$	1:35	$1:47^3$	4↑SnAntnoH-G2	**104**	3	4^2	$6^{3\frac{3}{4}}$	$6^{2\frac{1}{4}}$	$5^{5\frac{1}{2}}$	$4^{8\frac{1}{4}}$	Pincay L Jr	**LB**117	17.80	88- 18	$Congree123^{2\frac{1}{4}}$ *$MilwukeeBrew120^1$* $PlesntlyPrfct117^5$	Lacked late r
4Jan03-8SA	fst	$1\frac{1}{16}$	$:23^4$	$:47^3$	$1:11^2$	1:41	4↑SnPsqalH-G2	**102**	7	$8^{4\frac{1}{2}}$	$8^{3\frac{3}{4}}$	$8^{4\frac{3}{4}}$	$7^{5\frac{1}{2}}$	$4^{7\frac{1}{4}}$	Pincay L Jr	**LB**118	6.50	92- 05	*$Congaree121^6$* $Kudos119^{no}$ $Hot Market116^{1\frac{1}{4}}$	Improved
14Dec02-9Hol	fst	1⅛	$:47^1$	$1:10^4$	$1:35^3$	$1:48^2$	3↑NtvDivrH-G3	**105**	7	$6^{6\frac{1}{2}}$	$6^{5\frac{1}{2}}$	$6^{4\frac{3}{4}}$	$4^{1\frac{1}{2}}$	1^{hd}	Pincay L Jr	**LB**117	2.50	90- 10	$PiensSonndo117^{hd}$ $FleetstrtDncr112^1$ $NosThTrd116^{\frac{1}{2}}$	Came out 1/
24Oct02-5SA	fst	1	$:22^3$	:46	$1:09^3$	$1:34^3$	3↑OClm 100000N	**107**	6	6^6	$6^{4\frac{1}{2}}$	5^5	$4^{2\frac{1}{2}}$	1^{hd}	Pincay L Jr	**LB**118	*1.70	98- 12	*$Piensa Sonando118^{hd}$* *$Resolve118^{1\frac{1}{4}}$* $Truly a Judge118^{3\frac{1}{2}}$	Split foes 1
20Oct02-3SA	fst	7f	$:22^3$	$:44^4$	$1:08^2$	$1:21^1$	3↑OClm 100000N	**98**	5	4	$5^{5\frac{3}{4}}$	5^7	4^4	$3^{\frac{3}{4}}$	Pincay L Jr	**LB**118	10.50	98- 12	$Resolve118^{hd}$ $Siphonic116^{\frac{3}{4}}$ *$Piensa Sonando118^3$*	Inside turn,

Previously trained by Luis Urbina

Piensa Sonando was a prime example. A top horse in South America, he showed he could be a good horse in North America when he finished third in, then won, allowance races in his first two starts. But when Piensa Sonando was fully extended in the Grade 3 Native Diver, it was a sign that his future would not likely surpass the Grade 3 level.

In determining whether a horse is racing at the appropriate level, a handicapper notes if the horse has been successful at that level in the past—that is, whether he has won or finished in the money while also finishing within three lengths of the winner. A horse that is dropping in class can be supported if he is dropping after an acceptable effort, meaning he was competitive to the pace call or outfinished half the field.

A dose of common sense is required to determine if a third-place finish was a truly competitive effort. A horse that lollygags at the back of the field, and then passes a few tired horses in the stretch and clunks up for a distant third, cannot be deemed as having produced a competitive effort.

Typically, a horse is racing at the appropriate class level if he has hit the board and finished within three lengths of the winner in a recent race at the level. If the horse's competitive race was months ago, or several races back, chances are the horse will have a tough time running back to that race.

The subject of class is no less important—or more important—than current form, pace, or speed. Regarding class, you have everything you need for now.

It was not long ago that the definition of class often included purse earnings. The earnings information is shown in the past-performance career box, which also includes wins and starts, along with surface- or time-specific high Beyer figures. It seems like a long time ago that the amount of money a horse won in a category—lifetime, year, or surface—was used as a measure of class. But it was, and in 1982 an advertisement for a class-based handicapping system caught my attention. Written by L. D. Hurley, "The Winning Formula" promised to live up to its title. It was a mechanical handicapping procedure based on starts, wins, and earnings. It purported to determine "class."

It sounded good, and I bought it. Its arrival in the mail was greatly anticipated, and when it finally was delivered, along with a wagering scheme called the "5-for-5 plan," I knew it would not be long before I quit my job as a grocery-store clerk and became a full-time horseplayer.

The system was easily calculated. It started with the horse's earnings for the year. From that, two numbers were subtracted— number of starts, and number of wins (which had been multiplied by a special factor based on the class of the race). The formula did not apply to turf races, filly-and-mare routes, comebackers, or last-start maiden winners. It applied mainly to claiming horses. Perfect, I thought.

The method required no interpretation or creativity. It was all black-and-white, and I went along for the ride. Except that after an entire Del Mar season of "pretend" wagering by testing the system on paper, it had not produced the expected riches. Oh, darn. A lesson learned. Class is not measured by earnings, especially with so many races restricted to state-breds that offer purses disproportionately higher than the ability of the runners. Class is "current class," the level at which a horse is expected to be competitive. It is a broad assessment, like most of handicapping. After a few months I shelved "The Winning Formula" and went back to square one, which was trying to gain an understanding of the fundamentals of handicapping.

You already know from Chapter 2 how to determine if a horse is in form. And now you know how to determine if a horse fits on class.

But is he fast enough to win? Or will he battle for the lead, then wilt from the inevitable duel? That is the subject of Chapter 4, when we examine speed and pace.

4

SPEED AND PACE

Horseplayers have long tried to simplify the art of handicapping. And it sure would be easy if the athletic ability of a racehorse could be expressed as it is with human athletes—in a number. When a track-and-field athlete runs a 100-yard dash in 10 seconds, everyone knows he ran fast. A baseball player hits for a .300 batting average. A running back rushes for 100 yards in a football game. Good, solid benchmark numbers.

Familiar and comforting, statistics are something sports fans have grown accustomed to—quantitative, specific guidelines—as a means of athletic comparison. But horse racing is just a little bit more complex. The basic question may not change—which is the fastest horse?—but the clues certainly do.

An experienced horse typically does what he has done—reproduce previous performances. Assuming he is reasonably fit and competing at a suitable class level, a horse that ran six furlongs in 1:10 last time will run about 1:10 next time. A horse that ran six furlongs in 1:11 generally will run about 1:11 again.

Betting horses would be simple if six furlongs were the only race distance. A horseplayer would only need to consider current condition and class, compare final times, and wager on the fastest horse. It would be an easy game, right?

The catch is that horses do not always race the same distance, nor on the same type surface. A horse that ran six furlongs last time may run farther, 6½ furlongs, next time. A horse with a series of six-furlong races may face a horse whose recent races were farther, perhaps at 6½ furlongs. Now a handicapper is in a pickle. Which horse is faster? Is it the one that ran six furlongs in 1:10, or the one that ran 6½ furlongs in 1:16.60?

A handicapper could use help, some sort of common denominator, to compare those times and others at various distances. Thankfully, there is a standard: speed figures, which provide a measure of how fast a horse ran. *Daily Racing Form* publishes Beyer Speed Figures, developed by renowned handicapper Andrew Beyer. The figures allow quick, convenient contrast. They tell how fast a horse ran, and allow comparison of different horses' ability to meet the demands of a particular race. They help answer the question, is this horse fast enough to win?

Without speed figures, horseplayers would drift in a sea of mathematical computations, and here is why. At Santa Anita, a six-furlong race run in 1:10.40 is the same as a 6½-furlong race run in 1:17, or a seven-furlong race run in 1:23.40. It's the handicapping equivalent of $E = MC^2$.

6 Front Line
Own: Windmill Manor Farm
Black Red, Black Chevrons, Black And Gold
MELANCON L (41 3 8 6 .07) 2003: (460 58 .13)

Ch. f. 2 (Feb) SARAUG02 $25,000
Sire: Rodeo (Gone West) $3,000
Dam: Bounding Believer (Bounding Basque)
Br: Gus Schoenborn Jr (NY)
Tr: Werner Ronny(19 2 4 3 .11) 2003:(215 46 .21)

L 118

Life	3	1	1	0	$25,225	63	D.Fst	2	1	1	0	$19,2
2003	3	1	1	0	$25,225	63	Wet(337)	1	0	0	0	$6,0
2002	0	M	0	0	$0	-	Turf(263*)	0	0	0	0	
CD	0	0	0	0	$0	-	Dst(329)	0	0	0	0	

18Oct03-4Bel gd 1 :23³ :47¹ 1:13¹ (1:41¹) Ⓕ[S]MaidOTMist100k 43 6 1hd 1hd 2hd 3 1½ (4³) Guidry M L114 8.10 57- 26 Capeside Lady121nk Schemer114² ClarksburgQueen114¾ Vied inside,
4Sep03-3TP fst 5f :22² :46⁴ :59³ ⒻMd Sp Wt 25k 63 7 4 4 3½ 4⁴ 3² 1 2½ Butler D P L121 *.70 86- 13 FrontLine121 2½ SophiasHumor121 1½ StormClock121 2½ 4 wide, closed
13Aug03-7ElP fst 5f :23 :46³ :59⁴ ⒻMd Sp Wt 25k 59 3 2 2 1½ 3 2½ 2³ 2¾ Bejarano R L120 7.00 89- 17 Stoneway120¾ *Front Line*120 2¼ Melody Prospector120 1¾ 4w,gaining
WORKS: Nov9 CD 5f fst 1:03² B *22/28* Nov2 CD 5f fst 1:01 B *9/29* Oct10 CD 6f fst 1:14² B *3/9* Oct2 CD 6f fst 1:15² B *3/6* Sep18 TP 7f fst 1:33³ B *1/2* Aug24 ElP 4f fst :49³ B *5/12*
TRAINER: 2YO(150 .21 $1.83) Route/Sprint(20 .10 $0.84) Dirt(356 .21 $1.69) Sprint(351 .20 $1.68) Alw(81 .17 $1.27)

It's easy to determine how long it took a horse to complete a race—his final time. Add the margin of defeat (one length equals .17 seconds) to the time of the winner, as shown above. A horse that finished three lengths behind the winner of a mile race timed in 1:41.20 (or 1:41⅕) ran .51 seconds slower (.17 times three lengths = .51) than the winner, or 1:41.71. That is, the 1:41.20 final time plus .51 seconds. But now Front Line is entered in a seven-furlong race on November 16. Regarding her final time for the mile race, what relevance does it have?

In most races, there will be several horses that raced at different distances. A handicapper using only raw final time would spend all afternoon adding and subtracting margins of defeat to determine final time. Then it would be back to square one. Some horses raced at six furlongs, others at seven furlongs. Which horse is fastest? It's a mess.

Speed figures reduce the clutter. They quantify horses' past performances. When reasonably interpreted, speed figures also offer a sensible estimate of horses' future performances.

Beyer Speed Figures remove the drudgery of the beaten-lengths calculations, and also simplify another complication that concerns ever-changing racetrack surfaces. Dirt has a life of its own. A racing surface might be deep and slow one day, hard and fast the next day. The changing surface affects the speed at which horses run.

A horse that typically runs six furlongs in 1:10 may struggle over a deep, slow surface and complete the distance in 1:11. Now what? Did the horse run poorly, or was the slower time the result of the condition of the racetrack? Conversely, a horse that typically runs six furlongs in 1:10 may race over a hard, fast surface that produces unusually fast times. Now the horse bounces over the track and sizzles six furlongs in a quick 1:09. Was the performance as good as the fast time, or was it the result of the condition of the racetrack?

Beyer figures are calculated by considering the "speed" of the track. This fluctuation is called the track variant. At each class level, horses typically run within a certain range of final times. When they run faster or slower than the typical range, it can be because the track "played slow" or "played fast." In theory, a sprinter able to run six furlongs in 1:10.40 would run 6½ furlongs in 1:16.80, and seven furlongs in 1:23.20. Around two turns, the same caliber horse would run a mile in 1:37.10, and 1 1⁄16 miles in 1:43.80.

Here is how track variants work, using as an example a horse running on the first day of the racing week. Perhaps during the two previous "dark days" when there was no racing, weather conditions changed or the racing surface was renovated and new material (sand, for example) was added to the track. A shift in climate, or racetrack maintenance, can cause the track to become deeper than usual. Final times get slower.

A class level that typically runs six furlongs in 1:10 may run six furlongs over the deeper racetrack in 1:11. A class that typically runs six furlongs in 1:09 may require 1:10. On this day, the track "plays" one second slower than par. This is the track variant.

But a day later, the racetrack may have returned to normal. The dirt has more "bounce," and produces faster times. Now, the same class level of horse runs six furlongs in 1:10—one full second faster. So who ran better—the horse that ran 1:11 on the "dead" track that produced slow times? Or the horse who ran 1:10?

Speed figures furnish the answer. It's like a jogger on the beach. At high tide, he runs through sand that is deep and loose. A two-mile jog that normally takes 20 minutes may take 22 minutes. The next morning he jogs at low tide, over the hard surface that was covered by water the day before. The sand is tight, and the jogger requires only 18 minutes to complete his two-mile route. So which day did the jogger run faster? Probably, it was the same both days.

Handicappers regularly face this kind of question. A horse that required a longer time to race a particular distance may have run just as well as a horse that raced the distance in faster time on a different day. The speed of a racetrack fluctuates. Speed figures are calculated by considering the speed of the racetrack. They show if horses ran faster, slower, or the same, even if the final times were different.

Similarly, when horses that have been racing at different distances show up in the same race, a handicapper needs to know which horse is faster—the horse who ran six furlongs in 1:10, or the horse who ran 6½ furlongs in 1:17. Beyer contemplated the dilemma in the 1970's, and set out to quantify the speed of racehorses by assigning a speed figure to the times of races. This would allow a simple, direct means of comparing horses that ran at different distances or on different surfaces. Beyer's landmark 1975 handicapping book *Picking Winners* detailed the methodology.

A chart of average winning times at different distances is compiled, with a corresponding speed figure assigned to the times. At six furlongs, 1:10.40 equals a 100 Beyer Speed Figure; at 6½ furlongs, 1:16.80 equals 100. Faster times produce higher figures; slower times produce lower figures. In six-furlong sprints, one length equals 2.8 points on the Beyer scale; in routes, one length equals two points on the Beyer scale. A horse that raced six furlongs in 1:10 would receive a raw figure of 106.

A raw figure is assigned to each of the day's winning times, accompanied by the difference between the raw figure and the average figure for that class level. From this list, a track variant is created. This tells how fast or slow the track played relative to the average. If every sprint in the course of one racing day produced a raw speed figure that was five points faster than average, the track would be deemed to be faster than par by five points. As a result, five points are subtracted from the sprint figures, producing adjusted speed figures. It sure simplifies matters.

By assigning speed figures to the final time, a six-furlong race in 1:11 might earn, for example, an adjusted speed figure of 83. And the 6½-furlong race in 1:17.40 might also earn an adjusted speed figure of 83. Comparisons are simplified, and handicappers can easily assess horses' speeds.

The Racing Times was the first national publication to incorporate Beyer Speed Figures in past performances, and when *The Racing Times* ceased operation in 1992, *Daily Racing Form* began publishing them. Speed figures are perhaps the most widely used handicapping factor, and horseplayers who do not use speed figures are severely disadvantaged. A bettor does not always have to wager on the fastest horse, but one ought to know who the fastest horse is and what speed figure is typically required to win a specific race.

The utility of speed figures has gone beyond mere use as a handicapping tool. Speed figures often are the basis for establishing a horse's value. Horses are bought and sold based on how fast they have run. A lightly raced horse that runs an extraordinarily fast race becomes more valuable because of his potential to win more valuable races.

Beyer figures are the most widely distributed speed figures. In addition to using Beyer figures, many handicappers calculate personal speed figures. The daily process takes all of five minutes. I also consult figures generated by pace expert Tom Brohamer, and occasionally monitor other figures. Good speed figures accurately express how fast a horse ran. And a bettor that knows how fast a horse ran in the past is able to reasonably project how fast the horse will run in the future.

But horses are living, breathing animals that change daily. They do not always run the same race, which is why speed figures cannot be used as an isolated factor. In horse racing, no factor stands alone. Current condition and class, along with pace, affect horses' ability to achieve maximum performance—to run as fast as they can.

In boiling down final time to a number, handicapping is simplified. Regardless of distance, margin of defeat, or surface, figures allow easy comparison. They show how fast horses have run, and allow one to project how fast they may run again.

When conditions are right, horses generally run as fast as they are able. You already know from Chapters 2 and 3 how to recognize when conditions are right—when horses are physically fit and competing at an appropriate class level.

A beginning handicapper may have to accept on faith a lot of this speed-figure stuff. But know this—many horseplayers (speed handicappers) wish that figures had never been popularized. Figures provided their edge, and now their edge has been minimized because speed figures are so widely used. Chances are if you have read this far into *Handicapping 101*, you accept the premise of speed handicapping. The fastest horses win the majority of the races. It's true. If speed figures did not work, none of us would be wasting time with them. They do work. Speed is speed, and fast is fast.

Beyer figures show what "fast" is. It is fascinating that a single number can provide a direct measure of ability, particularly in a sport with so much built-in chaos. A horse that earns a Beyer figure of 83 does not do so automatically. A lot goes on between the start and the finish, yet surprisingly horses reproduce similar efforts time and time again. It all begins at the starting gate.

When a field is loaded into the gate, each horse is confined to a small stall that has swinging doors at the front and back. Both doors are closed after a horse enters the gate stall. After the entire field has loaded and is reasonably prepared, the starter (a track employee in charge of the gate crew) pushes a trigger that sends an electronic pulse to the gate. The metal doors at the front of each horse's stall spring open simultaneously. A bell rings, jockeys shout, and they urge their horses forward. The race is on.

The initial furlong of a six-furlong race takes approximately 11 seconds. Races reach top speed as the field runs down the backstretch, and after two furlongs—a quarter-mile—they bend into the turn. At about 40 miles per hour, the leaders begin to decelerate. Only one-third of the race—two of the six furlongs—has been run. The field races past the half-mile pole, a large green-and-white pole that indicates there is a half-mile to the finish wire. A critical part of the sprint is ahead. Jockeys maneuver for position as they enter the turn.

The turn is gently banked, and jockeys lean inward. As centrifugal force pulls horses outward—away from the rail—jockeys lean inward and use the bank of the turn to keep their horses on the course.

The turn at most tracks is between the half-mile pole and the quarter pole, a large red-and-white pole that indicates there is a quarter-mile to the finish. The middle segment of a sprint is where many races are won and lost. Front-runners that are unable to keep pace begin to wilt. They have expended much of their energy. Other front-runners, with energy in reserve, continue onward and fight off challengers.

Pace-pressers, horses whose running style is to race right behind the leaders, launch their attack. As the field races past the quarter pole and nears the homestretch, the pressers are at the leaders' throats. A quarter-mile remains. It is now or never. The pressers that have been running comfortably within striking distance begin to challenge. Other pressers have cracked. They fall back.

The stretch-runners are still lagging at the back of the field, as if they were never in the race. By the time the field passes the quarter pole and reaches the top of the stretch, the race is over for many of the entrants. The stretch may be the most exciting part of a dirt race, but what happens there is merely a product of what happened earlier. For many horses, the outcome has been determined. They have already been defeated. Depending on the rate of speed at which the race unfolded—the pace of the race—it will be won by a front-runner, a presser, or a closer.

The field races into the stretch, by which time many of the front-runners and pace-pressers are completely spent. The pace of the race was beyond their comfort zone. These horses are empty, and their jockeys ease them back. They will fight another day.

Other horses have been running comfortably. With energy remaining, these horses continue racing to the finish wire, and battle the remaining foes. As for the late-runners, they do what they always do. They pick up the pieces, and pass weary horses in the stretch. Except at the highest class levels, late-runners win only when everyone else loses.

The preceding scenario describes a typical sprint, and handicapping would be easy if every horse produced the same effort in every race, over identical surfaces, identical distances, at identical rates of speed, against similar competition. Yet circumstances are different every time a horse runs. The racing surface varies, the pace differs, the competition changes, and so does a horse's physical condition. Speed figures measure how fast a horse ran. And that is often dependent on the speed at which a race unfolded.

Pace, or rate of speed, has a powerful effect on final time. Picture yourself out for the two-mile jog that usually requires 20 minutes. Now sprint as fast as you can the first half-mile, and see how long it takes to complete the run. Longer than usual, for sure. It is the same with horses. Put two horses together in a race, and have them run head and head for the first half-mile. They will be spent, and will tire earlier than if they were cruising by themselves on a "lonely lead."

Only when the pace is comfortable can a horse be expected to produce a peak performance. When a horse faces intense early pressure (like the jogger who sprints the first half-mile), he will race faster than he prefers, expending energy reserves too soon. He subsequently tires. So why doesn't the jockey simply slow the horse down to conserve energy?

It is not that simple. Horses have peculiarities. When they are tinkered with, it often prevents them from performing well. Some horses are free-runners that cannot be held back. They want to race toward the front of the pack, run fast, and carry their speed as far as they can. When they "shake loose," they are more likely to carry their speed farther. But a pace battle will destroy them. In a race with several other front-runners who also are intent on racing to the front, the pace will be contested. The front-runners are more likely to burn each other out. The faster a horse runs early, the slower he will run late.

Sometimes a horse wins the battle, but loses the war. After battling early pace foes into defeat, a front-runner may be spent. He may not possess sufficient energy to withstand the rallies of pressers and closers.

Knowing how fast a horse ran in the past, the question becomes, how fast might he run in the future? How does the horse's best effort compare to the demands of the race, or even the rest of the field? Speed figures provide a key part of the overall picture, though they are only one part of the equation. Beyer discussed their significance.

"I always caution people that speed figures, our figures, do not purport to be a magic formula that tells you everything about a horse's capabilities. All they tell you are who has run fastest in a race. We know there are other elements, a lot of other elements, in handicapping. We also know that horses will run fast when they get perfect circumstances to do so. So, you have to offer a few caveats.

"Lots of things can happen to a horse during the course of a race—trouble, trips, the effect of track bias, going wide on the turns, that will compromise his performance. My feeling is that I can quantify how fast horses have run their race. The figures are a precise expression of [that]. But I have never been able to quantify to my satisfaction any other element of the game, including things that you would think would be easily quantifiable, such as weight or ground loss on the turns."

For example, looking at a horse who ran an 80 in his last race, Beyer said, "We know this is how fast he ran. And he ran faster than this horse who ran a 75. Now, let's look at the circumstances. Maybe the horse who ran a 75 was head and head for the lead in 44 and change, and tired and ran that 75. But the horse that ran the 80 did nothing remarkable. You'd look at these two performances and say, hey, I certainly prefer the horse who ran the 75. You should look at the circumstances under which a horse earned the number. Were the circumstances neutral? Where they favorable? Were they unfavorable?"

While Beyer figures are used to identify contenders, they can also eliminate noncontenders. For example, "When you see a horse who is not in the ballpark in terms of figures. A horse who got beat a length last time and he got a 60. And he's running against horses in the 80's. Horses who are just clearly overmatched, and not competitive in terms of figures, rarely win."

On the other hand, Beyer doesn't always advocate betting on the horse with the top figure. "When a horse's most recent race is a career best, and he just exploded and there is no reason, he's probably not going to do it again. I won't use the word 'bounce' in my handicapping, or my thinking about it, but just logically if a horse just ran his all-time best and it's out of whack with what he normally does, that probably was his peak."

Beyer popularized speed handicapping in the mid-1970's, and ever since then the issue for horseplayers has been how speed figures should be applied. Which of the horse's recent figures should be used, and what do they mean? If predicting the outcome of a race depends partly on identifying the fastest horse, it follows that an examination of Beyer figures will lead a horseplayer in the right direction. Most of the time, it does.

Beyer figures help separate contenders from pretenders by comparing horses' ability to the requirements of the race. That is, comparing horses' typical Beyer figures to the Beyer par—the average winning figure for the class. But what speed figures in a horse's past performances should be used? Which are less relevant? A little common sense goes a long way. Further, it cannot be overstated that speed figures are merely one part of handicapping, no more or less important than condition, class, or pace.

A horse is considered a contender on speed figures when he meets three requirements. The horse will have earned a Beyer figure within five points of par, which is the average Beyer figure for a winner at that class level. The horse will have earned the figure at least twice, and the figure will have been earned within the last six months.

Many handicappers compare one horse's Beyer figures to another horse's Beyer figures, but that is often misleading. Instead of comparing horses' figures to each other, speed figures should first be compared to the speed demands of a particular race. That is, is this horse fast enough to win a typical race at this level? The question forces a handicapper to interpret a horse's chances in the context of the class level.

Utilization of Beyer pars helps reduce the field to a manageable number of contenders. Handicapping is primarily a process of elimination. That's all. And speed figures help narrow the list. (Beyer Speed Figure pars are scheduled to be introduced into *Daily Racing Form* past performances as of this writing, and also are included in *Daily Racing Form*'s weekly publication, *DRF Simulcast Weekly*.)

For example, in a $25,000 claiming race for 3-year-olds and up at Belmont Park, the Beyer par is 89. A legitimate contender will have earned a figure within five points (84 or higher) of par, on more than one occasion, and will have done so recently.

Connie's Magic qualified as a contender on September 28, 2003, in race 6 at Belmont. He had exceeded the 89 Beyer par multiple times, and had done so recently. Based on speed figures, he was a contender.

A number of pitfalls lure horseplayers using speed figures. Sometimes, a big, fat speed figure will seduce a handicapper like a chocolate candy bar. Once in a while, everyone goes for the sugar. But in wagering on racehorses, the temptation of speed figures becomes a problem only if you let it. Speed figures can become a crutch. It is so easy to merely identify the "high-figure" horse and wager accordingly.

Unlike a horse's fluctuating condition or class, neither of which can be measured with a number, bold-type Beyer figures practically leap off the past performances. As a result, horses with high recent figures frequently are overbet. Find the horse with the highest recent figure, and often that horse will be favored. Whether he is the most likely winner depends on a host of circumstances, including interpretation of how the figure was earned.

The high-figure horse is the horse whose best recent speed figure is fastest in the field. For the figure to be reliable, it should have been earned under conditions similar to the race today. Let's look at another obvious contender.

Pearl
pp Steve

Gr/ro. f. 4 (Apr)
Sire: Salt Lake (Deputy Minister) $12,500
Dam: Great Pearl (Grey Dawn II)
Br: Morris Floyd & Chuck Givens (Ky)
Tr: Knapp Steve(0 0 0 0 .00) 2003:(275 32 .12)

SA	fst	6½f	:214	:444	1:102	1:172	4↑ ⒻClm 25000(25-22.5)	**73**	4	1	11	13	13½	11	Steiner J J	**LB**118 b	7.40	81- 15	SaltyPearl1181 DzzlingDimonds1184½ AllStrRunner1181	Strong hand ride	7
SA	fst	6f	:213	:444	:573	1:111	ⒻClm 16000(16-14)	**72**	1	2	11	12	12½	12	Steiner J J	**LB**117 b	8.90	83- 14	*Salty Pearl*1172 Mia Victoria1172¼ In a Daze112no	Speed, off rail, held	8
SA	sly	6½f	:213	:443	1:12	1:192	ⒻClm 12500(12.5-10.5)	**61**	7	1	2hd	2hd	1½	1nk	Steiner J J	**LB**119 b	8.10	71- 19	*Salty Pearl*119nk Angelis1171¼ Jane's Denial117½	Dueled,led,held	8
SA	fst	6f	:22	:453	:583	1:114	ⒻClm 16000(16-14)	**53**	7	2	21	21	43	67¾	Espinoza V	**LB**117 b	10.10	72- 17	EmrldPndnt1171½ BmshSwng1171 InsdStry117nk	Stalked outside,wkened	9
SA	fst	6½f	:22	:45	1:103	1:172	ⒻClm 12500(12.5-10.5)	**70**	8	2	1½	12	12½	12½	Alferez J O	**LB**117 b	17.00	81- 18	SaltyPearl1172½ RouteFiftySix1171 TsketBsket117½	Speed,off rail,driving	11
SA	fst	6f	:214	:45	:574	1:112	ⒻClm 16000(16-14)	**50**	2	5	2hd	21½	22½	56¾	Martinez F F	**LB**117 b	8.30	75- 13	TheLordsTune1174½ TableWine1172 *TizTnznite*117hd	Wkened,just lost 3rd	8
Hol	fst	5½f	:222	:462	:59	1:053	ⒻClm 12500(12.5-10.5)	**47**	6	1	2hd	21	32½	65¾	Solis A	**LB**118 fb	3.30	76- 14	FlmingCloud1181 MoreBubbls118no CiscoZstySuc1183	Dueled, weakened	6
Hol	fst	6f	:221	:454	:584	1:122	ⒻClm 12500(12.5-10.5)	**58**	5	1	12	13	12½	2¾	Solis A	**LB**118 b	2.70	74- 21	Baby Luck118¾ Salty Pearl1182 Queen Excess113¾	Speed,worn down late	6
Hol	fst	7f	:222	:454	1:12	1:244	ⒻClm 12500(12.5-10.5)	**57**	6	1	11	11½	31	45	Solis A	**LB**118 b	9.80	70- 19	InsideStory1182 *CleredtoLnd*111½ BmshSwing1182½	Drifted out, weakened	8

Salty Pearl found a new lease on life during the 2001 winter meet at Santa Anita, and won four races. A handicapper did not have to look far to find her attributes. For Salty Pearl, the most recent running line told just about everything.

Salty Pearl was fast. By the time she won on April 15, her style was known. A claiming filly, Salty Pearl was a breakneck front-runner—every race in her past-performance lines showed her either setting the pace or positioned second, within 1½ lengths of the lead.

The gray filly's consistency made her easily assessed, even when she was not the pick to win. As long as she continued to produce speed, remain competitive, and race at the same track, Salty Pearl's most recent performance—her last running line— would be the one handicappers needed to consider above all. It is like that with most horses. A horse's most recent start usually provides the greatest insight to his current ability, including his Beyer figures (speed), running style (pace), level of competitive ability (class), and current form (condition).

So if a horse's last start provides so much information, a beginning handicapper might wonder, why bother looking deeper into the horse's past performances? It's because the last start is not always the most relevant running line to consider.

Horses run well, or not, for a number of reasons. The distance of a horse's last start may not have been appropriate, or perhaps the surface was undesirable, or the horse may have been out-classed against opponents of superior ability. So which of a horse's recent running lines is most relevant to what he is trying to do this time?

The answer is surprisingly simple. It is the running line that most closely resembles the conditions of today's race. That is, a race within the past few months that was run under similar cir-cumstances. Most often, it is the horse's last start—similar dis-tance (either a sprint around one turn, or a route around two turns); same class (allowing for a one-level drop or raise); and familiar surface. When the conditions of a horse's most recent start are similar to today's, the last running line usually can be taken at face value.

After ascertaining the Beyer par for the class level, a handi-capper simply examines each horse's past performances and cir-cles the Beyer figures that match or exceed the par, as long as they were earned in races similar to the race at hand. The exer-cise points to the top contenders. A contender would have at least two Beyer figures circled that match or exceed par.

It is not that complicated. Sure, mistakes will occur, but the best handicappers simply commit fewer blunders. While circling Beyer figures that match or exceed par, check distance, class, and surface. The par-matching figures must have been earned under similar conditions.

's Rush In
Anderson & Cooperstone & Shapiro
w, Hunter Green 'sa' On Back, Green $22,500
43 3 3 5 .07) 2002:(916 95 .10)

Dk. b or br f. 4 (Mar)
Sire: Russian Courage (Nijinsky II) $1,000
Dam: Qui's a Lady(Qui Native)
Br: Milton Sydney Cohen (Cal)
Tr: Canani Nick(7 0 0 0 .00) 2002:(143 17 .12)

L 115

Life	19	2	5	0	$61,870	68	D.Fst	17	2	5	0	$61,870	68
2002	14	2	3	0	$52,290	68	Wet(271)	0	0	0	0	$0	–
2001	5	M	2	0	$9,580	59	Turf(245)	2	0	0	0	$0	55
SA	7	2	2	0	$39,860	68	Dst(210)	4	1	1	0	$23,960	68

ol fst 1 1/16 :241 :481 1:13 1:454 ⒻClm 25000(25-22.5) 65 2 1½ 1½ 1hd 31 64¾ Valdivia J Jr LB 120 b 12.80 69-24 LuxuryJwls116¾ **LuckySprt**118hd *I'mmchthbst*1183½ Inside duel,weakened 6
ol fst 1 1/16 :233 :471 1:124 1:471 ⒻClm 32000(32-28) 62 4 3nk 42 41½ 24 414½ Valdivia J Jr LB 118 b 14.00 52-28 GoGrlGo11812 **Pstr'sDutchss**1181 FrnkEylshs1181½ 3wd,btwn foes,wkened 6
A fst 1 :224 :461 1:112 1:383 ⒻClm 22500(25-22.5) 68 5 2hd 2hd 11 11½ 1hd Valdivia J Jr LB 115 b 4.30 78-19 Qu'sRshIn115hd CrvnCottg1153 TostOfThYr1171 Dueled,clear,held game 7
px fst 1 1/16 :221 :46 1:113 1:454 3↑ ⒻAlw 40000s 63 6 43 41¼ 51¾ 44½ 48½ Pedroza M A LB 114 b 6.10 74-16 AfterMyHeart114½ Aetha1221 SongOfBerndette1147 Off rail, no late bid 7
mr fst 1 :224 :462 1:111 1:382 ⒻClm c-(20-18) 67 1 1½ 1hd 2½ 42 54½ Berrio O A LB 118 7.90 78-16 SteamyDrems1181½ AfterMyHert118hd *PolyOle*1131 Inside duel,weakened 9
d from Cohen Milton S for $20,000, Perez Mag Trainer 2002(as of 08/14): (23 2 5 1 0.09)
mr fst 1 :222 :47 1:124 1:401 ⒻClm 25000(25-22.5) 62 6 32 3nk 2hd 1hd 22 Berrio O A LB 118 8.80 72-26 Semstress1182 Qui'sRushIn118½ **FncyBegining**1181 3wd bid,led,held 2nd 8
ol fm 1 1/16 Ⓣ :23 :463 1:103 1:414 3↑ ⒻAlw 40000s 55 7 32 32½ 44 88¼ 916 Berrio O A LB 115 59.90 70-16 Shalini1141 Battante1142½ Ace's Valentine1193 Stalked pace, weakened 10
ol fst 1 1/16 :232 :471 1:123 1:48 ⒻClm 22500(25-22.5) 59 1 1hd 1hd 1hd 2hd 21½ Berrio O A LB 116 5.10 61-37 **FncyBegining**1181½ Qui'sRushIn1161 BttyWho118nk Rail,led again,caught 6
ol fst 7½f :223 :454 1:11 1:312 ⒻClm 28000(32-28) 59 3 7 41½ 51¾ 43 65½ Krigger K5 LB 111 20.40 74-16 NormBee1181 Rightbyu111½ *PrettyAsAshly*118½ Btwn,angled in,wkened 7
A fm 1 Ⓣ :231 :473 1:121 1:37 3↑ ⒻAlw 40000s 50 6 31 31½ 85¾ 89¼ 814¼ Garcia M S LB 115 37.20 63-16 SterlingIdea122nk Bttnte115no *SunsetSerende*1221 Shuffled 1/4,weakened 8
A fst 1 1/16 :224 :47 1:132 1:481 ⒻⓈMd 35000(40-35) 54 7 1½ 1½ 11½ 21½ 21½ Nakatani C S LB 118 *3.60 61-27 Ⓓ*Calzada Kid*1201½ Qui's Rush In1185 Sharsanna1183 Steadied 1/8 & 1/16 10
irst through disqualification.
A fst 7f :222 :453 1:112 1:244 ⒻMd 28000(32-28) 58 6 3 3½ 31½ 42¼ 55½ Solis A LB 118 3.50 75-14 WtermelonWine1202 Monyindsbnk120no MothrFr1203 3 wide, weakened 12
Dec31 SA 5f fst 1:01 H *14/44* **Dec23 SA 5f fst 1:02 H** *36/48* **Dec11 SA 5f fst 1:002 H** *22/56* **Nov17 SA 4f fst :483 H** *15/42* **Oct30 SA 5f fst :593 H** *3/29* **Oct22 SA 5f fst 1:004 B** *8/30*
31-60Days(50 .12 $1.29) Dirt(74 .11 $1.75) Claim(60 .13 $1.51)

Based on the last-start running line of Qui's Rush In, a handicapper would have had a tough time making a case for her in the $25,000 claiming route for 4-year-old fillies on January 8, 2003. But handicappers sometimes need to dig deeper. In this case, one could have gone three races back, to her last start at Santa Anita, to find a race on which to base her chances.

Though she had been running at similar distances and class levels in her recent races, expectations were low at Hollywood Park. Qui's Rush In was 12.80-1 in her last start; 14-1 before that. But back on October 10 at Santa Anita, Qui's Rush In started at 4.30-1 against company similar to what she was facing today. The most appropriate running line to consider for Qui's Rush In was her last start at Santa Anita.

Based on the October 10 performance, a bettor might have considered Qui's Rush In a contender on January 8. Being a contender does not mean she was the top pick, only that she was one of a handful of possible winners. She did win, at a generous 15.30-1.

It is important to know how a figure was earned, and particularly important to recognize when a big figure was earned under abnormal circumstances. This includes a front-runner who raced unchallenged on the lead, or a closer who won a set-up, or a horse whose recent figures were earned on different surfaces or at dissimilar distances. Unless the circumstances are likely to be reproduced, the recent figure may not apply.

adringa
n:Ingalls Jim L
Black Cougar Emblem On Back, White
(78 4 7 8 .05) 2003:(128 7 .05)

Gr/ro f. 3 (Apr) BARMAY02 $40,000
Sire: Snowbound (Meadowlake) $1,000
Dam: Lou's Fast(Fast)
Br: Robert F Pulse (Wash)
Tr: Kenney Martin(16 0 1 1 .00) 2003:(73 6 .08)

L 114

Life	5	1	1	1	$35,520	94	D.Fst	3	1	1	1	$32,640	94
2003	5	1	1	1	$35,520	94	Wet(320)	0	0	0	0	$0	–
2002	0	M	0	0	$0	–	Turf(221)	2	0	0	0	$2,880	73
Hol Ⓣ	2	0	0	0	$2,880	73	DstⓉ(390*)	1	0	0	0	$2,880	73

ol fst 6f :214 :441 :563 1:09 3↑ ⒻAlw 58368N1X 94 3 5 21 21½ 21½ 23 Nuesch D LB 115 10.70 92-10 Ask Not1233 Madringa1154½ **Bold Roberta**1233 Stalked pace,held 2nd 7
ol fm 5½f Ⓣ :212 :441 :561 1:022 ⒻOClm 80000N 73 6 1 11½ 11 3nk 45 Nuesch D LB 118 8.20 87-08 *Katdogawn*1201 Sharpbill1222 *Fudge Fatale*1202 Speed,inside,wkened 6
ol fm 1 Ⓣ :234 :471 1:113 1:362 ⒻOClm 80000N 70 4 11 2½ 21½ 21½ 63 Nuesch D LB 118 8.00 79-12 VanillSky118½ Ldy'sMntle118nk ProvenForm118½ Rail,3wd into str,wknd 6
A fst 6f :22 :452 :574 1:101 3↑ ⒻAlw 51896N1X 90 4 3 11½ 11 1½ 33 Nuesch D LB 114 3.00 84-13 GoneExclusive1162½ Trckofthect122½ Mdring1143½ Angled in turn,wkened 5
A fst 6f :212 :442 :563 1:094 ⒻMd 50000(50-45) 89 5 3 11½ 12½ 16 19 Nuesch D LB 120 22.20 89-11 Mdring1209 **AmricnAnthm**1201 QuickNFncy1203 Speed, cleared,driving 7
Jun13 Hol 4f fst :471 H *3/31* **May27 Hol 4f fst :471 H** *2/24* **Apr9 SA 4f fst :504 H** *37/40* **Apr1 SA 4f fst :491 H** *18/30*
Dirt/Turf(12 .00 $0.00) Turf(24 .00 $0.00) Sprint(131 .08 $1.30) Alw(11 .00 $0.00)

Madringa crushed maidens by nine lengths in her March 21 debut (see previous page). She set fast fractions, ran her rivals silly, and powered home with a solid 89 Beyer. Four weeks later, she moved up in class, into a one-other-than allowance in which the Beyer par was 92. She was a contender, partly because her figure was within five points of par.

Handicappers correctly accepted the 89 that Madringa earned, and expected her to do it again. She was racing on the same footing, at the same distance, within a reasonable time frame. Although her debut figure was earned against easier company (maidens), Madringa did it setting fast fractions. She "earned" the figure, and was likely to run an 89 or better second time out, because circumstances were similar. She did earn an improved figure, ran well, and finished third. It was a good race, albeit a losing one.

Then followed an unusual twist in her career, one that drives horseplayers crazy and causes them to question the sanity of trainers. Following two promising dirt sprints, Madringa switched to a turf route. But her pedigree and fast-tempo running style hardly suggested a successful transition. Madringa merely possessed high figures, earned in dirt sprints. Now she was racing in a turf route. None of her rivals had exceeded 82. Madringa had a double advantage—both speed figures higher than her competition's. But you can see the problem.

The speed figures earned by Madringa could not be accepted at face value, for they had been earned on different footing, at a dissimilar distance, while setting a fast pace inappropriate to a turf route. Her dirt-sprint figures were not relevant to a two-turn turf race. They were pure sugar. Madringa pressed the pace, tired, and finished sixth. Speed figures are a functional tool, but apples must be compared to apples, and oranges to oranges. Mix the two together, and all you get is a stomachache at a short price.

Master of the Sea illustrates yet another trap. In his previous start, Master of the Sea ran the race of his life. He beat maidens by six lengths, and earned a career-best 89 Beyer. Those who accepted the figure at face value were locked into Master of the Sea as the selection in race 7 at Hollywood Park on April 27, 2003. No other starter had earned a recent figure anywhere close to 89.

Trouble was, the 89 was earned unexpectedly in the ninth start of Master of the Sea's career. His previous high was only 73. Furthermore, the 89 had been earned under abnormal circumstances. Master of the Sea had shaken loose on the lead after an opening quarter-mile in a slow 22.80. He was handed an easy lead, he got brave, and he romped.

Facing better company, the pace had to be faster. Master of the Sea had never successfully coped with fast fractions. It was unlikely he would cope now. He started at odds of 5-2, was unable to make the lead, tired, and finished 11th. It happens all the time. As horses move up in class, the pace quickens. Horses are foiled most when forced to cope with a faster pace. Quicker fractions frequently stymie horses trying to move up the ladder, which will be illustrated later in the chapter.

Winsome Dame	B. f. 4 (Apr)		Life	1 M 1 0	$10,000	86	D.Fst	1 0 1 0	$10,000 86
Own:Stronach Stable	Sire: Siphon*Brz (Itajara)		2002	1 M 1 0	$10,000	86	Wet(260*) 0 0 0 0		$0 –
Black, Black A/red Emblem On Gold	Dam:Distinct Habit(Distinctive Pro)	L 123	2001	0 M 0 0	$0	–	Turf(255) 0 0 0 0		$0 –
(42 6 4 9 .14) 2003:(666 119 .18)	Br: Adena Springs (Ky) Tr: Headley Bruce(9 2 0 1 .22) 2003:(85 21 .25)		Dmr	1 0 1 0	$10,000	86	Dst(300) 1 0 1 0		$10,000 86

5Dmr fst 6f :212 :442 :57 1:102 3↑ ⑩Md Sp Wt 50k   86 2 3 11½ 1² 1¹ 2² Solis A   LB 119 b   4.80 86−17 GoldenBnd119² WinsomeDme119½ ScrtApprov1197   Speed,rail,held 2nd 7
● Jly24 Dmr 5f fst :59 H 1/51   Jly18 Dmr 5f fst 1:00² H 4/26   Jly9 SA 6f fst 1:12¹ H 2/13 ● Jun30 SA 5f fst :58² H 1/55   Jun23 SA 5f fst 1:01³ H 24/56 ● Jun16 SA 5f fst :58 H 1/33
R: +180Days(15 .13 $0.51) 2ndStart(29 .28 $1.53) Dirt(239 .25 $2.22) Sprint(195 .25 $2.19) MdnSpWt(51 .29 $2.57)

Desert Pearls	B. f. 3 (Jan) FTSAUG01 $400,000		Life	0 M 0 0	$0	–	D.Fst	0 0 0 0	$0 –
Own:The Thoroughbred Corporation	Sire: Dixieland Band (Northern Dancer) $75,000		2003	0 M 0 0	$0	–	Wet(370) 0 0 0 0		$0 –
Green/white Stripes, Green Stripes	Dam:Pleasant Sunshine(Pleasant Colony)	⑬ 118	2002	0 M 0 0	$0	–	Turf(305) 0 0 0 0		$0 –
E (35 4 4 2 .11) 2003:(547 84 .15)	Br: Elia Simon Wallace White McBride (Ky) Tr: Baffert Bob(18 4 1 2 .22) 2003:(379 76 .20)		Dmr	0 0 0 0	$0	–	Dst(350) 0 0 0 0		$0 –

● Jly28 Dmr 6f fst 1:12 H 1/18   Jly22 Dmr 5f fst :59³ Hg8/59   Jly16 Hol 5f fst 1:00¹ Hg4/34   Jly9 Hol 6f fst 1:13⁴ H 4/11   Jly3 Hol 6f fst 1:12² H 2/10   Jun27 Hol 5f fst 1:00³ H 11/32
Jun21 Hol 5f fst 1:01² H 22/48   Jun15 Hol 4f fst :48 H 7/32   Jun12 Hol 4f fst :49 H 13/34   Jun6 Hol 4f fst :49² H 15/32   May27 Hol 3f fst :37³ H 7/10
1stStart(161 .13 $1.20) Dirt(898 .20 $1.47) Sprint(679 .19 $1.55) MdnSpWt(306 .18 $1.47)

A different trap was illustrated during the 2003 summer meet at Del Mar, in a two-race sequence that started with a maiden sprint on August 2. Winsome Dame's previous start had been a good second-place finish after setting a fast pace. Conditioned by Bruce Headley, she was training well for her comeback. Bob Baffert trained Desert Pearls, a fast-working first-time starter.

The morning before the race, Baffert was reading *Daily Racing Form* and noted Winsome Dame was listed as the analyst's "Best Bet," the most likely winner on the card. Baffert's filly, Desert Pearls, was picked second. The trainer was amused.

"How'd you come up with this one?" he said, jokingly. "My filly will run circles around the horse you picked."

"Wanna bet?" was the reply. "Sure, how much?" Baffert replied. "$100," was the answer. The trainer was surprised a public handicapper had $100 in his wallet. The challenge was accepted. Horse against horse, the winner collects.

Winsome Dame broke like a shot, opened up on the turn, and appeared on her way to victory. And then, she quit. Baffert was right. That day, his filly did run circles around her rivals. Desert Pearls ran past Winsome Dame as if she were standing still and galloped by more than seven lengths. She earned an outstanding Beyer figure of 91.

Based on that performance, Desert Pearls was sufficiently qualified to win a first-condition allowance in her next start. The Beyer par for a N1X filly-mare allowance was 92. But there was a problem. Instead of giving Desert Pearls sufficient recovery time of at least three weeks following the demonstrative maiden win, Baffert jammed her back in 13 days, on August 15. It was too soon. Baffert was flirting with danger, and so were bettors that took the short price.

Because she was wheeled back so soon, there was a chance Desert Pearls would regress. She did. Desert Pearls broke slowly (tired and unfit horses often break slowly), and finished fourth. The speed figure Desert Pearls earned in her debut was tops in the allowance field, but her subsequent effort shows there is more to predicting a horse's future performance than simply recognizing she was the fastest horse in the past. Current condition must be considered.

Since Beyer Speed Figures entered the mainstream, there has been much grumbling that it is impossible to get a square price (high odds) on a "high-figure" horse. High figures attract inordinate wagering action, but identifying the high-figure horse is only one part of the handicapping process. The fact that a horse has earned the highest Beyer figure in the race does not make him the automatic winner. It only means that in one area of handicapping, he is superior. Is it significant if one horse gets a 98, and another a 96? Not really; there are too many other considerations to quibble over a two-point difference.

avata
n:Tabor Michael B
yal Blue, Orange Ball, Orange Stripes
D (113 32 24 16 .28) 2003:(554 147 .27)

B. c. 3 (Feb) FTFFEB02 $575,000
Sire: Phone Trick (Clever Trick) $25,000
Dam: Pert Lady(Cox's Ridge)
Br: Mill Ridge Farm Ltd Jamm Ltd & Dr John A Chandler (Ky)
Tr: Biancone Patrick L(14 3 1 2 .21) 2003:(83 15 .18)

123

Life	9	5	1	1	$342,320	112	D.Fst	8	5	1	1	$340,640	112
2003	3	2	0	0	$116,280	112	Wet(345)	1	0	0	0	$1,680	75
2002	6	3	1	1	$226,040	102	Turf(245)	0	0	0	0	$0	–
Sar	3	2	0	1	$202,000	112	Dst(305)	1	0	0	1	$22,000	95

Sar fst	6f	:22 :443 :562 1:083	Amsterdam-G2	112	8	4	2hd	2hd	12½	15¼	Bailey J D	119	3.15	99–07	Zavata1195¼ Great Notion121½ Trust N Luck123nk	Vied inside, clear	7
Mth fst	6f	:214 :441 :561 1:084 3↑	OClm 40000N	100	2	4	2hd	2½	1hd	11	Farina T	114	*.80	95–15	Zavata1141 Rockin On Ready1142¾ SkipAGrade118nk	Inched clear final 1/8	8
Bel sly	6f	:212 :432 :55 1:074 3↑	Alw 56000C	75	2	1	1hd	34	411	515½	Farina T	L 112	3.15	84–11	True Direction1234¼ Well Fancied1134½ Vodka1152	Speed inside, tired	5
AP fst	1⅛	:46 1:094 1:354 1:493	B C JuvenileG1	—	9	105	117¾	1316	—	—	Stevens G L	L 122	14.00	— —	Vindication1222¾ Kafwain1222¼ Hold That Tiger1221¼	Pulled up	13
Sar fst	7f	:222 :453 1:102 1:23	Hopeful-G1	95	4	4	41½	42	32½	33¾	Bailey J D	122	*.35	86–13	Sky Mesa1221¾ Pretty Wild1222 Zavata1225¼	Checked shuffled early	6
Sar fst	6½f	:221 :453 1:104 1:173	Sar Special-G2	101	5	2	32	21	14½	17¼	Bailey J D	122	*.45	87–15	Zavata1227¼ Lone Star Sky1223¾ Spite TheDevil1167½	Wide, drew off, drive	5
Bel fst	5½f	:221 :442 :561 1:023	Tremont-G3	102	5	4	41¾	2½	11½	16¼	Bailey J D	114	*.50	99–08	Zavata1146¼ Hussar1144¼ Desert Warrior1143	4 wide, ridden out	5
Bel fst	5f	:223 :453 :573	Md Sp Wt 43k	89	5	3	12	1½	13	15½	Bailey J D	117	*.30	95–13	Zavata1175½ Lion Tamer1174¼ Pretty Wild117¾	Stumbled start, handy	6
CD fst	5f	:22 :451 :573	ThrChmnysJv121k	80	10	11	64¾	43½	32	21	Stevens G L	115	17.70	97–08	Holiday Runner1141 Zavata115¾ Posse1173¾	5w lane,closing	13

●Aug18 Sar 5f fst :59 H 1/20 Aug13 Sar 5f fst :594 H 3/46 ●Jly27 Sar 5f fst :583 H 1/52 Jly21 Sar tr.t(T) 5f fm :592 B 2/19 ●Jly15 Sar 5f fst 1:002 B 1/30 Jly9 Sar tr.t(T) 4f fm :51 B (d) 11/15
: Dirt(111 .23 $2.07) Sprint(73 .23 $1.89) GrdStk(29 .28 $1.94)

alid Video
n:Fehsenfeld Mack
ite, Blue Panel, Blue Diamonds
(—) 2003:(363 91 .25)

Dk. b or br g. 3 (Mar) OBSOCT00 $29,000
Sire: Valid Wager (Valid Appeal) $7,500
Dam: Miss Video(Star Gallant)
Br: Casey Seaman (Fla)
Tr: Manning Dennis J(2 0 0 0 .00) 2003:(88 14 .16)

L 121

Life	8	5	1	0	$445,700	110	D.Fst	5	4	0	0	$404,500	110
2003	5	3	1	0	$354,500	110	Wet(430)	3	1	1	0	$41,200	95
2002	3	2	0	0	$91,200	95	Turf(235)	0	0	0	0	$0	–
Sar	0	0	0	0	$0	–	Dst(380)	1	1	0	0	$137,500	100

Crc fst	6f	:213 :443 :57 1:10	Carry Back-G3	110	9	2	62½	3nk	11	12½	Bravo J	L 122	8.80	94–11	Valid Video1222½ Cajun Beat1171¼ Super Fuse117nk	3 wide, edged away	10
Mth sly	5f	⊗:221 :45 :57	Gilded Time50k	95	2	2	32½	33	23	22¾	Cruz C	L 122	*.90	94–13	Buzzy's Gold1132¾ Valid Video1224 Rockin On Ready1192	Inside, 2nd best	5
GP fst	1 1/16	:224 :462 1:113 1:43	Aventura250k	75	2	31	2½	2hd	32	614¾	Velasquez C	L 122	3.10	79–10	Dynever1223¼ Supah Blitz1226½ Massive1221	Saved grd, gave way	9
OTC fst	6f	:22 :45 :571 1:093	OBS Sprint50k	92	2	2	2½	1½	1hd	13½	Prado E S	L 122	-	97 —	VlidVideo1223½ SuperFuse1223¾ LughingLuke1223	Repulsed bid, drew off	7
GP fst	7f	:222 :443 1:091 1:221	(R)SnshnMilDash250k	100	1	5	31½	2hd	2hd	1½	Prado E S	L 120	2.70	97–08	VlidVideo120½ Excessiveplesur1203¼ SuphBlitz1207¾	Dueled rail, prevailed	7
Bel gd	1	:222 :452 1:101 1:361	Futurity-G1	77	3	2½	2½	44	49½	413½	Chavez J F	L 120	5.60	74–22	Whywhywhy1201¾ PrttyWild1205½ TruckIFtur1206¼	Ducked in start, bump	7
Mth fst	6f	:211 :442 :564 1:094	Sapling-G3	95	2	4	1hd	11	12½	12¼	Lopez C C	L 120	*1.90	90–10	Valid Video1202¼ Farno1205¾ Boston Park1201¾	Bumped start,inside	8
Mth sly	5f	:213 :452 :57	Md Sp Wt 32k	95	6	3	31	2hd	1hd	12½	Cruz C	L 118	4.10	95–14	Valid Video1182½ Farno1187 Max's Cat1182½	Outside bid,drew clear	7

Aug20 Mth 4f fst :492 B 5/31 Aug11 Mth 6f fst 1:132 H 1/1 ●Aug3 Mth 5f my 1:00 B 1/18 Jly27 Mth 4f fst :523 B 61/62 ●Jly9 Mth 4f fst :474 B 1/39 ●Jun29 Mth 6f fst 1:132 H 1/7
: 31-60Days(37 .14 $1.11) Dirt(164 .16 $1.86) Sprint(85 .14 $1.77) GrdStk(7 .43 $5.17)

osse
wn:Heiligbrodt Stables & Vinery Stables
hite, Burnt Orange Star, Orange Hoop
E C J (3 0 0 1 .00) 2003:(907 169 .19)

B. c. 3 (Feb) KEESEP01 $115,000
Sire: Silver Deputy (Deputy Minister) $40,000
Dam: Raska(Rahy)
Br: Robert E Low & Lawana L Low (Ky)
Tr: Asmussen Steven M(30 7 4 6 .23) 2003:(1167 275 .24)

L 123

Life	13	6	2	1	$498,581	111	D.Fst	10	3	2	1	$278,288	108
2003	6	4	1	0	$314,166	111	Wet(365)	3	3	0	0	$220,293	111
2002	7	2	1	1	$184,415	86	Turf(295)	0	0	0	0	$0	–
Sar	2	0	0	0	$18,000	96	Dst(370)	4	2	1	0	$219,398	111

8Sar fst	6f	:22 :443 :562 1:083	Amsterdam-G2	96	2	3	75¼	63¼	44	46	Lanerie C J	L 123	*1.05	93–07	Zavata1195¼ Great Notion121½ Trust N Luck123nk	Came wide, no rally	7
9Bel sly	7f	:221 :443 1:084 1:22	RivaRidgeBC-G2	111	5	6	710	79½	21½	1no	Lanerie C J	L 123	3.15	90–10	Posse123no Midas Eyes1236¼ Halo Homewrecker123hd	Resolute outside	8
9CD sly	6f	:21 :434 :561 1:092	Matt Winn111k	110	4	4	65¼	47½	33½	1½	Lanerie C J	L 120	*1.20	91–15	Posse120½ Bossanova1141¼ Coach Jimi Lee1205	5w lane,stiff drive	9
8Kee fst	7f	:213 :442 1:094 1:23	Lafayette-G3	108	2	5	55	44	2hd	12¼	Lanerie C J	L 118	*2.00	89–16	Posse1182¼ Roll Hennessy Roll1182¼ Bossanova1162¼	4w,hand urging	6
1GP fst	7f	:214 :441 1:082 1:21	Swale-G3	89	3	1	51½	43	36½	29¼	Meche D J	L 120	3.30	94–05	Midas Eyes1169¼ Posse1204½ Whywhywhy1222¼	Angled out, 2nd best	8
7FG fst	5f	:224 :454 :571	Alw 32000N2X	101	2	2	33½	32	11	16¾	Lanerie C J	L 118	*.50	103–14	Posse1186¾ Down Play1184¾ Cashmere Miss1151	Drew out, easily	5
4Hou fst	7f	:22 :44 1:092 1:223	GS Chal Juv263k	71	1	8	2hd	2hd	3nk	812½	Meche D J	L 122	8.00	82–05	Crackup1221¼ Supah Blitz1222¾ Cherokee's Boy122½	Dueled,rail, gave way	10
9CD fst	1	:222 :454 1:11 1:37	Iroquois-G3	49	7	4¾	71¾	62¾	89¼	819¼	Meche D J	L 121	4.40	63–18	Champali1181¼ Alke116nk What A Bad Day118no	5w lane,tired	10
8Sar fst	6f	:213 :444 :574 1:102	Sanford-G2	82	4	4	46	42	3½	44¼	Meche D J	L 122	3.60	86–13	Whywhywhy1222¾ WildcatHeir118no SpiteTheDevil1181½	Inside, split rivals	9
10CD fst	6f	:211 :45 :571 1:093	BshfrdManor-G3	86	6	1	41¾	1hd	11	23½	Meche D J	L 121	*.70	86–11	Lone StarSky1153½ Posse1211 CooperCrossing115nk	Stalked,led,no match	7
9CD fst	5½f	:213 :45 :57 1:033	Ky BC-G3	85	4	4	3nk	2hd	11½	13½	Meche D J	L 115	*.80	94–12	Posse1153½ Del Diablo1152½ Blackjack Boy1155	3abreast,hand urging	8
5CD fst	5f	:22 :451 :573	ThrChmnysJv121k	78	3	4	21½	1½	2hd	31¾	Meche D J	L 117	*.70	96–08	Holiday Runner1141 Zavata115¾ Posse1173¾	Forced pace,weakened	13
3Kee gd	4½f	:222 :452 :512	Md Sp Wt 50k	—	7	1	11		13½	113½	Meche D J	L 118	4.50	98–15	Posse11813 Hayes Road118¾ Wild Thrill118½	Ridden out,much best	8

●Aug18 Sar tr.t 4f fst :474 B 1/23 Aug11 Sar 4f sly :503 B 4/6 Jly28 Sar tr.t 4f fst :482 B 3/15 Jly21 Sar 5f fst 1:042 B 31/34 Jly14 Sar 5f fst 1:011 B 5/16 Jly7 CD 5f fst 1:032 B 17/20
R: Dirt(2411 .24 $1.67) Sprint(1869 .23 $1.58) GrdStk(79 .14 $1.09)

Identifying the fastest horses is a fundamental part of handicapping, and often leads to high-payoff winners. It happened in the 2003 King's Bishop Stakes for 3-year-olds on August 23 at Saratoga. Zavata was favored, partly because of his 112 last-start Beyer. But two others recently had earned lofty Beyers—Valid Video (110) and Posse (111). Those three were the fastest in the race. Zavata started at odds of 6-5; Valid Video was 7-1; and Posse was 6-1. Valid Video won by a neck and paid $17.60. It happens. High-figure performances still do lead to generous payoffs.

Beyond comparing a horse's Beyer figures to par, handicappers should view speed figures as part of a horse's overall history. A single figure that is either much higher or lower than what the horse typically earns could be an aberration. If the odds are high, a bettor can be forgiving. But when the odds are low, that is one reason why a handicapper should insist on a horse having earned par more than once.

What if, without warning or apparent reason, a horse that typically earns Beyers in the low 80's suddenly jumps up and runs a 90? What then? If the horse shows a previous series of races in which he typically earned a figure in the low 80's, chances are the horse will run back to that low-80's figure.

There are a number of reasons why a horse might jump up with a big figure, then regress. That is why a handicapper should insist on a horse having earned a par-matching figure more than once. Maiden races, of course, are an exception because many contenders will have raced only once. Some circumstances under which a big figure might be considered dubious include:

Unusual surface. A horse may catch a wet track he adores, but when he returns to dry land, his speed figure is not likely to be duplicated. Same with track bias. A horse flattered by circumstances such as a speed-favoring racetrack might not run as well under equable conditions.

Unusual pace. A horse may get loose on an easy lead (such as Master of the Sea). Faced with increased pace pressure, he is not likely to duplicate the high figure. It's the same with a closer who benefits from a pace meltdown. Unless a similar scenario reoccurs, the figure is not likely to be reproduced. In a race with less speed, the closer's figure is likely to drop.

Class change, multiple levels. Although claiming horses having par figures for the higher levels frequently will win on the rise, a nonclaiming horse that earns an outstanding figure against softer company cannot be expected to duplicate the performance when he steps up two or more class levels. It's because of the quicker pace or more exhausting finish. The faster-pace scenario is addressed later in this chapter.

Insufficient recovery time. When a first-time starter wins impressively (Desert Pearls, for example), the horse should be given at least three weeks before running again. Anything less, and trouble is possible. The same applies to horses returning from layoffs. When given insufficient time to recover following an all-out comeback, they often regress second start back.

At other times, a horse may suddenly improve, and the race can be taken at face value. Bettors can expect the horse to reproduce the effort. Some examples are listed below.

Barn change. A horse that improves following a trainer upgrade can be expected to reproduce the effort, if his subsequent placement suggests confidence by the trainer.

Maturity. A horse that returns from an extended layoff (three months or more) and is making his first start as a 3-year-old should improve. A suggested guideline is one length for every two months, or two points per month, when projecting improvement for a 2-year-old of last year that is now making his 3-year-old debut.

Explosive performances. Lightly raced 2-year-olds and 3-year-olds often improve dramatically, and handicappers can expect the performance to be repeated.

The flip side is when a horse regresses. Say a horse typically runs in the 80's, and suddenly drops to a 72. He might be tailing off, or the circumstances may have compromised his performance. He may have engaged in a pace battle with another front-runner and wilted. He may have encountered traffic trouble. He may have been racing at the wrong distance. He may have been simply outclassed.

It is a perpetual quandary for handicappers—determining if the horse's most recent speed figure is an accurate indication of the figure he will probably earn this time. While the horse's last start is the most likely gauge of what the horse will do again, a last start must be viewed in the context of today's race.

Other times, a horse's last disappointing speed figure can be disregarded and a handicapper may look farther back into the past performances for a more representative race. Disappointing efforts can be ignored under the following circumstances:

Pace battle. When a horse engages in a severe pace battle and wilts in the stretch, his speed figure suffers. Or, a horse may have been unable to keep up with a pace that placed him farther back than usual. When faced with a softer pace, the horse is likely to earn a higher speed figure.

Traffic trouble. A horse that encounters traffic trouble during the race will see his speed figure decline. Unless the trouble is the result of deteriorating form, a clean trip next time may allow the horse to earn his representative figure.

Normal fluctuation. Some horses are notoriously inconsistent. A horse whose history shows he frequently rebounds from poor efforts cannot be considered to be off form.

Other times, a poor speed figure may be taken at face value and the horse is considered to be in dubious form. These include the following:

Poor performance with no apparent alibi. If a horse runs poorly, without an excuse, a handicapper may be able to ascertain that the horse is tailing off. This is particularly true when a horse drops more than one class level following the subpar race, frequently a sign of surrender. When a maiden claimer runs poorly, the performance generally can be taken at face value.

Barn change or circuit change, followed by poor performance. A horse that changes barns and suddenly regresses can be viewed with skepticism. Likewise, when a racing circuit moves to a new track (Hollywood Park to Del Mar, for example) and a sharp horse produces a dull effort, it may be time to abandon ship.

Typically, a horse's most recent race is the most accurate measure of current ability. A horse that earns an 83 Beyer is likely to run a similar figure next time. And yet a horseplayer cannot accept it on blind faith, every time, just because it is his most recent. Particularly when a horse such as Foreign Accent romps when conditions are perfect.

reign Accent (GB)

Dk. b or br g. 4 (Mar) TATHOUOO $395,226
Sire: Machiavellian (Mr. Prospector)
Dam:Rappa Tap Tap*Fr(Tap On Wood*Ire)
Br: Meon Valley Stud (GB)
Tr: Spawr Bill(9 3 1 2 .33) 2003:(224 51 .23)

n:Lapera & Lane
pie, White HI On Baack, Purple $16,000
(60 10 9 14 .17) 2003:(887 107 .12)

Life	8	2	0	0	$28,739	86	D.Fst	3	1	0	0	$10,200 84
2003	4	1	0	0	$10,200	86	Wet(302*)	0	0	0	0	$0 –
2002	3	0	0	0	$12,289	–	Turf(330*)	5	1	0	0	$18,539 86
Fpx	0	0	0	0	$0	–	Dst(360)	2	0	0	0	$0 41

L 116

0mr fst 1½ :23 :462 1:112 1:45 3↑ Clm c- (20–18) 41 1 2½ 21 2hd 66 920½ Espinoza V LB 119 b *1.70 59 – 20 Potrilord119½ Para Usted119½ Tejan1193 Pulled,bid btwn,wkened 9
d from Girdner Paul K & Jones Reginald C for $20,000, Hines N J Trainer 2003(as of 08/23): (103 14 15 13 0.14)
0mr fst 1½ :473 1:112 1:502 3↑ Clm 10000 (10–8) 84 3 11 11 11 17 13½ Espinoza V LB 119 b 7.90 100 – 16 ForeignAccent1193½ GoldenBonus1092½ Smokvil/119hd Inside, held in hand 7
sly trained by Bray Simon
4ol fst 1½ :231 :463 1:113 1:451 4↑ Clm 25000 (25 –22.5) 40 2 1hd 41 87½ 812 822½ Lovato A J LB 118 b 7.60 55 – 14 The Poseur118½ Fly To The Lake118hd Dr. Hill1185 Fractious,off bit slow 8
5A gd 1 ① :241 :482 1:122 1:362 4↑ Alw 56000 N1x 86 9 42½ 42½ 54½ 54 77 Solis A LB 117 *2.80 73 – 23 MarshallRooster1194 Dvonic119¹ PcificColony119¹½ Stalked,empty lane 10
sly trained by John Gosden
ongchamp(Fr) gd *1¾① RH 2:022 Grand Prix de Paris-G1 6 13½ Fortune J. 128 14.00 Khalkevi128hd Shaanmer1281½ Without Connexion1286 6
m rating: 92 Stk 485000 Rank on lead,soon 5l clear,steadied 4-1/2f out,headed 2f out,wknd
urragh(Ire) hy 1 ① Str 1:471 Irish 2000 Guineas-G1 49½ Fortune J 126 11.00 Rock Of Gibraltar1261½ Century City1263 Della Francesca1265 7
m rating: 98 Stk 339000 Tracked in 4th,never threatened
ewbury(GB) gd 7f ① Str 1:234 Greenham Stakes-G3 7 13½ Fortune J⁵ 126 7.00 Redback1262½ Guys And Dolls126hd Maderno1263 10
oncaster(GB) sf 7f ① Str 1:342 • EBF October Maiden Stks(Div 1) 15 Carroll J 126 10.00 Foreign Accent1265 Zaajel1262½ Transit1264 12
Dwelt,angld right,prgrss hfwy,dueled 3f out,led 2f out,drew clear

Sep20 Fpx 4f fst :501 H 14/18 ● Sep14 Fpx 3f fst :354 H 1/6 Sep9 Dmr 3f fst :363 H 7/11 Aug17 Dmr 5f fst 1:03 H 65/65 Jly26 Dmr 5f fst :593 H 12/85 Jly19 Hol 5f fst 1:033 H 33/34

1stClaim(86 .33 $2.87) 31–60Days(171 .18 $1.90) Dirt(551 .21 $1.76) Routes(290 .15 $1.65) Claim(398 .21 $1.70)

When a front-runner is able to set the pace unchallenged, he will often "freak." It happened during the 2003 Del Mar summer meet. Foreign Accent dropped into a $10,000 claimer. His daylight victory earned an 84 Beyer, but when Foreign Accent returned three weeks later, up three class levels, he faced a different scenario. There was more speed in the field, the race was shorter and likely to be run at a faster tempo, and Foreign Accent was facing better horses. Even worse, and most important, his odds were much lower. A 7.90-1 longshot on August 1, he was only 1.70-1 on August 23.

Handicappers do get in trouble accepting everything at face value. Foreign Accent's 84 Beyer leaped off the page. But handicappers who recognized the career-best figure was earned under ideal circumstances (soft pace, soft foes) had to acknowledge the possibility that Foreign Accent might not reproduce the number. That is exactly what happened. Instead of gaining a clear lead, Foreign Accent was forced into a pace-pressing role, chasing the early leader. Foreign Accent proved counterfeit, and surrendered. He was vulnerable. His last start was produced under circumstances not likely to be duplicated.

In order to accept the horse's most recent speed figure at face value, circumstances must be similar. That means a class change within one level, up or down. It means racing on a similar surface, at a similar distance, with the likelihood of a similar pace. If those qualifiers are not met, a bettor needs to dig deeper into a horse's history to find races that were run under conditions similar to today's race.

1 El Vedado
Red
Own: Allen Joseph
Emerald Green/white Checks, White

ESPINOZA V (151 20 20 27 .13) 2003:(938 136 .14)

B. g. 3 (Mar)
Sire: Seattle Slew (Bold Reasoning) $300,000
Dam: Highest Glory (Damascus)
Br: Joseph Allen (Ky)
Tr: Drysdale Neil(14 4 2 2 .29) 2003:(125 22 .18)

(L) 119

Life	1 M 1 0	$9,800	88	D.Fst	1 0 1 0
2003	1 M 1 0	$9,800	88	Wet(330)	0 0 0 0
2002	0 M 0 0	$0	–	Turf(290)	0 0 0 0
Dmr	1 0 1 0	$9,800	88	Dst(310)	1 0 1 0

27Jly03–9Dmr fst 6½f   :22 :443 1:093 1:161 3+ Md Sp Wt 49k   88 3 7 41½ 43 4¾ 22½ Espinoza V   B 118   37.80 91–10 Montbretia1182½ElVeddo1183 ScenicWonder118¼   4wd into lan

WORKS: Aug14 Dmr 5f fst 1:052 H 65/66 Aug8 Dmr 4f fst :50 H 38/43 Jly24 Dmr 5f fst 1:004 Hg20/52 Jly18 Hol 5f fst 1:001 H 6/21 ●Jly12 Hol 3f fst :351 H 1/26 Jly6 Hol 6f fst 1:134 H 4/6

TRAINER: 2ndStart(22 .18 $1.77) 1stLasix(58 .21 $1.26) Dirt(78 .19 $0.98) Sprint(61 .11 $0.71) MdnSpWt(70 .20 $1.57)

---

2 Cyclotron
White
Own: Greenspun Headley & Molasky
White Green War Game Cock On Back

KRONE J A (143 25 14 18 .17) 2003:(427 63 .15)

Ch. c. 3 (Apr) KEESEP01 $220,000
Sire: Grand Slam (Gone West) $25,000
Dam: Eliot Chacer (Clever Trick)
Br: George Budig & R C Durr (Ky)
Tr: Headley Bruce(21 4 2 2 .19) 2003:(97 23 .24)

L 119

Life	1 M 0 0	$2,940	80	D.Fst	1 0 0 0
2003	1 M 0 0	$2,940	80	Wet(340)	0 0 0 0
2002	0 M 0 0	$0	–	Turf(415*)	0 0 0 0
Dmr	1 0 0 0	$2,940	80	Dst(325*)	1 0 0 0

27Jly03–9Dmr fst 6½f   :22 :443 1:093 1:161 3+ Md Sp Wt 49k   80 9 5 2hd 2½ 3¾ 46 Solis A   LB 118   5.00 88–10 Montbreti1182½ElVeddo1183 ScenicWonder118¼   Forced, 2wd, le

WORKS: ●Aug13 Dmr 5f fst :57 H 1/51 ●Aus6 Dmr 5f fst :581 H 1/59 Jly18 Dmr 6f fst 1:112 H 1/1 ●Jly6 SA 5f fst :574 H 1/51 Jun28 SA 6f fst 1:13 Hg2/9 ●Jun21 SA 4f fst :463 H 1/42

TRAINER: 2ndStart(31 .26 $1.43) Dirt(248 .25 $2.16) Sprint(202 .24 $2.14) MdnSpWt(55 .29 $2.53)

Young horses are often considered an unknown quantity. But even after only one good race, speed figures can be used to determine which horse is fastest. El Vedado and Cyclotron finished second and fourth, respectively, in their July 27 debuts at Del Mar. The final time of the race was a fast 1:16.29, and each 3-year-old earned a respectable Beyer Speed Figure—88 for El Vedado, 80 for Cyclotron.

But could they be expected to repeat the effort, or even improve? You decide. They both were trained by top horsemen (Neil Drysdale, Bruce Headley). Both had worked well since the race. El Vedado and Cyclotron met again August 23 and bettors established front-runner Cyclotron as the even-money favorite and El Vedado as the 2-1 second choice. They dominated the race, finishing 13 lengths clear of the field.

The key utility of speed figures is comparing them to the requirements of the race—par. Rather than comparing horses to one another, horses' speed figures are compared to the qualifications required for a particular race. This forces a handicapper to interpret a horse's chances in the context of the class level. It answers the question, is this horse fast enough to win a typical race at this level?

However, when none of the runners has matched par, speed figures should not be used. The absence of a par-matching horse means that speed figures are less likely to find the winner. In that case, other handicapping criteria become more important. Maiden races in particular are ripe to be won by first-time starters when none of the experienced runners has achieved par. Maiden races are further addressed in Chapter 5.

Here are the basic guidelines to using speed figures.

First, know par—the figure typically required to win a race at a particular class level. For example, in a $10,000 claiming race for older males at Santa Anita, one should be aware that it generally requires an 83 Beyer to win.

After ascertaining the Beyer par, the next step is to identify those horses that have "run to par"—horses that have demonstrated the ability to run the requirements of the race. A horse whose recent figures cluster around 83 would have little chance to win a $20,000 claiming race where the speed-figure par is 89.

After identifying which horses have run to par in similar races, the choice of contenders is narrowed. But this does not take into consideration whether the circumstances will be the same for the race to be run. Specifically, it does not take into account the one factor that ultimately will determine how fast a race will be run. That is, pace.

It's been said before that pace makes the race. Final time, you see, is merely a sum of the separate parts of the race. A race that unfolds with a slow early pace will usually result in a slower final time than a race run at a fast clip. When the pace is comfortable, a horse will continue on. An uncomfortable pace, one that is too fast, will cause him to wilt. So which is which? And how do you know? That is the next part of this chapter.

Pace

The strategy was crude. It was the 1982 Kentucky Derby, and my simple criterion was to bet a stretch-runner. Find a horse with a finishing kick. After all, at 1¼ miles, the Derby was a long race. None of the starters had raced that far, and to an inexperienced horseplayer it made sense to bet a horse that saved his best for last, a horse that would be running strongly through the lane.

That was the extent of my understanding, or perhaps misunderstanding, of pace. Back a stretch-runner in a long-distance race. Oh, brother. As a handicapper, I was in the Stone Age. Had I not been immediately lucky, I might have been saved much future heartache. But on that first Saturday of May 1982, ignorance was bliss.

The radio reception in our blue Ford Pinto was scratchy, but good enough to hear Dave Johnson's live call of the Derby. And when he called the field through the far turn, things were looking good. Front-runner Cupecoy's Joy was fading. El Baba, the second choice, was a tired horse turning into the stretch.

The whole picture changed as the closers took aim on the field and entered Churchill Downs' long stretch. Johnson spat out names in rapid-fire succession. The favorite, Air Forbes Won, briefly threatened and faded. Muttering made a move that he could not sustain. Water Bank rallied, briefly. Reinvested menaced. But the horse that caught Johnson's eye had unleashed a sweeping rally through the far turn. It was my stretch-runner. Gato Del Sol was on the move. "And down the stretch they come!"

Gato Del Sol had circled the field on the far turn, hit the stretch with a head of steam, powered to the lead in midstretch, and drew away. We were newlyweds renting a small apartment, and suddenly we felt rich. Our $15 investment ($5 across the board) was worth $182. Life was good. Handicapping genius and youthful enthusiasm all crammed inside an old used Pinto.

It was pure luck. Intelligent handicappers may have foreseen the likelihood of a pace meltdown, but not me. How naïve to be looking for nothing more than a stretch-runner in a route race. Gato Del Sol won the Derby not because he was a superior horse. He won because the front-runners burned one another out. The pace collapsed. A stretch-runner had to win.

Pace is the rate of speed at which a race unfolds. The fractions of a race complement some horses, compromise others. Front-runners generally perform best in races where there are few horses with a similar style. When the filly Winning Colors won the 1988 Kentucky Derby, her victory was partly the result of racing unchallenged on the lead. She got loose, and got brave, as did 2002 Derby winner War Emblem.

Conversely, fast fractions often spell doom for front-runners. In the 2001 Derby, Bob Baffert instructed jockey Gary Stevens to position Point Given close to the lead. The strategy backfired. Instead of biding his time early and producing his customary kick, Point Given expended his energy chasing a merciless pace. He finished fifth. Even good horses are affected by pace. When a horse is encouraged to chase intense fractions, he will grow tired, much sooner.

The essence of pace analysis is to determine a horse's preferred running style, and whether it is complemented by the dynamics of a race. The chief concern is whether the likely pace of the race suits the horse's preferred style. The questions of pace apply to dirt racing. On turf, early pace is less important, an issue that will be addressed in Chapter 5.

The initial consideration in pace analysis is identifying running style. Is the horse a front-runner who races straight to the lead? Is he a presser, typically positioned within a length or two of the lead? Or is the horse a closer, one that lags at the rear of the field?

Horseplayers able to envision how a race will unfold stand a greater chance of finding the winner. Handicappers must recognize which contenders will be flattered, or compromised, by the probable pace. Horseplayers can determine how fast, or slowly, a race is likely to unfold, and how the pace scenario will affect the contestants.

For horses, the general running styles are referred to as Early Pace (E), Pace-Pressers (P) and Early-Pressers (E/P), and Sustained (S).

Horses' styles rarely change. A speed horse remains a speed horse (until he wears down at the end of his career). Horses cannot adapt simply because the dynamics of a particular race happen to be wrong. A speedball front-runner cannot be rated off the pace when he enters a race with several other front-runners. In that case, as you can imagine, the front-runners may all be doomed.

Early Pace types (E) are horses whose best performances occur when they are able to lead the field in the early stage of the race. In determining a horse's preferred running style, the performances used are races that he won, or nearly won (within one length).

Pace Pressers (P) are horses whose best performances are in races when they are positioned within two lengths of the lead, and apply pressure on the pacesetters throughout the race. The most effective horses are Early-Pressers (E/P), whose versatility allows them to set the pace or press the leaders.

In a race with three or more "E" runners, a pace battle is likely to ensue. The "E" runners, intent on racing to the lead, will race faster and faster trying to get to the front. And then, they all wilt. But if there are fewer than three "E" types in the field, chances are the race will be won by one of those front-runners. Even in a race with two front-runners, there is less likelihood of a pace battle.

Finally, there are Sustained runners (S) such as Gato Del Sol. Sustained runners are typically positioned in the rear third of the field, and usually require a complete collapse of the pace in order to win. It does not happen often.

Front-running horses win more frequently than late-runners. In a study of more than 15,000 races, handicapping author William Quirin found that 26 percent were won by the horse who led at the first pace call—after the first quarter-mile in sprints, after the first half-mile in routes. Quirin further discovered that, lumped as a group, horses positioned first, second, or third win 57 percent of all races.

While early speed produces a high percentage of winners, handicapping goes beyond knowing which horse will be in front. How many front-runners are there? If there are two or fewer, it may be perfectly acceptable to back one or the other. Fewer speed horses means it is less likely a pace battle will transpire. Which presser will inherit the lead if the front-runners peel away? Are there so many front-runners in the field that the race figures to collapse in favor of a closer from the back of the pack?

In the 1991 Hollywood Gold Cup, front-runner Marquetry was seemingly overmatched against Farma Way. But Marquetry was the only other front-runner. Trainer D. Wayne Lukas instructed jockey Gary Stevens to conserve Farma Way's energy. Stevens rode Farma Way accordingly, and relinquished the lead to Marquetry. Although his credentials were less solid than Farma Way's, Marquetry became the lone speed. He exploited the pace advantage and a 12-pound weight concession and raced gate to wire. He paid $56.80. Lone speed, even when apparently outclassed, is always dangerous.

Pace analysis comes after analyzing condition, class, and speed. Only then is the determination made on how fast or slowly a race is likely to unfold. Then, contenders are assessed against the context of pace. If a horse appears a worthy form-class-speed candidate, the next question is whether his style suits the likely pace.

There are three segments to a race—early, middle, and late. The least important is the final segment. The closing fraction in dirt races, which is the final quarter-mile, is far less meaningful than the early fractions. Determining the horse that is first to the wire depends on what happened in the first and second segments of the race.

The dynamics of a six-furlong race are such that horses race at top speed throughout. By the time they reach the quarter pole (a quarter-mile remaining), two-thirds of the race is over and most of their energy has been spent. Because the opening half-mile is where the most work is done, it makes sense to emphasize that portion of a race. What happens in the stretch is merely a result of what happened earlier. In order to see how the race will unfold—how the game will be played—the place to begin is the first pace call. That is the opening quarter-mile in sprints, the opening half-mile in routes.

Many handicappers simply eyeball the field to identify which horses are likely to contest the pace. Others use a mechanical procedure called speed points, developed by Quirin and further examined in handicapping texts by James Quinn.

The procedure shows which horses are likely to control the early pace, and how many there are. When there are three or more front-runners, the race may be ripe for a closer. The assignment of speed points is based on the running position at the first call in the horse's last three qualifying races, and does not go farther back than five races. Horses end up with a speed-points total ranging from 0 to 8.

In sprints, speed points are added using criteria from the horse's last three starts. Each horse starts with 1 point, and gets:

1 point for each sprint in which he was positioned 1-2-3 at the first call.

1 point for each sprint in which he was within two lengths of the lead at the first call.

0 points for any other sprint.

0 points for any route, unless he ran within one length of the lead at the first call, in which case the race is disregarded.

In seven-furlong sprints, he may receive a point for position only if he led at the first call; if he was second or third, or merely within two lengths, he does not receive any.

1 bonus point if he led, or raced within a neck of the leader, in each rated race.

Minus 1 point if he has earned no points and did not finish in front of half the field in any of his rated races.

A horse with four or more points is likely to be among the early leaders. A horse with at least four points, and who ranks highest in the field, wins often. A horse with four or more points, and a two-point advantage, performs better yet. A horse with eight points is almost certain to battle for the lead. However, if others have six or more points, a duel is likely that may compromise horses with six or more points. The pace may unravel.

Speed points also can be used in routes (two-turn races at a mile or more). Points are awarded based on the horse's last three starts. Each horse starts with 1 point, and gets:

1 point for any route in which he was positioned 1-2-3 at the first call.

1 point for any route in which he was within three lengths of the lead at the first call.

0 points for any other route.

1 point for any sprint in which he was 1-2-3 at the first call, or within three lengths of the lead at the first call.

1 point for any sprint in which he was within six lengths of the lead at the first call.

0 points for any sprint in which he was neither 1-2-3 nor within six lengths, in which case the race is passed.

1 bonus point is added if a horse set the pace, or was within one length of the lead, in each rated sprint, or within three lengths of the lead in each rated sprint.

A horse with four or more speed points is likely to be among the early leaders. His chances to win depend on how many others have the same style. When three or more in a route have four or more speed points, the likelihood of a contested pace increases, and the chances of front-runners diminish.

The speed-points method is not devoid of flaws; mechanical procedures always require a dose of common sense. A front-runner that has been flattered by a series of unusually soft trips (slow pace) on the lead may earn a high speed-points total. But if the horse has been getting away with opening half-miles in a leisurely 50 seconds, or six furlongs in a slow 1:14, his high speed-points total may be a handicapping mirage. No pace analysis is complete without examining the fractions that a horse has been running. This is measured by the horse's position relative to the fractions of the pacesetter.

For the sake of simplicity in determining a horse's "interior fractions," one length is rounded to one-fifth of a second.

Smokey Glacken
Own: Susan and John Moore
White, Royal Blue Star, Blue Stars On
)S J A (41 9 4 7 .22) 2003: (1111 169 .15)
B. f. 2 (Mar) KEESEP02 $150,000
Sire: Forestry (Storm Cat) $50,000
Dam: Majesty's Crown (Magesterial)
Br: Jayeff B Stables (Ky)
Tr: Jerkens James A(11 2 2 4 .18) 2003:(168 40 .24)
L 118

Life	3	2	0	1	$73,500	79	D.Fst	2	2	0	0	$57,000 79
2003	3	2	0	1	$73,500	79	Wet(372*)	1	0	0	1	$16,500 78
2002	0	M	0	0	$0	-	Turf(317*)	0	0	0	0	$0 -
Aqu	0	0	0	0	$0	-	Dst(369)	1	1	0	0	$30,000 79

-10Bel sly 6½f :212 :442 1:102 1:17 ⒻAstarita-G2 78 1 7 4¾ 31½ 1hd 31½ Santos J A L117 4.20 86- 16 SpctclrMoon117nk FlnStory1201¼ SmkyGlckn11713 Wide move, weakened 9
-9Mth fst 6f :212 :441 :564 1:101 ⒻForwardGal50k 79 3 6 1hd 1hd 12 12½ Velez J A Jr L115 *1.10 88- 14 SmokeyGlacken1152½ BabaGonzo1214 Amzer1122½ Dueled 2w, drew clear 8
-4Sar fst 5½f :213 :453 :581 1:05 ⒻMd Sp Wt 45k 69 5 6 1½ 12 16 15 Santos J A L119 *1.45 91- 15 *Smokey Glacken*1195 *Storm Fleet*1191¾ Mystified119½ Widened when asked 10
S: Nov18 Bel tr.t 4f fst :493 B *21/47* Nov11 Bel tr.t 5f fst 1:01 B *2/16* Nov2 Bel tr.t 4f fst :49 B *8/33* Oct25 Bel tr.t 3f fst :363 B *2/11* Oct7 Bel tr.t 6f fst 1:15 B *1/1* Sep18 Bel tr.t 3f fst :362 B *8/24*
ER: 2YO(33 .27 $1.96) 31-60Days(104 .20 $1.47) Dirt(343 .25 $2.15) Sprint(189 .23 $1.98) GrdStk(54 .20 $2.84)

Stoic
Own: Jay Em Ess Stable
Fluorescent Green, Blue 'Js,' Blue
LLANO J J (84 13 9 15 .15) 2003: (1112 162 .15)
Dk. b or br f. 2 (May) KEESEP02 $250,000
Sire: Forestry (Storm Cat) $50,000
Dam: Brink (Forty Niner)
Br: Lance K Robinson (Ky)
Tr: Dutrow Richard E Jr(32 11 7 3 .34) 2003:(473 113 .24)
L 118

Life	5	2	1	1	$68,130	84	D.Fst	4	1	1	1	$42,330 84
2003	5	2	1	1	$68,130	84	Wet(384*)	1	1	0	0	$25,800 79
2002	0	M	0	0	$0	-	Turf(300*)	0	0	0	0	$0 -
Aqu	1	1	0	0	$28,200	77	Dst(392)	1	1	0	0	$28,200 77

-8Aqu fst 6f :221 :452 :574 1:11 ⒻAlw 47000N1x 77 1 4 51¾ 43 1½ 12½ Prado E S L119 2.60 85- 16 Stoic1192½ Sweet Vision1192 High Peaks1162¼ Took over when roused 7
-8Sar fst 7f :222 :452 1:103 1:24 ⒻSpinaway-G1 -0 5 2 62¾ 69¾ 621 641¼ Luzzi M J L121 24.75 46- 10 Ashado1211¼ *Be Gentle*1218¼ Daydreaming1211¾ Eased stretch 6
-5Sar fst 5½f :214 :45 :573 1:041 ⒻAlw 47000N1x 84 2 1 2½ 21½ 2½ 21 Prado E S L120 10.50 94- 08 Dixie Waltz1201 Stoic1201¾ *Ana's Lady Bird*1201¾ Bumped start, game 6
-6Bel gd 5f :214 :452 :582 ⒻMd Sp Wt 43k 79 3 1 2½ 21½ 2hd 11 Prado E S L118 *2.10 91- 17 Stoic1181 SelltheRallies1181¼ StormMinstrel1186¾ Speed outside, gamely 8
-3Bel fst 5f :223 :454 :583 ⒻMd Sp Wt 43k 64 1 1 59½ 57½ 512 36¼ Luzzi M J 118 12.20 84- 15 *Rodeo Licious*1154¾ *Dixie Waltz*1181½ *Stoic*1183¾ Going well late 7
: Nov16 Aqu 5f fst 1:01 B *2/7* Oct17 Aqu 5f fst 1:04 B *3/8* Oct7 Aqu 4f fst :504 B *6/7* Sep22 Aqu 5f fst 1:003 B *7/12* Aug25 Sar 4f fst :511 B *26/29*

'orest Music
wn: Michael J Gill
lue, White Ball, Blue 'Mcm,' Two White
E S (82 12 14 9 .15) 2003: (1437 255 .18)
Gr/ro. f. 2 (Apr) FTFFEB03 $325,000
Sire: Unbridled's Song (Unbridled) $100,000
Dam: Defer West (Gone West)
Br: Twin Hopes Farm Inc (Ky)
Tr: Shuman Mark(2 1 0 0 .50) 2003:(982 211 .21)
Blinkers ON
L 116

Life	2	1	0	0	$14,250	105	D.Fst	2	1	0	0	$14,250 105
2003	2	1	0	0	$14,250	105	Wet(361)	0	0	0	0	$0 -
2002	0	M	0	0	$0	-	Turf(323)	0	0	0	0	$0 -
Aqu	0	0	0	0	$0	-	Dst(383)	1	1	0	0	$14,250 105

3SA fst 1 1/16 :224 :464 1:104 1:423 ⒻBCJuvFil-G1 25 4 11½ 11 2½ 1430 1442 Prado E S LB119 7.10 49- 07 Halfbridled1192½ Ashado119nk *Victory U. S. A.*1199¼ Gave way 14
4Lrl fst 6f :22 :441 :56 1:082 ⒻMd Sp Wt 25k 105 4 1 14 17 18 18½ Karamanos H A L122 *.90 97- 14 ForstMusc1228½ *PrlousNght*12215¾ ExclsvPrnt122nk Quickly clear, driving 7
Nov17 Fai 4f fst :50 Bg *3/5* Aug27 Fai 4f fst :50 Bg *5/10*
R: 2YO(22 .14 $0.75) Route/Sprint(156 .17 $1.41) Dirt(1537 .20 $1.50) Sprint(878 .21 $1.51) GrdStk(30 .03 $0.69)

The Grade 3 Valley Stream Stakes on November 23, 2003, at Aqueduct featured three leading contenders, including Smokey Glacken and Stoic, who had earned almost identical Beyer figures in their last starts. However, comparison of their interior fractions indicated that Smokey Glacken had run a better race.

Using the approximation of one-fifth second for each length behind the pacesetter, Smokey Glacken's opening fractions were about 21.60 and 44.60, en route to a 78 Beyer. Stoic was farther behind a slower pace, and ran fractions of about 22.60 and 46 en route to a 77 Beyer. While the races were run at slightly different distances and at different tracks, the example applies.

Forest Music was a toss-out on principle. Her October 8 maiden win would bury the field, but she subsequently had shipped to California, been drilled in the Breeders' Cup Juvenile Fillies, then returned to the East. At odds of even money in the Valley Stream, Forest Music was a vulnerable favorite. The Valley Stream was all but over as soon as Smokey Glacken recovered from her stumble at the start. She sprinted to the lead, and dominated start to finish, winning by nearly four lengths. Stoic was unable to keep up with the fast pace and finished third. Forest Music was off the board.

When two horses with similar speed figures enter the same race, preference often goes to the horse that has been running faster in the early part of the race. Another means of pace analysis includes the use of pace figures. While a speed figure reflects a horse's time for the entire race, a pace figure reflects a horse's time only to the second pace call.

Pace figures, used in conjunction with speed figures, provide keen insight on how a horse earned his final time. A below-par pace figure often indicates weakness in the horse's running line. Pace figures can be made using methods outlined in Tom Brohamer's *Modern Pace Handicapping* or purchased privately. I subscribe to Brohamer's service, which provides figures for the Southern California circuit. But whether one uses speed points, fractional analysis, or pace figures, nothing beats good old-fashioned logic.

The 3-year-old claimer Ulloa illustrates what happens when a "need the lead" horse—an "E" horse—does not make it to the lead. Some horses get discouraged when they are unable to establish the early advantage. Every time that Ulloa failed to make the lead, he faded. Not coincidentally, Ulloa's best races were when he was able to outspeed his rivals to the front.

An "E/P" horse is the most effective type of runner. Versatile, they produce their best efforts when they are on the attack; Silver Charm was a good example. That is, until he lost his speed. Early-pressers cope with most pace scenarios, they are adaptable, and many are able to take control of a race in the absence of a true "E" horse.

"S" horses—deep closers—do not win their fair share on dirt. They do not commence their rally until after the pace call. It's tough to do—rallying past most of the field in the final quarter-mile. Closers win sometimes, but only when the front-runners collapse. After the 2001 Kentucky Derby, deep closer Monarchos never won another major race, nor did 1982 Derby winner Gato D(2003, Evening Attire, Puzzlement, and Saarland were handicap horses. But they were deep closers and rarely v

"S" runners are not entirely useless, however. Deep closers often pick up the pieces and hit the board even without winning. They frequently are the ideal type of horse to include in the two- or three-hole in a vertical wager such as an exacta or trifecta.

Speed points and running-style identification are good for the first portion of the race. Once the early-speed tendencies of a field are determined, one may turn to the second portion of a sprint race. The next part of pace handicapping is the distance from the half-mile to the quarter pole—the turn—on a one-mile racetrack. This is the far turn, where races typically are won and lost. The far turn is a key part of any race, particularly sprints.

Racing through the final turn, horses either handle the pressure, or succumb. To determine which horses are most likely to withstand the pressure, "turn time" and "ability time" can be considered. A horse's turn time is the time required to race from the half-mile to the quarter pole—around the turn. Ability time is the sum of the time is takes a horse to get to the pace call, added to the time the horse takes to negotiate the turn.

April Trust

Own: Stewart Hoffman
Royal Purple, Yellow 'Hsk,' Yellow Seams
P L JR (32 3 3 3 .09) 2003: (454 36 .08)

B. f. 3 (Apr)
Sire: Silver Ghost (Mr. Prospector) $10,000
Dam: Matter of Trust (Leo Castelli)
Br: Stewart L Hoffman (NY)
Tr: Jerkens James A(6 1 0 1 .17) 2003:(188 45 .24)

1157

	Life	3 1 0 1	$31,570	60	D.Fst	3 1 0 1	$31,570	60
	2002	0 M 0 0	$0	-	Wet(349)	0 0 0 0	$0	-
	Aqu ⊡	0 0 0 0	$0	-	Turf(270)	0 0 0 0	$0	-
					Dst(350)	3 1 0 1	$31,570	60

2Aqu fst 6f :224 :461 :583 1:122 3↑℗⑤Md Sp Wt 41k 60 5 5 3½ 1½ 1hd 1no Cotto P L Jr7 114 b 3.85 78– 12 April Trust114no Polonia1217½ Katies Danza1212½ 3 wide, prevailed 11
4Bel fst 6f :223 :471 1:003 1:14 3↑℗⑤Md Sp Wt 41k 45 6 8 3½ 1hd 2½ 37¾ Cotto P L Jr7 113 b *2.90 61– 29 Flying Pickle1205¾ Katies Danza1202 April Trust1131½ Vied 3 wide, tired 12
4Bel fst 6f :231 :471 :594 1:132 3↑℗⑤Md Sp Wt 41k 45 3 6 42½ 2½ 33 45 Velazquez J R 117 *1.45 67– 23 ValidPro1171½ ZatDarnCat1223¾ GataBePtient117nk Chased 3 wide, faded 9
Dec16 Bel tr.t 5f fst 1:04 B 4/9 Nov15 Bel tr.t 5f fst 1:041 B 29/34 Oct21 Bel 5f fst 1:014 B 9/27 Oct16 Bel tr.t 5f fst 1:03 B 8/10 Oct10 Bel tr.t 4f fst :492 B 6/15
R: Dirt(362 .25 $2.13) Sprint(195 .24 $2.05) Alw(168 .29 $2.39)

It's an easy pace-analysis calculation, and helps separate contenders, particularly in sprints. First, determine how fast a horse ran to the pace call by adding the pace-call fraction to beaten lengths. April Trust was on the lead, through a half-mile in 46.20.

Secondly, determine her turn time by subtracting her first quarter-mile from her half-mile. April Trust was one-half length behind an opening quarter-mile in 22.80, so she went the first quarter-mile in approximately 22.90. Subtracting that from her half-mile time of 46.20 means her turn time was 23.30.

Finally, add turn time (23.30) to the half-mile time (46.20) to determine ability time (69.50). Lower means faster. With only a little practice, a beginning horseplayer can calculate a horse's ability time in seconds. It provides a great tool for separating contenders.

That's what speed figures and pace analysis do, they separate contenders. And it pays to be a skeptic, particularly when a heavy favorite is moving up after a big win. A handicapper should know how fast a horse ran to the pace call, and whether it was fast enough to cope with the tougher pace demands at a higher class level.

At Santa Anita, the average half-mile fraction in a six-furlong sprint for one-other-than allowance horses is 44.40. That is par. A recent maiden winner may be moving into an allowance race after earning a lofty speed figure. But if he won the maiden race after running the opening half-mile in only 45, there is a good chance he will be outgunned against allowance foes. He will be forced to chase a faster pace than he did before, and his speed figure almost certainly will decrease.

So how do you know, specifically, if a horse is able to with-stand a class raise? One way is to become familiar with the pace requirements of different class levels. This may require advanced handicapping tools such as par times for both the pace call and final time. Another way is to use pace figures, which can be con-structed, or purchased from a number of reliable figure services.

We have only scratched the surface regarding pace. There is more to learn, and even expert handicappers continue to grapple with the subject. For now, this is plenty. A beginning handicapper possesses the basic tools to get started. Determine a horse's run-ning style, and compare it to the others. A lonely front-runner is dangerous. In a race with three or more speed horses, the time may be right to shop for a presser or closer. And calculating abil-ity time provides a tool to separate contenders.

The building blocks of the handicapping process have been identified—current condition, class, speed, and pace.

Is there more? You bet. These fundamentals are supported by the secondary factors, which are the subject of the next chapter.

5

SECONDARY FACTORS

It was a Friday night at Hollywood Park and I was getting killed, right in the middle of a festive, nighttime party atmosphere. The music between races was loud. The fun-loving crowd was boisterous. I was too young to feel old, but the distractions were annoying and my handicapping opinions were all wrong. It was going to be a long night.

It was 1995, and horseplayers were picking up on a new technique—pedigree handicapping, which focuses on considering the horse's lineage when he is trying something new. A horse "bred for grass" may improve when he changes from dirt races to turf. The horse's sire, or dam, or their offspring, may have been most effective on grass. Similarly, a horse "bred to run long" may improve when changed from a sprint to a route.

It was a broad assessment with no absolutes. A lot concerning pedigree had to be accepted on faith. That night, I was willing to try just about anything.

A handicapping guide called "Mudders and Turfers" was gaining popularity. It simplified the mystery of pedigree handicapping by assigning numerical ratings to horses that might project their capability on mud or grass. The biannual guide, written by Lee

Tomlinson, removed some guesswork. And it worked. It was pedigree handicapping for dummies, and I qualified. Another attribute of Tomlinson Ratings, beyond their helpfulness, was that even a novice could use them.

The first turf race on the Friday-night card was a sprint for $80,000 claimers, and the field included a shipper from small Yakima Meadows who was trying turf for the first time. Horses from the state of Washington usually are overmatched in Southern California, but Comininalittlehot's turf rating in "Mudders and Turfers"—a number that was based on his sire and damsire (maternal grandsire)—hinted he could improve on the grass. I had used Tomlinson Ratings with limited success, but this was new. The horse's high turf rating was completely out of whack relative to his odds of 21-1.

Apparently outclassed, with ordinary speed figures and no pace advantage, a bad post and a low-profile ex-jockey trainer in Frank Olivares, Comininalittlehot had turf potential and a fat price. He broke from post 10 in the 5½-furlong turf race, and stayed wide under jockey Gary Stevens. Unable to save ground on the turn, Comininalittlehot continued wide. It was not a good trip. Three Peat, the 8-5 favorite, opened up into the stretch and held a three-length lead with a furlong to go. But he was tiring. Comininalittlehot was narrowing the gap. He cut the deficit to two lengths, then a length, as both horses reached for the wire. Finally, in deep stretch, Comininalittlehot wore down his rival and won by a neck. He paid $44.20, and the $1 trifecta, with favorite Three Peat finishing second and a 13-1 longshot in third, came back $934.40. I had it. Friday night at the races was going to be fun after all.

It was my first decent score based solely on pedigree. And while few sensible horseplayers consider a secondary factor more important than the fundamentals, there are times when a handicapper can dig a little bit deeper. The elements of condition, class, speed, and pace can be accompanied by some creativity. Eventually, a handicapper will summon the courage, or desperation, to make a play based on auxiliary considerations.

The fundamentals remain true, but handicapping goes beyond the basics. "Mudders and Turfers" became so popular that Tomlinson Ratings now appear exclusively in *Daily Racing Form* past performances. As a pedigree guide, they work. So do trainer and jockey performance statistics that reveal peculiarities of the people closest to the horses. There are other incidentals, too, such as weight, medication, equipment changes, and workouts.

The past performances are filled with clues; there are lots of ways to find a winner. This chapter examines some of the "other" ways, beyond the fundamentals of condition, class, speed, and pace. None of the shortcuts is intended to supersede the basics. They are there only to consider. And it turns out there are a lot of factors beyond the fundamentals, particularly on grass.

Turf

The fact that the upset by Comininalittlehot occurred in a turf race at night might have been coincidental. Yet turf races and dirt races, especially long-distance races, are as different as night and day. Dirt racing is built on speed. Horses race as fast as they can for as far as they can, then peel away one by one. Some are finished at the half-mile pole, others surrender at the quarter pole, others at the eighth pole. The winner is the survivor, the horse who keeps going. Usually, dirt is less tiring, and speed carries.

Turf racing, however, is based on class and late speed. On grass, horses conserve energy, run more slowly around the course in a relatively tight cluster, then blast home with a furious late kick. In a typical turf race, the field is bunched and only a few lengths separate the pacesetter from the late-runners. Even at the quarter pole, most of the field is still in contention. The real running does not begin until the far turn and into the stretch. The winner is often the horse that can finish fastest.

Because the dynamics of a turf race—slow early, fast late—are so radically different from dirt, handicapping a grass race requires different techniques. It's similar to a card game. Five-card draw and seven-card stud are both poker, but they require different strategies.

After narrowing the list of contenders based on current form, the first consideration is class. A dirt horse may be qualified to move up in class based on speed figures, but figures are less relevant on turf. A horse's ability is shown in the class level at which he has been competitive, and how well he can finish. In

Class Drop

s on turf, any horse that ran well last time at a higher level ten holds a huge advantage. On grass, class is king, and it is the first thing to look for in a turf race—such as a horse dropping in class following an acceptable performance against better company. It's a powerful attribute.

```
7 Esmay (Aus)                    Dk. b or br f. 4 (Sep)                                          Life 10 1 1 2  $9,965 82 | D.Fst       0 0 0 0  $
  Own:Burns Mike & Kolbe Al      Sire: Desert King*Ire (Danehill)                                2003  3 0 0 1  $7,560 82 | Wet(305*)   0 0 0 0  $
Orange White, Black Horse Power Stables   Dam: Tycoon's Model*NZ(Last Tycoon*Ire)       L 121    2002  7 1 1 1  $2,405 -  | Turf(342*) 10 1 1 2  $9,96
ALMEIDA G F (45 4 7 4 .09) 2003:(293 30 .10)  Br: Austramore Pty, Codds Flat Bloodstock P/L & N Macintyre (Aus)  Dmr Ⓣ 2 0 0 1 $7,560 82 | DstⓉ(305*) 1 0 0 1  $7,56
                                 Tr: Carno Louis R(3 0 0 1 .00) 2003:(8 1 .13)

8Aug03-7Dmr fm 1 1/16 Ⓣ:23 :454 1:091 1:403 3↑ⒻOClm 62500N  82 5 410 410 410 44¾ 33¾ Almeida G F  LB 119  38.50 94-02 Top Spinner121nk Alozaina1213½ Esmay1192½  3wd into str,best
28Jly03-7Dmr fm 5f Ⓣ:212 :433 :55 3↑ⒻOClm 62500N  72 9 9 89¾ 811 811 611¼ Almeida G F  B 119  52.10 96 — Maria'sMirage1199½ RginTRex119½ RichMusique121½  Improved posi
2Jan03♦ Ellerslie(NZ)  gd *1¼Ⓣ RH 2:062  ⒻRoyal Stakes-G2  63¾ Bosson O P  121  -  Lafleur121hd Milzeel121nk Bramble Rose121
                                Stk 62700                                         Mid-pack on rail,awaited room,mild la
11Dec02♦ Matamata(NZ)  gd *1¼Ⓣ LH 2:03 3↑ Intermediate Conditions Race  52¾ O'Sullivan L A  118  -  Kajema121¾ Tanor Manor1211 Mighty Valiant121
                                Alw 3010                                          Towards rear,wide turn,mild la
24Nov02♦ Te Rapa(NZ)  gd *1 Ⓣ LH 1:38 3↑ ⒻIntermediate Conditions Race  2hd O'Sullivan L A  121  -  Diamond Hill119hd Esmay1211 Telsa121
                                Alw 3020                                          Tracked leader,bid 1f out,just
28Oct02♦ Te Rapa(NZ)  yl *1 Ⓣ LH 1:384 3↑ Intermediate Conditions Race  62½ O'Sullivan L A  117  -  Hamish123hd Tuscany Reign123nk Tunzi123
                                Alw 4890                                          Wide in mid-pack,finished well without threa
9Oct02♦ Te Aroha(NZ)  gd *7f Ⓣ RH 1:244 3↑ Maiden Race  1nk Waddell J L3  114  -  Esmay117nk Governor's Pearl1203¾ Twinkleovani117
                                Maiden 2400                                       Tracked in 3rd,dueled 1f out,led n
18Sep02♦ Avondale(NZ)  yl *7f Ⓣ RH 1:254 3↑ Maiden Race  115¼ O'Sullivan L A  117  -  Sweet Pearla1201½ Cornflower120½ Courtezan117
                                Maiden 2360                                       Towards rear thro
4May02♦ Te Rapa(NZ)  yl *6f Ⓣ LH 1:12  Conditions Race  65¼ O'Sullivan L A  119  -  Cheetie1133½ Lessthanasong119nk Von Ryans119
                                Alw 4500                                          Rated towards rear,wide turn,eve
17Apr02♦ Arawa Park(NZ)  gd *6f Ⓣ LH 1:132  Maiden Race  37¼ O'Sullivan L A  120  -  Deautche Express1206¾ Under Cover Angel120½ Esmay120
                                Maiden 2230                                       Wide in 5th,3rd 2f out,lost duel
WORKS: Aug15 Dmr 6f fst 1:152 H 11/14  Aug4 Dmr 4f fst :494 H 54/64  Jly20 Dmr 5f fst 1:012 H 14/27  Jly5 SA 5f fst 1:01 H 18/44  Jun27 SA 5f fst 1:013 H 30/45  Jun21 SA 5f fst 1:012 H 14/45
TRAINER: Turf(17 .12 $5.73) Routes(5 .00 $0.00) Alw(11 .18 $8.85)
```

Esmay raced above her conditions (over her head) on August 8 in a two-other-than/$62,500 optional claiming race. She ran well at odds of 38-1, finishing third in the seven-horse field. It was an "acceptable" performance, which means finishing in the top half of the field or within three lengths of the winner, or being competitive at a late stage of the race. Following the third-place finish, Esmay dropped into a one-other-than allowance on August 22. The favorite for the race was a well-bred import who had not raced in nearly a year. Esmay held the edge in current class and current form, and rallied to a half-length win at $16.20.

SIXTH RACE
Del Mar
AUGUST 22, 2003

1 1/16 MILES. (Turf)(1.40) ALLOWANCE. Purse $58,000 (plus $17,400 CBOIF – CA Bred Owner Fund) FOR FILLIES AND MARES THREE YEARS OLD AND UPWARD WHICH HAVE NOT WON $3,000 OTHER THAN MAIDEN, CLAIMING, OR STARTER OR WHICH HAVE NOT WON TWO RACES. Three Year Olds, 118 lbs.; Older, 123 lbs. Non-winners Of A Race Other Than Claiming Or Starter At A Mile Or Over Allowed 2 lbs. (Non-Starters for a claiming price of $32,000 or less in the last 3 starts preferred). (Rail at 7 feet).

Value of Race: $61,480 Winner $34,800; second $15,080; third $6,960; fourth $3,480; fifth $1,160. Mutuel Pool $452,670.00 Exacta Pool $258,405.00 Quinella Pool $33,176.00 Trifecta Pool $242,140.00 Superfecta Pool $102,918.00

Last Raced	Horse	M/Eqt.	A.Wt	PP	St	¼	½	¾	Str	Fin	Jockey	Odds $1
8Aug03 7Dmr3	Esmay-AU	LB	4 121	7	9	61	74	61	31	1½	Almeida G F	7.10
7Aug03 8Bmf1	Moscow Burning	LB	3 116	2	4	2½	31	5hd	2hd	2½	Espinoza V	19.00
4Aug03 7Dmr2	Runway Lollipop-ARG	LB	4 121	6	1	3hd	2½	1hd	11½	31	Valenzuela P A	2.90
23Jly03 2Dmr7	Vamos Nina-CHI	LB	6 121	5	2	41	4hd	4hd	5½	4nk	Nakatani C S	17.80
27Jly03 7Dmr7	La Perfecta-CH	LBb	4 123	3	6	9	9	85	6½	53½	Valdivia J Jr	36.50
17Jly03 7Hol1	Icee Cheaspeake	LBf	4 123	1	5	11	11	21	41	62½	Smith M E	4.20
27Jly03 7Dmr6	Issaqueena	LB	4 121	4	3	82	81	9	9	7hd	Solis A	10.30
27Jly03 7Dmr5	Honeypenny	LB	4 123	8	7	5hd	5½	3hd	71½	81½	Flores D R	6.60
27Sep02 ML2	Dubai Belle	LBb	4 123	9	8	72½	61	72	83	9	Krone J A	2.60

OFF AT 6:05 Start Good. Won driving. Course firm.
TIME :232, :473, 1:113, 1:354, 1:414 (:23.40, :47.79, 1:11.79, 1:35.95, 1:41.98)

$2 Mutuel Prices:			
7-ESMAY-AU	16.20	8.20	4.00
2-MOSCOW BURNING		14.40	6.60
6-RUNWAY LOLLIPOP-ARG			3.00

$1 EXACTA 7–2 PAID $147.40 $2 QUINELLA 2–7 PAID $183.20 $1 TRIFECTA 7–2–6 PAID $690.20 $1 SUPERFECTA 7–2–6–5 PAID $8,214.90

Dk. b. or br. f, by Desert King*Ire–Tycoon's Model*NZ, by Last Tycoon*Ire. Trainer Carno Louis R. Bred by Austramore Pty, Codds Flat Bloodstock P/L & N Macintyre (Aus).

ESMAY (AUS) jostled in tight between horses in the chute, chased a bit off the rail, went up three deep between horses on the second turn, bid three wide past midstretch, and gamely prevailed under some urging. MOSCOW BURNING pulled her way between horses then stalked a bit off the rail, was between foes again on the second turn, had the leader slip away in the stretch then finished with interest while splitting rivals late. RUNWAY LOLLIPOP (ARG) three deep early, stalked outside a rival, bid outside the pacesetter and took a short advantage on the second turn, inched clear in the stretch, fought back toward the inside but could not quite match the top pair late. VAMOS NINA (CHI) angled in and saved ground stalking the pace, awaited room off heels leaving the second turn, split rivals in midstretch and finished with interest. LA PERFECTA (CHI) unhurried along the inside early, came out into the stretch and found her best stride late. ICEE CHEASPEAKE took the early lead, set the pace inside, drifted out a bit midway on the second turn, angled back in and weakened in the stretch. ISSAQUEENA pulled between horses in the chute then was rank and steadied toward the inside in the run to the first turn, chased a bit off the rail, came out in the stretch and lacked the needed rally. HONEYPENNY stalked outside then between horses on the backstretch, bid three deep on the second turn, steadied when a bit crowded midway on that bend, came four wide into the stretch and weakened. DUBAI BELLE widest in the chute, chased outside, went four wide on the second turn and into the stretch and also weakened.

Owners— 1, Burns Mike & Kolbe Al; 2, Van Kempen Dallas; 3, Triple B Farms; 4, Becker Barry & Judith; 5, Abumohor Roberto & Wright Robert J; 6, Ladin Marty; 7, Stoneside Stable LLC; 8, Straeter Terry; 9, Darley Stud Management LLC

Trainers—1, Carno Louis R; 2, Doyle Casey; 3, Hines N J; 4, Robbins Jay M; 5, Polanco Marcelo; 6, Aguirre Paul G; 7, McAnally Ronald; 8, Canani Julio C; 9, Harty Eoin

$2 Daily Double (6–7) Paid $69.20; Daily Double Pool $28,525.
$1 Pick Three (2/6/7–6–7) Paid $48.00; Pick Three Pool $101,572.

The class-drop angle applies to all levels on turf. While they do not always generate payoffs as generous as Esmay's at 7-1, the class distinctions on grass usually are clear.

Irish Warrior
Own:Coleman & Dasaro & Thompson
Orange, White/brown Sash, White
(161 24 23 27 .15) 2003:(791 137 .17)

Ch. h. 5
Sire: Irish River*Fr (Riverman)
Dam: Spiritofpocahontas(Alleged)
Br: Robert B Berger (Ky)
Tr: Dollase Wallace(7 0 0 1 .00) 2003:(69 16 .23)

L 116

Life	18	5	6	3	$319,500	101	D.Fst	0	0	0	0	$0	–
2003	6	1	2	3	$154,800	101	Wet(290)	0	0	0	0	$0	–
2002	6	2	2	0	$91,400	99	Turf(345)	18	5	6	3	$319,500	101
Dmr (T)	3	1	0	1	$77,400	99	Dst(T)(445)	0	0	0	0	$0	–

8Dmr fm 1⅛ (T) :472 1:11 1:342 1:454 3↑ EddieRead H-G1 99 6 53½ 54½ 52¼ 43 35¼ Krone J A LB 114 8.30 99-03 Special Ring1175 Decarchy117nk Irish Warrior114hd 3-4w, willingly late 6
7Hol fm 1⅛ (T) :474 1:11 1:341 1:461 3↑ American H-G2 101 2 43 41¾ 42 32½ 32¾ Solis A LB 116 4.40 99-07 *CandyRide120¾ SpecialRing1182* IrishWrrior1161 Stalked btwn,best rest 5
5Hol fm 1 1/16 (T) :24 :471 1:112 1:41 4↑ Alw 65348C 100 1 713 714 79¼ 73¾ 1no Solis A LB 116 3.00 91-15 Irish Warrior116no Decarchy1222½ Native Desert1221 Swung out,rallied,up 8
6Kee yl 1⅛ (T) :513 1:172 1:414 1:532 4↑ Alw 63822C 94 2 32 2hd 31½ 3½ 2½ Day P L 118 *.60 69-27 *Honor InWar117½ IrishWarrior118¾* HolyConflict1164¾ Coming again late 4
7SA fm 1⅛ (T) :481 1:12 1:344 1:463 4↑ OClm 150000N 101 5 54 53½ 53½ 31½ 31¼ Almeida G F LB 118 6.90 95-11 Blue Steller1181 Kappa King118nk Irish Warrior1183½ Off rail, willingly 5
7TuP fm 1 1/16 (T) :233 :474 1:12 1:422 3↑ TuP BC H150k 101 6 73½ 73¾ 72¾ 4¾ 2nk Almeida G F L 116 12.30 100 — Century City117nk Irish Warrior116nk Hataab116¾ 5wide 1/4,bid 6w,closd 9
5SA fm 1 (T) :233 :473 1:114 1:354 3↑ Alw 70420N$mY 93 7 87 85½ 74¼ 76 63¾ Desormeaux K J LB 117 f 12.50 79-17 Night Life119no Lord Jim1172½ Sumitas117nk In tight into stretch 10
2Dmr fm 1⅛ (T) :491 1:133 1:37 1:482 3↑ OClm 125000N 84 5 32 32½ 31½ 54¼ 66½ Solis A LB 117 2.50 84-09 *DvidCopprfld117no* Admnnstrtor1211 *DltForm1192* 4wd into lane,wkened 6
7Hol fm 1 1/16 (T) :242 :474 1:104 1:404 4↑ OClm 100000N 98 2 33 43 44½ 41¼ 1½ Solis A LB 118 *1.20 91-12 Irish Warrior118½ GeoQuercus116no Kachamandi119hd Swung wide,rallied 6
2Hol fm 1 1/16 (T) :242 :482 1:114 1:403 4↑ OClm 80000N 99 4 57 56 54½ 32½ 2hd Solis A LB 120 1.70 92-08 MostLikly118hd *IrishWrrior1202* Adminnistrtor1203 Off slow,4wd into str 5
5Hol fm 1 (T) :23 :453 1:094 1:342 4↑ Alw 55330N2X 99 5 57 59 54¼ 11½ 11 Solis A LB 118 3.60 92-08 Irish Warrior1181 Amicable1182 Euribor118hd Came out,rallied,held 8
7SA fm 1 (T) :22 :444 1:084 1:333 4↑ OClm 80000N 92 3 714 816 87¼ 54 2½ Solis A LB 118 9.40 93-06 *ApchWings118½ IrishWrrior118hd ThPricSpirit118no* Came out 1/8, surged 10

: Aug25 SA 6f fst 1:161 H *3/3* Aug19 SA 5f fst 1:022 H *9/12* Aug12 SA 5f fst 1:011 H *9/22* Aug6 SA 4f fst :482 H *7/26* Jly24 Dmr (T) 3f fm :363 H (d) *1/3* Jly15 Hol 4f fst :492 H *11/24*
R: 31-60Days(61 .21 $1.24) Turf(102 .21 $1.58) Routes(140 .26 $2.11) GrdStk(39 .26 $1.57)

Irish Warrior was soundly beaten in a Grade 1 on July 27. But he did finish third in the six-runner field—an acceptable performance—and was dropping into a Grade 2. Irish Warrior paid

$8.20. The class-drop angle is particularly effective with 3-year-olds in spring and summer. By that time of year, the owners and trainers of second-tier 3-year-olds become realistic regarding their horses' ability, and drop them from allowance races into claiming races. The horses wake up, often at overlaid odds.

5 Winning Stripes
Own:Robinson & Shustek & Stanley
Green Pink, Black Horse Emblem On Green
SOLIS A (127 18 17 22 .14) 2003:(751 131 .17)

B. c. 3 (Mar) CALAUG01 $50,000
Sire: Candy Stripes (Blushing Groom*Fr)
Dam: Ali's Dancer(Marshua's Dancer)
Br: Thomas W Bachman (Cal)
Tr: Morey William J Jr(9 3 0 3 .33) 2003:(111 20 .18)

L 118

Life	11	3	1	1	$121,805	90	D.Fst	7	0	1	1	$41,8
2003	7	2	1	0	$93,595	90	Wet(280*)	1	1	0	0	$23,5
2002	4	1	0	1	$28,210	72	Turf(330)	3	2	0	0	$56,3
Dmr Ⓣ	1	1	0	0	$36,300	86	DstⓉ(335)	2	1	0	0	$20,0

28Jly03-4Dmr fm 1 1/16 Ⓣ :23² :47 1:11³ 1:42 Clm 62500 (62.5-55) 86 6 97¾ 811 85¾ 42½ 1no Desormeaux K J LB 118 b 5.50 91-06 WnnngStrps118no DrmOfDshng118nk **ByndInfnty**1181 Came out,ralli
2Jly03-4Pln fst 1 1/16 :23² :46⁴ 1:11 1:41³ Pleasanton49k 83 2 46 44½ 32 47½ 411½ Alvarado F T LB 116 b *.90 83-06 Obermeister1153½ *Allwood*1166½ Commercant Vic1161½ Bid turn, weak
25May03-8Hol fm 1 Ⓣ :24¹ :48² 1:12¹ 1:35² WillRogers-G3 82 5 44½ 42½ 33½ 45½ 65½ Solis A LB 119 b 10.00 81-13 Private Chef115¾ *BansheeKing*1151¼ Singletary1173 Angled in, weak
26Apr03-4Hol fst 1⅛ :46² 1:10⁴ 1:36 1:49 Ⓢ Snow Chief250k 25 7 41¼ 42 45 819 844 Desormeaux K J LB 117 b 3.40 45-10 ChifPlnnr1167 Excssivplsur1242½ TizACoup1172 Stalked,gave way,e
8Mar03-8GG fst 1 1/16 :22³ :45² 1:09² 1:42¹ ElCamnoRlDbyG3 90 6 77 79 77½ 55½ 42½ Baze R A LB 115 b 11.30 89-12 OcenTrrc1151½ MinistrsWildCt117no *TnMostWntd*1151 Fanned 4w, ra
9Feb03-8GG fst 1 :23 :46² 1:10⁴ 1:36⁴ GldnStateMle66k 90 6 65¾ 66 52¾ 31½ 21¼ Alvarado F T LB 117 b 6.30 85-19 MinistersWildCt1161¼ WinningStrips1173 ClovrSitution117½ Late bi
24Jan03-3GG wf 1 :23³ :47³ 1:12 1:36 OClm 50000N 87 2 42 42 42½ 2½ 12 Alvarado F T LB 118 b *2.60 90-17 WinningStripes1182 BridgBuildr1189 BluSti118½ Shifted out 1/4p,d
28Nov02-5GG gd 1 Ⓣ :22⁴ :47 1:12² 1:37² Md Sp Wt 33k 72 8 43 32 42 2hd 1no Alvarado F T LB 118 b *1.10 87-15 *WinnngStrps*118no DrctMl1183½ RnsomThKroonr1181½ Bid 3w,dueld, d
17Oct02-6BM fst 1 :23¹ :47 1:11¹ 1:36³ Md Sp Wt 31k 72 6 43½ 34 43¾ 43½ 31¾ Duran F5 LB 113 b 8.80 85-10 *Buddy Gil*1181¼ Onebigbag118½ *Winning Stripes*113½ Rallied ir
26Sep02-3BM fst 1 :22² :46 1:10⁴ 1:37⁴ Md Sp Wt 30k 58 4 33 42 42¼ 35 42½ Lumpkins J LB 118 b 12.80 78-17 Attack Force1131¼ Smokin Mike1181 Direct Male118nk Even late, ga
9Sep02-4Dmr fst 6f :21⁴ :45² :58 1:11² Md 62500 (62.5-55) 42 1 9 923 919 916 812½ Flores D R LB 120 b 31.30 71-16 *Zayed*1201½ Fly To The Wire120no *Mr Joe B*1201 Inside, ou
WORKS: Aug16 Dmr 4f fst :47³ H *3/63* Aug9 Dmr 5f fst 1:02² H *57/62* Jly25 Dmr 4f fst :49¹ H *37/64* Jly19 GG 6f fst 1:14³ H *5/8* Jly12 GG 5f fst 1:00¹ H *6/31* ●Jun28 Pln 4f fst :46 H *1/9*
TRAINER: Turf(25 .24 $1.91) Alw(37 .24 $1.36)

Horses who drop into age-restricted claiming races after banging heads with allowance or stakes horses repeatedly hold the upper hand, assuming that they are dropping in class following an acceptable performance. Winning Stripes had shown speed on July 2, an indication of sharp form, and was only two lengths off the lead at the pace call. He dropped into a claiming race for 3-year-olds, and woke up at $13.

In turf routes without a dropper, preference goes to horses that have run well at the level of today's race. The class barriers in turf racing are steeper than on dirt. On grass, it is simply more difficult to climb the ladder. Big winners of preliminary allowance races (N1X) frequently stall on the way up; turf races most frequently are won by horses that have established credentials at the level.

5 Expresso Bay
Own: Bruce Hochman
Green Gold, Purple Circle 'Bh' On Back, Purple
PEDROZA M A (5 0 0 1 .00) 2003: (826 122 .15)

Dk. b or br g. 6 (Feb)
Sire: Metfield (Seattle Slew) $3,000
Dam: Cappucino Bay (Bailjumper)
Br: Albert Bell & Joyce Bell (Ky)
Tr: West Ted H(2 0 1 1 .00) 2003:(155 34 .22)

L 119

Life	29	8	7	5	$239,890	99	D.Fst	14	2	4	2	$61,
2003	8	4	2	0	$123,620	99	Wet(278)	1	0	1	0	$6,
2002	5	1	1	2	$28,900	93	Turf(256)	14	6	2	3	$172,
Hol Ⓣ	4	2	1	0	$52,140	90	DstⓉ(311)	6	3	0	3	$80,

23Oct03-7SA fm 1 Ⓣ :22⁴ :46 1:09² 1:33³ 3↑ OClm 80000N 92 8 21½ 2hd 2½ 1hd 23 Pedroza M A LB118 6.20 91-06 BucklandManor1173 ExpressoBay1181 Sequoian1183 Bid,led,lost w
5Sep03-6Dmr fm 1 1/16 Ⓣ :25¹ :51¹ 1:15 1:43³ 3↑ Clm c-(50-45) 95 7 11½ 11 11½ 11½ 1½ Pedroza M A LB121 *1.80 83-17 Expresso Bay121½ Albatros1192 Quake1191 Inside,held g
Claimed from Lake Forest Stable for $50,000, Carava Jack Trainer 2003(as of 9/5): (260 37 37 43 0.14)
17Aug03-7Dmr fm 1 Ⓣ :22⁴ :46 1:09² 1:33¹ 3↑ Clm 50000(50-45) 99 3 11 1hd 11½ 2hd 1nk Pedroza M A LB119 8.00 97-08 *Expresso Bay*119nk *Dell Place*1191 Albatros1193 Fought back rail
20Jly03-9Hol fm 1 1/16 Ⓣ :24¹ :49 1:12⁴ 1:42¹ 4↑ Clm 40000(40-35) 90 5 11½ 11 12 13½ 13½ Pedroza M A LB120 4.30 85-13 *Expresso Bay*1203½ Euribor1182½ Navel118½ Strong han
2Jly03-5Hol fm 1 Ⓣ :23² :46³ 1:10¹ 1:35 4↑ Clm 40000(40-35) 86 6 2½ 2hd 2hd 1½ 1hd Nakatani C S LB118 4.60 89-11 *Expresso Bay*118hd Big Future118no Adham1161 Held game btw
31May03-7Hol fm 5½f Ⓣ :22¹ :44² :56² 1:02² 4↑ Clm 40000(40-35) 83 9 6 55¾ 54¼ 42 23½ Nakatani C S LB118 16.20 88-08 LousExpectation1183½ *ExpressoBay*118hd Pachar1181 Angled in,gan
10May03-2Hol fm 1⅛ Ⓣ :48⁴ 1:12⁴ 1:37¹ 1:49² +4↑ Clm 40000(40-35) 81 5 31 21 2½ 11 54¼ Espinoza V LB118 2.70 78-12 Red Briar116no Fuse Quick120hd Boomslang1183½ Pulled,bid,led,w
20Apr03-5SA fm *6½f Ⓣ :22¹ :44² 1:07² 1:13¹ 4↑ OClm 32000 87 11 1 3½ 33½ 52¾ 42½ ♦Espinoza V LB118 40.30 88-10 Thundermann1182 **Vacamonte**118½ Solitario118no 4wd into lane,
22Jun02-6Hol fst 1 1/16 :23² :46² 1:10⁴ 1:42² 4↑ Clm c-(25-22.5) 68 8 2hd 2hd 21½ 68½ 618 Lumpkins J LB119 *2.50 73-10 JklnsLstKn1163 ThDnvrDrm1164 Clcupbond1161 Pressed pace, we
Claimed from Bell Joyce for $25,000, Martin John F Trainer 2002(as of 6/22): (138 38 30 20 0.28)
25May02-3BM fst 1 :22 :45 1:09⁴ 1:36 4↑ Clm c-(25-22.5) 88 5 1hd 1hd 12½ 1½ 21 Lumpkins J LB119 *.80 89-10 AlmostGolden1191 ExpressoBy1194½ DrPingo1121 Fast fractions,
Claimed from Bell Joyce for $25,000, Peery Chuck Trainer 2002(as of 5/25): (133 21 33 21 0.16)
9May02-2BM fst 1 :23¹ :47 1:11¹ 1:36 4↑ Clm 30000(32-30) 93 1 11½ 11 12 12 12 Lumpkins J LB115 *1.70 90-14 ExprssoBy1152 *AlmostGldn*1171½ TctclAllsn1176½ Stmbld strt,jmpd
24Apr02-4BM fm 1 1/16 Ⓣ :23⁴ :48¹ 1:12¹ 1:43³ 4↑ Clm 25000(25-22.5) 88 4 21 21 2½ 32 31½ Lumpkins J LB117 1.70 86-14 Lucayan Indian117no Califo1171½ *Expresso Bay*1171 Pressed, bid, ou
WORKS: Nov15 SA 6f fst 1:13⁴ H *6/21* Nov8 SA 4f fst :47⁴ H *7/31* ●Nov1 SA 3f fst :36² H *1/8* Oct13 SA 5f fst :58⁴ H *2/38* Oct6 SA 6f fst 1:12² H *2/18* Sep30 SA 4f fst :49² H *29/39*
TRAINER: 2Off45-180(31 .32 $3.45) Turf(59 .20 $2.25) Routes(87 .18 $2.01) Alw(58 .22 $2.17)

old Sphinx
B. c. 4 (Mar)

vn: Wertheimer Farm
Sire: Storm Cat (Storm Bird) $500,000

yal Blue, White Pinstripes On Back
Dam: Gold Splash (Blushing Groom*Fr)

0 R (19 16 1 .05) 2003: (950 142 .15)
Br: Wertheimer et Frere (Ky)
Tr: Mandella Gary(1 0 1 0 .00) 2003:(71 11 .15)

						Life	10 2 3 1	$85,945	94	D.Fst	0 0 0 0	$0 –
						2003	3 2 1 0	$69,800	94	Wet(449)	0 0 0 0	$0 –
					L 121	2002	5 M 0 1	$8,801	–	Turf(371)	10 2 3 1	$85,945 94
						Hol ⑦	0 0 0 0	$0	–	Dst⑦(405)	0 0 0 0	$0 –

SA fm 1	⑦ :22³ :46	1:09⁴ 1:34³	3♠ Alw 49000n1x	94 5	3¹½ 2²	2¹	1ʰᵈ 1¹½	Flores D R	LB120	*2.00	89– 04 Gold Sphinx120¹½ Six Numbers115¹ Rock N Rosh115ⁿᵒ Stalked,bid,led,clear 9
SA fm 1	⑦ :23 :45⁴	1:10 1:34¹	3♠ Alw 50176n1x	89 9	4⁴ 44½	41½ 41½	2ⁿᵒ	Flores D R	LB120	6.70	91– 09 BucklandMnor117ⁿᵒ GoldSphinx120½ Tombstone118ⁿᵏ Blockd 1/4 to past 1/8 9
Dmr fm 1	⑦ :21³ :45⁴	1:10² 1:34²	3♠ Md Sp Wt 51k	87 8	4² 2ʰᵈ	1ʰᵈ 1¹½	1¹	Flores D R	LB123	4.20	91– 08 GoldSphnx123¹ ButofCours118¹½ AmrcnLbrty118¹½ Bid,led 1/4,clear,held 8

usly trained by Christiane Head-Maarek

auville (Fr)	sf *⁷f	⑦ Str 1:25³	Prix de Balleroy Hcp 55100		5³½	Thomas R	123	34.00	Seditieuse117ⁿᵒ Mushroom Countess121²½ Negueva117ⁿᵏ 17 Towards rear,bid 1-1/2f out,lost duel for 3rd & 4th
ichy (Fr)	sf *1	⑦ RH 1:44¹	Prix des Arvernes Alw 22100		11	Doleuze O	126	8.20	Massigann123¹ Binya122ʰᵈ Brother Buck128² 14 Stumbled start,towards rear throughout.Mushroom Countess 4th
ongchamp (Fr)	gd *1	⑦ RH 1:37²	Prix du Grand Palais Alw 28200		5²½	Doleuze O	126	4.50	Riverse Angle126ⁿᵒ Am Brose126¹½ Brother Buck126ⁿᵏ 7 Rated at rear,brief progress over 1f out,hung
nantilly (Fr)	sf *1	⑦ RH 1:41	Prix du Puits aux Chiens Alw 20600		3²	Doleuze O	123	5.20	Am Brose123ⁿᵒ Never Regret123² Gold Sphinx123ⁿᵒ 8 Rated at rear,late gain into 3rd
nantilly (Fr)	gd *6f	⑦ Str 1:22	Prix de Billy Alw 25500		5⁵½	Doleuze O	126	*1.70	General Ridge126½ Avranches122¹½ Sforza130³ 7 Tracked in 3rd,faded through last quarter
eauville (Fr)	yl *5½f	⑦ Str 1:04³	Prix de Saint-Arnoult-EBF Alw 24000		2ⁿᵏ	Doleuze O	125	*1.50	Sforza128ⁿᵏ Gold Sphinx125¹ Wheater125⁴ 6 Tracked in 4th,bid 1-1/2f out,dueled 150y out,outgamed
nisons-Laffitte (Fr)	sf *5½f	⑦ Str 1:08¹	Prix Fier-EBF Maiden 12700		2⅔	Doleuze O	128	2.20	Go One128¾ Gold Sphinx128ⁿᵏ Point d'Honneur128⁵ 7 Rank tracking leaders,bid 1f out,held by winner

Nov15 Hol 6f fst 1:15 H 15/20 ●Nov8 Hol 6f fst 1:13⁴ H 1/6 Nov3 Hol 3f fst :36⁴ H 12/17 Oct22 Hol 3f fst :36⁴ H 3/12 Oct16 Hol 5f fst 1:03 H 22/24 Oct10 Hol 3f fst :36⁴ B 5/21

: Turf(53 .17 $1.54) Routes(62 .18 $1.92) Alw(29 .21 $1.16)

Gold Spinx was razor sharp, and his N1X victory on October 25 looked even better after the second- and third-place finishers returned to win their next starts (as highlighted above). But Expresso Bay was sharp also, and his most recent performance was a second-place finish at the level of today's race. Nevertheless, bettors went for Gold Sphinx. He ran well. But the winner was the horse whose ability had been established at the level. (See chart on next page.)

It happens all the time. A horse that finished third or better in a N2X turf route frequently holds an advantage over a horse moving up from a N1X win. Even though it is only a one-level class rise from N1X to N2X, the climb is severe. Pace analysis is less critical on turf, where late speed is far more important than early speed. Yet pace remains a consideration. A turf horse able to gain an easy lead—assuming he is fit and realistically spotted— can race gate to wire. However, there are fewer front-running winners on turf than on dirt.

A turf horse should be able to supply a finishing kick. A horse's closing fractions in turf races provide a means of comparison, and are a simple calculation. In the past-performance line of a horse that ran a mile on turf, the last two times are the six-furlong time, and the finish. The difference between the two is the final quarter-mile of the race. The time in which an individual horse completed the distance is computed by subtracting or adding the number of lengths gained or lost.

SEVENTH RACE
Hollywood
NOVEMBER 21, 2003

$1\frac{1}{16}$ MILES. (Turf) (1.38^3) ALLOWANCE. Purse $46,000 (plus $13,800 CBOIF – CA Bred Owner Fund) FOR THREE YEAR OLDS AND UPWARD WHICH HAVE NEVER WON $3,000 TWICE OTHER THAN MAIDEN, CLAIMING, OR STARTER OR WHICH HAVE NEVER WON THREE RACES. Three Year Olds, 120 lbs.; Older, 123 lbs. Non-winners Of Two Races Other Than Claiming, Or Starter At A Mile OrOver Since September 15 Allowed 2 lbs. One Such Race Since Then Allowed 4 lbs.

Value of Race: $46,000 Winner $27,600; second $9,200; third $5,520; fourth $2,760; fifth $920. Mutuel Pool $271,913.00 Exacta Pool $129,176.00 Quinella Pool $14,059.00 Trifecta Pool $167,245.00

Last Raced	Horse	M/Eqt.	A.	Wt	PP	St	¼	½	¾	Str	Fin	Jockey	Odds $1
23Oct03 ^{7}SA^2	Expresso Bay	LB	6	119	5	1	$1^{1\frac{1}{2}}$	$2^{2\frac{1}{2}}$	1^1	1^1	1^{nk}	Pedroza M A	3.30
25Oct03 ^{12}SA^1	Gold Sphinx	LB	4	121	1	3	4^1	4^2	$3^{1\frac{1}{2}}$	2^1	2^2	Flores D R	1.30
11Nov03 ^{7}Hol^3	White Buck	LB b	3	117	6	6	7	7	7	5^{hd}	3^1	Nakatani C S	8.80
19Apr03 ^{3}SA^6	Holdthehelm	LB b	4	119	2	2	$2^{\frac{1}{2}}$	3^{hd}	$2^{\frac{1}{2}}$	$3^{2\frac{1}{2}}$	4^3	Fogelsonger R	45.80
23Oct03 ^{7}SA^4	Vacamonte-GB	LB	5	119	3	4	$6^{2\frac{1}{2}}$	5^{hd}	5^{hd}	6^{10}	$5^{\frac{1}{2}}$	Solis A O	7.50
5Sep03 ^{7}Dmr^4	Marina Minister	LB b	3	116	7	5	5^{hd}	6^6	6^3	4^{hd}	6^{11}	Valenzuela P A	22.50
30Apr03 ASC^7	Tikkun-Ire	LB	4	119	4	7	3^{hd}	1^4	4^{hd}	7	7	Krone J A	3.20

OFF AT 9:57 Start Good. Won driving. Course firm.

TIME :24^3, :47^1, 1:11^3, 1:35^2, 1:41^4 (:24.68, :47.37, 1:11.60, 1:35.51, 1:41.85)

$2 Mutuel Prices:			
5 – EXPRESSO BAY	8.60	3.40	2.40
1 – GOLD SPHINX		2.80	2.20
6 – WHITE BUCK			3.00

$1 EXACTA 5–1 PAID $9.30 $2 QUINELLA 1–5 PAID $6.60
$1 TRIFECTA 5–1–6 PAID $39.30

Dk. b or br. g, (Feb), by Metfield – Cappucino Bay, by Bailjumper. Trainer West Ted H. Bred by Albert Bell & Joyce Bell (Ky).

EXPRESSO BAY sped to the early lead and angled in, relinquished command on the backstretch, took over again into the second turn, inched away and held on gamely under urging. GOLD SPHINX stalked the pace inside, came out a bit into the stretch, bid outside the winner past midstretch and continued willingly but could not get by. WHITE BUCK off a bit slowly, settled outside a rival then was carried out some into the first turn, angled in on the backstretch, advanced inside into the stretch, came out late and edged a rival for 3rd. HOLDTHEHELM was in a good position stalking the pace outside the runner-up to the stretch, drifted in a bit in the drive and lost the show. VACAMONTE (GB) chased along the inside, came out in upper stretch, was between horses in midstretch and lacked a further response. MARINA MINISTER off a bit slowly, angled in and chased outside a rival, split horses on the second turn and did not rally. TIKKUN (IRE) broke slowly, was very rank and steadied off heels into the first turn, tugged his way to the front outside foes on the backstretch, lugged out badly nearing the second turn and gave way.

Owners– 1, Hochman Bruce; 2, Wertheimer Farm LLC; 3, Manoogian Jay; 4, Carmel Judith and Bradley; 5, Juddmonte Farms Inc; 6, Rosenberg Richard A and Zakaryan Eugene; 7, Myers Martin

Trainers– 1, West Ted H; 2, Mandella Gary; 3, Mitchell Mike R; 4, Assinesi Paul D; 5, Frankel Robert J; 6, Nor Fabio; 7, Cecil Ben D

4 Zentsov Street
Yellow
Own: Robert B & Beverly J Lewis
Green, Yellow Hoops And Sleeves, Yellow — **$80,000**
SOLIS A (—) 2003: (985 174 .18)

B. h. 6 (Apr)
Sire: Nureyev (Northern Dancer) $100,000
Dam: Storm Fear (Coastal)
Br: Bemak N V dba Ashford Stud & John T L Jones Jr (Ky)
Tr: McAnally Ronald (1 0 0 0 .00) 2003: (283 41 .14)

L 119

Life	14	3	2	3	$205,916	100	D.Fst	0	0	0	0
2003	2	0	1	0	$12,200	90	Wet(359)	0	0	0	0
2001	3	0	0	0	$2,160	93	Turf(349)	14	3	2	3
Hol Ⓣ	2	0	0	1	$61,080	100	DstⓉ(374)	1	0	0	0

17Aug03– 1Dmr	fm	1	Ⓣ :23^3	:47^4	1:11^2	1:34^3	3↑ Clm 80000(80–70)	90	1	$6^{2\frac{3}{4}}$	$6^{2\frac{1}{2}}$	6^3	$5^{2\frac{3}{4}}$	2^1	Solis A	LB119	12.00	89– 08	**Sweet Stepper**117^1 Zentsov Street119$^{\frac{1}{2}}$ [D]Surprized119^1	Rail trip	
25Jly03– 6Dmr	fm	$1\frac{1}{16}$	Ⓣ :24^1	:49^1	1:12	1:41^4	3↑ Clm 80000(80–70)	82	4	$4^{2\frac{1}{2}}$	$5^{3\frac{3}{4}}$	$6^{7\frac{3}{4}}$	$7^{9\frac{1}{2}}$	$7^{6\frac{1}{2}}$	Valdivia J Jr	LB119	27.90	85– 08	ReelEmIn119^{no} ***SweetStepper***115^{nk} Kachmndi119$^{1\frac{1}{2}}$	Pulled,chase	
24Oct01– 7SA	fm	1	Ⓣ :24^2	:47^3	1:11^1	1:33^4	3↑ Alw 54000N3x	93	2	5^5	$5^{5\frac{1}{2}}$	5^5	$5^{3\frac{1}{2}}$	$5^{4\frac{1}{2}}$	McCarron C J	LB118 b	6.00	93– 02	Decarchy122$^{2\frac{1}{2}}$ Wallace118^{nk} Night Life120^{nk}	Saved groun	
5Sep01– 8Dmr	fm	1	Ⓣ :22^2	:45^3	1:09^1	1:33^2	3↑ LiveDreamH76k	84	4	7^5	7^{10}	$9^{8\frac{1}{2}}$	$9^{9\frac{1}{2}}$	9^9	McCarron C J	LB115	9.90	89– 09	LonesomeDud114^{hd} SpkinPssing116$^{1\frac{1}{4}}$ LordJim117^{no}	Saved grou	
12Jly01– 5Hol	fm	1	Ⓣ :23^4	:46^4	1:10^3	1:33^3	3↑ OClm 80000N	81	1	5^{10}	5^{12}	$6^{6\frac{1}{2}}$	$5^{6\frac{1}{2}}$	5^9	McCarron C J	LB117	*1.70	87– 04	I've Decided119^{no} *Cagney*117$^{2\frac{1}{2}}$ Anzari117^2	3wd into la	
26Nov00– 8Hol	fm	1⅛	Ⓣ :48	1:11^4	1:34^3	1:46^3	ETHolDby-G1	100	3	$6^{2\frac{1}{4}}$	$8^{3\frac{3}{4}}$	$4^{1\frac{1}{4}}$	$3^{1\frac{1}{2}}$	$4^{1\frac{1}{2}}$	McCarron C J	LB122	5.70	93– 09	[D]DesignedforLuck122^{hd} Brahms122$^{\frac{1}{2}}$ DvidCopperfield122^1	Stea	
Placed third through disqualification																					
4Oct00– 3SA	fm	1	Ⓣ :24^1	:48^2	1:12	1:35	[R]InExcess72k	99	1	3^2	$3^{2\frac{1}{2}}$	2^1	$1^{\frac{1}{2}}$	1^4	McCarron C J	LB114	1.80	84– 17	ZentsovStreet114^4 DvidCopperfield118$^{2\frac{1}{2}}$ GreyMmo116^2	Steady	
18Aug00– 7Dmr	fm	1	Ⓣ :22^3	:46^3	1:10^3	1:35^1	[R]Relaunch64k	97	2	$2^{\frac{1}{2}}$	2^1	2^{hd}	$1^{\frac{1}{2}}$	4^1	McCarron C J	LB120	4.40	88– 08	DesignedforLuck118$^{\frac{1}{2}}$ Schotis122$^{\frac{1}{2}}$ *Wlkslikeduck*120no	Dueled, ou	
14Apr00– 3SA	fm	1	Ⓣ :23^4	:48	1:12^2	1:35^4	Alw 58710N1x	96	5	1^{hd}	1^{hd}	1^{hd}	1^{hd}	$1^{\frac{1}{2}}$	McCarron C J	B118	*.40	80– 16	Zentsov Street118$^{\frac{1}{2}}$ Pizza N Beer120^4 Ceeband118^4	Inside due	
17Mar00– 4SA	fm	*6½f	Ⓣ :20^4	:42^2	1:06^4	1:12^4	Alw 53000N1x	96	4	9	7^8	6^{10}	$4^{8\frac{1}{2}}$	$3^{1\frac{1}{4}}$	McCarron C J	B120	*2.50	93– 07	FinlRow120^{no} *DesignedforLuck*118$^{1\frac{1}{4}}$ *ZentsovStreet*120^4	Split foes	
Previously trained by Aidan O'Brien																					
23Oct99♦Doncaster (GB)	sf	1	Ⓣ LH 1:45				Racing Post Trophy-G1 Stk 298200							$5^{10\frac{1}{4}}$	Kinane M J	126	5.50		Our Aristotle126$^{1\frac{1}{4}}$ Lermontov126^{nk} Ekraar126^7	*Rated in 5th,ridden without res*	
Timeform rating: 91																					
16Oct99♦Newmarket (GB)	gd	7f	Ⓣ Str 1:26^4				Dewhurst Stakes-G1 Stk 334000							3^3	Kinane M J	126	14.00		Distant Music126^1 Brahms126^2 Zentsov Street126$^{2\frac{1}{2}}$	*Led to over 1-1/2f out,one-paced to line.Ki*	
Timeform rating: 109																					

WORKS: Nov4 Hol 5f fst 1:01 H *11/26* Oct28 Hol 5f fst 1:02^1 H *15/20* Oct21 Hol 4f fst :48^3 H *7/32* Oct14 Hol 4f fst :50^1 H *12/20* Sep30 Hol 6f fst 1:16^2 H *11/11* Sep23 Hol 5f fst 1:04^2 H *34/35*
TRAINER: 61-180Days(109 .16 $1.68) Turf(391 .12 $1.26) Routes(422 .13 $1.39) Claim(63 .17 $1.88)

In Zentsov Street's last race, the final quarter-mile was run in 23.20 (1:34.60 minus 1:11.40). Zentsov Street gained two lengths. At the quarter pole he was positioned sixth, three lengths behind. At the finish, he was second, one length behind. By subtracting the two lengths (one-fifth, or .20, per length) that Zentsov Street had gained during the 23.20 final quarter, we see that he ran his final quarter-mile in 22.80, or 11.40 seconds per final furlong.

The most recent turf route by Sweet Stepper was September 7 at 1¹⁄₁₆ miles. He gained 2½ lengths during a final five-sixteenths of 29 seconds (1:41.20 minus 1:12.20). Therefore, Sweet Stepper ran the final five-sixteenths in 28.50 (29 seconds minus 2½ lengths, or .50 seconds). Dividing the 28.50 by the 2½ furlongs, Sweet Stepper's final furlongs were run in an average of 11.40 seconds per furlong, the same as Zentsov Street's. But there was one difference.

Beyer Speed Figures showed that Sweet Stepper was a faster horse. In every recent route he had earned a Beyer above 90; Zentsov Street had exceeded 90 only twice in the last five races, and he had not won a race in three years. The *Daily Racing Form* handicapper botched the selection for the race, which unfolded in predictable fashion. (See chart on next page.)

Even though class is the prime factor on grass, Beyer Speed Figures provide a measure of comparison. Then there are times when none of the turf-race runners has performed well at, or above, the level of today's race. Perhaps the best strategy is to simply pass the race. No one can find every winner in every race.

SIXTH RACE
Hollywood
NOVEMBER 16, 2003

1 1/16 MILES. (Turf) (1.38³) CLAIMING . Purse $45,000 (plus $5,400 CBOIF – CA Bred Owner Fund) FOR THREE YEAR OLDS AND UPWARD. Three Year Olds, 120 lbs.; Older, 123 lbs. Non–winners Of Two Races At A Mile Or Over Since September 15 Allowed 2 lbs. Such A Race Since September 15 Allowed 4 lbs. Claiming Price $80,000, For Each $5,000 To $70,000 2 lbs.(Maiden And Claiming Races For $62,500 Or Less Not Considered). (Rail at 15 feet).

Value of Race: $45,000 Winner $27,000; second $9,000; third $5,400; fourth $2,700; fifth $900. Mutuel Pool $332,147.00 Exacta Pool $189,634.00 Quinella Pool $20,580.00 Trifecta Pool $193,237.00 Superfecta Pool $61,433.00

Last Raced	Horse	M/Eqt. A. Wt	PP	St	¼	½	¾	Str	Fin	Jockey	Cl'g Pr	Odds $1
22Oct03 ³SA⁴	Sweet Stepper	LB 4 115	3	1	2²	2½ 1	2¹	1½	1nk	Krone J A	70000	2.30
25Aug03 7Dmr⁴	Leprechaun Kid	LB b 4 119	4	4	6⁴	5½ 1	3½	3hd	2½	Valenzuela P A	80000	7.20
26Oct03 7BM⁵	Bonaguil	LB b 6 121	7	5	5hd	6½ 1	6½ 1	5½ 1	3no	Flores D R	80000	6.00
13Oct03 8SA¹	Tombstone-Arg	LB 6 121	1	6	4½ 1	4hd	4¹	4hd	4nk	Almeida G F	80000	5.60
11Oct03 6SA¹	San Nicolas	LB 5 119	2	2	1½	1hd	1hd	2²	5½ 1	Desormeaux K J	80000	3.90
17Aug03 1Dmr²	Zentsov Street	LB 6 119	4	7	7	7	7	7	6²	Solis A	80000	4.30
20Oct03 7SA⁷	Sex Machine-Aus	LB 6 117	5	3	3½	3½	5½	6hd	7	Baze T C	75000	10.80

OFF AT 3:06 Start Good . Won driving. Course firm.

TIME :24¹, :48, 1:11², 1:35², 1:41⁴ (:24.24, :48.06, 1:11.49, 1:35.57, 1:41.84)

$2 Mutuel Prices:

3 – SWEET STEPPER	6.60	3.60	2.60
7 – LEPRECHAUN KID		5.80	3.60
8 – BONAGUIL			3.00

$1 EXACTA 3–7 PAID $18.80 $2 QUINELLA 3–7 PAID $19.00
$1 TRIFECTA 3–7–8 PAID $88.30 $1 SUPERFECTA 3–7–8–1 PAID $310.30

Ch. h, (Feb), by Candy Stripes – Ali's Dancer , by Marshua's Dancer . Trainer Canani Julio C. Bred by Taylor Made Farm Inc (Ky).

SWEET STEPPER prompted the pace, took a short lead leaving the second turn and held on gamely. LEPRECHAUN KID off a bit slowly, angled in and saved ground chasing the pace, moved up inside leaving the backstretch and into the second turn, was shuffled back midway on that bend, came a bit off the rail past midstretch and split foes with a late bid to just miss. BONAGUIL also a bit slow to begin, chased outside a rival then angled in leaving the backstretch, came out nearing the stretch and found his best stride late. TOMBSTONE (ARG) a half step slow into stride, chased inside then between horses on the backstretch and into the second turn, continued outside a foe leaving that bend, then split rivals with a late bid. SAN NICOLAS had good early speed and set a pressured pace inside, fought back through the stretch but weakened a bit late. ZENTSOV STREET off a bit slowly, saved ground off the pace, came out into the stretch and lacked the needed rally. SEX MACHINE (AUS) well placed stalking the pace three deep to the stretch, weakened in the drive.

Owners– 1, Beck Robert L; 2, Ed and Natalie Friendly Trust; 3, Red Baron's Barn LLC; 4, Blau Pellman Schechter et al; 5, Lake Forest Stable; 6, Lewis Robert B and Beverly J; 7, Vasili Angelo

Trainers– 1, Canani Julio C; 2, Machowsky Michael; 3, Vienna Darrell; 4, Aguirre Paul G; 5, Carava Jack; 6, McAnally Ronald; 7, McAnally Ronald

Sweet Stepper was claimed by Alesia Bran Jam Stable and Carr; trainer, Eurton Peter.

Scratched– Labamta Babe (22Oct03 7SA⁶)

$2 Daily Double (3–3) Paid $48.40 ; Daily Double Pool $31,475 .
$1 Pick Three (6–3–3/5) Paid $129.10 ; Pick Three Pool $71,174 .

Pedigree

Pedigree becomes a consideration when a horse tries something new. A horse's sire and dam pass on attributes to their foals. Pedigree handicapping provides clues to a horse's potential to handle an unfamiliar surface or distance, and is particularly effective on turf with maidens and lightly raced horses. Those that are bred for grass frequently improve many lengths over their dirt form. The dilemma arises in deciding if the potential is worth wagering on.

The odds determine the course of action. Comininalittlehot was 21-1 that evening at Hollywood Park. It does not require that much courage to back a longshot with potential. A winning horseplayer is less concerned with frequency of winners, and more concerned with being suitably rewarded when the winners do run in. And they will. Had Comininalittlehot started at 5-2, he would not have been a good bet. The potential reward would not have justified the risk.

Pedigree handicapping is a double-edged sword. The benefit is that the information can be subjectively interpreted, and therefore is less likely to be considered by bettors who need quantitative, specific guidance. As a result, pedigree-based overlays regularly occur. The disadvantage in considering pedigree is its fluctuating significance. It is more important at some times than at others. Pedigree is a consideration when a horse attempts something for either the first or second time.

After two starts on an unfamiliar surface, a horse's performance should speak for itself. So why give a horse even a second chance? It's because the initial experience is not always the most accurate depiction of a horse's ability. Horses do need assurance; they need to gain confidence that something new will not lead to harm. Horses can improve the second time they try something.

The Tomlinson Ratings included in each horse's past performances provide a gauge of potential in three areas—turf, wet tracks, and distance. The ratings are based on a review of more than 10,000 stallions, and their inclination to pass on certain characteristics to their offspring. As a general guideline, a turf rating of 280 or higher suggests the horse be given additional consideration when trying grass for the first or second time. A rating of 320 or higher on a wet track or at today's distance suggests the horse may run particularly well in mud or over a certain route of ground.

Tomlinson-based pedigree analysis is most telling on grass. Wet-track pedigrees may have less relevance than even 10 years ago, at least in California, partly because of modern maintenance procedures. Now, before a heavy rain, racing surfaces are "sealed" (packed tight by steamrollers) to prevent water from seeping in. Instead, the water rolls off, and the sealed track resembles a fast track. Whereas rain once led to deep mud and slow times, it happens less often today.

Wet weather is a good time for a bettor to hibernate. While Tomlinson Ratings for wet tracks provide a gauge to potential wet-track ability, wet-track wagering often is little more than unmitigated gambling. Few serious players look forward to a rainy day at the track. The fields are small, turf racing is canceled, the sealed track often plays like a paved highway, and value is difficult to find.

For handicappers who insist on playing in the rain, established ability on a wet surface is worthy of note. Once a horse has run well on a different surface (wet or turf), pedigree ratings are less significant. A horse that has raced three times on a wet track, without success, probably would prefer dry land. No kidding. Horses and handicappers do have shortcomings; wet weather remains troublesome for many. So be it. It's not like the sun will never shine again.

Jockeys

On turf, more riding strategy is required. Whereas dirt horses rip early and fade late, turf races place a premium on positioning and jockeys' skill. Turf races expose a jockey—for better or worse. There is nowhere to hide. To win on turf, a jockey must save ground, avoid traffic, gauge the horse's finishing rally, and do it all in the blink of an eye. Jerry Bailey earned his reputation as a premier jockey due in part to his command of turf. He described the difference between riding on dirt and turf.

"The biggest difference is that the accent on saving ground and being patient is a lot more evident in turf racing that it is in dirt racing. If you use your horse early in a dirt race you might be able to get away with it. If you use your horse too early in a turf race, you'll pay the price the last quarter-mile. It's a more tiring surface to run on. You have rare exceptions like Belmont in July when it hasn't rained in two weeks and you run three-quarters in 1:07. Speed will carry then. In fact you want to send them to the lead. Dirt horses will run good on a turf course like that; you don't have to be a grass horse. Other than that, in general . . . if you move too soon on a grass course you pay the price. [On dirt] I might steal off turning for home, or at the three-eighths pole I might try to get a couple more lengths, but I wouldn't do that on the grass. [You wait] as long as you can."

No one doubts the importance of jockeys, yet their abilities are not easily quantified because their performances hinge mostly on the horses. "I would say 90 percent of it is [the horse]," Bailey said. "A good rider can't make a bad horse win. But a bad rider can get a good horse beat. Therein lies your difference. You don't have 10 good riders every time. So if you're between two or three horses, you have to factor in the rider. I think the ability of the horse is the major factor in a race. A loaded gun is dangerous in anybody's hands."

Even when a jockey appears to be in a slump, the reason might be that the trainers he rides for are in a slump. A slow horse is a slow horse. The handicapping dilemma is ascertaining a jockey's current ability. A good jockey stays out of a horse's way, and allows the horse to perform at his peak. As a handicapping factor, it's comforting to have a hot jockey on your horse. But by itself, the presence of a top rider is insufficient reason to back a horse.

It's no knock. A good jockey goes a long way. A good jockey rarely encounters trouble, usually is in the right spot, and horses respond to his touch. But it is rare when a wager can be made because of the rider. Got a hot jockey on your horse? That's good; chances are the jockey will not get in the horse's way. Other handicapping factors are more accurately quantified, and more important.

On the other hand, a cold jockey may be reason to steer clear of a horse. Jockeys do go cold, as handicappers do, and sometimes nothing works out right. When a jockey slumps, his horses break poorly, encounter trouble, get caught wide, are blocked behind others, and lose repeated photo finishes. One measurement of a jockey's performance is his ratio of wins to seconds. A top jockey should have a credible win percentage, but even more important, he should have more wins than seconds. The idea is that a rider whose mounts are running well and hitting the board should also be winning his fair share.

If a low-odds horse is ridden by a slumping rider, it may be time to pass. When you are wagering at a short price, everything must be perfect.

Past performances in *Daily Racing Form* include two sets of statistics that can be used as a broad tool in analyzing jockeys. Both sets of numbers are listed after the jockey's name. The first is the jockey's record at the current meet; the second is the jockey's record for the year. The statistics paint a picture of a jockey's short- and long-term trends. Win percentage is less important than ratio of wins-seconds-thirds. And it's okay to back a low-percentage jockey when the odds are high enough.

Much time is spent debating the attributes of jockeys. It is a fun topic, open to great subjectivity. By 2002 in Southern California, Pat Valenzuela had reemerged as the circuit's dominant rider. Valenzuela was doing more than winning—he was affecting how races unfolded. Horses produced more speed when he rode for the first time. During the same period, Julie Krone came out of a 3½-year retirement to emerge as a leading rider in California with a patient, sit-still style. So who was better—Valenzuela on the lead, or Krone from behind? The answer is obvious: It depended on the horse.

From a national perspective, Bailey's reputation as the premier jockey of the early 2000's will not be debated. His mounts are rarely in trouble, he rides the best horses, and everyone knows it. Bailey is good, among the best ever. But for a beginning handicapper to recognize the fact, the benefit is minimal. Top jockeys ride the best horses; those horses usually are among the favorites. That's all you need to know.

A horse that was ridden by a low-profile jockey and is switching to a top rider may be given a second look. That's all. The leading jockeys rarely ride hopeless outsiders. So when a top rider gets on a horse that initially appears to have little chance, a handicapper might dig a little deeper in the past performances. If the jockey has ridden the horse successfully in the past, his mere presence may be an indication the horse is coming back around. And when a leading jockey accepts a mount on a horse that also is dropping in class, it is definitely worth consideration.

It is the horse that carries the jockey, not the other way around. Want to gamble on a jockey? Go ahead. Your energy will be misdirected, because it is another individual who should be garnering most of the attention.

Trainer

The trainer is the most important person associated with the horse. That fact is directly related to form, class, speed, and pace. The trainer is responsible for the training methods and frequency of races; for placing the horse at the proper level; and for plotting race strategy with the jockey. The trainer also employs the grooms and exercise riders, and consults with veterinarians. A trainer is the coach, manager, and team president rolled into one.

A trainer decides when and where a horse runs, or works out. The trainer communicates with owners, deals with jockeys and their agents, negotiates with bloodstock agents (people who buy and sell horses), talks with racing secretaries, entertains owners, handles media interviews, and interacts with stewards. No single person has as much influence.

There are low-profile trainers that win at high mutuel payoffs, and high-profile barns that win at low mutuel payoffs. The problem for handicappers is quantifying a trainer's proficiency beyond win percentage.

Trainer statistics are highly useful, particularly when there is insufficient information about the horse, or when a handicapper is unfamiliar with the circuit. It helps to know the guys behind the horse, especially when the horse is unfamiliar. It happens every spring with first-time starters.

The April meet at Kentucky's historic Keeneland track offers a festival of top-class racing and the highest purses in the country. The 16-day meet also brings out the first premier 2-year-old maiden races of the year. Most 2-year-old maiden races at Keeneland's spring meeting are filled with first-time starters. In addition to workouts and pedigree, the role of the trainer is highly important.

Some trainers prefer to race their horses into shape in actual competition. These horsemen do not bear down on young horses in workouts leading to their first start. Other trainers come out firing with first-time starters that have been honed to deliver a top effort. The trainer's tendencies are shown at the bottom of each horse's past-performance lines. These trainer statistics reveal the trainer's competency in specialized areas, including first-time starters.

Hasslefree	Dk. b or br c. 2 (Apr) FTSAUG02 $425,000		Life	0 M 0 0	$0	–	D.Fst	0 0 0 0	$0	–
Own: Lewis Robert B & Beverly J	Sire: Forestry (Storm Cat) $50,000		2003	0 M 0 0	$0	–	Wet(326)	0 0 0 0	$0	–
Green; Yellow Hoops Yellow Sleeves	Dam: Belle of Abruzzi(Time for a Change)		2002	0 M 0 0	$0	–	Turf(292)	0 0 0 0	$0	–
(—) 2003:(255 43 .17)	Br: Lynn B Schiff (Ky)	118	Kee	0 0 0 0	$0	–	Dst(307)	0 0 0 0	$0	–
	Tr: Lukas D Wayne (—) 2003:(124 12 .10)									

S: ●Mar29 SA 1f fst :12¹ Hg 1/10   Mar23 SA 3f fst :35² Hg 5/27   Mar13 SA 3f fst :35 H 2/20   Mar3 SA 2f fst :22⁴ H 3/7
ER: 1stStart(72 .10 $0.82) 2YO(150 .15 $1.14) Dirt(516 .15 $1.38) Sprint(363 .17 $1.44) MdnSpWt(202 .16 $1.28)

In the first 2-year-old maiden race of the 2003 Keeneland spring meet, the public supported 8-5 Hasslefree, a first-time starter with high-profile connections. The expensive ($425,000) colt was sired by a promising young stallion, Forestry, whose stud fee was a lofty $50,000. Further, Hasslefree was trained by D. Wayne Lukas and ridden by Pat Day. He had trained fast, but there was more to his story than pedigree and works. Over the course of a 35-year Thoroughbred training career, Lukas had typically allowed young horses to develop in races, rather than being jacked up to win first time.

It was background information anyone could know by looking at Hasslefree's past performances. Below the colt's workouts was the section on trainer statistics that showed Lukas's tendencies: TRAINER: 1stStart (72 .10 $0.82).

Since the beginning of the previous year, Lukas had sent out 72 first-time starters. He had won with 10 percent, mostly at low odds, producing a return on investment (ROI) of just 82 cents per $2 win wager. It equaled one winner every 10 starts, at an average $2 win payoff of only slightly more than $8. Lukas firsters were being overbet in relation to their true chances. There were alternatives in the race. Of the 10 starters, four had trainers with positive data regarding first-timers. One of those trainers was saddling a colt named Palpen.

5	Palpen		

5 Palpen
Own: Heiligbrodt Racing Stable
Grees White; Burnt Orange Star, Burnt Orange
MECHE L J (—) 2003:(318 31 .10)

Ch. c. 2 (Jan) OBSOCT01 $25,000
Sire: Pentelicus (Fappiano) $5,000
Dam: Darned If You Dont(Darn That Alarm)
Br: Joseph Barbazon & Helen Barbazon (Fla)
Tr: Asmussen Steven M (—) 2003:(416 109 .26)

	Life	0	M	0	0	$0	–	D.Fst	0	0	0	0
	2003	0	M	0	0	$0	–	Wet(360)	0	0	0	0
118	2002	0	M	0	0	$0	–	Turf(245)	0	0	0	0
	Kee	0	0	0	0	$0	–	Dst(345)	0	0	0	0

WORKS: Mar22 Hou 4f fst :49 Bg 4/41 Mar16 Hou 4f fst :50¹ Bg 41/73 Mar9 Hou 3f fst :36⁴ Bg 11/32

TRAINER: 1stStart(198 .18 $2.37) 2YO(377 .22 $1.89) Dirt(1801 .24 $1.69) Sprint(1397 .23 $1.61) MdnSpWt(366 .23 $1.78)

Steve Asmussen had run 198 first-timer starters since the beginning of 2002, winning 18 percent (nearly twice Lukas's win rate), while producing a gawdy ROI of $2.37. Asmussen firsters generally were cranked and ready. And so was Palpen. Though favorite Hasslefree ran well and finished second, Palpen benefited from a rail-skimming trip to win by nearly two lengths. He paid $18.40. The trainer statistics published in *Daily Racing Form*—even as a stand-alone factor—suggested that Palpen was a prime contender.

Trainer statistics help complete the story, beyond past performances. Particularly in specialized contests such as springtime 2-year-old races, trainer statistics can put a bettor one step closer to an educated wagering decision. *Daily Racing Form* past performances cover 29 categories of "trainer form," listing up to six of the most relevant categories underneath the horse's workouts. The trainer-form categories show the rate of success with horses in the following situations:

First North American start
First race after claim
First race with trainer
180 days since last race
60-180 days since last race

31-60 days since last race
1-7 days since last race
First-time starter
Second start of career
First-time turf
First-time blinkers
First-time Lasix
2-year-olds
Dirt to turf
Turf to dirt
Blinkers on
Blinkers off
Sprint to route
Route to sprint
Dirt
Turf
Sprints
Routes
Maiden claiming
Maiden special weight
Claiming
Allowance
Stakes
Graded stakes

The categories cover the trainer's starters since the beginning of the previous year, and allow horseplayers to view a trainer's performance in a specific situation. The most important categories deal with change, because change of any type has a potential influence on performance. In fact, most of the categories listed deal with change—a horse trying to do something different. That includes making the first start after changing stables, returning from a layoff, adding or removing equipment, or changing surface.

European imports, as another example, can be difficult to assess. It's often tough to know where a horse fits on the North American class ladder when he is shipping in from another continent. Trainer form provides a clue. In using trainer form, a horseplayer must place a great deal of faith in the trainer. Which is fine.

Trainer form is intended to provide support to past performances. The inherent ability of a horse remains the most important factor. Trainer form merely offers supplemental information. Trainer form may provide clues to a horse's condition—the first eight categories deal with current form.

Is a horse that has not raced in North America ready for a top effort in his first start back? His workout pattern provides evidence. So does his trainer. A trainer who wins at 15 percent or higher in a particular category is doing well, and when his ROI exceeds the $2 break-even point he is doing better yet. A trainer who wins less than 9 percent in a particular category may be performing below expectations, though win percentage must be considered in light of the ROI.

Expectations vary. The average field size in North America is slightly more than eight starters per race. A random sample would produce a win rate of slightly higher than 12 percent (one in eight). A competent trainer should do better than the random sample, so a benchmark of 15 percent is considered relevant— above average.

A trainer winning at 15 percent, or 3 percent higher than average, is doing well. A trainer winning at 9 percent, or 3 percent lower than average, is not. High-volume stables that generally rank in the top 10 by starts and wins at the meet should win at least 15 percent. Horses trained by guys such as Bobby Frankel and Steve Asmussen commonly are prepared to deliver a peak effort every time, because those trainers have dozens more horses waiting in the wings. Big stables frequently have more than one horse available for a specific race, maiden races in particular, and therefore take their best shot most of the time. Conversely, low-volume barns may allow maidens to develop gradually and improve as they gain experience.

Beyond win rate, ROI can be considered. In the example with Lukas-trained firsters, there is nothing inherently "wrong" with an ordinary, slightly below-par 10 percent win rate. But it becomes wholly relevant when the accompanying ROI also is subpar. In backing Lukas first-start maidens, bettors were getting back 82 cents for every $2 win bet.

A benchmark for ROI is $1.70. The takeout on win bets is approximately 15 percent; random wagering would produce a 15 percent loss per dollar wagered, or 30 cents per $2. That equates to an ROI of $1.70. It's a matter of opinion how far the mark can be deviated from. An ROI of $1.90 or more is reason for enthusiasm; an ROI of $1.50 or less suggests the trainer's horses tend to run below expectations.

It's not easy to balance win percentage and ROI, which is why trainer form is merely a broad gauge. A trainer who wins with a particular move at 15 percent or more and produces an ROI of $1.90 or more is cause for wagering enthusiasm. Conversely, a trainer who wins at 9 percent or less and produces an ROI of $1.50 or less is a trainer whose inefficiency in that category is reason for caution.

A new order has emerged among modern trainers. Win percentage has become the standard by which trainers consider themselves judged, and a handful of the nation's trainers are noted by their horsemanship and ability to win at high-percentage rates. Wayne Catalano (30 percent), Jeff Mullins (30 percent), Anthony Dutrow (30 percent), Bobby Frankel (29 percent), and Cole Norman (27 percent) neared the end of 2003 with outstanding win rates. Their achievements far exceeded the 15 percent standard. Trainer statistics allow a handicapper to objectively evaluate a trainer's performance. And trainers, of course, are spokespersons for their horses.

Except for the messages they send through body language, horses do not talk. It is unfortunate, because in most sports, the athletes speak well enough to be quoted. But the week before the 2002 Kentucky Derby, no one was asking War Emblem any questions. He could not have answered. He was just a high-figure shipper from Chicago, aiming for the biggest race in America. Instead of interviewing the actual athletes—the horses—racing journalists must rely on trainers for quotes and anecdotes. It creates an interesting and awkward situation, because trainers are not always entirely forthright.

Considering what is at stake, there are reasons to stay private. A trainer with a longshot front-runner often maintains a low profile before a big race. Strategically, it makes sense. If attention is called to the front-runner—if he is considered a serious contender—there is increased likelihood the horse will be challenged early in the race. However, if the front-runner is not considered legitimate—if others believe he will tire regardless—there is a greater chance he may shake loose, race uncontested, and lead gate to wire.

The week of the 2002 Derby, War Emblem's trainer, Bob

Baffert, was saying very little about his colt. Baffert is among the most widely recognized figures in horse racing—accessible, quotable, clever. But he was not singing the praises of War Emblem. Weeks earlier, Baffert had advised owner Prince Ahmed Salman to purchase a 90 percent interest in War Emblem, who had won the Illinois Derby in a romp. But Kentucky was a different story, and Baffert was playing it close to the vest. "I wanted to talk about him, but I couldn't. He was doing soooo good. But if I started talking about him, if I started bragging on him, they might have taken him seriously," Baffert said later.

Instead, he stayed quiet. The only headlines Baffert made during Derby Week resulted from the surprise entry of overmatched Danthebluegrassman. Baffert's understated approach regarding War Emblem helped soften the Derby pace scenario. Had Baffert publicized War Emblem the week of the race, it was less likely he would have made such an easy lead. Everyone knows what can happen when a front-runner shakes loose early, and slows down the pace. His heart grows, he gets brave, and he is gone. That is exactly what happened.

The colt established a comfortable and unchallenged lead. The underpublicized front-runner stole the biggest race in America. It happens all the time—front-runners stealing races, and trainers managing journalistic spin. Give them credit—horsemen are in a tough spot. It can be self-defeating to publicize strategy, or physical condition. This is why handicappers must also be skeptics, not only during Derby Week, but also the other 51 weeks of the year.

Workouts

A horseplayer who follows the same methods as everyone, and believes everything he reads, eventually will lose. This includes misinterpreting fast workouts, which matter far less than believed. A healthy workout pattern is just that—a pattern. It can be every five days, or every six days, or every seven days. The only requirement is that the pattern be regular and steady. Some horseplayers are "private clockers," individuals whose income (from wagering and from more reliable consultation fees) is based on their observations of horses in the morning. Gary Young, one of the most widely respected and opinionated clockers in California, admits that there is more to the job than punching a stopwatch.

"The biggest misconception people have about this part of the game is they think that because we clock horses, we immediately walk in and know who to bet on. They don't know that before every racing day, you might be looking up workouts for three hours the night before. The amount of hours that goes into it is quite a bit. You have to go through [workout notes], you have to do your final calculations for the races, scratches might make a difference.

"We often joke that if every horse ran like they worked, we'd be in Hawaii playing golf every day. They don't all run like they work. There are others that know the difference between practice and game day, and they just go through the motions out here in the morning. [Good ones] float over the ground. There's not an exact science to it.

"You have to know the horse. There are some horses that are sore all over. If you came out and saw Kona Gold jog or gallop, and were asked if you want to buy that horse for $15,000, you'd say 'No thank you.' That's just the way he is. The part where recognizing soreness really comes into a real benefit is to know a horse that you've seen train all year and all of a sudden . . . you can see the aches and pains coming on him."

Young does not publish his observations, and earns his living by advising owners and trainers on potential purchases. That, and wagering. Young is not always right. No clocker, or handicapper, is accurate every time. Yet because workout "information" is such a highly specialized area of expertise, the tendency is for bettors to exaggerate its importance.

Lindero
Own: Cubanacan Stables
White, White Cs In Red Triangle
OA G F (36 2 6 4 .06) 2003:(284 28 .10)

Ch. c. 2 (Jan) KEESEP02 $9,000
Sire: Boundary (Danzig) $15,000
Dam: Mrs. Highness(Alydar)
$40,000 Br: Hickory Tree Farm Inc (Va)
Tr: Garcia Juan(21 2 2 1 .10) 2003:(146 7 .05)

Life 1 M 0 0 $560 25 D.Fst 1 0 0 0 $560 25
L 120 2003 1 M 0 0 $560 25 Wet(410) 0 0 0 0 $0 –
2002 0 M 0 0 $0 – Turf(300) 0 0 0 0 $0 –
Dmr 1 0 0 0 $560 25 Dst(365) 0 0 0 0 $0 –

- 30mr fst 5½f :22² :46¹ :58³ 1:05 Md 50000 (50-45) 25 3 3 52½ 53¼ 69¼ 51⁴ Almeida G F LB 119 b 32.00 76–13 FebEleven119½ FiercKnight119²½ Prsumption119³ 3wd into lane, wkened 9
: Aug6 Dmr 6f fst 1:14² H 5/8 Jly23 Dmr 5f fst 1:02 Hg34/45 Jly13 SA 5f fst 1:01 H 16/48 Jly6 SA 4f fst :49¹ H 33/55 Jun29 SA 3f fst :35⁴ H 4/27 Jun11 SA 5f fst 1:01 H 18/37
ER: 2ndStart(39 .05 $0.58) 2YO(68 .10 $1.39) Dirt(286 .12 $1.54) Sprint(242 .08 $1.21) MdnClm(125 .11 $1.07)

A second-time starter in a weak maiden race looked tempting during the 2003 summer meet at Del Mar. He was the 20-1 longshot Lindero, facing a field of $40,000 maiden claimers. A clocker proclaimed that Lindero had little chance. His reasoning was that Lindero's six-furlong workout one week earlier was too slow—1:14.40. He was right about one thing—the workout was slow. But works are not meant to be a measure of ability. All they do is allow a handicapper to ascertain condition. The clocker's workout-too-slow analysis failed to consider factors that are the heart of handicapping—condition, class, speed, and pace.

Lindero was physically fit—he had finished in midpack in his debut, after racing within three lengths of the lead to the pace call. Further, it was expected that Lindero would improve second time out. Most second-time starters do improve. Lindero fit on class—after pressing the pace in a $50,000 maiden claiming race, he was dropping one level to $40,000 maiden claiming. It was the best kind of class drop—a horse dropping sensibly one notch following an acceptable performance against better.

The speed figure earned by Lindero in his debut was dreadful. But first-time starters and speed horses often run to the point of exhaustion before falling apart. They often generate subpar speed figures. Finally, pace. Lindero had raced within striking range of the lead against better.

Lindero was a contender, nothing more and nothing less. The clocker did not like Lindero because of a slow work. It was like saying Michael Jordan would not make any free throws because he missed a few during practice. But horseplayers who viewed Lindero's slow workout as merely a measure of condition did the right thing. There were reasons to like the slow horse, not the least of which was the fact that he was running against other slow horses. (See chart, opposite page)

FIRST RACE

Del Mar

6 FURLONGS. (1.07³) MAIDEN CLAIMING . Purse $24,000 FOR MAIDENS, TWO YEAR OLDS. Weight, 120 lbs. Claiming Price $40,000, if for $35,000, allowed 2 lbs. (Clear. 79.)

AUGUST 13, 2003

of Race: $24,000 Winner $14,400; second $4,800; third $2,880; fourth $1,440; fifth $480. Mutuel Pool $247,063.00 Exacta Pool
09.00 Quinella Pool $18,834.00 Trifecta Pool $148,107.00 Superfecta Pool $43,071.00

Raced	Horse	M/Eqt. A. Wt	PP	St	¼	½	Str	Fin	Jockey	Cl'g Pr	Odds $1
03 3Dmr⁵	Lindero	LB b 2 120	7	2	4½	3²	2²	1²	Almeida G F	40000	20.10
03 5Dmr⁵	Fortune Catcher	LB bf 2 120	2	4	1ʰᵈ	1½	1¹½	2²	Krone J A	40000	1.20
	Exploited	LB 2 120	6	6	5⁸	5⁶	4³	3¹	Stevens G L	40000	3.20
03 5Dmr⁹	Something Fierce	LB b 2 120	4	3	3½	2ʰᵈ	3²	4⁸	Solis A O	40000	2.60
03 2Dmr⁸	B B Saunter	B 2 118	5	7	6¹	6³	6²½	5¹	Ziesing S	35000	85.50
	Royal Photographer	LB b 2 118	8	1	7³½	7⁸	7¹⁰	6¹	Valenzuela F H	35000	30.90
03 2Dmr⁴	Let's Belly Up	LB b 2 118	3	5	2ʰᵈ	4½	5¹	7¹½	Martinez F F	35000	6.40
	Toketee	B 2 120	1	8	8	8	8	8	Leyva J C	40000	77.00

OFF AT 2:01 Start Good . Won driving. Track fast.
TIME :22², :46, :58², 1:11³ (:22.53, :46.10, :58.51, 1:11.76)

2 Mutuel Prices:	7 – LINDERO	42.20	11.00	4.60
	2 – FORTUNE CATCHER		3.20	2.40
	6 – EXPLOITED			3.00

$1 EXACTA 7–2 PAID $69.20 $2 QUINELLA 2–7 PAID $40.60
$1 TRIFECTA 7–2–6 PAID $313.50 $1 SUPERFECTA 7–2–6–4 PAID $929.10

h. c, (Jan), by Boundary – Mrs. Highness , by Alydar . Trainer Garcia Juan. Bred by Hickory Tree Farm Inc (Va).
INDERO stalked the pace off the rail on the backstretch, bid four wide into the turn and three deep leaving the bend, then
down the runner-up under some urging to prove best. FORTUNE CATCHER had good early speed and dueled inside,
d clear into the stretch but could not hold off the winner. EXPLOITED stalked the dueling leaders off the rail on the
stretch and into the turn, continued outside a foe leaving the bend and picked up the show. SOMETHING FIERCE forced
ace three deep then between horses leaving the turn, dropped back into the stretch and weakened, then returned bleeding
e mouth. B B SAUNTER broke a bit slowly and was squeezed, settled off the rail, angled in on the turn and did not rally.
AL PHOTOGRAPHER also settled off the inside without early speed, angled in some on the turn and was outrun. LET'S
LY UP a bit fractious in the gate, vied for command between horses, dropped back on the turn and weakened. TOKETEE a
ow to begin, saved ground off the pace, came out into the stretch and was outrun.
Owners– 1, Cubanacan Stables; 2, Dolindale Farm and O'Neill Richard; 3, Hughes B Wayne; 4, Class Racing Stable Freitas Richard and
man Art; 5, Rodriguez Jose M; 6, Johnston E W and Judy; 7, Meadowbrook Farms Inc; 8, Zamora Ricardo
Trainers– 1, Garcia Juan J; 2, Peterson Douglas R; 3, Stute Warren; 4, Sherman Art; 5, Soto Antonio; 6, Warren Donald; 7, La Croix
; 8, Zamora Ricardo
Exploited was claimed by Leotti Thomas; trainer, Delia William.

There is now an entire cottage industry that peddles "workout information." A lot of hard-working clockers beat the crack of dawn to time horses in morning works, and sell their published observations. These clockers do a fine job, and there can be reasons to consider workout analyses after addressing the basics. But workout information is not a magic ingredient. And yet even experienced handicappers are prone to alter wagering strategy when they hear that a clocker "liked so-and-so's workout."

The first Saturday of the 2001 Del Mar meet, I botched a pick-four wager for that very reason. Based on the recommendation of a clocker, I "singled" 7-1 first-time starter American System in the first leg of the pick four, even though second-time starter Saturday Hero was the most logical winner at odds of 2-1. American System ran well, but finished third. You can guess what happened. Saturday Hero won in a romp, but my pick-four ticket already was dead. It was too bad, because I had the next three longshot winners and the pick four paid $18,580.60 for $1. It was the type of painful lesson that can happen when you buy into someone else's opinion instead of sticking with your own.

Workouts are important only in the context of the overall picture. The purpose of viewing workouts is to gauge a horse's condition, not his ability. A slow horse will work in slow time. When he is entered against other slow horses, the workouts only offer an estimate of his physical fitness. That was the Lindero mistake. Slow horses do win races. Workouts are a secondary factor to support the handicapping basics, and far less important than the horse's most recent race.

This is not intended to incriminate workout analyses. Yet not every handicapping factor means the same thing to everyone. A good clocker may be able to measure a horse's ability by seeing how the horse trains in the morning. Hats off to the clocker. The mistake is to accept a clocker's opinion and interpret it as fact. Not qualified to make an interpretation? Don't lose money chasing someone else's. A good workout pattern does not get any more obvious than the patterns of four debut sprint winners trained by Rafael Becerra during the 2003 Oak Tree meet at Santa Anita.

All four had:

A five-furlong workout within seven days of their debut
A six-furlong workout as their next-to-last work
A workout from the gate as their third-to-last work
At least two gate works leading to the debut.

A gate work familiarizes a horse with the starting gate, and allows him to be taught what to do when the stall doors open and the bell rings. When a trainer works a horse twice from the gate, it suggests an all-out effort is forthcoming the first time the horse enters a race.

Workout patterns can be supplemented with clocker reports or handicapping analyses that disclose the names of other runners the horse has trained with "in company," a workout that imitates race conditions. St. Averil and Rahy Dolly worked together on November 2. Further, the 2-year-olds were joined in the workout by the older horse Tizbud, and both St. Averil and Rahy Dolly finished in front of Tizbud.

The plain fact that one horse finishes in front of another in a workout is a broad consideration, and in this case it did not mean that St. Averil or Rahy Dolly was better than Tizbud. It only meant that they held their own in a workout. But the day before the Becerra-trained 2-year-olds made their debuts, Tizbud romped to a three-length win in the $250,000 California Cup Classic. His performance made the workouts of St. Averil and Rahy Dolly look even better. The colt and the filly both started at 5-2, and ran like they could have been odds-on. St. Averil won his debut by three lengths; Rahy Dolly won by 11.

Another clue to intent could have been found in Becerra's trainer form, below the workouts. Since the beginning of 2002, Becerra had started 21 firsters, won with 29 percent, and produced an ROI of $2.18 for each $2 bet to win.

A good workout pattern for a first-time starter would include a work at least once every seven days, and a recent workout within one furlong of the distance of the race, preferably at the distance. A horse making his debut at six furlongs will have worked at least five furlongs within his last three workouts. A well-intended firster also would have at least one recent gate workout. These are only general guidelines, not hard-and-fast rules. Regarding first-time starters, trainer statistics are more relevant.

Workout patterns also can determine a horse's likely success following a layoff. A sensible work pattern for a horse who has been off 45 days or more would include a series of increasingly longer workouts, preferably at least one workout at a distance within a furlong of the race, and finalized by a shorter drill. A guideline used by some handicappers is that a first-time starter or a comebacker should work an average of one furlong a day over the past month. For example, a workout pattern in the past 30 days may include a half-mile work as the last work, two six-furlong works, and two five-furlong workouts. That is a total of 26 furlongs (4 + 6 + 6 + 5 + 5), reasonably close to the furlong-a-day requirement. As with first-timers, the tendencies of the trainer are relevant.

A sensible work pattern must always be viewed in conjunction with other components. With a comebacker, that means returning at an appropriate class level—for example, a class drop of no more than one level from his most recent competitive race. A drop of more than one level suggests the horse has gone downhill since his last race, notwithstanding a series of fast works. A comebacker that returns at a class level higher than his previously established ability would probably be in tough.

The distance and surface at which a comebacker returns should be a distance and surface at which the horse has run well previously. And, the trainer statistics below the workouts show a trainer's proficiency with comebackers. With some guys, it's automatic. Bobby Frankel's 29 percent win rate in 2003 was partly due to the fact that he does not waste starts. His horses, comebackers included, are ready to roll.

Imports

An estimated 800 European imports make their way to the U.S. for racing each year, and pose a dilemma for U.S. handicappers. Most European races are on turf, and therefore most European imports are turf horses. Their chances are based on traditional turf handicapping principles that emphasize class. A European that has run well against stronger company overseas must be viewed as a contender in the U.S. That is one reason why some horses are purchased and imported from Europe. Because the class hierarchy in Europe is structured differently from that in the U.S., many European imports are able to face easier company here than they have been meeting overseas.

tatement (Ire)
n: Highclere Stable
nt Blue, Royal Blue Hoop On Sleeves
A (71 10 12 8 .14) 2003: (959 145 .15)

B. c. 3 (Mar) TATHOU01 $309,960
Sire: Singspiel*Ire (In the Wings*GB)
Dam: Last Spin*GB (Unfuwain)
Br: Mrs E B L Long (Ire)
Tr: Clement Christophe(14 1 3 1 .07) 2003:(288 62 .22)

Ⓛ 118

Life	4	M	2	1	$9,627	-	D.Fst	0	0	0	0	$0	-
2003	2	M	1	0	$4,168	-	Wet(160*)	0	0	0	0	$0	-
2002	2	M	1	1	$5,459	-	Turf(396)	4	0	2	1	$9,627	-
Bel(T)	0	0	0	0	$0	-	Dst(T)(405)	0	0	0	0	$0	-

sly trained by Sir Michael Stoute

rk (GB) n rating: 94+	gf 1 5/16 (T) LH 2:082	RoyalYrkshreRatedH(1-1/4m,85y) Hcp 45500	42½	Fallon K	126	4.50	Black Falcon121½Nuit Sombre1201¾Mubeen132nk *Led to over 1f out, one-paced to line*	9
tterick (GB) n rating: 78+	gf 1½ (T) LH 2:302	Barton Maiden Stakes Maiden 9500	21½	Lynch F	120	*.60	Rahaf1201½Statement12015Promising1258 *Led til approaching final furlong, gave ground grudgingly*	6
down Park (GB) n rating: 90	gf 1 (T) RH 1:442	Missing Piece S. Alw 18900	33	Norton F	123	*1.00	Cat Ona High127hdChoir Master1233Statement1231¾ *2nd after 3f, bid 2f out, faded final furlong*	7
ndown Park (GB) n rating: 90+	gf 7f (T) RH 1:312	Attheraces Telebet Novice Stk Alw 16900	23	Dettori L	121	1.75	Al Jadeed1313Statement121½Binanti1262 *Dwelt, soon 3rd, roused over 2f out, gained 2nd 100y out*	5

Sep10 Sar tr.t(T) 4f gd :501 B(d) *9/17*
1stNA(50 .20 $1.19) 1stW/Tm(66 .21 $1.22) 61-180Days(113 .21 $1.44) 1stLasix(110 .23 $1.29) Turf(484 .23 $1.70) Routes(539 .22 $1.65)

A European import that has run well against better company generally holds the advantage in his first U.S. start. Statement had raced credibly against the equivalent of allowance company and held the class edge when he met a field of maidens at Belmont Park in his first U.S. start on September 25, 2003. Trainer Christophe Clemente's win rate with "first start in NA" was 20 percent. Statement returned $7 in the 12-horse field. No big deal, but you get the idea.

oyal Price (Ger)
n: Michael Bello
e, Yellow Hoop And Sleeves, Blue Cap
(69 11 10 11 .16) 2003: (911 158 .17)

B. c. 3 (Feb)
Sire: Oxalagu*Ger (Lagunas*GB)
Dam: Rhabea*Ger (Stanford*Ire)
Br: Dr K Graf (Ger)
Tr: Frankel Robert(14 3 2 2 .21) 2003:(320 96 .30)

Ⓛ 119

Life	8	M	4	1	$76,351	-	D.Fst	0	0	0	0	$0	-
2003	5	M	3	1	$73,694	-	Wet(280)	0	0	0	0	$0	-
2002	3	M	1	0	$2,657	-	Turf(221)	8	0	4	1	$76,351	-
SA(T)	0	0	0	0	$0	-	Dst(T)(257)	6	0	2	1	$60,077	-

sly trained by Daniela Thomas

ologne (Ger) m rating: 95	gd *1 (T) RH 1:373 3↑	Winterfavorit-Revanche Alw 33800	33¼	Pietsch A	128	*.60	*Wild Advice*1282 Action Fighter128¼ Royal Price1281¼ *Tracked in 3rd,lacked rally*	6
ortmund (Ger) m rating: 108	gd *1 1/16 (T) RH 1:472 3↑	GP der Wirtschaft(1-1/16m,55y)-G3 Stk 63800	2¾	Pietsch A	117	3.20	War Blade130¾ Royal Price117½ Arlecchina111¾ *Trckd ldrs,2nd 3f out,pressed winner 2f out,gamely.Valdoura 6th*	8
ologne (Ger) m rating: 105	gd *1 (T) RH 1:393 3↑	Mehl-Mulhens-Rennen(Ger2000Gn)-G2 Stk 231000	26	Pietsch A	128	46.20	Martillo1286 Royal Price1282½ *Ransom O'War*128nk *Tracked in 3rd,2nd 100y out,no chance with winner.Wild Advice 8th*	9
ulheim (Ger) m rating: 80	yl *1 (T) RH 1:35 4↑	Orakel der Dreijahrigen (Lstd) Stk 21700	46¼	Czachary C	119	23.30	*Martillo*1232 Wild Advice1231¼ Rajpute1213 *Bumped start,towards rear,mild late gain*	9
rankfurt (Ger)	sf *7½f (T) RH 1:352 3↑	Pr IntlGalloprennenBaden-Baden Maiden 5300	2¾	Palik J	128	6.10	Bros126¾ Royal Price128¾ Finora1214 *Rated in 5th,bid 1f out,held by winner*	9
ologne (Ger)	gd *1 (T) RH 1:39	Preis der Winterfavoriten-G3 Stk 153000	1016½	Schikora A	128	60.40	Eagle Rise1282 Glad Hunter1281 *Minley*1281 *Trailed throughout.Encanto 6th*	10
ologne (Ger) rm rating: 78	gd *1 (T) RH 1:383	Winterfavorit-Trial Alw 25500	44	Bouleau A	121	11.80	Encanto128½ Anolitas1211½ *Senex*1212 *Towards rear,some late progress*	7
Frankfurt (Ger)	gd *6½f (T) RH 1:202	Mercedes-Benz C-Klasse Cup Maiden 5100	2½	Bouleau A	123	3.60	One Touch123½ Royal Price12312 *Arc en Ciel*1231¾ *Tracked in 4th,bid over 1f out,held by winner*	6

Oct13 Hol 5f fst 1:011 H *12/27* Oct6 Hol 6f fst 1:141 H *2/8* Sep29 Hol 5f fst 1:021 H *21/36* Sep23 Hol 6f fst 1:141 H *3/10* Sep17 Hol 5f fst 1:011 H *7/35* Sep8 Dmr 4f fst :483 H *6/32*
R: 1stNA(53 .43 $3.18) 1stW/Tm(76 .39 $3.14) 61-180Days(156 .28 $1.84) Turf(546 .25 $1.75) Routes(646 .27 $1.85) MdnSpWt(99 .19 $1.40)

A horse that placed in European stakes frequently holds a distinct class advantage in the U.S. It doesn't get much more clear than Frankel-trained Royal Price, who had placed in two group stakes (equivalent to graded stakes) overseas before facing maidens in the sixth race at Santa Anita on October 19, 2003. He only paid $4.20.

Beyond credentials of the horse, the trainer remains a key. The trainer form that is published below the workouts provides a clue. Some trainers—Frankel and Clemente, for example—do well with European imports, largely because their imports are realistically placed. Many are dropping in class, as in the previous examples.

Golden Dragon (GB)
Own: Cobra Farm Inc
Green, Gold Cobra On Back, Green
GOMEZ G K (83 13 8 8 .16) 2001:(691 104 .15)

Ch. g. 4 TATOCT99 $46,379
Sire: Piccolo*GB (Warning*GB)
Dam: Aunt Judy*GB(Great Nephew*GB)
Br: Wates M E (GB)
Tr: Puype Mike(3 1 0 0 .33) 2001:(38 5 .13)

Ⓛ 118

Life	8	2	2	0	$18,410	–	D.Fst	0	0	0	0	
2001	8	2	2	0	$18,410	–	Wet(350*)	0	0	0	0	
2000	0	M	0	0	$0	–	Turf(321)	8	2	2	0	$
SA Ⓣ	0	0	0	0	$0	–	DistⓉ	0	0	0	0	

Previously trained by Michael Jarvis

5Oct01♦ Newmarket(GB)	gd	7f	Ⓣ Str	1:26	3↑	Fitzwilliam Rated Handicap	$8^{7\frac{1}{4}}$	Robinson P	119	9.00	Free Rider $130^{1\frac{1}{4}}$ Point Of Dispute $122^{2\frac{1}{2}}$ Wahj 131^{hd}
Timeform rating: 82						Hcp 24500					*Rated in mid-pack,ridden without response*
31Aug01♦ Chester(GB)	yl	7f	Ⓣ LH	$1{:}27^4$	3↑	Chronicle Newspapers Rated Hcp	5^8	Robinson P	118	*3.50	Wahj $128^{3\frac{1}{2}}$ Forever Times 114^{nk} Glenrock 119^3
Timeform rating: 79						Hcp 24200					*Rated in mid-pack,*
18Aug01♦ Newbury(GB)	gd	7f	Ⓣ Str	$1{:}23^3$	3↑	Stan James Handicap	2^{nk}	Robinson P	119	25.00	A Touch Of Frost 119^{nk} Golden Dragon $119^{1\frac{1}{4}}$ Raheibb 126^{nk}
Timeform rating: 96+						Hcp 18000					*Soon steadied at rear,sharp run 1f out,hung.Wa*
29Jly01♦ Newmarket(GB)	fm	1	Ⓣ Str	$1{:}38^2$		Mail on Sunday Mile Hcp Qlfr	10^{10}	Robinson P	132	9.00	Momentum 133^{hd} Halland $128^{2\frac{1}{2}}$ Dennis El Menace 117^{nk}
Timeform rating: 74						Hcp 23300					*Rank towards rear,progress 2f out,soo*
30Jun01♦ Chester(GB)	gd	*7½f	Ⓣ LH	$1{:}32^3$		Farndon Classified Stakes	$1^{1\frac{3}{4}}$	Callan N	129	2.50	Golden Dragon $129^{1\frac{3}{4}}$ Dusty Carpet 126no Montana Miss 123^1
Timeform rating: 88						Alw 9100					*Tracked leader,led over 1f*
30May01♦ Southwell(GB)	gd	6f	Ⓣ LH	$1{:}15^1$	3↑	HBLB NSPCC Maiden Stakes	1^1	Robinson P	124	*.55	Golden Dragon 124^1 Another Victim $130^{1\frac{1}{2}}$ Justafancy $124^{1\frac{1}{2}}$
Timeform rating: 70+						Maiden 8500					*Tracked leaders,led 150y*
7May01♦ Doncaster(GB)	gd	7f	Ⓣ Str	$1{:}25^3$	3↑	Unicyclist Maiden Stakes	$2^{2\frac{1}{2}}$	Tebbutt M	124	5.00	Alnahaam $124^{2\frac{1}{2}}$ Golden Dragon $124^{\frac{1}{2}}$ Far Note 124no
Timeform rating: 81+						Maiden 9800					*Tracked in 3rd,bid 2f out,bumped and angled right 1f*
19Apr01♦ Newmarket(GB)	sf	7f	Ⓣ Str	$1{:}28^4$		Alex Scott Maiden Stakes	6^8	Robinson P	123	20.00	Smirk 123^5 Indian File $123^{\frac{3}{4}}$ Anadonis $123^{1\frac{1}{4}}$
Timeform rating: 72						Maiden 10900					*Tracked leaders,weakened*

WORKS: Feb7 SA Ⓣ 5f fm 1:00 H (d)*2/8* Feb2 SA Ⓣ 6f fm 1:16 H (d)*4/7* Jan27 SA Ⓣ 5f fm $1{:}04^1$ H (d)*5/6* Jan17 SA Ⓣ 5f fm $1{:}02^4$ H (d)*7/8* Jan9 SA Ⓣ 4f fm $:48^2$ H (d)*2/4* Jan2 SA Ⓣ 4f fm $:50^2$ H (d)*2/5*
TRAINER: 1stW/Trn(10 .10 $1.10) 61-180Days(6 .00 $0.00) Turf(13 .15 $3.17) Sprint(25 .16 $2.06) Alw(13 .23 $3.43)

Success with European imports is not confined to major stables; smaller outfits can do just as well and often at higher prices. During the 2002 winter meet at Santa Anita, a nugget was uncovered based on decent European form. Golden Dragon had shown himself to be a good European sprinter, and when he made his U.S. debut for trainer Mike Puype he was overlooked by bettors at odds of 17-1 despite meeting easier foes than he had raced credibly against overseas.

SEVENTH RACE
Santa Anita
FEBRUARY 13, 2002

ABOUT 6½ FURLONGS. (Turf) (1.11) ALLOWANCE OPTIONAL CLAIMING . Purse $54,000 (plus $16,200 CBOIF – CA Bred Owner Fund) FOR FOUR–YEAR–OLDS AND UPWARD WHICH HAVE NOT WON EITHER $3,000 TWICE OTHER THAN MAIDEN, CLAIMING, OR STARTER OR WHICH HAVE NEVER WON THREE RACES OR CLAIMING PRICE OF $80,000. Four–year–olds 122 lbs.; Older 123 lbs. Non–winners of two races since December15 allowed, 2 lbs. A race since then, 4 lbs. (Races for $62,500 or less not considered). (Allowance horses preferred). (Rail at 30 Feet).

Value of Race: $54,324 Winner $32,400; second $10,800; third $6,480; fourth $3,240; fifth $1,404. Mutuel Pool $352,445.00 Exacta Pool $234,695.00 Quinella Pool $27,520.00 Trifecta Pool $245,447.00 Superfecta Pool $96,106.00

Last Raced	Horse	M/Eqt. A. Wt	PP	St	¼	½	Str	Fin	Jockey	Cl'g Pr	Odds $1
28Jly01 8Dmr12	Romanzo	LB 5 119	9	1	4hd	5½	31	11	Stevens G L		14.30
5Oct01 NEW8	Golden Dragon-GB	LB b 4 118	7	8	10	8½	71	2½	Gomez G K		17.90
3Sep01 8Dmr7	Euribor-Ire	LB 4 118	4	10	53½	42	4½	31	Smith M E		3.30
1Jly01 DPP3	Alyzig	LB b 5 119	2	6	2½	21½	21	42½	Desormeaux K J		13.30
12Jan02 5SA4	Flying Rudolph	LB b 5 119	8	2	62½	62½	6½	5hd	Espinoza V		5.10
11Jan02 7SA4	Pacing the Cage	LB 4 118	1	9	91½	9½	93	61	Enriquez I D		7.50
11Jan02 7SA2	Devil's Roar	LB 4 118	3	5	12½	11½	1hd	71	Pincay L Jr		1.90
5Jan02 7SA7	Lampedusa	LB b 5 119	10	3	8hd	7½	8hd	8hd	Valdivia J Jr		41.30
10Jun00 9Bel8	Hugh Hefner	LB b 5 119	5	4	33	3hd	51½	91	Nakatani C S		9.80
23Jun01 4Hol3	Winston Chi	LB b 4 118	6	7	7½	10	10	10	Delahoussaye E		27.50

OFF AT 4:12 Start Good . Won driving. Course firm.
TIME :211, :431, 1:063, 1:122 (:21.28, :43.21, 1:06.60, 1:12.50)

$2 Mutuel Prices:

9 – ROMANZO	30.60	13.80	8.40
7 – GOLDEN DRAGON–GB		17.80	11.20
4 – EURIBOR–IRE			4.20

$1 EXACTA 9–7 PAID $263.10 $2 QUINELLA 7–9 PAID $279.80
$1 TRIFECTA 9–7–4 PAID $1,959.10 $1 SUPERFECTA 9–7–4–2 PAID $10,958.80

B. g, (Apr), by French Deputy – Nightatmisskittys , by Al Mamoon . Trainer Greenman Dean. Bred by Northwest Farms (Ky).

ROMANZO chased outside a rival down the hill, swung out four wide into the stretch and closed gamely under left handed urging to gain the lead in deep stretch, then held. GOLDEN DRAGON (GB) settled off the rail then three deep, angled in some on the hill, also came out four wide into the stretch and closed with a rush on the far outside. EURIBOR (IRE) squeezed a bit at the start, saved ground chasing the leaders, came off the rail for room in midstretch and continued willingly. ALYZIG stalked the leader a bit off the rail, bid outside that one in the stretch, had the rider lose the whip past the eighth pole and was outfinished. FLYING RUDOLPH chased three deep then off the rail, came four wide into the stretch and lacked the needed rally. PACING THE CAGE saved ground unhurried down the hill and improved position in the stretch. DEVIL'S ROAR broke through the gate before the start, sped to a clear early lead, set the pace inside, fought back when challenged in the stretch but weakened late. LAMPEDUSA settled three deep then angled in down the hill, came out in the stretch and did not rally. HUGH HEFNER stalked outside a rival or off the rail down the hill, came out into the stretch and weakened. WINSTON CHI chased between horses early then dropped back outside a rival and had little left for the stretch.

Owners– 1, Greenman Jean; 2, Cobra Farm Inc; 3, Robins Shirley; 4, Taub Steve; 5, Alpert David and Herb; 6, Desperado Stables Inc; 7, Columbine Stable; 8, Bloodstock Management Services Inc and Preston Wood Farm LLC; 9, King Edward Racing Stable; 10, Reddam J Paul

Trainers– 1, Greenman Dean; 2, Puype Mike; 3, Drysdale Neil; 4, Pinfield Timothy; 5, Stute Melvin F; 6, West Ted H; 7, Greely C Beau; 8, Canani Julio C; 9, Jones Martin F; 10, Dollase Craig

Scratched– Lookn East (27Jan02 1SA 1) , Al Mamaaliq (06Oct01 221707CUR7)

$2 Daily Double (4–9) Paid $140.00 ; Daily Double Pool $25,264 .
$1 Pick Three (2–4–9) Paid $420.20 ; Pick Three Pool $64,754 .

Golden Dragon fired, but missed by a length. Darn. The example still applies. When a logical contender starts at high odds, a bettor does not have to be right often. Here's an example that occurred during the 2001 summer meet at Del Mar. Trainer Ben Cecil's record with European imports was already an unqualified success. But it was an astute observation made by a retired schoolteacher named Easy Hellerstein at a handicapping seminar 10 years earlier that pointed the right way. Hellerstein had noticed European imports making their U.S. debuts had performed spectacularly at Del Mar over the years. His angle referred primarily to imports from France.

Like most "angles," Hellerstein's was based in logic. Turf racing is stronger in Europe than in the U.S., where the top horses generally gravitate to dirt. Research provided validation: European imports have tended to outperform expectations in the

ﬨ Del Mar. So when Cecil brought in a 3-year-old filly
her U.S. debut in one of the strongest turf stakes of the
ﬨe Grade 1 Del Mar Oaks—a dilemma arose because she
ﬨally did not fit the system. She was from England, not
France. But the reasoning was sound—European imports often
have outrun their odds. Cecil was no dummy, nor were the advis-
ers for owner Gary Tanaka. They recommended the purchase of
the filly in Europe, with the aim of running in the Oaks.

It was not an easy race; few Grade 1's are. And turning for
home, the 21-1 longshot import had only one horse beat. But
then she swung to the far outside, lowered her head, and produced an electrifying stretch run. Golden Apples scorched the
Del Mar turf, sizzled her final three furlongs in less than 34 seconds, outfinished Affluent by a length, and returned $44. I had
her. Well, sort of. In what ranks as an utterly moronic wagering
decision, I had singled her in a pick-three sequence that did not
end until one race later. I still had to sweat out one more race.
Fortunately, the pick three landed at $1,056.70 and I won. But I
felt like an idiot for allowing a 21-1 longshot to slip past without betting on her to win. Clever handicapping was nearly
spoiled by absent-minded wagering strategy (a subject that will
be discussed in a later chapter).

Daily Racing Form past performances for European imports
include Timeform ratings, which are subjective assessments
based on a horse's performances and provide a broad appraisal
of ability, which can be used to measure the class level at which
he may fit in the U.S.

A Timeform rating of 130 or higher denotes the horse is an
above-average Group 1 winner; 125-129 means an average
Group 1 winner; 115-120, an average Group 2 winner; 110-115,
an average Group 3 winner; 100-105, an average listed-race
winner. Timeform ratings are not speed figures. However, some
handicappers compare them to Beyer figures by subtracting 14
points from the Timeform rating.

Southern Hemisphere imports, too, have made their mark in
the U.S. Grade 1 winners such as Candy Ride, Bayakoa, Paseana,
and Lido Palace all started their careers in South America;
Happyanunoit started in New Zealand. All were south of the
equator, which presents a handicapping enigma. Dozens of
Southern Hemisphere horses are imported each year to the U.S.,
and they often require lengthy acclimation periods before return-

ing to the form they established in their native land. The transition period often requires several races.

A demanding handicapper will insist that a Southern Hemisphere horse reestablish his credentials in North America. Unlike an import from Europe, a Southern Hemisphere import faces too many variables to be expected to reproduce his best form in his first North American start. After all, a Southern Hemisphere horse is accustomed to a winter that begins in June, and a summer that begins in December. Until he shows something in the U.S., let him prove what he can do. The new shooters will beat you sometimes. So what?

Weight

One of the most talked-about subjects in handicapping is the amount of weight that a horse is assigned to carry in a race. The impost includes the jockey, saddle, and lead weights. Weight assignments generally range from 113 to 122 pounds. In most cases, the conditions of the race mandate weight assignments and are based on recent performance, age, or gender.

For example, in an allowance race for 3-year-olds and up, older horses may be assigned to carry 123 pounds while 3-year-olds may be assigned only 117. In theory, the disparity allows younger horses to run faster than they would if they were carrying a higher weight. Because older horses generally are faster than younger horses, the weight difference narrows the gap. Weight will slow down a horse.

Fillies and mares often receive a five-pound weight concession when entered against colts and geldings. Horses also can receive weight concessions when they have not won a certain type of race within a specified period of time. For example, the conditions of a race may read "nonwinners of a race since July 1 . . . two pounds." That means if a horse that has not won a race within the period of time, he gets an additional two pounds off his assigned weight.

Weight assignments are written into the conditions of the race, but in handicap races, the racing secretary assigns weights based on the perceived ability of the runners. In the 1991 Hollywood Gold Cup for example, Marquetry had a 12-pound weight advantage over Grade 1 winner Farma Way. Marquetry won. The weight helped make a difference.

Usually, it does not. The truth is, weight is a relatively minor handicapping factor. Better horses carry more weight than lesser horses. Better horses also win more races. Weight does become important, however, when there is a significant change from a previous assignment and/or a large difference between horses' weights.

For example, a horse carrying 123 pounds wins by a half-length over one carrying 118. Now they meet again, and the winner carries 126 while the runner-up carries only 116. The five-pound shift can make a difference. It is unclear exactly how much difference it makes, and handicappers should not get bogged down in petty details. That is, unless the disparity is slapping you in the face.

Apprentice jockeys receive "weight allowances" that theoretically compensate for their inexperience. A horse ridden by an apprentice carries less weight than horses ridden by experienced journeyman riders. A California apprentice begins with a 10-pound allowance, which lasts until he wins his fifth race, after which he rides with a seven-pound allowance until he wins his 40th race, or for one full year following his fifth win. If the apprentice has not won 40 races during that time, he rides with a five-pound allowance for one more year or until his 40th win, whichever comes first.

Few doubt that the less weight a horse carries, the faster he may run. However, less weight rarely compensates for a jockey's inexperience. During the 2003 Del Mar summer meet, apprentice Mick Ruis rode with a seven-pound allowance. He won just four races from 69 starts, and his mounts repeatedly found traffic trouble or were weakly handled. The ratio of wins, seconds, and thirds posted by Ruis told all: four wins, nine seconds, three thirds. He finished second more than twice as often as he won, which was less than 6 percent.

On a more positive note, Ruis left the competitive Southern California circuit following the Del Mar meet and relocated to Phoenix, where he rode at Turf Paradise and became the leading rider. When he returned to California, he was a better jockey.

Equipment and Medication

Equipment and medication can affect a horse's performance. A significant piece of equipment that is listed in past-performance lines is blinkers. These are plastic eye cups of varying size and configuration, attached to a nylon hood, which fits on the horse's head and restricts his lateral vision. The purpose of blinkers is to keep a horse focused on what is in front of him, rather than being distracted by peripheral views. A horse that adds blinkers often produces more early speed than in previous races. Leading rider Jerry Bailey discussed what adding blinkers can do.

"The two things it generally does is make them focus, and make them more aggressive, which translates into a little more speed. They're like kids. It's hard to keep them concentrated on one thing for an extended period of time. So, some of them you have to help out by equipment; blinkers. Once they get the idea, you can remove them. Sometimes they'll become too aggressive and it'll hinder their running style." In spring 2003, Bailey recommended that blinkers be added to Empire Maker's equipment.

e Maker
monte Farms Inc

Dk. b or b. c. 3 (Apr)
Sire: Unbridled (Fappiano) $200,000
Dam: Toussaud (El Gran Senor)
Br: Juddmonte Farms, Inc. (Ky)
Tr: Frankel Robert J(0 0 0 0 .00) 2003:(388 113 .29)

Life	8	4	3	1	$1,985,800	111
2003	6	3	3	0	$1,936,200	111
2002	2	1	0	1	$49,600	92
	0	0	0	0	$0	-

D.Fst	6	2	3	1	$935,800	110
Wet(383)	2	2	0	0	$1,050,000	111
Turf(306)	0	0	0	0	$0	-
Dst(0)	0	0	0	0	$0	-

;ar	fst	1⅛	:47	1:10³	1:35	1:48	JimDandy-G2	**110**	5	5⁶	5⁶½	5³½	2²	2ⁿᵏ	Bailey J D	L123	b	*.30	95-11	Strong Hope121ⁿᵏ Empire Maker1232½ Congrats1151	Game finish outside	6
3el	sly	1½	:48³	1:13²	2:02³	2:28¹	Belmont-G1	**110**	1	2¹	2ʰᵈ	1¹	1¹½	1¾	Bailey J D	L126	b	2.00	91-14	EmpirMkr126¾ TnMostWntd1264¼ FunnyCid1265¼	Stalked 4wide, gamely	6
;D	fst	1¼	:46¹	1:10²	1:35³	2:01	KyDerby-G1	**106**	11	8⁵½	8⁴	3¹½	3½	2¹¾	Bailey J D	L126	b	*2.50	92-06	*Funny Cide*1261¾ *Empire Maker*126ʰᵈ Peace Rules126ʰᵈ	5w bid,2ndbest	16
\qu	my	1⅛	:47¹	1:11	1:35⁴	1:48³	WoodMem-G1	**111**	8	3²½	3²	3¹½	1ʰᵈ	1½	Bailey J D	L123	b	*.55	93-12	Empire Maker123½ *Funny Cide*1237½ Kissin Saint1231	3 wide, drift in late	8
;P	fst	1⅛	:46¹	1:10³	1:36	1:49	FlaDerby-G1	**108**	6	4²½	3¹½	2¹	1½	1⁹¾	Bailey J D	L122	b	2.10	97-10	*Empire Maker*1229¾ Trust N Luck122½ Indy Dancer1222½	Drew off, driving	7
;A	fst	1⅛	:46¹	1:10²	1:35³	1:48¹	ⓇSham81k	**98**	5	6⁶½	7⁵½	5²¾	3²	2¹	Bailey J D	LB115		*.40	92-11	ManAmongMen1201 *EmpireMaker*1152 Spensive1205½	Split foes,inside bid	7

"He would get his position early, and he would lose position throughout the middle of the race. He would lose focus. He would be closer going into the first turn than he would be at the half-mile pole. Somewhere in that space he would lose position. For him, it was lack of focus. [Blinkers] made him more attentive, which translated into him being more aggressive."

The "blinkers on" category of trainer form provides a clue to potential improvement of a horse that is adding them. Sometimes, as in the case of Empire Maker, blinkers on can be a reason for improved performance. Second-time starters that add blinkers often produce significant improvement. The addition of blinkers generally has a greater impact than removal of blinkers, though taking the blinkers off can make an aggressive horse relax.

A piece of equipment that some consider a source of alarm is "front wraps." These are supportive bandages that can indicate weakness in a horse's front legs. The addition of front wraps often means the horse is less physically sound than in previous races. However, addition or removal of front wraps is not a stand-alone factor. As with any change, front wraps (on or off) must be considered in the context of other more important factors.

Southern California trainers Paul Aguirre and Carla Gaines use front wraps on nearly every horse they start. And so what? Fusaichi Pegasus wore front wraps, and all he did was win the Kentucky Derby. There are so many other standards by which to measure a horse's current form that it can be a study in frustration to guess the motive behind the addition or removal of front wraps. Sometimes, wraps are merely a decoy.

Captain Squire was entered in a $62,500 claiming race for 3-year-olds on January 9, 2002, following an impressive daylight maiden win. However, trainer Jeff Mullins did not want Captain Squire to be claimed, so he added front wraps, hoping potential buyers would consider them a sign of a possible weakness. No one claimed Captain Squire, who won by eight lengths, and as of late 2003 he was closing in on the million-dollar earnings mark. From 2001 through late 2003, Captain Squire wore wraps only that once.

Some handicappers have legitimate concerns regarding front wraps, and believe their addition is a negative handicapping factor. It's no point debating the issue. However, incidental details such as front wraps and blinkers have to be analyzed in the context of the overall situation. There is usually more to the story.

Medication is a similar consideration, though less relevant because most horses already are treated with Lasix, Butazolidin ("Bute"), or both. Lasix, the trade name for furosemide (also called Salix), acts as a diuretic and reduces pressure on capillaries. This helps prevent hemorrhaging in the lungs, or "bleeding." A front-runner that has been tiring in his races, possibly because of bleeding, may improve when treated with Lasix. Butazolidin, the trade name for phenylbutazone, is an anti-inflammatory medication. The impact of these permissible medications—Lasix and Bute—is not a primary handicapping factor.

The upper-right corner of a horse's past performances—the career box—includes a plethora of information, divided in two segments. The area on the left side contains the horse's records for his lifetime, the current year, the previous year, and at the track at which he is running today. The right side of the career box includes his record on different track surfaces—dirt (fast), wet, turf—and at today's approximate distance. Each segment also includes the highest Beyer Speed Figure a horse has earned in that category.

A useful aspect of the lifetime-record segment is determining the ratio of wins, seconds, and thirds. A horse whose second-place finishes outnumber his wins may be a perennial "hanger" who never quite gets there.

The best-Beyer listing can be compared to the horse's most recent figure, although a veteran who just ran his all-time best might be considered unlikely to repeat it. Or, the best-Beyer listing can be a signal of potential improvement for a horse whose recent figures show an upward pattern.

An older horse whose current-year ratio of wins to seconds has declined relative to his career totals may be growing wise. Horses sometimes lose their will to win, and become mere pack animals who are content to race alongside other horses. They maintain position, even without trying to win.

Specific-surface records (fast, wet, turf) may show distinct preferences for a particular footing, while the horse's record at today's distance and track can reveal other patterns. A "horse for the course" is one whose record on the surface of today's race is out of proportion and superior to his lifetime record. Horses often perk up at certain tracks or times of year when that track is running. When a horse is returning to a course over which he has had success in the past, a handicapper must recognize the possibility of improvement over recent races. Should you take a short price based on a horse's course record? No. Short prices should be accepted only when the fundamentals of handicapping are in alignment.

The patterns in racing repeat again and again. Workouts and weight assignments are insignificant relative to condition, class, speed, and pace.

When you see something happen at the racetrack, it's probably not the first time it has happened. And you can bet that it will not be the last. The question is, how do you put it all into play? That is the subject of the next chapter.

6

BETTING
THEORY

Every horseplayer has a handicapping workshop that is a little bit different. It might be a quiet office desk, the kitchen table, or the living-room sofa—a comfortable place to spread out *Daily Racing Form* and start marking the past performances.

My first was an old wooden desk in my bedroom. It had a small green lamp in the corner, under a bulletin board filled with photographs, a traffic citation, a presidential campaign button, a rock concert advertisement for Ted Nugent, a spring-semester sign-up schedule for classes at Pasadena City College, and the 1976-77 winter racing schedule at Santa Anita. A lot of miscellaneous junk that 18-year-olds save. It was a little corner of my own little room, and it was cool.

It turned out to be a place of discovery and refuge. It was January 1977, and I had graduated six months earlier from Arcadia High, a mile from Santa Anita. College would wait until spring. I was saving money while working as assistant manager at McDonald's, and living at home. Not exactly a rocket launch for a high school graduate, though there were two reliable places to escape—my old wooden desk and the racetrack. The Santa Anita winter meet had opened a few weeks earlier, and I had the next day off. That night I bought a copy of *Daily Racing Form* and spread it across my desk. Pen in hand, I dove in.

The first race was a $12,500 claiming sprint for fillies and mares, and there she was—Fresh Fruit. She had not raced in almost three months, but was dropping one class level for a good trainer, Hal King. A sharp five-furlong workout (59.20) only a few days earlier signaled Fresh Fruit's readiness. She figured to be one of the favorites.

The second race was another filly-mare claiming sprint. Lady Nephilim's form was erratic, but she was cutting back to a sprint after fading in a series of routes against better company. She was sure to be overlooked—a live longshot. One other contender was Tif Tif. The next day I would be going to the track with $20, and planned to invest $4 in the daily double. The entire handicapping process took an hour. Only two races and I was beat. I turned out the lights, and went to sleep.

The guy I was supposed to meet in the Santa Anita clubhouse was a no-show. Too bad for him. Post time for the first race was approaching. I wagered as I'd planned—two $2 daily-double tickets keying Fresh Fruit in race 1, to Lady Nephilim and Tif Tif in race 2. The worst-case scenario? I would have just $16 for the rest of the card. Fresh Fruit, back from a three-month layoff with a fast work four days earlier, showed unexpected speed in race 1 and was on the lead at the quarter pole. She shook off every challenge, and held by a nose over stretch-runner White Jade.

My double ticket was halfway home, from a $10.20 winner to two longshots. Tif Tif fell to the rear in race 2 and stayed there, but 27-1 Lady Nephilim was forwardly placed and positioned fourth down the backstretch. This time she did not quit in the stretch, as she had done in her two-turn races. Lady Nephilim was a half-length from the lead at the quarter pole, and the same margin at the eighth pole. The co-favorites were running one-two, and Lady Nephilim kept grinding. And grinding, and grinding. Would she get up?

At the wire, Lady Nephilim dropped her head in time, nailed the favorite, and won by a nose. I was a teenage handicapping genius, with a $415.40 daily double to prove it. It was big bucks in 1977. Bet a little, win a lot. And I still remember exactly what it smelled like in the corner of my room, at the old wooden desk with the small green lamp. It was there that I realized I would always be a horseplayer. I might as well learn to be a better handicapper.

The $415 jackpot has long since been spent, and countless wagers have flamed out since. But that 1977 triumph left an impact. Beyond paying for spring-semester tuition, it cemented the notion that a small bettor did stand a chance. And some of the old-school handicapping maxims still work 25 years later. Fresh Fruit was a comebacker dropping one level with a fast recent work and a winning trainer. Lady Nephilim had been fading going long. This time she was going short—the familiar route-to-sprint play. Both angles still work. I doubt I was that clever that day. More likely, I just got lucky.

Winning at the races seems relatively easy in a peaceful study or the pages of a book, where everything is clean and tidy and quiet. There are no distractions, no pressure, and no such thing as real money. Real-time racetrack chaos is a whole different story. Perhaps you have felt it on a bad day when every handicapping opinion has been wrong. You've lost the first seven races, and your money is almost gone, and a 15-1 longshot is enticing but the 8-5 favorite looks safe. The choices are to wimp out and bet the chalk, or wager on the outsider. Are handicappers as brave for the last race as for the first? The urge to cash a ticket—to be right just once—is what pulls many horseplayers into playing it safe. And it's too bad.

Horseplayers who win often must choose between the most likely winner and the most sensible wager. The contradiction is a major sticking point and one reason most horseplayers do not sustain long-term profit. Many lose, even though they do not have to. Horseplayers bet too many underlays—horses whose chances of winning are lower than their odds. Good handicapping goes beyond picking winners. Novice horseplayers may wonder, why the contradiction? Why not simply find the horse you like and bet that horse to win? It's a good question.

The quandary is that not every horse is "priced" the same, nor do they all have the same chance to win. Horses' odds differ based on public perception. A horse with the most perceived positive attributes will attract the most wagering action. There are few surprises. The favorite's advantage usually is recognizable, and bettors wager accordingly. Lopsidedly, sometimes. The horse may be so heavily favored that his odds are disproportionate to his real chance to win. He may have a 50 percent chance, but his odds may be 4-5.

See the problem? At 4-5, long-term losses are guaranteed, even for a horse that wins half the time. A 4-5 shot returns only $3.60 for each $2 win wager. Make the same bet 100 times, for a total investment of $200. Win 50 times, and receive total payoffs of $180 (that is, 50 winning bets at $3.60 each; 50 x $3.60 = $180). It's a loss of $20, notwithstanding a 50 percent win rate.

Purchasing a sensible bet is a matter of considering risk and reward. The sooner a bettor accepts the reality that most wagers are losers, the greater his chance to win long-term. It is not necessarily a bad thing to lose a bet. Losses are a reminder of what we still have to learn; wins provide confidence to continue. Most illustrations in this text are winning examples, but for every horse that won, there were many others that did not. Sometimes a horse runs up the track for no apparent reason. It is not a problem. The key is managing risk and reward. A winning bettor will wait until the potential reward outweighs the risk—when a payoff is disproportionately high. It does not happen often with a horse that wins half the time.

At odds of 4-5, losses are guaranteed. But in the same race, for example, another horse may be estimated to have a 10 percent chance. Perhaps his positive attributes are not easily recognized, and his odds are 14-1 (he would pay $30). See the possibility? If the 10 percent win estimate is reasonably close, profits are assured, even winning just one out of 10. Make the same $2 bet on that horse 100 times, for a total investment of $200. Lose 90, win 10, and receive total payoffs of $300, for a profit of $100. It works in theory. In reality, it is considerably more difficult.

Handicappers must be sharp enough to recognize a longshot that has more than just a prayer. The opportunity does not occur every race. Furthermore, few bettors possess the necessary discipline to forsake frequent winners (favorites win one of three) in favor of a longshot that may win only one out of 10. It's one of the hardest parts of the game. The favorite is the horse on which most others have wagered, and happy cheers of bettors who backed the favorite seemingly grow higher, along with a longshot bettor's stack of losing tickets. When wagering on low-probability, high-return horses, it is not unusual to go an entire afternoon, even a week, without winning a bet.

It may not sound like much fun. But what is fun? For some, it may be cashing tickets on winning horses. Fine, bet the favorite every race and spend the rest of the afternoon socializing. There is nothing at all wrong with that. For others, fun is being ahead of the game at the end of the month, meet, or year.

The way to accomplish this is by accepting risk (making a bet) only when it is justified by the potential reward. Low risk generally translates to low reward in the form of low payoffs. And because most horseplayers sacrifice reward in order to cash tickets, "overlays" in low-odds ranges rarely occur. An overlay is when the horse's odds are higher than his actual chance to win. An 8-5 shot ($5.60) with a 50 percent chance to win is an overlay. An underlay is when the horse's odds are lower than his actual chance to win. A 4-5 shot ($3.60) with a 50 percent chance is an underlay.

Low-odds runners occasionally offer "value." There are a thousand examples—Tiznow winning the 2001 Santa Anita Handicap at even money, or Fusaichi Pegasus winning the 2000 Kentucky Derby at 2.30-1. Some thought Empire Maker, the 2-1 second choice, was a cinch in the 2003 Belmont. There is nothing wrong with betting on favorites. A beginning horseplayer will handicap a race, find a horse he likes, and bet him regardless of odds. It's okay, for now. There is a learning curve to handicapping, however, and sooner or later a bettor may realize that backing short prices is not doing much good in the long run. And so, a winning bettor must learn to lose.

Defeat in a single race means nothing. It is merely a by-product of betting. And while selection-based, pick-the-winner handicappers collect more often than value-minded (bet-the-overlay) handicappers, selection-oriented methods eventually must surrender. Favorites win one out of three. When the payoffs on favorites exceed the cost of the wagers ($18 on a nine-race card), it's a winning day. A New York bettor who wagered on every favorite during the 2003 fall meet at Belmont would have won 120 of 355 races, enjoyed 12 winning days, and cashed at least one ticket every day but one during the 38-day meet. But at the end of the meet, the bottom line would have been $710 invested, only $612.80 returned—86 cents on the dollar. It was a losing meet, typical for any race meet in which a bettor wagers on every post-time favorite.

It's a reliable long-range percentage—and it's a losing proposition. Even so, bettors often prefer the relative comfort of a favorite.

ightseek
wn: Juddmonte Farms
een, Pink Sash, White Sleeves, Pink
J D (—) 2003: (730 196 .27)

Ch. f. 4 (Feb)
Sire: Distant View (Mr. Prospector) $20,000
Dam: Viviana (Nureyev)
Br: Juddmonte Farms Inc (Ky)
Tr: Frankel Robert(19 5 3 2 .26) 2003:(325 98 .30)

L 123

Life	12	8	4	0	$1,319,866	115	D.Fst	10	7	3	0	$1,130,266	115
2003	7	4	3	0	$1,057,888	115	Wet(352)	1	1	0	0	$180,000	110
2002	5	4	1	0	$261,978	100	Turf(332)	1	0	1	0	$9,600	85
SA	3	0	3	0	$140,000	108	Dst(356)	4	2	2	0	$700,000	115

Bel fst	1⅛	:474	1:122	1:363	1:491	3↑ⒻBeldame-G1	**107**	2	51½	53	3nk	12½	14½	Bailey J D	L123	*.30	84-26	Sightseek1234½ Bird Town1204¾ **Buy the Sport**120¾	When asked, in hand	7
Sar fst	1⅛	:491	1:132	1:38	1:504	3↑ⒻGoFWandH-G1	**115**	5	31½	21½	2½	18	111½	Bailey J D	L121	*.15	81-27	*Sightseek*12111½ *ShesGotthBt*1125 NonsuchBy1134	When ready, ridden out	6
Bel sly	1 1/16	:222	:451	1:091	1:404	3↑ⒻOPhippsH-G1	**110**	2	2½	2½	2hd	11½	15	Bailey J D	L118	*1.05	96-18	*Sightseek*1185 **TakeChrgeLdy**1195 MndysGold1181¾	Drew clear under drive	5
CD fst	7f	:222	:452	1:10	1:22	4↑ⒻHmnaDstH-G1	**107**	2	5	51¼	51½	11½	14½	Bailey J D	L116	*.80	92-08	*Sightseek*1164½ Gold Mover119hd Miss Lodi1142¼	Split foes,3w,driving	8
SA fst	1⅛	:47	1:103	1:353	1:481	4↑ⒻSMrgrtaH-G1	**108**	4	11	11	11½	2hd	22	Valdivia J Jr	LB116	2.50	91-16	Starrer1212 *Sightseek*1163 Bella Bellucci1165	Inside, 2nd best	5
SA fst	1⅛	:463	1:104	1:353	1:482	ⒻLaCanada-G2	**105**	1	1½	1hd	1hd	1½	2¾	Valenzuela P A	LB118	*.90	91-11	**Got Koko**121¾ Sightseek1181½ Bella Bellucci1183	Bit off rail,worn down	5
SA fst	7f	:22	:443	1:092	1:22	4↑ⒻSntMncaH-G1	**101**	5	6	41½	3nk	11	2½	Bailey J D	LB115	*.70	95-07	Affluent119½ Sightseek1151½ Secret of Mecca1103	Bid 3wd,led,willingly	7
Aqu fst	1	:23	:45	1:093	1:352	3↑ⒻTopFlgtH-G2	**100**	7	2½	41½	2½	2½	11¾	Bailey J D	L113	*1.40	89-19	Sightseek1131¾ *Zonk*116¾ Nasty Storm1165½	Stalked wide, clear	9
Kee fst	7f	:223	:454	1:112	1:234	ⒻRavenRun-G3	**98**	7	11	52¼	41¾	21	13¼	Bailey J D	L117	*.90	85-23	*Sightseek*1173¼ Miss Lodi123hd Respectful1176¼	Slow start,between,drv	12
Bel fst	1 1/16	:231	:461	1:104	1:411	3↑ⒻAlw 48000N1X	**99**	1	21	1½	1hd	18	112	Bailey J D	L117	*.35	94-11	*Sightseek*11712 ClerDestiny1171¼ *TresureBech*1192	When asked, ridden out	7
Sar fm	1 Ⓣ	:231	:461	1:11	1:354	3↑ⒻAlw 48000N2L	**85**	1	23	28	2½	2½	2¾	Bailey J D	L117	*.85	88-11	Title Nine119¾ *Sightseek*1171¼ Marquet Rent1175¼	Dug in gamely inside	6
Sar fst	6f	:222	:46	:582	1:11	3↑ⒻMd Sp Wt 45k	**89**	7	6	51½	31	11½	17¾	Bailey J D	L118	1.70	87-14	Sightseek1187¾ Truly a Legend1181¼ Adversity1182¾	Going away, driving	7

●Oct19 Hol 5f fst :591 H *1/26* **Sep29 Bel 4f fst :50 B** *9/11* **●Sep21 Bel 6f fst 1:103 H** *1/10* **Sep14 Bel 4f fst :492 B(d)** *3/22* **●Sep6 Bel 5f fst :582 H** *1/63* **Aug27 Sar 5f fst 1:022 B** *3/5*
: 2Off45-180(228 .33 $2.20) Dirt(256 .31 $1.95) Routes(649 .27 $1.86) GrdStk(302 .29 $1.94)

Favorites frequently are underlaid; their odds do not accurately reflect their chances. The potential reward is less than the risk, and an example occurred in the first Breeders' Cup race of 2003. Most horseplayers expected Distaff favorite Sightseek to win, and she was hammered to odds of 3-5. She had much in her favor—sharp current condition, multiple Grade 1 wins, high Beyer Speed Figures, and a versatile running style adaptable to any pace scenario. Sightseek, however, offered negligible value at 3-5. To profit in the long run backing horses at 3-5, a bettor would have to win at least 63 out of 100 races (63 x $3.20 = $201.60).

Few handicappers win consistently at such a high rate, and backing low-odds horses leaves virtually no margin for error or chaos. While racing is predictable over the long term, unpredictable things occur in the short term, and they did in the Distaff. Sightseek lost position early, bled, and floundered. Few predicted her fourth-place finish, but no reasonable horseplayer could expect Sightseek to win 63 out of 100, either.

While it is easy to look back on a loser as an illustration, the reality is that horses such as Sightseek win often. They do. Studies show that favorites at 7-10 and lower win slightly more than half their starts. There is no getting around it. Yet high win percentage does not necessarily correlate to a sensible wager.

One unique quality of racing is that the odds are not predetermined; they are merely the consensus opinion of the wagering public. It is the opposite of the fixed odds of a casino game. On a roulette wheel, black always pays even money, regardless of how much money was bet on the color. But at the track, the odds are determined by bettors. A further explanation of wagering pools is found in Chapter 7. In short, the more money that is wagered on a horse, the lower the payoff. There are more winning bettors to pay off. The less money wagered on a horse, the higher the payoff. There are fewer winning bettors to pay off. The idea is to find discrepancies between a horse's odds and his actual chance to win.

Horses often are more heavily favored than they should be. Every race has a favorite, no matter how weak the race might be. And bad favorites do win. It does not mean they were good bets. Perhaps the most frustrating part of wagering on low-odds horses is that it leaves no margin for error. To make money backing short prices, a bettor must be right an awful lot of the time. Which makes it tough when chaos steps in. In the Breeders' Cup, Sightseek bled, which was an unpredictable occurrence. In the 1990 Breeders' Cup Sprint, favorite Dayjur was on his way to victory when he inexplicably jumped a shadow in deep stretch, lost his momentum, and got nailed by longshot Safely Kept.

Nothing in racing is preordained. At the Hollywood Park press-box betting window, in autumn 1998, I waited behind trainer Julio Canani as he bet several thousand dollars on his runner in a minor stakes. While it can be useful information to know a trainer is backing his horse at the window, I stayed with the horse I liked. She finished a bad third. Meanwhile, Canani-trained Tranquility Lake, who later won a Grade 1, could not get it done in the Matiara Stakes. At 6-5, she lost by a nose. Even when the trainer likes his horse, everyone else is also trying to win. No race can be predicted with 100 percent certainty. Too many things happen. But over time, patterns emerge. A horse with speed, dropping one class level, may be a legitimate winner in a claiming-race sprint. But one day, he may break slowly and be eliminated at the start. It does not mean he was a poor bet, only that in one chaotic instance, something unexpected happened.

Luck plays a factor in individual races, but over time, luck evens out. I took comfort in that thought after the 2003 Clark Handicap at Churchill Downs. I had keyed 19-1 longshot Aeneas in the exacta and trifecta, under likely winner Evening Attire. It worked out perfectly—Evening Attire won, and Aeneas finished third behind longshot runner-up Quest. The trifecta would pay several hundred. Then Evening Attire was disqualified for interference, and my winning trifecta was worth zero.

I thought it was a questionable call by the stewards, but whether or not Evening Attire should have been disqualified is moot; the fact is that he was. Differences of opinion abound at the track, including interpretations of races yet to be run. Not every handicapper views a race the same way. One person may like a horse because he expects the horse to gain a lonely lead. Another may expect a pace battle to transpire. Someone will be wrong. In order to stand a chance at winning, a bettor must acknowledge the possibility his analysis is the one that is erroneous, and factor that possibility into his wagering scheme. Mathematical wizardry is not required. Simply insist on being paid a fair reward when the wins do occur. And they will. The simple requirement is the ability to recognize when a horse's odds are out of whack. At every price range, there is a possibility a horse has a greater chance, or less, than most believe.

A sensible practice is to rank selections in order of preference, then compare them to the betting public's choices. When the first, second, and third selections correspond to the first, second, and third selections of the public, there may be no advantage. That is, unless bettors have gone overboard.

For example, say Horse A is the most likely winner, yet his advantage over Horse B is considered minimal. Further, bettors hammer Horse A to even money, while Horse B's odds drift to 6-1. It's pretty clear which horse to bet. A horseplayer that can estimate a particular horse's chances to win is miles ahead of the crowd. But it may require waiting out a series of races until one's opinion is unique from the crowd's. The public often makes mistakes. Sometimes, the horse is not as good as his low odds suggest. Other times, a horse may not be as bad as his high odds suggest.

tswhatimtalknbout
vn: Hughes B Wayne
ange/purple Quarters, Orange
D R (361 58 53 43 .16) 2003:(336 54 .16)

Dk. b or br c. 3 (Mar) FTFFEB02 $900,000
Sire: A.P. Indy (Seattle Slew) $300,000
Dam: Lucinda K(Red Ransom)
Br: R&R King Stables (Ky)
Tr: Ellis Ronald W(39 5 6 6 .13) 2003:(37 5 .14)

L 122

Life	4	2	1	1	$119,120	105	D.Fst	3	2	0	1	$69,120 105
2003	4	2	1	1	$119,120	105	Wet(410)	1	0	1	0	$50,000 102
2002	0	M	0	0	$0	–	Turf(335)	0	0	0	0	$0 –
SA	4	2	1	1	$119,120	105	Dst(380)	0	0	0	0	$0 –

SA gd 1 1/16 :22 4 :46 2 1:10 4 1:43 3 San Felipe-G2 102 7 106½ 106¾ 74¾ 62½ 2no Flores D R LB 116 3.20 86 - 19 **BuddyGil**119no Atswhtimtlknbout116¾ Brncusi1161¼ Furious outside rally 10
SA fst 1 1/16 :23 :46 2 1:10 1 1:41 4 Alw 56000N1X 105 2 5 4 54½ 41½ 2½ 1¾ Flores D R LB 118 *.80 95 - 15 Atswhtmtlknbout118¾ *Durng*1183½ BuckIndMnor1202½ 3wd bid,led,gamely 5
SA fst 1 :22 3 :45 1 1:09 3 1:36 Alw 56000N1X 92 6 76¾ 46 3 5 3 5 32½ Flores D R LB 118 *1.70 88 - 16 AplchnThndr1182 NtnWdNs118½ *Atshtmtlnbt*1188½ 4wd 7/8,late bid at 2d 7
SA fst 6f :21 2 :44 2 :57 1:10 1 Md Sp Wt 48k 87 2 11 10 11 109½ 7 5 1½ Flores D R LB 120 *1.50 87 - 11 Atswhtmtlknbot120½ *BckIndMnor*120½ MchImg1201 Off slow,late surge 11

Mar31 SA 5f fst :58 4 H *2/49* Mar25 SA 4f fst :48 4 B *16/29* Mar9 SA 6f fst 1:13 B *9/31* ●Mar3 SA 4f fst :46 2 H *1/47* Feb17 SA 3f gd :36 2 B *2/8* ●Feb9 SA 6f fst 1:11 2 H *1/16*
: Dirt(108 .17 $1.32) Routes(83 .16 $1.92) GrdStk(14 .14 $1.41)

Atswhatimtalknbout was supposed to win the 2003 Santa Anita Derby. He was lightly raced, and well-suited for the 1⅛-mile distance. Atswhatimtalknbout had only one major flaw—he was not particularly fast. In five of the previous six years, the Santa Anita Derby winner had earned a Beyer figure of 108 or higher. Atswhatimtalknbout had yet to run that fast. His last-start Beyer was only 102, down from 105 one race earlier. While many handicappers projected improvement for Atswhatimtalknbout, the reality was he had not run fast enough yet. It was a conspicuous defect, which would have been acceptable if his odds were reasonable. They weren't. At 3-2, Atswhatimtalknbout finished fourth. He simply was not that good.

Conversely, Came Home was not supposed to win the 2002 Pacific Classic at Del Mar. A 10-1 outsider racing against older for the first time, Came Home was not believed to be a genuine mile-and-a-quarter horse. Further, he had yet to earn a Beyer figure good enough to win the Pacific Classic (116 or higher the previous six years). The upside included Came Home's high odds, improving form, and a speed-favoring Del Mar racetrack that frequently carries milers to victory in mile-and-a-quarter races. Came Home won by three-quarters of a length and paid $23. In retrospect, he simply was not that bad.

Ultimately, a bettor who accepts low odds must be reasonably sure the horse qualifies on the fundamentals—current form, class, speed, and pace. When a horse such as Atswhatimtalknbout starts at 3-2 despite a deficiency on a key factor such as speed, it may be time to seek an alternative, or pass the race.

A horseplayer's top selection usually will be the same as everyone else's. There is no shame in sharing the same opinion. It is the nature of the game. Opportunities result when one's opinion differs from the crowd. One benchmark is to insist on a 50 percent overlay—for example, when you believe a horse has a 1-in-5 chance (his odds should be 4-1), and he is hanging on the board at 6-1. A 50 percent overlay allows sufficient leeway for bad luck or mistaken analyses.

Other handicappers wager on any overlay, however minimal. For example, when a horse's odds should be 5-2 and the horse instead is 3-1, they bet. The problem is few handicappers are skilled enough to slice it that thin. A 20 percent overlay does not leave much room for being wrong. And that will happen a lot.

If a horse is 6-5 for reasons unknown, a reexamination of the race is required. And remember, one does not have to wager on every race. Some races are simply inscrutable. It's quite all right to let the race pass without a bet. There is another race in just a few minutes. On the other hand, if it is perfectly evident why a horse's odds are low, and a negative opinion is still held, one may proceed with a wagering strategy against the favorite.

The same applies to longshots. Before wagering on a high-odds horse, one should understand why no one else likes the horse. There will be times when a handicapper believes a horse should be 3-1, but the horse instead is 12-1. It could indicate a faulty analysis. Chances are something has been missed. But what? Look again, and find out. Most middle-priced horses have at least one fundamental flaw. Either their current form appears below par, or they are outclassed, or their speed figures are inferior, or the pace scenario is all wrong.

It does require courage to separate from the crowd, and back a horse no one else likes. And it's fine to do, if one knows the reason why. Things generally fall into place once a handicapper separates reasonable contenders from hopeless pretenders.

A mistake is jumping too far ahead of one's own handicapping skills. It's hard not to after hearing about the South Dakota bettor who wagered $8 on the pick six in the 2003 Breeders' Cup, and won $2.6 million. Or the Petaluma Five, a Northern California quintet that wagered $128 and hit a $1.6 million pick six during the 2003 summer meet at Del Mar. These lovely yarns of human interest rarely happen. And for every small bettor who wins big, a thousand losers shuffle away.

Every horseplayer would love to start winning money right away. If the other guy is doing it, then why not? Usually, the other guy is not doing it. Sorry to break the news, but more horseplayers lose money than win. Success at the races is not as easy or glamorous as it often sounds. The winning pick six at the 2003 Breeders' Cup was funded by thousands of losers, the ones no one heard about.

Take it easy. It's okay for a handicapper to be coldhearted. It might be a necessity. There is more to winning than simply picking the right horses. Yet that is the first step to handicapping—identifying contenders and eliminating noncontenders. The game hinges primarily on the ability of the horse. At the first stage of the handicapping process, odds are not even a consideration. A quick review of the handicapping steps follows.

- Examine the current condition of the entrants. Identify those in acceptable form, and those that are not.
- Ascertain the class level by reading the conditions of the race. Identify which horses are racing at an appropriate level, and those that are not.
- Know the speed-figure par for the type of race, and identify horses that have earned Beyer Speed Figures recently that are reasonably close to par.
- View the likely pace scenario, and identify which horses may be flattered or compromised.

At this stage, contenders emerge. Throw-outs eliminate themselves. The noncontenders will be off form, outclassed, or not fast enough. Usually, a handful of contenders remain, which a handicapper will rank in order of preference. In a field of 10, there may be three or four main contenders. If, as post time nears, there is a 15-1 longshot among those four, a handicapper must know why the odds are that high. When there is a rational explanation (apparently subpar recent races, for example) accompanied by valid reasons to still consider the horse a contender, the situation may provide an opportunity.

Those horses can rescue a patient bettor. The 2003 spring-summer Hollywood Park meet was a losing one for me. I was in action only 39 days of the 65-day meet, wagered a total of $4,942, and got back only $4,001. It translates to an ROI of only 80 cents per dollar. Not a good meet. It would have been worse if not for the last race on a quiet Thursday. It was a race I did not plan to bet, with a horse I did not expect to win.

It was a cheap 2-year-old maiden claiming sprint, with 10 starters and no one special. Lil Bro Eddie was one of a handful with some sort of shot. Nothing more, or less. He looked like an ordinary 10-1 borderline contender with about a 1 in 10 chance. These types of ambiguous horses tend to go one of three directions in the betting. Sometimes they are bet down, and a bettor who used creative handicapping to find the horse may not have been so clever after all. Other times, midpriced horses stay right where they figured to. At about 10-1, they probably are priced in accord with their true chances. Then there are times when a middle-priced longshot is completely ignored, for no good reason. It was happening to Lil Bro Eddie.

Until 10 minutes to post, I planned to sit out the race. But the odds on Lil Bro Eddie were going in only one direction—up. He was 30-1, then 35-1, then 40-1. Lil Bro Eddie was not this bad. He was one of those middle-priced outsiders that occasionally slip through the cracks. He was a contender, nothing more, in a modest field. Lil Bro Eddie was a contender, at a giant price—53-1.

I made three bets on Lil Bro Eddie—to win, keying him in the two-hole in the exacta, and keying him in the three-hole in the trifecta. If Lil Bro Eddie hit the board, I would make a stack. I expected Lil Bro Eddie to show speed, and finish off the board. It would be typical for a 10-1 shot. But the odds on Lil Bro Eddie were five times that high.

Lil Bro Eddie did not win. He pressed the pace inside, and appeared to be struggling on the turn. Stalking Tiger was running away from the field, but Lil Bro Eddie did not give up. He continued to grind away, he kept digging, and in deep stretch he surged into second. The $2 exacta paid $847.20. It was parimutuel salvation; suddenly my wagering deficit was not quite so deep. One never knows when the opportunity for a score will arise. Preparation, and narrowing the contenders beforehand, was the key. It happens in racing, almost every day.

The best handicapper is the public, which sets the odds by wagering on horses according to their approximate chance to win. In fact, horses' odds correspond to their chances with amazing accuracy. Over time, the public has proven to be deadly precise. Horses run to their odds. Jim Cramer of Handicappers Data Warehouse ran a computer study in late 1999 that covered 200,000 races. The study, published in the January 2000 issue of *Meadow's Racing Monthly,* illustrated the public's accuracy.

From 200,000 races:

Horses at 1-5 won 71.9 percent
Horses at 2-5 won 61.3 percent
Horses at 3-5 won 51.6 percent
Horses at 4-5 won 45.1 percent
Horses at 1-1 won 40.4 percent
Horses at 6-5 won 37.3 percent
Horses at 7-5 won 33.9 percent
Horses at 8-5 won 31.0 percent
Horses at 9-5 won 28.8 percent
Horses at 2-1 won 26.9 percent
Horses at 2.20-1 won 25.1 percent
Horses at 2.40-1 won 23.0 percent
Horses at 2.60-1 won 22.6 percent
Horses at 2.80-1 won 20.5 percent
Horses at 3-1 won 19.4 percent

The table suggests it might be impossible to beat the races. It *would* be impossible, for a gambler picking horses by throwing darts. The takeout rate, the 15 to 20 percent that comes off the top before anything is returned, makes random wagering a losing proposition. But horses do not run to their odds every time. Surprise—the public makes mistakes. There are plenty of horses that start at even money when their odds should be higher. People bet anyway on these types of horses, because they want to win a bet, often at any price. An individual handicapper can win money betting at the right price. And not being afraid to lose.

Lil Bro Eddie was not a horse many expected would win, or even run second. Horses with a 1-in-10 chance usually lose. A horseplayer who is able to cope with the inevitable losses will discover that profits are attainable. Discipline and creative thinking are required. And a horseplayer must be willing to swim against the tide when circumstances warrant. A bettor must remain confident, regardless of how the bet turns out.

There is no parimutuel wagering in Dubai, site of the $6 million Dubai World Cup each spring. Still, a determined horseplayer can find action. English bookmakers attend the event to take care of wagering needs. I met one such bookmaker in Dubai, days before the 2002 World Cup. The representative, from a reputable bookmaking firm in England, posted odds for the World Cup and supporting races. Bookmakers try to balance the action, so that no matter which horse wins, the bookmaker will make a profit after paying winning bettors.

In the $2 million Golden Shaheen, a six-furlong sprint, the bookmaker goofed. Echo Eddie had been facing mostly state-breds, and had never run outside California. Yet he was emerging as one of the premier sprinters in the West. His career-best Beyer figure was 114, close to Grade 1 par. Echo Eddie's lack of "class" was a non-issue. In sprints, class may not always be a primary consideration. Sprints are all about speed, and Echo Eddie was fast. I thought he was at least as good as, and possibly better than, the American sprinters he would face in Dubai, including Xtra Heat, Caller One, Men's Exclusive, and Bonapaw. The bookmaker had Echo Eddie at 25-1. Trying to keep a straight face, I bet $100. It was going to be a betting coup. Echo Eddie should have been no higher than 6-1, in my opinion. I was set up for a $2,500 score.

Sprint races at Nad Al Sheba Racecourse in Dubai are torturous to watch. The start of the six-furlong straightaway is six furlongs away. The field runs almost directly toward the grandstand, and it is impossible to tell who is in front. The field broke from the gate, and the gray outline of Echo Eddie was in contention. The track announcer was calling his name among the leaders. Echo Eddie was ready to pounce on Caller One, whose form, I thought, had had gone downhill. A few days earlier, I declared to a Japanese television crew that Caller One was "yesterday's horse." They thought that was funny. Boy, was I clever.

Echo Eddie battled Caller One, pressing him as hard as he could. But Caller One was not yesterday's horse. He had another good one in him and refused to let Echo Eddie get past. The margin was a head. My betting coup had been thwarted by the resolve of one of the world's best sprinters. Darn. And it was such a good bet. It just so happened to be a losing one.

Every day, there are horses whose odds are out of whack with their chances. The public makes mistakes because so many are afraid to lose. Yet even with a takeout rate that ranges from 15 to 20 percent, people do win money at the races. It just requires some work.

The parimutuel system was invented in France in the 1860's as a means to compete with bookmakers. Loosely translated, the term *parimutuel* means "mutual wagers"—betting among ourselves. Bettors do not wager against the bookmaker or the racetrack.

Rather, they wager against one another. The track has no vested interest in the outcome of a race, but merely holds the money for redistribution to the winners. And the odds are a reflection of how bettors perceive the chances of each horse. The horse perceived to have the "best chance" will have the most money wagered on him. The horse perceived to have the least chance has the least money. The racetrack collects the wagers, takes out 15 to 20 percent (depending on the jurisdiction and the type of bet) for taxes, purses, and operating expenses, and returns the rest to the winning bettors.

To win money requires identifying weak spots in the betting. If the second-most-likely winner is the fifth betting choice, it may be an opportunity. When the public miscalculates a horse's chances, an individual horseplayer can tilt the odds in his favor.

Odds correspond to percentages. Even money (1-1) corresponds to 50 percent; 3-1 (one out of four) corresponds to 25 percent. In a mythical parimutuel system with no takeout—all the money bet returned to winning bettors—the percentage of one pool would add to 100. Because of the takeout, the points add to more than 100. In a state with 15 percent takeout, percentage points add to roughly 120.

This is the odds percentage table.

1-5 equals 83.33 percent
2-5 equals 71.42 percent
1-2 equals 66.67 percent
3-5 equals 62.50 percent
4-5 equals 55.56 percent
1-1 equals 50.00 percent
6-5 equals 45.45 percent
7-5 equals 41.67 percent
3-2 equals 40.00 percent
8-5 equals 38.46 percent
9-5 equals 35.71 percent
2-1 equals 33.33 percent
5-2 equals 28.57 percent
3-1 equals 25.00 percent
7-2 equals 22.22 percent
4-1 equals 20.00 percent
9-2 equals 18.19 percent
5-1 equals 16.67 percent

6-1 equals 14.29 percent
8-1 equals 11.11 percent
10-1 equals 9.09 percent
12-1 equals 7.69 percent
15-1 equals 6.25 percent
20-1 equals 4.76 percent
30-1 equals 3.23 percent

Total the percentages from a race chart. In a state with a 15 percent take, the total will be close to 120.

If no takeout existed, the odds on each starter would be slightly higher and the total would be 100 points. Takeout eats players alive. When only 85 percent of the money wagered gets returned, somebody is going to lose. It does not have to be you.

Bookmakers structure odds similarly to the parimutuel system, except that bookmakers offer fixed odds. If a bookmaker offers 25-1 on a horse such as Echo Eddie, the bettor who wagers at that price gets the full odds at 25-1. The bookmaker in Dubai lowered Echo Eddie's odds after I made the bet; subsequent backers of Echo Eddie would have been paid considerably less. The bookmaker did not want additional action on the horse at such a high price. In a parimutuel system, bettors are paid based on final odds, which are determined after betting has closed and the race has begun.

It would be great if a beginning handicapper could simply sit back and cherry pick overlaid longshots such as Echo Eddie or Lil Bro Eddie. But it's not going to happen. Sorry about that. A beginning handicapper cannot find sensible longshots until after he knows how to find reasonable contenders.

Think of the betting pools as the stock market. The efficient-market theory holds that the stock market is accurately priced at any given time. That is, the price of stocks is a reflection of the combined wisdom of the market—all investors. Microsoft stock was trading at $26 per share in late 2003, a price that was established by the collective sentiment of the market as a whole. At $26, there were an equal number of buyers and sellers. It was what the stock was worth. A wagering pool is similar. The odds that are on the board are a reflection of the handicapping opinions of bettors that have invested in the race.

An even-money shot is even money because the majority of bettors recognize that horse to be the most likely winner. A horse at 30-1 is that high because few bettors consider that horse to be a contender. Most of the time, the betting market has priced the horses in accord with their actual chances. It sometimes takes a while to wait until a mistake is made.

Winning does require reasonable determination of the probability of an outcome, comparing it to the odds being offered, and wagering accordingly. A bettor will be right sometimes, wrong most of the time. A bet should never be made because of a conviction a horse will win. It's nice to have confidence in one's selection, but few bettors sustain long-term profits by merely picking winners.

I did not realize that in the late 1980's when I started picking horses for a living. I thought that if I could simply select a lot of winners I could generate win payoffs that would compensate for my losers. But that's not the case. Finding the most likely winner is a fine place to start, and every bettor should be able to do just that. But "likely winners" rarely return double-digit payoffs. Successful bettors do not win by selection-based handicapping. Public handicappers do not make money betting their top selections. Rather, winning horseplayers are able to estimate a horse's true chances, and back that horse when the odds do not correlate. It happens, often.

Even though the ability to pick a high percentage of winners is not the key to parimutuel success, it is the only place to start. A beginner should first find the most likely winner, but not stop there. One also should identify the second-most-likely winner, and the third. The eventual winner should be among one's top three contenders at least two-thirds of the time. A handicapper's top three contenders will be in acceptable current condition, and racing at a proper class level. They will have demonstrated sufficient ability (speed figures) to handle the demands of the particular race, and have a running style that suits the likely pace dynamics of the race. Those fundamental factors are all one needs to find the winner among a trio of contenders in two out of three races. It's an easy game? Well, not quite.

After ranking the top three horses in order of preference, a bettor can begin to consider the concept of fair value by assigning win probability to those selections. If the race were run 100 times, how often would the top choice win? How often would the second choice win? The third choice? A horseplayer who can do this can win money, because the important decisions are made. After the handicapping and assigning odds, it is only a matter of wagering on the overlay.

For example:

Top selection A has a 33 percent chance.
Second selection B has a 20 percent chance.
Third selection C has a 10 percent chance.

Correlate the percentage to odds.
33 percent equals 2-1
20 percent equals 4-1
10 percent equals 9-1.

Horse A would represent "fair value" at odds of 2-1;
    a break-even proposition.
Horse B would represent "fair value" at odds of 4-1;
    a break-even proposition.
Horse C would represent "fair value" at odds of 9-1;
    a break-even proposition.

Does anyone really do this—assign probabilities? It sounds like theoretical nonsense. Yet people do assign probabilities, in a variety of ways. Experienced handicappers do it by intuition. Beginning handicappers can follow the mechanical method outlined.

Horse A represents value at any price above 2-1. He will win 33 percent, and the payoff would be $6. Break-even. Bettors should insist on a 50 percent overlay. That is, Horse A would not be wagered on unless his odds were 3-1 or higher. Horse B, the 4-1 shot, would not be wagered on unless his odds were 6-1 or higher. Horse C would be not wagered on unless he was 14-1.

The reason for insisting on a 50 percent premium is to allow margin for error. It is entirely possible that one's handicapping is imprecise. Maybe a horse believed to have a 33 percent chance has only a 25 percent chance. Anyone can be wrong. By insisting the horse be 3-1 or higher, it lessens the chance of long-term losses. A horse that wins one out of four, and pays $8 (odds of 3-1) will result in a bettor's breaking even over the long haul.

If assigning specific probabilities is too complex, it will be necessary to narrow the field to three leading contenders. A handicapper who can do that, and bet the contender whose odds are highest, will form a winning strategy. The top selection rarely results in overlays. That's okay. There will be more overlays among the second and third choices. The positive attributes of those horses are less evident, and there is a greater chance the public will mistake their chances. Sometimes, the public overdoes it on the favorite, which allows the odds on second selections to drift up. Determining when to forsake the top choice, and bet on a second or third choice, is a matter of allowing the odds to mandate the play.

When a second choice has a 20 percent chance (4-1) but his odds are 8-1, make the play. Four out of five times it will lose. So what? The one-in-five win ratio will lead to handsome payoffs. Still more discipline is required to wager on one's third preference when odds on the top two are unacceptable. A third choice with only a 10 percent chance (9-1) is a reasonable wager when the odds are at a 50 percent premium. That is, 14-1. Overlays are often difficult to find in small fields. Whereas a 5-1 shot may be the second choice in a 12-horse field, a 5-1 shot may be the longest price in a five-horse field.

A bettor must be prepared to lose most of his wagers. It is part of horse racing. This is not flipping a coin, where anyone can win 50 percent. It is important to realize that most horse bets are losers.

Trouble is, many horseplayers are not risk-takers. They wager on predictability, and sacrifice value for the notion that they can win by picking winners. It does not happen. In making an odds line on top contenders, bettors can determine both value and anti-value. The latter is when a horse's odds are beneath his actual chance to win. The next chapter, on wagering, will illustrate methods by which to exploit a favorite whose odds are underlaid.

A dilemma arises in the case of a legitimate favorite that has no apparent flaw. If the horse is solid, some suggest not betting against the horse. He is likely to win anyway. However, no horse is invincible. There is no such thing as a sure thing. Horse racing is about probabilities. If a horse has a 50 percent chance of winning, but his odds are 1-10, it would be sensible to find an alternative, despite the high likelihood of the favorite winning.

The mighty Cigar shipped to Del Mar in 1996, seeking the modern-day record for consecutive wins. He had won 16 in a row, and the Pacific Classic was expected to be a mere formality. A good time to crown the king. No one could envision his getting beat, even though nearly all horses get beat sooner or later.

Cigar was hanging on the board at odds of 1-10. He was the biggest cinch of the year. Simultaneously, he was the year's worst underlay.

Five others were entered in the Pacific Classic. They were not slouches. The field included Siphon, winner of the Hollywood Gold Cup in his previous start; Tinners Way, seeking his third straight Pacific Classic upset; Dare and Go, who won the 1995 Strub; and hard-knocking Dramatic Gold. Cigar was the likely winner, but he also had shipped cross-country to race over an unfamiliar track. He was not a lock.

At odds of 1-10, Cigar would need to win 90 out of 100 for a bettor to break even. I figured Cigar might win "only" two out of three (66 percent). His odds should have been 1-2. Yet an underlay does no good without a sensible alternative. Horseplayers sometimes make the mistake of betting a race for the simple reason that the favorite's odds are too short. It should not be done unless an overlay can be found among the other contenders. In the Pacific Classic, there was at least one, and he was hitting the Pacific Classic on an upward pattern.

But no one beats Cigar, right? Except this time, the pace was cruel, and Cigar went after the front-runner Siphon too soon, on the backstretch. Then Dramatic Gold attacked Cigar from the outside, applying even more pressure on the 1-10 favorite. Suddenly there was a three-way duel with intense fractions. The horse I wagered on was alone in fourth.

It was the perfect trip, behind three dueling leaders. At the quarter pole, the question was not whether Dare and Go would win, but what the margin would be. He swept past a weary Cigar in midstretch, and rolled home by 3½ lengths. Dare and Go paid $81.20.

The bet, which I did not expect to win, actually did win. I was a temporary genius, again, yet melancholy. I had made the bet by telephone, from my new home in Phoenix, Arizona. It was a long way from Del Mar, and the 1996 season was the first seaside meet I had missed in years. I wondered if I had made a mistake by giving up my California racetrack position to work in the editorial offices of *Daily Racing Form*. It was a calculated risk, and a story for the next chapter.

7

THE WAGERING MENU

It was early 1996, and my head was spinning. A newspaper handicapper for 10 years, I was supposed to know it all. But in horse racing, no one ever does. I was on the brink of parimutuel disaster.

The exotic-wagering explosion had reached full speed. It was no longer enough merely to find winners. A horseplayer had to know what to do with them. That is, how to bet them. The game had changed. Betting to win was old school.

The wagering choices had become so numerous that a successful bettor needed to spend as much effort on strategy as on handicapping. Bet to win? Boring. Pick the first two finishers in order, and play an exacta? Now one needed two opinions on the same race. The trifecta—picking the first three finishers in order—was becoming increasingly popular, as the betting menu expanded to include more and more home-run-style wagers.

Multiple-race bets required a bettor to pick the winner of successive races. The promise of jackpot pick-six payoffs helped usher in a new, swing-for-the-fences wagering mentality. Win the lottery at the racetrack. The pick three was emerging as a popular wagering vehicle, and when it was first offered once a day in

Southern California, on races 6 through 8, the choice was simple. To play, or pass?

Bettors clamored for more. They asked for and received rolling pick threes that covered the entire race card. The pick three requires a bettor to pick the winner of three successive races. With a rolling pick three, if you get blown out in the first leg of a wager that includes races 1 through 3, there's no worry— another pick three on races 2 through 4 will rev up in only a half-hour. And another on races 3 through 5 a half-hour later. All day. Along with exacta and trifecta wagering, the menu seemed unlimited.

The game had shifted radically, and I was being swept away by the seemingly infinite number of wagering choices. It was sensory overload. I could have stood strong, raised my fist, and defied the game's new direction. Either that, or run for cover.

I gave up a dream job as Southern California handicapper for *Daily Racing Form,* and requested a transfer to the paper's editorial headquarters in Phoenix, Arizona. We sold the house, packed up the kids, and hit the road. No more working at the racetrack to battle a game that I thought could be beaten. Exotic wagering was beating me.

Hundreds of miles from where I grew up at Santa Anita, Hollywood Park, and Del Mar, the Phoenix hiatus provided relief. The daily parimutuel bleeding stopped. It helped to step back and recognize personal flaws. There were plenty, including the most blatant—an utter lack of discipline, a reluctance to pass a race. The attempt to overpower the game by sheer volume of winners was not working. My wagering strategy was broken and needed fixing.

Isolated from major-league racing, I rediscovered that one element of winning is not betting. It sounds contradictory. It was okay to skip a race, a day, even a week. At the very least, a horseplayer must be willing to shun the jackpot mentality. Keep things simple. Do what you do best. Horseplayers cannot get rich every day. Some die broke trying. For those that survive, distinct strengths and weaknesses are recognized. They are not the same for every bettor.

Two and a half years after leaving California, we were ready to come home. Once again we sold the house and packed up the kids, and we headed back to Southern California. For a second chance.

In autumn 1998 I regained my former position as *Daily Racing Form* handicapper in Southern California, and tiptoed back into the parimutuel pools. The wagers stayed small and simple. They had to. This time, there was no place to hide.

It was make-or-break time. Temptation had to be resisted. No rolling pick threes, all day. No shoot-for-the-moon trifecta every race. If I made only one serious bet all day, so be it. Tomorrow would be here soon enough, with another wagering menu filled with opportunity. Discipline, apparently, is a skill that can be learned. By choice, or by necessity. It's not that tough to pass a race. Even today, temptations remain—like pick-six carryovers and potential five-figure superfecta payoffs. Mistakes? They happen, too. I still bet, almost daily, but at least now I have a plan. Do you?

The mere application of handicapping basics—condition, class, speed, and pace—will not necessarily result in winning at the races. A horseplayer must take the next step after the handicapping is done. There are a lot of ways to go, and a lot of traps to avoid. The choice of wagers is vast. In order to survive, a horseplayer must learn to navigate.

Most wagers fall into one of two groups—"vertical" wagers based on the outcome of a single race, and "horizontal" wagers based on the outcome of two or more races. Single-race wagers include exactas (picking the first two finishers in order), trifectas (first three), and superfectas (first four). These wagers require picking the vertical placement of the runners. Multiple-race wagers include the daily double (picking the winners of two successive races), the pick three (three successive races), the pick four, and the granddaddy of horizontal wagers—the pick six. All you have to do is pick six consecutive winners.

Wagers that include two or more horses are called exotic wagers, and the potential rewards correspond to the degree of difficulty. The greater the difficulty of a wager—the more potential outcomes—the more likely it will produce a high payoff. The less difficult a wager—the fewer potential outcomes—the more likely it will produce a low payoff. For example, in a 10-horse field, there are 10 potential win payoffs. Winning bettors receive money lost by those who backed the nine losers, minus takeout.

An exacta in a 10-horse field includes 90 possible combinations (10 possible winners, multiplied by nine possible runners-up). The money wagered on the 89 losing combinations, minus takeout, is distributed to winning exacta bettors.

The exponential increase in combinations often creates bomber payoffs. In a pick four in which each leg has 10 runners, there are 10,000 possible combinations (10 x 10 x 10 x 10). The pick-four pool is spread thin; fewer dollars are wagered on the winning combination. There is one winning combination and 9,999 losers. The resulting score can be a bonanza. It is what bettors want.

In 2002, more than $15 billion was wagered on Thoroughbred horse racing in the United States, and bettors clearly prefer exotics. Win, place, and show betting (WPS) accounted for less than one-third of the total bets, while the remaining two-thirds was geared toward higher-paying exotic wagers.

(2002 Wager Types by Percentage of Total Wagering; U.S. commingled pools)

WPS	32.9129
All Exotics	67.0871

Exotics

Exacta	27.6951
Trifecta	24.0109
Superfecta	03.9625
Pick Three	03.4077
Daily Double	03.2725
Quinella	01.2724
Pick Six	01.2056
Perfecta	01.0579
Pick Four	01.0459
All Others	00.1565

("All Others" includes Place Pick All, Twin Trifecta, Classix, Future Wager, Head2Head, Consolation Double, Trifecta Super, Pick Nine, Place Pick Nine, Consolation Pick Three, Jockey Challenge, and Pick Five.)

The sheer number of alternatives is enough to confuse anyone. Horseplayers must decide which bets make the most sense. It's not the same for everyone, every time. Let's examine the choices.

Win Betting

Here is where we all got started; wagering in its purest form. For you to cash a win bet, your horse only needs to win the race. The takeout rate (the percentage of the betting pool "taken out" for taxes, purses, and fees before winners are paid) varies from 14 to 20 percent in U.S. racing jurisdictions. (New York has the nation's lowest win takeout at 14 percent; California's is 15.43 percent; Kentucky's is 16 percent.) Relative to the higher takeout rates of exotic wagers (generally 20 to 25 percent), win bets are fairly inexpensive. Win bets are easy to understand. The expected payoffs are posted on the odds board—odds of 3-1 mean $3 profit for every $1 wagered, or an $8 payoff for a $2 bet.

The right time for a win bet is when a horse's chance of winning is higher than the odds—for example, a horse whose odds are 3-1, but who has a 33 percent chance to win. If the analysis is accurate, profits result.

Win payoffs, like most bets, correlate to field size. Larger fields include more possible results and higher payoffs. The effect of field size is significant. A computer study of more than 42,000 races nationwide, by Southern California handicapping author Barry Meadow, shows a direct correlation between median win payoff and field size. Median means half the payoffs are higher, and half are lower. Rounded to the nearest 20-cent payoff, the overall median was $8.40. As the list indicates, the median payoff increased along with field size.

Median payoffs

Five-horse fields:	$6.00
Six-horse fields:	$7.00
Seven-horse fields:	$7.60
Eight-horse fields:	$8.40
Nine-horse fields:	$9.00
Ten-horse fields:	$9.80
Eleven-horse fields:	$10.60
Twelve-horse fields:	$11.00

Win odds are calculated by subtracting from the betting pool the takeout and the money wagered on the winner, then dividing by the amount wagered on the winner. As an illustration, look at a win pool with a 15 percent takeout rate. From $100,000 in the win pool, $15,000 (15 percent takeout) is subtracted, leaving $85,000. From that amount, the money bet on the winner ($25,000 in this example) is subtracted. That leaves $60,000, which is divided by the amount bet on the winner ($25,000), resulting in odds of 2.40-1. On a $2 bet, the win payoff is $6.80, which includes the original investment.

The effect of takeout is significant. The winner in the preceding example would have returned $8 in a mythical pool with no takeout. In a jurisdiction with a 20 percent take, the win payoff would have been only $6.40. Takeout is the reason many horseplayers lose. They wager without an advantage. Picking winners is not enough. A bettor must back only horses whose odds are higher than their chance to win.

To recommend the most effective technique for win betting is akin to suggesting how to vote. It is matter of personal choice. The obvious guideline is never bet underlays, and only bet overlays. There is more to it, of course, because horses' odds vary greatly, and opinions differ. A rock-solid favorite at 5-2 may seem perfectly acceptable to one bettor and simultaneously be considered a severe underlay by another.

This is what works for me, and I admit—finding overlays among obvious selections does not happen with any great regularity. I still bet an occasional 3-1 shot that I believe should be 2-1, mainly because I enjoy the action. However, I do not make serious money betting low-odds overlays. My winning seasons are rarely due to an unusual hot streak betting 33 percent winners at odds of 3-1. Rather, winning seasons usually result from a handful of big scores.

I win when the public commits a major blunder. It happens in high odds ranges—at least 8-1. When I make a significant win bet, it is with reasonable confidence that the public has badly underestimated a horse's chances. Most of those bets, I lose. But overlay payoffs compensate. Atswhatimtalknbout was the most likely winner of the 2003 San Felipe Stakes, but it was close between him and Buddy Gil, who I thought had about a 1 in 5 chance. Buddy Gil won by a nose and paid $21.60. Victory U.S.A. was equal to Halfbridled in the 2003 Breeders' Cup Juvenile Fillies, in my opinion (misguided, as it turns out). I thought both had about a 1 in 4 chance. Victory U.S.A. finished third at almost 8-1; Halfbridled dominated at 2-1.

There were plenty of other losers that were up the track. So what? Losing is no big deal if the win payoffs make up for it. It would be great if handicapping were precise, which would allow one to profit by betting 2-1 overlays. That has not happened. What is the recommended technique for win betting? For me, it is betting high-odds overlays. For you, it might be medium- or low-price overlays. The operative word is *overlays,* at whatever price.

Place Betting

To cash a place bet, your horse must finish first or second. The place payoff is the same regardless of finish position. There are two payoffs in each race, and payoffs vary depending on the amount of money bet to place on the one-two finishers. When a favorite finishes first or second, the place payoffs are depressed. The place pool is separate from the win pool, but most of the time the favorite in the win pool also is favored in the place pool. That horse has the most money wagered on him to place.

Place payoffs are small relative to win odds; the odds to place generally are about one-third the odds to win. The percentage is even lower for horses that are longshots to win. Place payoffs are calculated after subtracting takeout and wagers on the two winners. The remainder is distributed to winning place bettors. The payoffs depend on which horses finish one-two. For example:

$100,000 in place pool:

$40,000 to place on Horse A
$20,000 to place on Horse B
$10,000 to place on Horse C
$30,000 to place on remainder of field

Horses A and B finish one-two. The place payoffs are calculated as follows:

From $100,000 in the place pool, $15,000 (15 percent takeout) is subtracted, leaving $85,000. From that amount, the money bet on the two "winners" (the one-two finishers, in this case $40,000 and $20,000) is subtracted. That leaves $25,000, which is divided equally between the one-two finishers. That is, $12,500 is returned as winnings to Horse A and B place bettors, along with original bets. Place odds are calculated by dividing the $12,500 by the amount wagered to place on each horse.

The place odds on Horse A would be 3-10 ($12,500 divided by $40,000), or $2.60 for each $2. The place odds on Horse B would be 6-10 ($12,500 divided by $20,000), or $3.20 for each $2.

If Horse A, the favorite, finishes off the board, payoffs increase. For example, Horses B and C finish one-two. That would result in place odds on Horse B of 1.375-1, or $4.70 for each $2. The place odds on Horse C would be 2.75-1, or $7.50 for each $2.

Place betting is like walking on a treadmill. It gets a bettor nowhere, unless all that one wants to do is cash tickets. The favorite finishes first or second 55 percent of the time, so place bets on higher-odds horses merely subsidize place payoffs for favorites. The exception is when a favorite is vulnerable, and the rest of the field is evenly matched. There are more effective means of protection, including the "exacta as place bet" strategy explained later in this chapter. Betting to place is tedious, payoffs are low, and it is difficult to formulate a winning strategy. A similar assessment applies to show wagering.

Show Betting

A show bet is a winner if the horse finishes first, second, or third. Show payoffs are the same regardless of finish position, and payoffs vary depending on the amount wagered to show on the horses that finish first, second, or third. When a favorite finishes first, second, or third, the show playoffs are depressed because the favorite usually has the most money bet on him to show. There are three show payoffs each race—for the first-, second-, and third-place finishers. The show pool is independent of the win pool.

Show payoffs are minuscule, and rarely worthwhile. The odds to show are roughly one-sixth the odds to win. Why bother? Show payoffs are calculated after takeout is applied, and after original wagers on the winning horses are deducted from the pool. The remaining dollars are divided by three, and distributed to winning show bettors. There isn't much left.

While betting to place and show may seem safe, it merely allows bettors to cash small tickets while delaying the inevitable—death by taxes (takeout). There are precious few situations when place and show betting make sense. That is because favorites finish in the money (first, second, or third) in 67 percent of all races. A horseplayer contemplating a show bet against a heavy favorite would be better served simply betting to win on more than one horse. Wagering to place and show is futile, and beginning horseplayers would do themselves a favor by forsaking those bets altogether.

Exactas

To win the exacta, a bettor selects the first two finishers in order. In a 12-horse field, $2 exacta payoffs routinely return from $75 to $100. During the 2002 Saratoga meet, $2 exacta payoffs for 8-, 9-, 10-, and 11-horse fields clustered around a median of about $60. The median exacta payoff in seven-horse fields was $37; six-horse fields, $25; and five-horse fields, $19. A winning exacta that includes the favorite typically will be low. The exacta combination that attracts the most wagering dollars is the combination with the favorite over the second favorite.

Though exacta payoffs correspond to win odds, the exacta pool is independent of the win pool. The exacta payoffs conform to win odds merely because of a horse's perceived attributes. A horse favored in the win pool based on standard handicapping usually will be favored in the exacta pool for the same reasons.

Here is a typical exacta pool, in which Horse A was favored, Horse B was the second favorite, and Horse C was the third favorite.

$100,000 in pool, distributed as follows:

$5,000 on A-B combination
$4,000 on B-A combination
$3,000 on A-C combination
$2,000 on C-A combination
$1,000 on B-C combination
$500 on C-B combination
$84,500 on remaining combinations

Exacta payoffs are calculated as follows, assuming the winning exacta is A-B:

From $100,000 in the exacta pool, $20,000 is subtracted (20

percent takeout), leaving $80,000. From that amount, the money bet on the winning A-B combination ($5,000, in this example) is subtracted, leaving $75,000. That amount is divided by the amount bet on the winning combination ($5,000), which equals odds of 15-1. A $2 exacta would pay $32. A $2 exacta on the C-B combination would pay 159-1, or $320 for $2.

While the exacta is a two-horse bet, another approach is to view the exacta as two win bets in the same race: First, find the horse (or horses) to win; then, find the horse (or horses) to "win" the race for second. It generally takes more than one ticket to hit the exacta because of the bet's difficulty.

In a 10-horse field, a bettor may settle on one horse to win. That's good—halfway home. Next, he identifies the candidates to finish second and employs a strategy called a partial wheel, or part wheel. That is, he keys one horse to win, and uses other horses in the runner-up slot—the "two-hole." The part wheel compels a distinction between the winner and potential runners-up.

Part wheels allow bettors to leverage their handicapping opinion when one of the two favorites can be tossed out. For example, a 2-1 favorite is rock solid, but the 3-1 second choice is considered vulnerable. A part wheel that keys the favorite on top of the fourth, fifth, and sixth betting choices (a $6 investment) may result in a $2 exacta payoff of $24, effectively turning a 2-1 shot into a 3-1 shot.

In a race with solid co-favorites, it might not make sense to bet an exacta. Exactas that combine the first two favorites typically pay less than they should. As a general rule, one should avoid playing two favorites in an exacta.

Exacta wagering is not roll-the-dice gambling, and order of finish often depends on pace. For example, take a race in which a front-runner is preferred despite the presence of other front-runners. In that case, likely candidates to finish second certainly would not be other pure-speed horses, who have cracked from the chase. So who might finish second? Clunk-up closers who pick up the pieces. Though they are not candidates to win, the dynamics of the race may allow them to be sensible choices to finish second.

The one-two finishers in an exacta generally will consist of:

Speed-speed (a front-runner or pace-presser wins; another front-runner or pace-presser finishes second).
Speed-closer (a front-runner or pace-presser wins; a late-runner finishes second).

Closer-closer (a late-runner wins; another late-runner finishes second).

Closer-speed (a later-runner wins; a front-runner or pace-presser finishes second).

Understanding the pace dynamics can allow a bettor to fashion an exacta from the bottom up. There are plenty of clunk-up horses who are not considered candidates to win, but whose style is flattered by the pace. A similar example would be a race in which a handicapper likes three speed horses at short prices. On the premise that two of the front-runners will burn out from the duel, a bottom-up exacta strategy can be formulated. Simply use the three speed horses in the one-hole, and two or more longshot closers to complete the exacta. This technique also can be used for trifectas.

Other scenarios include keying a front-runner in a race likely to be run at a tepid pace. Then, the runner-up may be another horse complemented by the slow pace. A closer-closer exacta may be forecast when the pacesetters are expected to collapse. An exacta part wheel would insist on other late-runners to complete the order of finish. Finally, when a closer is preferred despite the possibility of a slow pace, it may be front-runners most likely to finish second. Exacta strategy must be formed while considering the pace of the race.

Part wheels offer an effective way to play the exacta, yet some bettors wheel a key horse to the remainder of the field, and pray for a longshot to finish second. Prayer has no rightful place in wagering. In a wheel, a bettor is simply trying to get lucky, hoping that a longshot finishes second. Most of the time, a logical contender will finish second, the exacta payoff will be relatively low, and the bettor will be fortunate to break even. Rather than wheeling a horse in an exacta, one would be better off simply betting a key horse to win.

Another popular exacta strategy is a "box." Boxing horses in the exacta means betting two or more of them to finish one-two without regard to order of finish. In a three-horse exacta box, two must finish one-two. The cost of an exacta box is the number of horses, multiplied by the number of horses minus one, and multiplied again by the base bet.

A two-horse box includes two combinations (2 x 1)—either horse can finish first, the other must finish second. At $2 each, the cost of the bet is $4. A three-horse exacta box covers six possible combinations (any of the three may finish first, one of the other two must finish second); a four-horse exacta box includes 12 combinations (4 x 3).

Boxing fails to differentiate contenders from outsiders. In a four-horse exacta with horses that are 2-1, 4-1, 8-1, and 12-1, a bettor would spend as much on the 12-1 shot as on the 2-1 shot. It does not make sense. If the 12-1 shot is the overlay in the race, a sensible strategy would be betting that horse to win, and keying him in the exacta under the other three contenders.

Although network television rarely offers meaningful wagering strategy, there was an exception during the broadcast of the 2003 Preakness Stakes. On the premise that one of the favorites— Kentucky Derby winner Funny Cide or third-place finisher Peace Rules—would misfire, NBC analyst Bob Neumeier recommended an exacta play, structured so that Funny Cide or Peace Rules must win; the other must run out. Neumeier figured that Funny Cide had benefited from a perfect trip in the Derby and possibly was not as good as he looked, while Peace Rules, back on short rest and lacking a solid foundation of races, might regress.

The exacta was a part wheel, using Funny Cide and Peace Rules to win, and three longshots to finish second. The bet would lose if Funny Cide and Peace Rules finished one-two, which was the combination that attracted the most action. It was a clever strategy—taking a stand against the most probable exacta combination, and one that would result in an underlay payoff if it did run in.

The play—six combinations at $2 each—turned out to be an overlay winner. Funny Cide won in a romp, while Peace Rules staggered in fourth, and 20-1 longshot Midway Road finished second. The $2 exacta combining Funny Cide and Midway Road returned $120.60, not bad for a $12 investment.

Beyond favorites producing underlay payoffs in exactas, a combination that typically produces lower-than-expected returns is when two longshots make up the exacta. Bettors shooting for the moon combine longshots in the exacta more often than their actual probability of finishing one-two warrants. Rather than combine two longshots in the exacta, it makes more sense to wager on each of them to win.

A favorite strategy of mine is using the exacta as a place bet on a longshot. I wager to win on the longshot, but rather than backing it up with a place bet, I instead use a one-way exacta with the favorite over the longshot, or with a couple of other contenders over the longshot.

A longshot is more likely to finish second than win. And when the longshot does finish second, one out of three times it is the favorite that wins the race. An exacta combining a favorite and a longshot pays far more than the place price on the longshot. Of course, a bettor will cash only one in three times when the longshot finishes second. The exacta must pay at least three times the place payoff, and usually does.

EIGHTH RACE **5 FURLONGS. (.56^2) MAIDEN CLAIMING. Purse $21,000 FOR MAIDENS, TWO YEAR OLDS. Weight, 119 lbs. Claiming Price $40,000, if for $35,000, allowed 2 lb.**

Hollywood

MAY 29, 2003

Value of Race: $21,000 Winner $12,600; second $4,200; third $2,520; fourth $1,260; fifth $420. Mutuel Pool $325,767.00 Exacta Pool $206,458.00 Quinella Pool $22,687.00 Trifecta Pool $237,679.00 Superfecta Pool $128,466.00

Last Raced	Horse	M/Eqt.	A.	Wt	PP	St	3/16	3/8	Str	Fin	Jockey	Cl'g Pr	Odds $1
	Stalking Tiger	LBb	2	119	4	3	1^{1}	1^{1}	$1^{3\frac{1}{2}}$	$1^{4\frac{1}{2}}$	Almeida G F	40000	5.40
14May03 ^{3}Hol^{6}	Lil' Bro Eddie	LBbf	2	119	3	2	$3^{\frac{1}{2}}$	$4^{1\frac{1}{2}}$	3^{1}	$2^{\frac{1}{2}}$	Ziesing S	40000	53.80
14May03 ^{3}Hol^{3}	Areyoutalkintome	LB	2	119	6	7	$4^{2\frac{1}{2}}$	$2^{\frac{1}{2}}$	2^{hd}	$3^{1\frac{1}{2}}$	Valenzuela P A	40000	7.10
14May03 ^{3}Hol^{2}	Anthony Eats	LB	2	119	8	4	$7^{2\frac{1}{2}}$	5^{hd}	5^{5}	4^{2}	Leyva J C	40000	5.60
14May03 ^{3}Hol^{4}	Lago Maggiore	LB	2	119	9	1	$2^{\frac{1}{2}}$	$3^{1\frac{1}{2}}$	$4^{1\frac{1}{2}}$	5^{3}	Espinoza V	40000	9.40
7May03 ^{8}Hol^{4}	Five Wild Cats	LBb	2	119	2	9	$8^{1\frac{1}{2}}$	8^{3}	7^{1}	$6^{2\frac{1}{2}}$	Solis A	40000	2.30
	Caperex	LB	2	119	10	6	$9^{2\frac{1}{2}}$	$9^{\frac{1}{2}}$	9^{1}	$7^{1\frac{1}{2}}$	Berrio O A	40000	31.90
	Trickinthepark	LBb	2	119	1	10	10	10	10	8^{1}	Pedroza M A	40000	14.10
7May03 ^{8}Hol^{5}	Wolf Class	LBbf	2	117	5	5	$5^{\frac{1}{2}}$	$6^{\frac{1}{2}}$	6^{hd}	$9^{1\frac{1}{2}}$	Atkinson P	35000	3.30
7May03 ^{8}Hol^{9}	Mr. Lee	LBb	2	119	7	8	6^{hd}	$7^{1\frac{1}{2}}$	8^{hd}	10	Valdivia J Jr	40000	53.80

OFF AT 4:54 Start Good. Won driving. Track fast.
TIME :22, :45, :57^2 (:22.04, :45.13, :57.48)

$2 Mutuel Prices:				
	4-STALKING TIGER	12.80	9.40	5.20
	3-LIL' BRO EDDIE		52.40	14.20
	6-AREYOUTALKINTOME			5.00

$1 EXACTA 4–3 PAID $423.60 $2 QUINELLA 3–4 PAID $458.40 $1 TRIFECTA 4–3–6 PAID $2,672.00 $1 SUPERFECTA 4–3–6–8 PAID $10,254.10

B. g, (Apr), by Twin Spires–Just Plain Fancy, by Falstaff. Trainer Aguirre Paul G. Bred by (Cal).

STALKING TIGER sent between horses to the early lead, set the pace a bit off the rail, angled in on the turn and drew clear under some left handed urging. LIL' BRO EDDIE close up stalking the pace inside, fell back a bit leaving the turn, continued a bit off the rail in the stretch and gamely got the place. AREYOUTALKINTOME chased outside a rival then between horses into and on the turn, was bumped in upper stretch and edged for second. ANTHONY EATS chased between horses then outside on the backstretch, continued three deep on the turn and bested the others. LAGO MAGGIORE close up stalking outside on the backstretch and three deep on the turn, was bumped in upper stretch and weakened. FIVE WILD CATS broke in and bumped a rival, went between horses the a bit off the rail on the backstretch and turn, steadied off heels leaving the bend, swung three deep into the stretch and was not a threat. CAPEREX chased outside on the backstretch, angled in off the rail on the turn and did not rally. TRICKINTHEPARK bumped at the start, saved ground off the pace, came out into the stretch and failed to menace. WOLF CLASS chased off the rail then angled in for the turn and weakened in the stretch. MR. LEE a bit crowded at the start, chased off the inside then between horses on the turn and weakened in the stretch.

Owners— 1, Aguirre Paul G; 2, Costello John London Dick & Lovinge; 3, Belmonte Philip Gerson Racing & Gul; 4, Moreno Robert B; 5, Steinmann Heinz; 6, Aizenstadt Foltz Lopez Et Al; 7, Haras El Palenque & McNeil; 8, Warren Benjamin C; 9, Carmel Judith & Bradley; 10, Lanning Curt & Lila

Trainers—1, Aguirre Paul G; 2, Duncan Leonard M; 3, Mitchell Mike; 4, Sadler John W; 5, Harrington Mike; 6, Dominguez Caesar F; 7, Avila A C; 8, Sise Clifford Jr; 9, Assinesi Paul D; 10, Moger Ed Jr

$2 Daily Double (5–4) Paid $35.00; Daily Double Pool $87,732.
$1 Pick Three (5/7–5–4) Paid $60.90; Pick Three Pool $103,717.
$1 Pick Four (7–5/7–5–4) Paid $625.30; Pick Four Pool $185,691.
$2 Pick Six (9–2–7–5/7–5–4) 5
Correct Paid $543.00; Pick Six Pool $176,902. $2 Pick Six (9–2–7–5/7–5–4) 6
Correct Paid $19,768.40 $1 Place Pick All (8–OF–8) Paid $1,181.20;
Place Pick All Pool $32,558.

Hollywood Park Attendance: 5,198 Mutuel Pool: $1,193,156.00 ITW Mutuel Pool: $2,939,004.00 ISW Mutuel Pool: $3,962,527.00

In an inscrutable race without a legitimate favorite, it is acceptable to "back-wheel" the longshot—that is, use the long-shot to finish second under several others, or even the entire field. We saw in the previous chapter that runner-up Lil Bro Eddie, who returned $52.40 to place, keyed a $2 exacta payoff of $847.20. Had I used that same exacta investment ($22) and wagered to place instead, the place payoff would have been $576.40, or $270 less than the exacta. Of course, if Lil Bro Eddie had won, the place bet would have paid off, but the exacta would have been lost.

A bet called the quinella is similar to the exacta, but requires picking the first two finishers without regard to order. It is like an exacta box, but pays the same regardless of which horse wins. A quinella in a 10-horse field has half as many combinations (45) as an exacta (90). Quinellas fail to consider the very reason that exactas can be profitable—not every horse in an exacta wager has the same chance to win. Some are more likely to finish second. Quinellas do not distinguish between the one-two finishers. A quinella is basically an exacta box for dummies. You are smarter than that. A "perfecta" is the same as an exacta, but with a different name.

Trifectas

Winning the trifecta requires picking the first three finishers in order. The larger the field size, the tougher it gets—there are 720 potential trifecta combinations in a 10-horse field, and 1,320 combinations in a 12-horse field. Determining the number of combinations is easy. A horse that finishes first cannot finish second, so the number of potential runners-up is reduced by one. Likewise, a horse that finishes first or second cannot also finish third; the number of potential third-place finishers is further reduced by one. Multiply the three together. Multiplying 10 x 9 x 8 will equal 720 possible combinations. In a six-horse field, there are only 120 combinations. As one might expect, trifecta payoffs correspond to field size and odds of the first three finishers.

During the 2002 Del Mar meet, trifecta races with 11 or 12 starters produced median payoffs of more than $600 (for $2). Trifecta races with nine or 10 starters produced median payoffs of more than $400. Eight-horse fields produced a median of approximately $300; seven-horse fields produced a median of less than $200.

Winning the trifecta usually requires buying more than one ticket. Few handicappers are good or lucky enough to identify the first three finishers with absolute precision. A bettor must spread out to pick up the marginal horses that can totter into third while never seriously threatening the winner.

A sensible trifecta strategy mandates a using a key horse. For the same reason boxes and full wheels are not advised in exactas (no distinction between main contenders and fringe contenders), boxes and wheels make little sense in trifectas. While there are a number of techniques to play a trifecta, a bettor should start with a horse on which to build the wager.

The trifecta was a relatively new bet in California in 1991. It was spring at Santa Anita, and a 3-year-old claiming horse, Lazarito, looked interesting. Although he had blown leads in several recent starts, I was willing to give him one more chance in a race that figured to unfold at a slow pace. I invested $40 in the trifecta, in effect making 40 separate $1 wagers that keyed Lazarito (No. 9) in the one- and two-holes with five others. They were Fiesta Fair (No. 5), a 12-1 shipper from Northern California; Capirazza (No. 1), a wacky 48-1 longshot who had a tough trip in his previous start; and three other contenders—Nos. 10, 11, and 12.

The bet with Lazarito in the one-hole was structured like this:

9 with 1, 5, 10, 11, 12 with 1, 5, 10, 11, 12.
That is, 1 x 5 x 4 = $20.

A second ticket used Lazarito in the two-hole:

1, 5, 10, 11, 12 with 9 with 1, 5, 10, 11, 12.
That is, 5 x 1 x 4 = $20.

The forecast of an easier pace proved accurate. It was about a second slower. Capirazza jumped out to the lead, pressed from the outside by Lazarito. The opening quarter went in 22.40 and the half in 45.60. If Lazarito could not win this time, he was a bum. Well, he didn't win. But he ran well enough. He wore down 48-1 Capirazza in deep stretch; both were nailed by Fiesta Fair. The $2 trifecta, a 12-1 shot over a 7-1 shot over a 48-1 shot, paid $15,095.20. I had it for $1, a payoff of $7,547.60.

The only unfortunate by-product of the score was that it set the stage for a chase that would prove futile. I squandered plenty trying to hit another similar-sized trifecta. It never happened. Most of the time, trifectas simply do not pay that much. At least the strategy was sound—a $40 play that keyed a medium-priced horse to finish first or second, with five other contenders.

Trifectas are not likely to produce a life-changing score. No point chasing rainbows. But the trifecta is still a good bet that typically returns $300 or more in large fields. A trifecta that includes the top wagering choices is almost always overbet. During the 2002 Del Mar summer meet, 41 trifectas were composed of the first three favorites. The average $2 payoff was $74.48. A bettor who made a three-horse trifecta box using the first three favorites the entire meet would have won back just 68 cents on the dollar. Trifectas are best played when a handicapping opinion is separate from the public's.

A trifecta generally is structured from the top down. Start with a horse to win, and add contenders to fill out the bet. But it also can be built from the bottom up, which is my favorite way to play. When fashioning a trifecta from the bottom up, the key horse should be a longshot with little chance to win or finish second. Circumstances are such the longshot has a better chance to finish third than most believe. Longshot late-runners typically fit the description.

In constructing a partial back-wheel trifecta, the longshot goes in the three-hole under obvious contenders. In the 2001 Pacific

Classic at Del Mar, for example, the logical contenders were Futural, disqualified winner of the Hollywood Gold Cup; Skimming, a Del Mar specialist and Pacific Classic winner the year before; and hard-trying graded stakes winner Dixie Dot Com. Captain Steve would take action, but his form was in conspicuous decline. He was a throwout. Meanwhile, 44-1 longshot Dig for It was intriguing. He had a valid excuse for his abysmal last start—a minor foot injury—had trained super since, and was ignored by bettors.

Dig for It had little chance to win. He was short on class, and lacked suitable speed figures. He was not even a logical candidate to run second. The Pacific Classic was one tough race. Further, whatever chance Dig for It had to finish third depended on one of the three logical runners misfiring. It was a gamble worth taking, though, because each contender had a potential flaw. Skimming was possibly not the same horse he had been the year before, Dixie Dot Com had never won a race as strong as the Pacific Classic, and Futural looked as if he might have peaked.

If any of that trio were to come up short, Dig for It might sneak into the trifecta. The wager was structured from the bottom up, keying Dig for It in the three-hole under the three logical contenders. At $2 per bet, the cost was only $12. The race played out just as I had hoped. Second choice Skimming raced gate to wire, his fourth straight win at Del Mar. Dixie Dot Come finished second at 7-1. Futural misfired and ran last. Captain Steve was flat, just as expected. Dig for It threatened briefly on the far turn, lost his punch, and held third. It was right where I wanted him. The $2 trifecta returned $319.40 in the six-horse field.

Trifecta strategy is a matter of preference. Some never play without a key. Others box every closer in a race that figures to unfold at a torrid pace and doom the front-runners. Others use three horses in the one-hole, the same three in the two-hole, then wheel the field in the three-hole. Wheeling the field means praying for a longshot to run third. Might as well play the exacta.

While the payoffs in most of the examples are for $2 wagers, payoffs are shown differently in various parts of the country. Some jurisdictions post exacta payoffs in $1 increments, others use $2 as the base. In the next example, the base bet will be $1. You will soon see why.

Superfectas

Here is the chance to hit a grand slam. A superfecta requires picking the first four finishers in order. In a 10-horse field, there are 5,040 combinations (10 x 9 x 8 x 7). In a 14-horse field there are 24,024 combinations (14 x 13 x 12 x 11). No wonder that in the 2003 Breeders' Cup Juvenile Fillies, won by 2-1 favorite Halfbridled, the $1 superfecta paid $2,995.10.

To have a realistic chance to hit, it requires significant money, perhaps at least $60. It can be worth it. The median $1 super-fecta payoff is well into four figures.

The superfecta is not for those who are faint of heart or insufficiently bankrolled. Bettors who merely fool around with the superfecta without taking it seriously are destined to fail. It is a bet in which extended losing streaks are normal. The superfecta wager makes exactas and trifectas look downright tame.

An effective superfecta strategy requires two key horses: a "win key"—a horse that must win—and a "board key," a horse that must finish second, third, or fourth. The two remaining spots are spread with at least five other horses. Here is how the wager is constructed:

Win: Horse A (win key)
Place: Horse B (board key)
Show: Horses C, D, E, F, G
Fourth: Horses C, D, E, F, G
Cost of $1 bet: 1 x 1 x 5 x 4 = $20

Now, the board key is dropped into the third- and fourth-place spots:

Win: Horse A (win key)
Place: Horses C, D, E, F, G
Show: Horse B (board key)
Fourth: Horses C, D, E, F, G
Cost: 1 x 5 x 1 x 4 = $20

Win: Horse A (win key)
Place: Horses C, D, E, F, G
Show: Horses C, D, E, F, G
Fourth: Horse B (board key)
Cost: 1 x 5 x 4 x 1 = $20

That totals $60. A bettor may consider adding another ticket that allows the "board key" to finish in front of the win key.

Win: Horse B (board key)
Place: Horse A (win key)
Show: Horses C, D, E, F, G
Fourth: Horses C, D, E, F, G
Cost: 1 x 1 x 5 x 4 = $20

The total cost of this play is $80, and three things must happen. The win key must win (or finish second behind the board key); the board key must hit the board; and the remaining spots must be filled by two of the other five selections. The size of the bet can be pared to $36 or $48 by using only four other horses with the win key and board key.

A superfecta bettor should know what to aim for. Unless the field size is at least nine (approximate median payoff $1,000), why bother? Secondly, a superfecta that includes the first two betting choices often produces an underlay payoff. That is generally what happens when your opinion is the same as everyone else's. Unless one of the two favorites can be tossed, the chance for a major score decreases. Finally, a large bankroll is required. A bettor must count on extended losing streaks. Unless one's bankroll can withstand prolonged punishment, it makes more sense to focus on bets with a higher rate of success.

It is up to the individual to find a preferred technique to play vertical exotics. Here is what works for me. Bet structure depends on odds. In a vertical wager, I rarely position a higher-odds horse on top of a lower-odds horse in an exacta or trifecta. This would be a typical strategy for wagering on a 15-1 longshot:

- Win bet on the longshot.
- Exacta bet, using one or two favorites over the longshot.
- Trifecta bet, using three or four logical contenders in the one- and two-holes, and keying the longshot in third.

The amount of money allocated to each wager would depend on the level of confidence. If it was a horse I loved, I would invest most to win, and use the exacta and trifecta merely to recoup the win bet if the longshot finished second or third. If the horse was 15-1 and simply an overlay shot, I might allocate more funds to the horse finishing second or third, and use the win bet as the saver. No two situations are alike, and a horseplayer must maneuver according to circumstance.

The above strategy prevents cashing all three bets (win, exacta, and trifecta) in the same race. That is fine. The fact is, 15-1 shots finish third more often than second, and second more often than first. As for choosing not to put higher-odds horses over the longshot in the exacta or trifecta, a bettor cannot cover everything. If a 20-1 shot finishes in front of my 15-1 shot, then my analysis of the race was wrong and I deserve to lose. So be it.

When betting a wacky 50-1 longshot, a bettor might deviate from the recommendation against wheeling, and buy a $2 exacta using the entire field over the longshot. In a 12-horse field it costs $22. This is sometimes referred to as suicide insurance. When a bettor's 50-1 shot runs second, he should have the exacta for $2 regardless of which horse wins the race. Obviously, the lower the odds on the longshot, the fewer alternatives there are. If the longshot is only 8-1, it probably makes sense to only bet him to win.

A bettor cannot cover ever eventuality, every time. You must give yourself chances to make a score with a limited investment. And sometimes one cannot expect the horse to finish any higher than third anyway. If he does, you lose. Fine, turn the page.

Over time, strategy is likely to change. That is good. It means a bettor has adjusted to his personal strong suits. Looking back on my first pedigree score in 1995, I probably would not make the same play today. I would not have had the $1 trifecta that paid $934.40. But I would have had the $44.20 win mutuel on Comininalittlehot more than once. One bettor's preference is not law for another. As long as you are playing the overlays, in exotic pools and straight pools, good things can happen.

Up to this point we have covered win, place, and show betting and the vertical exotics, all of which deal with the outcome of a single race. Horizontal exotics link multiple races, and attract about 10 percent of total wagering. When horizontals are attacked with efficient strategy, they add another weapon to a bettor's arsenal. Let's move ahead, beginning with the most familiar horizontal of all—the old man called the daily double.

Daily Double

To win the daily double requires picking the winners of two consecutive races. Win odds and field size are the most influential factors in determining payoffs. In exotic-wagering pools, horses generally are bet in proportion to their odds to win. In a daily double, two races with 10 horses would mean there are 100 potential combinations—10 starters multiplied by 10 starters.

In the daily double, two $6 winners may return $20 or more, depending on field size and the odds of the other starters. The payoff is similar to a parlay, in which proceeds from one race are placed entirely on the next race. In a parlay, the $6 payoff on the first race would be carried over to the second race. When that horse wins at odds of 2-1, the payoff would be $18 ($6 bet to win at odds of 2-1). The daily double usually pays more than a parlay because the wager is subjected to takeout only once, whereas a win parlay is subjected to takeout twice.

A daily double is calculated the same way as every other wager. The takeout rate, which is higher for exotics than for win-place-show, is subtracted, as is money bet on the winning combination. The resulting amount is divided by the amount of money bet on the winning combination to determine the odds.

Daily doubles and exactas are reasonable exotic wagers for a novice to start with, because of medium- to high-priced rewards, and a reasonable chance of winning. However, a bettor should have an opinion that differs from the crowd's.

The best-case scenario for the daily double is finding a favorite or favorites to wager against—low-odds runners to throw out completely. In so doing, one can eliminate a sizable percentage of the pool and create the possibility of an overlaid payoff.

A purpose of the double is to leverage against low-odds runners, or on high-odds runners, to create a magnified payoff. That means taking a stand against a favorite in at least one leg of the bet.

The issue in constructing a double is the number of combinations that a bettor should use. When one race uses a favorite as a "key," no more than four horses should be used in the other leg, and the favorite should be excluded. A bettor going four-deep is acknowledging the favorite's vulnerability. Daily doubles that link two favorites generally are underlaid.

In a double that does not use the favorite in either leg, the suggested number of combinations is six. Two-deep in one leg and three-deep in another is plenty. It's a conservative strategy that can be adjusted to the situation. If one of the favorites that a bettor is taking a stand against is odds-on, it might be acceptable to go deeper than three horses. Regardless, the three-deep guideline is sensible. A bettor who goes any deeper is admitting to utter confusion. If one can eliminate the favorite, but not find reasonable alternatives among three other horses, then the race is tougher than it originally looked. Skip it.

Finally, as with many other exotic wagers, combining two longshots in the daily double typically produces underlay payoffs. It seems weird. Combined longshots are supposed to produce bonanza payoffs. They do, but less than they should. Their payoffs rarely correspond to fair value. It is more advisable to wager on both longshots separately to win.

As a general guideline, bettors should reconsider the wager if more than six daily-double combinations are needed. If it takes more than six to be confident the winner was included, perhaps one's understanding of the race is not so great, after all.

Pick Three

Winning the pick three requires winning three consecutive races, and typically requires purchasing more than a single combination. Few handicappers are good enough to nail three straight winners.

A typical pick-three play might look like this:

Race 1: Horse A
Race 2: Horses A, B
Race 3: Horses A, B, C, D

The above ticket demands precision in the first leg. Use just one horse, and that one horse must win. In the second leg, either of the two horses must win for the ticket to stay alive. Finally, any of the four horses used in the final leg must win. At $2 per bet, the cost of the ticket is $16. That is, eight combinations (1 x 2 x 4).

Pick-three payoffs generally correspond to the odds of the winner, and are influenced by the size of fields. The pick three is a terrific wager for economy-minded bettors, offering a chance to hit a good-sized payoff with only small money. Payoffs are calculated the same as with every other wager. First takeout is subtracted, then money wagered on the winning combination is subtracted. The remainder is divided by the amount on the winning combinations to determine the odds.

When the pick three was instituted in California in 1986, it was called the Daily Triple. It was a $3 bet offered once a day, and required a disciplined approach. The cost of the ticket increases exponentially, so the preceding example (1 x 2 x 4) would cost $24. The minimum bet gradually decreased to $1, and the wager was expanded to cover the entire card.

Because the base bet is so small, bettors get reckless. The shotgun approach (spread-spread-spread) is not advised. The pick three should be played only with a complete understanding of each race in the sequence. It means narrowing the list of contenders to a manageable number, or having the confidence to take a stand against a short-priced favorite.

At some tracks, pick threes can "roll" all day (a new pick three starts with every race), and it is easy to get caught up in the wave. For a bettor who plays rolling pick threes the entire card, only one miscalculation—or upset—means all three bets die. Of course, it also means that a "single" can be a single in three separate sequences.

Pick-three bets should be confined to series of races that a bettor understands. There are plenty of events that are indecipherable messes. Some pick-three bettors play right through those legs, and wheel the entire field. Good luck. It rarely makes sense to invest in an incomprehensible race. Bettors should almost never wager on situations that are not understood. That is particularly true for exotic wagers that have a low rate of success anyway. The worst thing for a bettor to do is lose money on races in which he does not have an opinion. There will be plenty of losing even when one does have an opinion.

A nine-race card with rolling pick threes will include seven sequences, beginning on each race from 1 through 7. If races 3 and 7 are too tough, then there is only one possible pick three to play—the one covering races 4 through 6.

Pick-three wagers can be kept small, and limits are encouraged. It is beneficial to have a nonfavorite single in at least one leg, and leave out the favorite altogether in two of the three legs. A single allows for greater leverage in the other two legs. The cost of the ticket doubles when any two horses are used in a race.

In a race without a single, a bettor should think twice before going more than three-deep. If one cannot find the winner, or the overlay, among three horses, it may reveal some misunderstanding. Skip the race. The reason to play the pick three is to magnify potential payoffs on a horse one prefers, or exploit the vulnerability of a flawed favorite. The pick three is not a bet to play just for action.

An overlay pick-three payoff depends on beating favorites in at least two of the three legs. That is because most pick-three tickets are built around the logical contenders. A pick three with three favorites rarely produces an overlay payoff. Bettors frequently play the pick three with the idea of trying to hit it regardless of the payoff, and often overbet short-priced contenders.

Like the daily double, the pick three is simple enough that it can be built around a specific horse. That means taking a stand somewhere. It might be against a low-odds favorite, or in support of a not-so-obvious overlay. Either way, the race has to be accompanied by two other legs that can be reduced to a manageable number of contenders.

Perhaps the deepest one should go is one-third of the field. In a 12-horse race, no more than four runners should be used. None of those four should be the favorite. Using the favorite and three others defeats the purpose. It would be like betting to win on a favorite, and also betting to win on three others in the same race. In a 10-horse field, a bettor should not go more than three-deep. These are arbitrary limits. A bettor must have boundaries. Without them, one might continue to add horses to a leg of the pick-three series. Next thing you know, you have wheeled the entire field.

When the pick three is too tough, a bettor may consider confining wagers to the daily double or individual races and forsake the horizontal, multiple-race wager.

In the most frequently played horizontal wagers—the pick three and the double—the idea is to leverage a single horse, or bet against a bad favorite. A slightly different approach is required for pick fours and pick sixes. Key horses—singles—are important in those bets. But in my opinion, when leveraging a key horse, a pick three is as far as one should push the envelope.

Pick-four and pick-six bets can be structured around a single horse, but are best viewed as a series of races rather than races that surround one horse. It's a different dynamic.

Pick Four

The pick four requires picking the winners of four successive races, and was first instituted regularly on the autumn 2000 wagering menu at Hollywood Park. The bet quickly gained momentum, and is now offered at most major racetracks. There is good reason for the popularity. The pick four has everything—attainable win rates, affordability, and an opportunity for good-sized scores for relatively small investments. Horseplayers nationwide poured more than $150 million into pick-four pools in 2002.

The bet pays well. The 2003 median $2 payoff was $1,840 during the Santa Anita winter meet; $1,510 at Del Mar; and $1,288 during the Belmont fall meet. Keeneland offered two pick fours daily at its 2003 spring meet, with a $1,878 median for the early pick four and a $700 median for the late pick four, which usually included a stakes race with a heavy favorite and a small field.

The pick four does not discriminate. Whereas a massive bankroll that is able to sustain long losing streaks might be required to attack the pick six or superfecta, the pick four requires a fraction of the investment. Pick-four payoffs are too small for big-ticket players to overwhelm the pool, yet big enough that winning only two or three in a season can make a bettor's year. The pick four allows small bettors to compete equally with the heavy hitters. No one "buys" an advantage.

Few bettors win the pick four by using only one horse in each race. Rather, the popular strategy is to "spread" by using several horses in some or all of the races. The cost of the wager escalates accordingly. Here is an example:

Race 1: Horse A (one horse)
Race 2: Horses A, B (two horses)
Race 3: Horses A, B, C (three horses)
Race 4: Horses A, B, C, D (four horses)

With 24 possible combinations (1 x 2 x 3 x 4 = 24) at $2 each, this hypothetical bet would cost $48.

Most pick-four bettors structure their ticket similar to the example, but it is an inefficient way to play. The reason to use multiple horses is because several have a chance. However, they do not all have the same chance. By including multiple horses in one leg, a bettor makes no differentiation between runners. The most effective pick-four strategy is to play more than one ticket, keying certain horses and relegating others to backup status.

As an example, consider a pick-four sequence in which every race has three main contenders. What if a fourth runner in each leg possesses borderline qualities? He is a fringe contender, not as good as the others, but one that cannot be completely thrown out, either. If the ticket used the fringe contender in each leg, going four-deep, the $2 ticket would be structured 4 x 4 x 4 x 4, and cost $512. Rather steep.

A more efficient strategy is to play one "main" ticket with the three top contenders, along with four "backup" tickets using the fourth horse in each leg along with the three top contenders in the other three legs. This allows a bettor to be "wrong" once in the sequence.

The tickets are easily structured, with a "top and bottom" strategy that is written out as follows. A horizontal line separates main contenders from secondary contenders.

	Race 1	Race 2	Race 3	Race 4
Main contenders	**A,B,C**	**A,B,C**	**A,B,C**	**A,B,C**
Secondary contenders	D	D	D	D

Five separate tickets are purchased, for a total cost of $378. In filling out the tickets, the bettor would dip "below the line" once on each ticket.

Main ticket:
    ABC, ABC, ABC, ABC (3 x 3 x 3 x 3) = $162

Backup tickets:
    D, ABC, ABC, ABC (1 x 3 x 3 x 3) = $54
    ABC, D, ABC, ABC (3 x 1 x 3 x 3) = $54
    ABC, ABC, D, ABC (3 x 3 x 1 x 3) = $54
    ABC, ABC, ABC, D (3 x 3 x 3 x 1) = $54

ple is for illustration; a $378 investment is high for
ays under $2,000 most of the time. Further, few pick-
nces will include exactly three main contenders and
contender. Still, the concept of backup tickets is sensi-
b.   strategy allows a bettor to miss in one of the pick-four
legs, and still have a chance to win the bet, as long as one of the
backup horses wins.

A variety of combinations can be used to structure the bet.
There may be one race in which a bettor uses no backup whatso-
ever; for example, a 5-1 medium-price horse that is singled. A bettor willing to take a stand on one horse at a fat price might stand
alone in that leg. Be right, or be knocked out. It's a bold strategy.

Let's structure a mythical pick four in which the total cost
does not exceed $100.

Race 1 main contenders: A (2-1 favorite), B (4-1), C (6-1).
   Fringe contenders: D (8-1), E (8-1).
Race 2 main contenders: A (2-1 favorite), B (4-1), C (6-1).
   Fringe contenders: D (8-1), E (8-1).
Race 3 main contenders: A (8-5 favorite), B (5-2). Fringe
   contender: C (6-1).
Race 4 main contenders: A (6-5 favorite), B (5-2). Fringe
   contender: C (6-1).

A ticket that used every horse would $450 (5 x 5 x 3 x 3).

One way to structure the bet would be to insist that at least
two favorites lose. Otherwise, the payoff will be minimal. The
intention of the pick four is to exploit overlays. It won't happen
using all favorites.

ABC, ABC, B, B = $18
ABC, BC, A, B = $12
ABC, BC, B, A = $12
BC, ABC, A, B = $12
BC, BC, A, A   = $8

That is $62, and takes care of the main contenders. That
leaves $38 to spend on backups. Same strategy: insist two
favorites lose.

```
DE, ABC, A, B   = $12
DE, BC, A, A    = $8
ABC, DE, A, B   = $12
ABC, DE, B, A   = $12
```

That gets in the backups for the first two legs. But with back-ups still left in races 3 and 4, the $100 limit has been exceeded. Concessions must be made. One of the backups will have to be scrapped. In this example, there will be no backup in race 4. Too bad. And it will also be necessary to single the race 4 favorite, the lowest price in the sequence. The logic remains sound. By allow-ing only two favorites to win, the bet would still pay well. The last two tickets will bring the cost of the bet to $114. Can you live with going $14 over budget? If not, scrap the last two tickets.

```
BC, A, C, A     = $4
A, BC, C, A     = $4
```

That is a total of 11 tickets, and seems like an awful lot of labor to spend just a little more than $100 on the pick four. And who wants to work while gambling? You know the answer—winners do. A successful pick-four strategy makes distinctions between main contenders and backups. Sound too complicated? Then don't play the bet.

Gambling on horses is supposed to be fun, and it is. The way to have fun is to win. And the way to win is by playing smart, steering clear of underlay combinations, and keying potential overlays that might be pick-four singles. Before the 2001 Del Mar meet, Southern California syndicated handicapper Bob Ike and I set out to prove that the pick four was a winnable wager.

We lost at that first meet, hitting 8 of 43. Our average daily investment was $158 (we were betting in $1 increments). At the end of the meet, we had wagered $6,823 and won back $5,192. It was a loss of $1,631. Still, only two things prevented a win-ning meet—a questionable disqualification, and botched strategy (our own fault) opening weekend. At the fall Oak Tree meet at Santa Anita, we scaled back our average daily investment to $100, yet boosted the win rate and won 8 of 30. By the end of the meet, we had invested $2,619 and won back $4,788. It was a profit of $2,169. Ahead for the year, we skipped Hollywood Park fall, and regrouped for Santa Anita.

It was a banner season. Betting an average of $184 a day into the pick four, we won 19 of 60 plays and more than doubled our investment. From $11,073 wagered, we won back $22,724. All good things eventually come to an end, and the remainder of the year we won just 5 of 52, lost back $7,706, and finally called it off early in 2003. It was a good run. Overall, we won 40 of 185 pick-four wagers, bet $30,206, and got back $34,689 for a profit of $4,483 and a return on investment of $1.14 for each dollar wagered.

Any reasonable horseplayer can do the same thing. The bet worked by using fundamental handicapping, structuring multiple tickets, and taking aggressive stands when the situation warranted. Of course, the same thing applies to the pick six. And that is a bet to which I admit—I'm in the hole.

Pick Six

The pick six is not a sensible wager for novice horseplayers. It's too tough to win, and heavy hitters willing to spend $1,000 or more daily often have an insurmountable advantage over small bettors trying to get by on nickels and dimes. Winning the pick six requires picking winners of six consecutive races. The cost of the bet increases exponentially each time more than one horse is used in a race.

A ticket that uses two horses in each race would cost $128 (2 x 2 x 2 x 2 x 2 x 2 = 64 combinations, multiplied by the $2 cost of the bet). Assuming the standard 33 percent win rate for favorites, a ticket like the one above that used the first two favorites in each leg would win only about 2.5 percent of the time. And it would not pay much if it did hit.

The pick six makes mathematical sense when there is a carryover. When no one wins the pick six, most of the pool is carried over to the following race day. It creates "positive expectation" for bettors—more money is paid out than is taken in. For example, a $100,000 pick-six carryover may generate wagers the following day of $400,000. After the 20 percent takeout is subtracted, $320,000 would be paid out. Added to the $100,000 carryover, a total of $420,000 would be paid to winning bettors, though only $400,000 was wagered into the pool. It works in theory. A bettor still has to hit the thing.

Pick-six experts suggest not bothering with the bet for less than $128. It's a lot of money for one bettor. With four other friends each chipping in a few cents more than $25, however, the bet is manageable. It should only be played on carryover days.

The pick six can be structured similarly to the pick four, with backup tickets that account for the preferred ranking of horses. A borderline contender in one race should not be used with as much "strength" as a rock-solid single in another race. Further, it is not advised to use the two-horses-in-each-race strategy. Rather than go 2 x 2, experts suggest going 1 x 4. And when a 3-5 shot is staring you in the face, go with it. There is a misimpression that one must beat the favorite every race to create a memorable payoff. It is not the case. When reasonable horses win on a carryover day, the pick six can pay $1,000 to $5,000.

A recent marketing ploy is the "guaranteed pick-six pool," in which the racetrack guarantees a minimum amount in the pool. It creates no advantage for bettors, however. It simply guarantees more money in the pool, and more winning tickets because more people play the bet. There is no positive expectation.

A small bettor who chips away at the pick six with a $16 ticket every day would be better off making a $320 play once a month. At least then, he would have a chance to hit. A novice may prefer sticking to bets in which there is a reasonable chance to win.

A few other miscellaneous bets need to be mentioned, though they have not caught on. The "place pick all" requires having a horse finish first or second in every race. The twin trifecta requires winning two consecutive trifectas. Future wagers on the Kentucky Derby and Kentucky Oaks are marketing tools used by Churchill Downs, just as the Breeders' Cup Future Wager is a marketing vehicle for the Breeders' Cup. These bets attract more publicity than handle.

There are many choices, and every bettor has an individual preference. No one horseplayer can tell another what to prefer. It's all a matter of taste and bankroll. A guy who goes to the track with $20 probably ought to stick to win bets, with an occasional double or exacta.

A horseplayer who goes in with $100 can aim a little higher, or wager more aggressively on standard bets. A pick-three or trifecta strategy is not out of line. At $200 a day, the pick four and an occasional superfecta can be considered. At $500 daily, a bettor can be as aggressive as he sees fit. Everything is fair game, including the pick six.

Regardless of how much money a bettor is willing to risk, one still must win an occasional bet to stay in action. Higher bankrolls provide cushions to ride out the extended losing streaks that are inherent in exotic wagers.

It's okay to tiptoe into the parimutuel pools, and fine to make only win bets. A novice bettor soon gets comfortable, and summons the courage and confidence to wade deeper into the exotics. Along the way, he will learn there is more to the game than mere handicapping. There is an awful lot that is strictly mental. And that is a subject for the final chapter.

8

CONCLUSION

There are many different components to handicapping successfully, and horseplayers may want everything all wrapped together, somehow. Trouble is, there is no neat-and-tidy procedure that combines the key handicapping factors—condition, class, speed, and pace—into a simple method for picking winners.

Handicapping concepts offer broad guidelines, not specific directives. There are no hard-and-fast rules, and a bettor needs to be flexible. The basic principles are relevant only when accompanied by logic and discipline. There is no "right way" to handicap, or to wager. It has taken an entire career for me to figure out that successful handicapping means you have to, well, keep trying to figure it out. This is one journey that never ends.

The whole key to playing the races successfully is to do what other bettors do not, within reason. That means respecting the crowd, but not necessarily following it. The crowd makes mistakes. So will you. And along the way, you will discover specialties. Every bettor has them. Are high-odds horses your forte? Claiming sprinters on dirt? Many horseplayers do not know the answer. That's too bad. If a bettor does not know where he is going (which races to bet), how is he ever going to get there (profit)?

Horseplayers must learn to recognize advantageous situations. Yours and mine are not the same. One way of finding specialties is to keep wagering records. It's the best way to determine mastery in certain circumstances, as well as befuddlement in others. At the very least, records let a bettor know where he stands relative to the bottom line. Horseplayers have selective memories, but wagering records do not lie. They allow a bettor to review and recognize patterns. Maybe exacta betting is a losing proposition. Perhaps the trifecta is producing an admirable 10 percent profit. Maybe a handicapper is getting killed in $10,000 claimers.

Wagering records can be as advanced as computer-generated spreadsheets, or as simple as a couple of columns in a spiral notebook. Bets are recorded by wager and race type, and provide fodder for self-analysis. No one will do it for you. Sooner or later, a bettor must accept the reality that certain types of bets, or situations, should be left alone.

Even more important, wagering records allow a bettor to identify strengths. Handicapping fundamentals do not change, but a bettor who keeps records will discover a class, surface, distance, or wager at which insight is particularly keen. It allows a greater chance of exploiting strengths, and steering clear of weak spots.

Do you know what you are good at? How much you have won or lost this year? What part of your game needs improvement? Do you habitually wager on overly ambitious exotic bets that erode your bankroll? By how much? There is no substitute for writing down every wager you make. And since most horseplayers do not keep records, the practice puts you a step ahead of the crowd, regardless of handicapping proficiency.

Want to have fun playing the races? It is not that complicated. Bet horses that are in top physical shape, and racing at proper class levels. Bet them when they possess appropriate speed figures, and have suitable running styles for the likely pace of the race. And only bet them at square prices. You are risking your own real money. Bettors who refer to winnings as "the track's money" are certain to give it right back. Know this—wagering profit is yours. It results from hard work, intelligent analysis, and managed risk. Someone who considers it anything less is destined to lose.

SEVENTH RACE

Santa Anita

FEBRUARY 28, 1999

1 MILE. (1.33²) 19th Running of THE SAN RAFAEL. Grade II. Purse $200,000 Guaranteed. 3–year–olds. By subscription of $200 each to accompany the nomination, and $2,000 additional to start, with $200,000 guaranteed, of which $120,000 to first, $40,000 to second, $24,000 to third, $12,000 to fourth and $4,000 to fifth. Early bird nominations to the 1999 Santa Anita Derby (closed Friday, December 4) are automatically eligible to the San Rafael Stakes with all fees waived. Weight, 121 lbs. Non–winners of $70,000 at one mile or over, allowed 3 lbs. Of a race of $40,000 at any distance, 6 lbs. Starters to be named through the entry box by the closing time of entries. A trophy will be presented to the owner of the winner. Closed Thursday, February 18 with 9 nominations.

Value of Race: $200,000 Winner $120,000; second $40,000; third $24,000; fourth $12,000; fifth $4,000. Mutuel Pool $745,410.00 Exacta Pool $440,979.00 Quinella Pool $58,641.00 Trifecta Pool $478,466.00

Last Raced	Horse	M/Eqt. A.Wt	PP	St	¼	½	¾	Str	Fin	Jockey	Odds $1
7Feb99 6SA1	Desert Hero	LB	3 116	4	2	4¹	4ʰᵈ	5¹½	4²	1ⁿᵏ	Nakatani C S	10.40
12Dec98 8Hol2	Prime Timber	LB	3 115	7	8	7½	6¹	4¹	1ʰᵈ	2ʰᵈ	Stevens G L	2.30
22Jan99 6SA1	Capsized	LBf	3 115	3	6	8¹	8ʰᵈ	6¹½	5²½	3ⁿᵏ	Solis A	8.70
27Jan99 6SA1	Love That Red	LBb	3 115	2	7	5ʰᵈ	5ʰᵈ	3ʰᵈ	3¹	4½	Gomez G K	19.80
24Jan99 8SA1	Honest Lady	LBb	3 115	5	3	2¹	2¹	1½	2ʰᵈ	5¹¹	Desormeaux K J	1.40
31Jan99 8SA2	Buck Trout	LB	3 121	6	5	3½	3¹½	2ʰᵈ	6⁵	6²½	Delahoussaye E	18.60
6Feb99 5SA2	Aristotle	LBb	3 115	1	1	6¹½	7¹	7¹	7²	7²½	Valdivia J Jr	6.20
6Feb99 7TuP1	Eagleton	LB	3 118	8	4	9	9	8⁶	8¹²	8	Enriquez I D	28.50
6Feb99 7TuP2	Patrick's Exit	LBb	3 117	9	9	1¹	1ʰᵈ	9	9	—	Higuera A R	99.60

Patrick's Exit:Eased

OFF AT 3:51 Start Good. Won driving. Track fast.

TIME :22², :45⁴, 1:10, 1:23, 1:36² (:22.41, :45.92, 1:10.19, 1:23.10, 1:36.45)

$2 Mutuel Prices:

4–DESERT HERO	22.80	9.00	6.40
7–PRIME TIMBER		3.60	3.00
3–CAPSIZED			5.60

$1 EXACTA 4–7 PAID $42.60 $2 QUINELLA 4–7 PAID $40.60 $1 TRIFECTA 4–7–3 PAID $261.90

B. c, (Feb), by Sea Hero–Multiply, by Easy Goer. Trainer Dollase Wallace. Bred by Sexton Hargus & Vinery (Ky).

DESERT HERO tracked the leaders while saving ground for six furlongs, lacked room inside and forced to steady sharply passing the eighth marker, was yanked to the outside and finished furiously under right hand pressure to collar PRIME TIMBER reserved while four wide on the backstretch, caught five wide into the final bend, challenged four wide around the second turn, forged to the front passing midstretch, inched away late but could not stave off the winner. CAPSIZED settled off the early pace, was caught three wide around the final bend, angled out further entering the lane and produced a strong stretch surge from the outside to narrowly miss. LOVE THAT RED eased out slightly early on the backstretch, loomed boldly three deep around the final turn, continued to battle bravely between foes thru a grueling stretch duel and narrowly missed. HONEST LADY pressed the early pace and grabbed a short advantage late on the backstretch from the inside, continued along the rail into the lane, dug in very gamely but gave ground grudgingly late. BUCK TROUT caught three wide through the opening half, outside HONEST LADY on the final turn then weakened. ARISTOTLE bobbled leaving the gate and was rank around the first turn, saved ground but failed to menace. EAGLETON three wide early, caught five wide into the final turn and tired. PATRICK'S EXIT broke a step slow, then crossed over the grab the lead, relinquished control late on the backstretch and was later eased.

Owners— 1, The Thoroughbred Corporation; 2, Jones Aaron U & Marie D; 3, Gold Spur Stable Quartucci & Stoner; 4, Wells Terry D; 5, Juddmonte Farms Inc; 6, Steinmann Heinz; 7, Paraneck Stable; 8, Weir Dennis E; 9, Bango Casby & Flansburg

Trainers— 1, Dollase Wallace; 2, Baffert Bob; 3, Lewis Lisa L; 4, Duncan Leonard M; 5, Frankel Robert; 6, Harrington Mike; 7, Bradshaw Randy; 8, Lewis Kevin; 9, Lockwood Richard L

Scratched— Lethal Instrument (14Feb99 3SA3)

Filtering out the Noise

There is a lot of stuff to weed out in order to develop a winning approach. An objective handicapper must filter out irrelevant noise, including useless tips and hyperbole. Skepticism is a good thing, because there is plenty in racing that gets overblown simply because of drama. It happened in February 1999 when the West Coast 3-year-olds were beginning their push toward the Santa Anita Derby. Desert Hero was a maiden sprint winner going into the Grade 2 San Rafael Stakes. By the time the mile race was over, the colt was billed as a superstar. All because of some traffic trouble.

"Trip handicapping" looks at how races were run, and will be run. It begins with a subjective analysis of "trouble," such as getting off to a slow start, racing wide on turns, or being checked in traffic. The challenge is quantifying the severity of the trouble, and deciding if the trouble was even relevant. No question, Desert Hero overcame trouble to win the San Rafael.

Another element of trip handicapping is analyzing a horse's past performances to see how he did what he did. If he raced alone on the lead, he may have run better than expected. If he battled through testing fractions, he may have run worse than expected. What type of trip will the horse get this time—a lonely lead, or a head-and-head duel?

In the case of Desert Hero, the primary question was, what did his traffic trouble really mean? Buried inside and behind horses as the field entered the stretch, Desert Hero was stuck, hopelessly blocked along the rail. Finally, in deep stretch, jockey Corey Nakatani jerked Desert Hero's reins to the right, steered him into the clear, and the colt exploded to win by a neck. It was courageous and dramatic. Few winners overcome trouble at such a late stage of a dirt race. But was it significant? When Desert Hero returned five weeks later, as the 5-2 second favorite in the Santa Anita Derby, that was the question facing handicappers. By some accounts, Desert Hero now was a leading Kentucky Derby contender.

Skeptics pointed out that the final quarter-mile of the San Rafael had been run in a laggardly 26.26. The field was bunched at the wire, which (on dirt) often indicates a weak race. The Beyer Speed Figure earned by Desert Hero was a subpar 95. Bottom line? The trouble was incidental relative to the slow final time of 1:36.45. Desert Hero was brave in the San Rafael, that is all. He proceeded to lose the Santa Anita Derby by seven lengths; so much for the relevance of his trouble. Drilled in the Kentucky Derby and subsequently overmatched in three other graded stakes, Desert Hero won a two-other-than allowance race in January 2000 and never raced again.

Have you messed up a similar analysis? No problem. Handicapping blunders are tolerable as long as the odds provide a guideline. It is okay to be wrong if the price is right. Go ahead and bet against vulnerable favorites at low odds. When they occasionally win, so what? High-odds horses, however, are another story.

An Open Mind

Handicappers should learn something every day. Sometimes the mistakes hurt, whether the horse was a bad favorite, such as Desert Hero, or an obtainable longshot, such as the 2003 Breeders' Cup Juvenile winner. In the weeks after Action This Day won a slow (1:45.67 for 1⅟₁₆ miles) maiden race in a three-way blanket finish, the colt blossomed. His works improved, his focus intensified, and he acted like a seasoned professional. Trainer Richard Mandella told anyone who listened that the colt had changed, and was on course for the Breeders' Cup Juvenile even though his maiden-race Beyer Speed Figure was a dreadful 79.

More than a week before the Breeders' Cup, Mandella was quoted in the October 17 *Daily Racing Form* about Action This Day. The trainer said, "He was an ugly duckling . . . that's turning into a swan. . . .Then you wonder, well, is he fast enough? I breezed him and he went in [1:12] and went 22-and-change for his last quarter. He's turning into a man."

The colt was on his way up. Mandella's confidence was encouraging—so encouraging that as the week went on it began to seem that the colt, instead of being an intriguing longshot, might actually go off as an underlay. The same bettors who had considered wagering on him began to discount him, on the premise that Mandella's hype would depress the odds, and started to look elsewhere. Once you have gotten off a horse you once liked, it is awfully hard to go back, and by race day, Action This Day was all but forgotten. Unfortunately, when it comes to keeping an open mind, some lessons are more difficult to learn than others. The odds were not depressed. Action This Day rallied from last, won the Juvenile by 2¼ lengths, and paid a whopping $55.60. Sometimes, the noise means something. The higher the odds, the more closely one should pay attention.

Action This Day was not the most likely winner going in. He was just a big, fat overlay. Stubborn handicappers have no one to blame but themselves when making decisions without considering the most important factor—the odds. Action This Day would have been a poor risk at 10-1. But his odds were 26-1. He figured to improve, and did. It was a wasted opportunity. After considering condition, class, speed, and pace, the determining factor must always be odds.

Daily Wagering Plan

Beyond understanding the handicapping requisites, successful bettors plan ahead, before getting to the track. Bettors that approach each race card with a plan of attack have a head start. A wagering plan entails a thorough review of the card beforehand, and identification of potentially advantageous situations—a race that is a specialty, or a vulnerable favorite to bet against. Field sizes are key. The smaller the field, the less chance the public will commit a mistake in assigning odds. Small-field races are good races to pass. But middle-priced contenders sometimes get lost in the shuffle in a big field.

A wagering plan merely identifies races with potential, and allows bettors to allocate capital accordingly. If the last race of the day is appealing, it makes sense to have funds available for that race. Similarly, bettors may find that the first race is the only reasonable wagering opportunity on the card. This poses a dilemma. A bettor with $100 to wager that day might play it safe and bet only $10, figuring that if he loses, there is still $90 to gamble on the rest of the card. It is not a smart way to play.

It is a sticky predicament, as a group of novice bettors discovered on Santa Anita Handicap Day 2003. The group, invited for a day at the races by the Thoroughbred Owners and Breeders Association, listened as I conducted a pre-race seminar. There was one problem—my analysis of the card included only one forceful opinion, and it coincided with the first race of the day. The entire afternoon was keyed to that one race. If I lost, I would be done for the day. But win or lose, I would be back tomorrow. The TOBA group would not. Their weekend wagering was limited to the 11 races on the Big 'Cap card.

Trekking
Own: Juddmonte Farms Inc
Green, Pink Sash, White Sleeves, Pink
ES D R (228 40 32 21 .18) 2002:(813 143 .18)

Ch. f. 4 (Jan)
Sire: Gone West (Mr. Prospector) $125,000
Dam: Didina*GB(Nashwan)
Br: Juddmonte Farms Inc (Ky)
Tr: Frankel Robert(47 13 11 6 .28) 2002:(480 117 .24)

L 118

Life	5	1	2	0	$13,635	82
2003	1	0	0	0	$2,240	82
2002	4	1	2	0	$11,395	–
SA Ⓣ	1	0	0	0	$2,240	82
D.Fst	0	0	0	0	$0	–
Wet(350)	0	0	0	0	$0	–
Turf(350*)	5	1	2	0	$13,635	82
DstⓉ(350)	0	0	0	0	$0	–

03–7SA fm 1¼ Ⓣ :48^4 1:13^4 1:37^3 2:01^4 4↑ ⒻOClm 40000N 82 8 6$^{4\frac{3}{4}}$ 6^5 6^5 5^4 4$^{3\frac{1}{2}}$↓ Flores D R LB 117 3.20 80–16 Splendeur117½ Absolute Charmer117$^{1\frac{1}{2}}$ Java119$^{1\frac{1}{2}}$ Shuffled 1/4,stdy late 10
eviously trained by Roger Charlton
02♦ Brighton(GB) gd 1¼Ⓣ LH 1:59^2 3↑ ⒻVirginia Rated Hcp (Listed) Stk 42500 12$^{24\frac{1}{2}}$ MacKay J 111 6.50 Averted View133^2 Mubkera125^{no} Celtic Ballet111$^{2\frac{1}{2}}$ 13
Rank tracking leaders,weakened 3f out
02♦ Beverley(GB) sf 1¼Ⓣ RH 2:10^2 Hull Daily Mail Maiden Stakes Maiden 11100 1¾ Darley K 121 *.50 Trekking121¾ Tanaji121¾ Alnahda121^3 4
neform rating: 76+ *Led throughout,held well*
02♦ Newmarket(GB) gd 1¼Ⓣ RH 2:05^2 Bjorn Again Maiden Stakes Maiden 9600 2no Hughes R 121 *2.75 Distinction126^{no} Trekking121$^{2\frac{1}{2}}$ Transit126^2 16
neform rating: 82 *Led for 1f,led again over 2f out,caught on line*
02♦ Newmarket(GB) gd 1¼Ⓣ Str 2:06^3 ⒻNGK Spark Plugs Maiden Stakes Maiden 11100 2$^{2\frac{1}{2}}$ Hughes R 123 5.00 Mount Street123$^{2\frac{1}{2}}$ Trekking123$^{2\frac{1}{2}}$ Ishtak123^5 14
neform rating: 82 *Led or dueled to 100y out,outpaced late by winner*
KS: Feb24 Hol 4f fst :49 H *8/36* Feb17 Hol 5f fst 1:00^2 H *7/52* Jan31 Hol 3f fst :35^3 H *2/17* Jan25 Hol 6f fst 1:13 H *2/11* Jan18 Hol 6f fst 1:14^2 H *7/15* Jan11 Hol 5f fst 1:01^1 Bg*6/24*
NER: Turf(379 .24 $1.69) Routes(413 .25 $1.70) Alw(185 .27 $1.79)

Trekking deserved a second chance after an ordinary U.S. debut. The comment lines from her first three starts included the word *led.* She had employed that front-running style to win once and finish second twice in Europe. In her first local start, however, she was rated early and unable to show speed. On Big 'Cap Day, the thought was Trekking would use her speed and race to the front. In a field without pace, she was a potentially dangerous, lonely front-runner at odds of 6-1. The group of novice bettors listened as the handicapper suggested that they unload on the race.

The group was reluctant. Who wouldn't be? A fellow they met a half-hour earlier was advising them to swing for the fences on the first race. It turned out that the recommendation was solid. Trekking made the lead, raced unchallenged out front, and won by four lengths at $14.60. The novice bettors were off to a good start on what became a good day. They won 5 of 11 races, and finished with modest profits. Most wagers, including the first race, were similarly sized. Meanwhile, I had one of my best days of the meet, based on making my biggest bet in the very first race.

This is the dilemma facing casual fans. Spread wagers thin in order to stay in action? Or play to win? It depends on the objective. Most successful bettors view each race as merely one in a series of races. No race is more important than the others. The first race on a Wednesday is the same as the last race on a Sunday. But a casual fan that simply wants to gamble all day will just have to get lucky.

Wagering plans do not need to be set in stone. There are always unexpected opportunities. One never knows when a logical contender will start at overlaid odds. A wager may not have been planned, but the situation mandates a bet. As for the type of wager, the key is to stay consistent and play to your strengths.

Strategic wagering decisions are made long before the racing begins. Handicapping author and fervent horseplayer Andrew Beyer talked about strategy.

"You should have a fairly consistent philosophy of how you play races so that you're not constantly going from one approach to another and [leaving yourself] open for second-guessing. Whenever I see the opportunity to go for the jugular—trifectas, superfectas, or whatever—I will do it. And I know that a certain percentage of the time my key horse will win and I'm going to blow. But I rarely kick myself and say, geez, I should have taken that 5-to-2. Because that's the way I play.

"The worst thing [is] if somebody half the time is going to bet the 5-2, and 50 percent of the time key him in the superfecta. You know that his head is going to be spinning with second-guessing. That is when you start getting rattled; the worst thing you can do is let yourself get thrown off track emotionally, when you're banging your head against the wall [saying] I should've done this, or I should have done that. That just sort of opens the gate for more mistakes. I don't think there's a right way or a wrong way to approach betting strategy. But have a reasonably consistent one. Okay, here's the way I play, and it didn't work out this time, but I'm not going to get upset about it because that's the consequence of my actions.

"The worst strategy is to be defensive. Lots of people say geez, I'll make some across-the-board bets, and try to be defensive. The best chance of making money over a long period of time is not because you have successfully ground out a profit. I don't know anybody who succeeds by grinding it out. It's by making the occasional big score. In the course of a single day maybe you have one decent exacta in an eight-race card and there is your whole profit. Or in the course of a year maybe there is one pick six, or a twin tri. When you look back, one or two bets in a whole year, a good year, may be your profit. But you don't want to just swing for the fences in every at-bat."

Self-Analysis

Knowing the types of races you are good at, and the bets you plan to make, will save much grief. So go ahead. Do what other people are not doing—keep records and plan ahead. And allow time for post-race analysis. Did the race unfold as expected? If not, why not? Was the expected pacesetter on the lead? If not, why not? What did you miss? Post-race examination does not necessarily include building a case for the winner, only becoming aware of the winner's attributes.

Wagering habits must be constantly evaluated. Everyone makes mistakes. Learn from them. During the 2003 summer meet at Del Mar, I engaged in a full-scale superfecta experiment. The average wager was close to $80 on the 32 plays. It was a serious test devoted to one wager. Unintentionally, I got scared and was reluctant to bet additional money in the same race as the superfecta. It cost me at least twice during the meet when super-fecta key horses finished one-two. The $1 exactas paid $35 and $22. Too bad I did not bet them.

I had surpassed my psychological wagering limit spending $80 on the superfecta, a low-percentage, single-race bet that I was pre-pared to lose. What I did not expect was how the superfecta exper-iment would affect other bets. Those two exactas for $35 and $22 were ones that should have been nailed cold. Lesson learned. When you are in over your head on one bet, other bets may suffer.

Having a Bankroll

There is an old joke about two guys walking into a racetrack.

"I hope I break even," says one.

"Why?" asks the other.

"Because I need the money."

The guy who needs the money is almost certain to lose. He may not even realize it, but he will play like a frightened kitten. Bold, potentially advantageous wagering decisions will be col-ored by the play-it-safe desire to "not lose." The bettor is likely to forsake a 15-1 shot and instead back the 8-5 favorite. It is one racetrack truth that can be supported purely by anecdotal evi-dence—scared money rarely wins.

Horseplayers who are reluctant to risk losing are virtually guar-anteed to do exactly that. Bettors must accept the possibility of defeat. If the money was budgeted for wagering, a losing day is tol-erable. But a horseplayer gets in trouble when he reaches into "other" money for a day of gambling. Don't do it.

The allocation of wagering dollars depends on several factors.

A person who goes to the races and bets two times a year may not need to put money aside for betting. Infrequent track visits will be funded from the entertainment budget. But someone who wagers frequently must plan his wagering, and eliminate the "need to win" pressure. There are enough distractions already, without being forced to deal with the outside ramifications of a losing day.

A horseplayer needs the freedom to make a wagering decision without having to consider its potential effect on the household budget. If a relationship is involved (a spouse or significant other), that person must be aware of the wagering situation. Certain disaster awaits those who wager on horses while hiding the play from a partner.

A portion of income might be allocated to "parimutuel investing." What is the appropriate amount? The only person who can answer that is you. It may depend on how one categorizes oneself as a player. A bettor that attacks low-probability, high-reward wagers such as the superfecta may need to replenish his wagering bankroll monthly. Another bettor that bets primarily to win and has a greater chance of short-term success may not need to replenish his bankroll as often.

This is a worst-case scenario, of course. Ideally, a horseplayer wins consistently, his bankroll mushrooms, and there is money even after a losing day. Bettors should have wagering funds beyond what is in their pockets. There is nothing like a stack of $100 bills that provides renewed confidence. The important thing is to separate wagering money from living expenses. There is more than enough second-guessing in handicapping. When the household budget fails to balance because of overextension at the betting windows, a reevaluation of priorities is in order.

Losing streaks are inevitable, regardless of expertise. With a steady source of wagering capital, losing streaks need not destroy. The duration of losses depends on the types of bets. A bettor whose play centers on low-odds horses will not lose as many consecutive races as a bettor playing exotic wagers or longshots. The essentials to survive a losing streak are consistent strategy and a separate bankroll.

One should have an idea of bet size. One recommendation is "percent of bankroll" wagers on win bets, up to 3 percent of overall bankroll. No argument, though the rigidity of the scheme may be ill-suited for a bettor who plays a variety of wagers such as pick threes, exactas, and win pools. As difficult as it can be during a long string of losses, a horseplayer must be able to view the long-range picture. Then, short-term losses are merely a nuisance, rather than a problem.

Confidence While in a Slump

It is not always easy to shake a slump. In early 2001, I was mired in a wagering funk. The Santa Anita winter meet came and went, and nothing happened worth bragging about, or crying about. I lost $584, certainly not the worst meet of my career. But it was all plain vanilla. No hits, no scores. On average, I was getting back 88 cents for every dollar wagered. A public handicapper should do better. But I wasn't. Having wagered $5,114 at the meet, I had won back only $4,530. I could have done as well betting favorites every race. The doldrums continued into the spring-summer racing season. Two months into the Hollywood Park meet, my return on investment had dwindled to 72 cents on the dollar. Talk about a tailspin. My average daily handle declined still further.

D Scott		

It was July 1, Hollywood Gold Cup Day; the track was giving away Chris McCarron bobble-head dolls. McCarron was riding the favorite in race 4—Von Stauffenberg, who had shown promise in his only start. My eye was on a first-time starter with higher odds. I liked his pedigree, he had worked well, and his trainer occasionally struck with longshot first-timers. Ran D Scott was the second-likeliest winner, yet his odds were a whole lot higher than the favorite's.

I planned my only wager that day on the firster, and arrived minutes before the race. I looked at the odds board and was stunned. Ran D Scott was an open secret. His odds had dropped to just 3-1. It is foolish to wager on a first-time starter at such low odds, but I did so anyway. Sometimes, you lose your senses in the middle of parimutuel freefall. I made the bet—$50 to win—and shuffled up to the Hollywood press box feeling embarrassed. By the time I sat down and looked at the program again, the horses had almost reached the starting gate.

That is when I realized my blunder. I had mistaken the program numbers and wagered on the wrong horse. What a moron. In fact, the horse I originally planned to bet was totally ignored. Ran D Scott was hanging on the tote board at odds of nearly 30-1. Now what? I had about 90 seconds to decide.

First, I canceled the mistaken wager. But how much should I bet on the longshot? Moments earlier I had been willing to risk it all at odds of 3-1. Did I have the courage to do the same at odds of 30-1? The field loaded into the gate. I changed my bet—$50 to win on a longshot first-time starter. It was a good-sized swing, and here I was, in an extended slump.

The firster was bred for speed, but he had none. Down the backstretch of the six-furlong sprint, he was next-to-last. Jockey Eddie Delahoussaye was sitting chilly, and Ran D Scott picked up steam into the turn. He began passing horses rapidly, one after another. Suddenly, an emergency. He ran up on the heels of a rival and steadied hard at the quarter pole. His momentum was lost. I muttered something obscene.

The field turned for home, and Ran D Scott was next-to-last again. But he had gathered himself, and starting running. With a furlong remaining, seven horses were in front of him. He was flying on the outside, eating up ground. It was going to be close. Then, it wasn't. Yards from the wire, Ran D Scott hit the front and won going away. He paid $60.20 for $2, and set the stage for one of the longest win streaks of my wagering career—nine months. From ice-cold to red-hot in 1:10.40. This game will turn that quickly.

Later that day, the crowd overlooked another appealing long-shot, in the Grade 2 Triple Bend Handicap. He was moving up in class after a better-than-it-looked effort at lower odds in a weaker race. Ceeband won the Triple Bend and paid $91.80. I had him, and only because of Ran D Scott. Lucky streak? Call it what you want.

The mere use of the term *streak* implies an element of luck. It is true that luck plays a factor in individual races, but fortune—ill or good—usually evens out over the long haul. Employ the handicapping fundamentals, use imagination, bet the overlays, and good things will happen.

est Secrets									
Oxley Debby M		B. f. 3 (May) Sire: Forest Wildcat (Storm Cat) $40,000 Dam: Garden Secrets (Time for a Change) Br: William Patterson & James Glenn (Ky) Tr: Ward J T Jr(0 0 0 0 .00) 2003:(90 17 .19)							
1–7CD fst 1	:23 :46³ 1:11²1:36¹	ⓅAlw 44200n1x	87	1	2ʰᵈ 1ʰᵈ 1½ 1ʰᵈ 2ⁿᵒ	Albarado R J	L121	*1.20 86– 14 DsignrPhon118ⁿᵒ ForstScrts121⁷½ SvnFourSvn118¾	Drft out late,good try 6
1–3Kee fst *7f	:22² :46 1:11⁴1:28²	ⓅMd Sp Wt 50k	76	7 1	11½ 1ʰᵈ 12½ 14¼	Chavez J F	L118	*1.30e 82– 15 Forest Secrets118⁴¼ About Respect113¹ Oval118ⁿᵏ	Pace, ridden out 11

ory Ride									
umphrey G W Jr		B. f. 3 (Mar) Sire: Seeking the Gold (Mr. Prospector) $150,000 Dam: Young Flyer (Flying Paster) Br: Mr. & Mrs. John C. Mabee (Ky) Tr: Arnold G R II(0 0 0 0 .00) 2003:(259 34 .13)							
–5Bel fst 7f	:23 :45³ 1:09⁴1:22	3↑ⓅAlw 43000n1x	101	1 1	1½ 11½ 1⁷ 1⁷	Samyn J L	L117 f	*.20 93– 15 Victory Ride117⁷ Quick Blue115¹½ Kiss a Miss115⁵	When ready, hand ride 5
–4Kee fst 7f	:22¹ :45¹ 1:10²1:22¹	ⓅMd Sp Wt 48k	108	10 3	2¹ 11¹ 1³ 114¼	Day P	L119 f	*1.40 91– 14 VictoryRide119¹⁴½ LauriesBld119⁷ PrdisePond119³¼	Ridden out,much best 11

Hard Lessons

Many lessons are learned the hard way. A special daily double linking the 2001 Acorn Stakes on June 8 and the Belmont Stakes the next day served as a reminder that pairing two long-shots in an exotic wager often produces underlay payoffs. It is better to wager separately on each longshot. The Acorn field was evenly matched, with several qualified to win. Victory Ride was the high-figure filly. Bettors stuck on speed figures had only one decision—bet or pass? On numbers, no one else was close. But at 1.45-1, Victory Ride offered minimal value, which was no surprise. Most horseplayers never seem to get enough of speed. Value-oriented handicappers, however, often find themselves wagering against the figure. It was not difficult in the Acorn.

There were a number of "value" possibilities among the seven other starters. One filly embodied an angle that, year after year, produces staggering payoffs: Back high-odds horses moving up in class following a loss at lower odds, on the provision the maneuver is reasonable and executed by a winning stable. (Triple Bend winner Ceeband also fit the angle.)

On every inspection, it makes sense. The high-odds guideline allows a comfortable margin for error. The up-in-class criterion addresses the issue of condition. Horses moving up in class usually have accompanying good form, or reason for improvement.

The "lower odds in last start" component adds further assurance to the issue of condition. A horse whose odds are relatively low generally is in acceptable current form. The "reasonable-maneuver" warning must be loosely interpreted. Bettors must determine if a move makes sense. An in-the-money finish last out, for example, gives horse and trainer license to move on. Finally, the move must be done by a reputable trainer. This weeds out starry-eyed dreamers with borderline credentials. The procedure does not attempt to address the credentials of the favorite; it only offers a longshot alternative.

Forest Secrets was 50-1 and moving up in class following a second-place finish at 6-5. The maneuver made sense. Aside from speed figures, her past performances mirrored Victory Ride's. Both had scored runaway debut victories, and followed with sharp efforts versus allowance foes. Finally, Forest Secrets was trained by John Ward. Just five weeks earlier, he had won the Kentucky Derby with Monarchos, a high-odds horse moving up in class after a loss at a lower price.

Forest Secrets outran expectations and paid $102.50. Genius? Hardly. The score was nothing more than reasonable application of a tried-and-true wagering angle—betting high-odds horses moving up after a loss. The celebration lasted only until the Acorn-Belmont "will-pays" were posted later on the *Daily Racing Form* website. From a 50-1 winner in the first leg, the $2 doubles were paying as follows.

Point Given, $417

Monarchos, $600

A P Valentine, $710

Balto Star, $748

Dollar Bill, $903

Invisible Ink, $973

Thunder Blitz, $992

Dr Greenfield, $1,184

Buckle Down Ben, $1,923

In shopping for a price, I had keyed the wrong longshot in the Belmont—Balto Star at 12-1. While the front-runner was never going to beat 6-5 favorite Point Given, expectations were for a greater discrepancy in daily-double payoffs. Balto Star went to post in the Belmont at nearly nine times the odds of Point Given, but the daily double would have paid less than twice as much.

Bettors clever enough to find Forest Secrets only needed to accept Belmont favorite Point Given to win a $417 daily double. Others were left with a $2 win ticket on a $100 horse, and a daily-double story about the one that got away.

Of course, there also are the unforgettable bets that you land against all odds. One of the great things about betting horses is that you never know when several details will add to something memorable. Every day is filled with opportunity, even when least expected. You cannot force parimutuel victory. Sometimes you have to take a deep breath, relax, and let the game come to you.

It happened in 1996 at Santa Anita, when trainer D. Wayne Lukas entered a 3-year-old in a one-other-than allowance sprint on February 15. It would be the colt's first start in seven months. Unexpectedly, Lukas scratched the colt from the sprint, and entered him in a mile race around two turns the following day. It was unusual; the colt had never raced a route of ground. At the time, Lukas typically started a layoff horse in a sprint, then stretched him to two turns for his next start.

THIRD RACE													

THIRD RACE
Santa Anita
FEBRUARY 16, 1996

1 MILE. (1.33²) ALLOWANCE . Purse $46,000 FOR THREE–YEAR–OLDS WHICH ARE NON–WINNERS OF EITHER $3,000 OTHER THAN MAIDEN, CLAIMING OR NON–WINNERS OF TWO RACES. 120 lbs. Non–Winners of a race other than maiden or claiming at one mile or over allowed 3 lbs.; of such a race other than claiming, 5 lbs.

Value of Race: $46,000 Winner $25,300; second $9,200; third $6,900; fourth $3,450; fifth $1,150. Mutuel Pool $301,846.00 Exacta Pool $251,282.00 Quinella Pool $45,719.00

Last Raced	Horse	M/Eqt.	A.	Wt	PP	St	¼	½	¾	Str	Fin	Jockey	Odds $1
18Jan96 3SA¹	Budroyale	LB	3	116	5	2	11½	11	1½	12½	13	Delahoussaye E	2.70
1Jly95 9CD⁴	Grindstone	B	3	115	6	7	7	5½	4½	2½	2¾	Stevens G L	1.60
12Jan96 3SA³	Tibet	LB	3	117	2	4	3½	4½	5½	3hd	3nk	Desormeaux K J	2.10
26Jan96 4SA¹	Homecoming Flag	LB	3	115	4	1	2½	2¹	2hd	43	47½	Nakatani C S	8.70
12Jan96 3SA⁹	Oblomov–GB	LB b	3	115	3	5	5hd	7	64	5½	51	Douglas R R	34.40
3Feb96 6SA¹	Pugnacious	LB b	3	115	7	3	41½	3hd	3½	67	69	Antley C W	18.40
12Jan96 8SA¹	Case History	LB b	3	115	1	6	6hd	6½	7	7	7	McCarron C J	28.80

OFF AT 2:00 Start Good For All But. Won . Track fast.

TIME :22⁴, :47, 1:11², 1:36 (:22.95, :47.01, 1:11.40, 1:36.01)

$2 Mutuel Prices:

5 – BUDROYALE	7.40	3.60	2.40
6 – GRINDSTONE		3.40	2.20
2 – TIBET			2.20

$0 EXACTA 5–6 PAID $26.00 $0 QUINELLA 5–6 PAID $11.80

B. g, (Jan), by Cee's Tizzy – Cee's Song , by Seattle Song . Trainer Puhich Michael. Bred by Cecilia Straub Revocable Trust (Cal).

Owners– 1, Kirkwood Al and Saundra S; 2, Overbrook Farm; 3, Dizney Donald R; 4, Arrias Fred and Restaino Robert; 5, Cronin Robert J and Golden State Stable; 6, Garber Gary M; 7, Stull Tom and Wilson James R

Trainers– 1, Puhich Michael; 2, Lukas D Wayne; 3, Hess R B Jr; 4, Baffert Bob; 5, Walsh Kathy; 6, Cross David C Jr; 7, Machowsky Michael

That was the first indication that Grindstone might have been more advanced than expected. There was no doubt after he ran over a track that produced a series of front-running, rail-skimming winners. It was an inside-speed bias of the highest magnitude. Grindstone lacked speed, raced four-wide, made a run at pacesetter Budroyale into the lane, and finished second. His runner-up effort was nothing short of sensational. Racing wide, against the grain of the bias, he was defeated by only three lengths in a solid time of 1:36. The notations went into my race chart. A single plus mark indicates a better-than-it-looked effort. Grindstone got three of them.

There was only one thing to do—check Grindstone's future-book odds in Las Vegas. He was 40-1 to win the Kentucky Derby. I bet. One month later, Grindstone was on his way to Fair Grounds for the Louisiana Derby, only the second start of his 3-year-old year. It was already March, by which time Lukas's other 3-year-olds—Honour and Glory, Editor's Note, Prince Of Thieves, and Victory Speech—were much further developed. Grindstone was merely an afterthought, and though he would start at 2.40-1 in the Louisiana Derby, his Kentucky Derby odds in Las Vegas remained fat. At 40-1, I bet again.

Grindstone crushed the Louisiana Derby field by 3½ lengths, beating no one of consequence, but doing it impressively. He received scant recognition, however, because one day earlier, Breeders' Cup Juvenile winner Unbridled's Song had roared to a 5¾-length triumph in the Florida Derby, earning a 114 Beyer Speed Figure, compared to the 102 Beyer earned by Grindstone in Louisiana. Another month passed, and Grindstone maintained form. On the eve of the April 13 Arkansas Derby at Oaklawn Park, Grindstone was 30-1 to win the Kentucky Derby. I bet, for the third time.

Breaking from the impossible post 12 in a 1⅛-mile race at Oaklawn, Grindstone came up a neck short and finished second. It did not matter; he had done enough. It was on to Churchill Downs, along with the other four Lukas colts. Unflattering rumors about Grindstone's suspect physical condition floated coast to coast during Derby Week. I could only hope he would be in the starting gate, because the Derby was coming apart. Unbridled's Song had foot trouble. Blue Grass winner Skip Away was training poorly over the Churchill Downs surface. The race suddenly was wide open.

You can guess the rest. Jerry Bailey produced a flawless ride, guiding Grindstone from 15th to first, winning the Derby by a nose over Cavonnier. Grindstone never ran again, and I have not cashed a Derby future wager on an individual horse since. But I landed that jackpot, which was based on Lukas's management of the colt (scratching from a sprint to go in a route), and recognition of a blatant racetrack bias that compromised Grindstone in his sterling runner-up comeback.

You never know when you will get lucky. Preparation meets opportunity when least expected. I often remind myself that while performing the repetitive tasks required of a handicapper. A lot of mundane stuff goes on behind the scenes. The fundamentals covered earlier in this text remain more important than incidental details, but a successful horseplayer often looks beyond condition, class, speed, and pace.

A handicapper must change in order to stay abreast of—or ahead of—the competition. My first season as a full-time turf writer and handicapper was the 1988 winter meet at Santa Anita, before Beyer Speed Figures were widely published. I subscribed to the Southern California publication "Handicapper's Report," which provided speed figures, race commentary, and workout reports from a private clocker. The HR figures were an elixir. That winter, my interpretation of the figures enabled me to become the leading California newspaper handicapper, in my first year on the job. But after Winning Colors buried the Santa Anita Derby field and won the Kentucky Derby, I realized I had an awful lot to learn.

A turf writer ought to be able to recognize brilliance. But if there is a learning curve to handicapping, there also is one to reporting on the sport. The only thing I saw when Winning Colors won the Santa Anita Derby was a big filly beating males by a large margin—7½ lengths. I missed the significance of her sizzling half-mile in 45.60, and six furlongs in a blazing 1:09.40. That spring was my first trip to Churchill Downs. I could have brought some California expertise to Kentucky, if I had any.

All I had was wide-eyed wonder. And when the field for the 1988 Kentucky Derby came onto the track and the band started playing "My Old Kentucky Home," I got all choked up. California turf writer Bob Mieszerski was in front of me while the band played, and the horses paraded by. My only hope was that Mieszerski would not turn around to say something. Thank goodness, he didn't. There is absolutely no proof that I cried at my first Kentucky Derby.

I had a lot to learn when I got home from Kentucky. "Handicapper's Report" was selling a telephone handicapping analysis of each day's card, which they replayed for free every night. It became part of my evening ritual—listening to handicappers Jeff Siegel and Bob Selvin explain why they liked certain horses, and how the races should be played. It was a 10-minute handicapping seminar, five nights a week, and it taught me a lot.

As Beyer Speed Figures entered the mainstream and payoffs dropped on high-figure horses, it became clear that an additional edge was required. I was introduced to the computerized handicapping program All-in-One. After much experimentation, I determined I could handicap better than a computer. The oddity is that I still use All-in-One, though not to handicap. The program is based partly on "track profiles," which is the early running position of winners. They show if a particular distance favors early speed, or another distance favors pressers. There may be a post-position bias that has been overlooked.

Data is inputted from race charts (a five-minute daily chore) into the All-in-One program, which sorts and provides up-to-date track profiles. It sounds like drudgery. But at least for me, track profiles are a necessity. I need to know what is happening on the track, by more than memory.

The handicapping portion of All-in-One taught an invaluable lesson—the importance of assigning fair odds at which a horse should be bet. The program produced an odds line on the top contenders. If they went off any higher, it was acceptable to make a bet. The program underscored the essence of successful betting—wagering on horses whose odds are out of whack with their true chances to win.

I was rusty when I returned to Southern California in 1998, after a 2½-year hiatus in Phoenix. To prepare for my return, I imitated New York colleague Dave Litfin, a meticulous record-keeper. Litfin clipped past performances of each winner and filed them under the trainer's name. Great, still more tedious paperwork. Before returning to California, I clipped and filed each winner's past performances for the three previous race meets. The one-season experiment has grown to years of data—past performances of every Southern California winner, filed under trainer, since 1998. There is no better way to get familiar with the nuances of a trainer, or a class level. The time-consuming procedure offers keen insight to trainer idiosyncrasies that is unavailable anywhere else.

ddy Grace (17½) Dk. b or br g. 3 (May) Life 0 M 0 0 $0 – D.Fst 0 0 0 0 $0 –
Everest Stables Inc Sire: Petionville (Seeking the Gold) $7,500 2002 0 M 0 0 $0 – Wet(450*) 0 0 0 0 $0 –
, Red Mountain Emblem On Back, Red (§/) $32,000 Dam: Too Charming (Capote) 120 2001 0 M 0 0 $0 – Turf(257) 0 0 0 0 $0 –
EZ G K (28 4 6 3 .14) 2001:(691 104 .15) Br: Everest Stables Inc (Ky) SA 0 0 0 0 $0 – Dist 0 0 0 0 $0 –
Tr: Carava Jack(14 1 3 0 .07) 2001:(355 74 .21)

KS: Dec31 S A 4f fst :483 H 18/46 Dec20 S A 4f fst :484 Hg 17/44 Dec13 S A 6f fst 1:14 H 17/25 Dec6 S A 5f fst 1:012 H 15/40 Nov28 S A 5f fst 1:01 H 14/56 Nov21 S A 4f fst :483 H 12/40
Nov14 S A 3f fst :353 H 6/25 Sep27 Ell 2f fst :261 B 2/5
NER: 1stStart(19 .26 $3.28) Dirt(314 .21 $1.90) Sprint(267 .21 $1.96) MdnClm(61 .26 $2.47)

It takes courage to embrace a first-time starter. Who really knows how good he will be in competition? But after clipping and filing dozens of past performances on trainer Jack Carava's horses, a pattern emerged with his debut winners. They all had increasingly longer works leading up to a six-furlong drill, followed by consecutive four-furlong works before the debut. Carava struck twice during the 2000-01 Santa Anita winter meet with longshot firsters that fit the pattern, and Daddy Grace, on January 10, was the first one of the 2001-02 winter meet. Based on this knowledge—call it inside information—and contempt for the rivals that Daddy Grace was facing, he was my top selection in *Daily Racing Form*. He won by three lengths, and returned $22.20. It was a winner I would not have had without imitating Liftin's procedure.

Video race replays are another invaluable reference tool. While one can visualize a race by merely examining past performances or race charts, there is no substitute for watching exactly what happened, either live or on video. Many racetracks have kiosks that offer push-button replays of races at their tracks, while a number of websites offer race replays.

Watching a race replay allows a handicapper to note subtleties that may not show up in published data. A horse that is uncomfortable racing behind and between horses may not be "rank," but if he is running with his head held high in the air and his jockey is having an uneasy time controlling him, the horse might be worth a second chance under different conditions. You never know what you might find while watching a replay. It was during summer 2000 when something looked unusual on the video of American Lady's last start. It was not entirely clear—in handicapping, what is?—but her odds were sufficiently appealing to find out.

American Lady	Dk. b or br f. 2 (Apr)	Blinkers ON	Life 2 M 0 0	$0	D.Fst 2 0 0 0	$0 27
Own: Marshall Robert W	Sire: Latin American (Riverman) $2,500					
	Dam: Unconditionally (Silver Hawk)		2000 2 M 0 0	$0	Wet 0 0 0 0	$0 —
	$28,000 Br: Robert W Marshall (Ky)	L 116	1999 0 M 0 0	$0	Turf 0 0 0 0	$0 —
. MARTINEZ F F (49 8 10 5 .16) 2000:(108 13 .12)	Tr: Marshall Robert W (16 5 1 1 .31) 2000:(36 9 .25)		Hol 2 0 0 0	$0	Dist 1 0 0 0	$0 27

7Jun00–8Hol fst 5f	:22² :46¹	:59	⑦Md 40000 (40–35)	27 6 3 4½ 7⁷½ 8¹² 9¹⁴½	Jauregui L H	LB 118	21.80 72–19 SilkyGoose118⁶ ThunderValley118⁵ BetsAFlying113ⁿᵏ	Weakened outside 1H
3May00–4Hol fst 4½f	:21⁴ :45³	:52	⑦Md Sp Wt 46k	22 6 7 8¹⁰	8¹⁵ 8¹⁵½	Desormeaux K J	B 118	24.00 79–16 ShineUpC(e)118ⁿᵒ NotbleCreer118² GoldnBilt118²½	Off bit slow,gave way H
WORKS: Jun22 Hol 3f fst :36³ Hg4/11	Jun1 Hol 5f fst 1:02¹ H 19/25	May26 Hol 4f fst :49³ H 19/33	May14 Hol 3f fst :37 Hg7/22	Apr27 Hol 4f fst :50 Hg23/28	Apr21 Hol 4f fst :49 H 16/28			

The past performances showed that American Lady "popped and stopped" in her second start. No big deal. But the video was more revealing. Between the start call and the first pace call, American Lady produced a burst of speed that could not be conveyed in black and white. I thought the filly might be able to carry her speed farther next time. At worst, she figured to set the early pace.

In the *Daily Racing Form* handicapping analysis, she was the third preference, with the comment: "American Lady is either the best longshot gamble on the card, or a complete waste of time . . . might be able to run more than she has shown so far. She now gets blinkers, switches to a jockey that this barn has had success with, and she will start at a huge price." American Lady broke on top while half the field got wiped out by trouble at the start, and raced gate to wire, winning by 6½ lengths at $75.20. American Lady was a winner I never would have found without watching video.

Nor would she have been found without first considering the handicapping basics. American Lady's rivals were weak—off form, outclassed, too slow, or unsuited to the pace demands of a maiden-claiming sprint. The winner was a gold nugget in a bad field, uncovered through handicapping logic and creative interpretation. In racing, you never know when you will find treasure. There is no shortage of parimutuel gold if you dig in the right places.

The nuggets are not always easy to find, of course, and using the right tools is essential. For a horseplayer, it begins with sensible application of the fundamentals. Good handicapping usually boils down to condition, class, speed, and pace. Most winners are physically fit, racing at an appropriate level of competition, fast enough for that level, and suited to the likely rate of speed.

It's not that difficult. A little common sense goes a long way. Sensible handicapping that dares to be different affords bettors a reasonable chance to win. Sometimes, being different means nothing more than being prepared. Even a beginning handicapper can recognize what a logical contender looks like in the past performances. Most races include more than one contender. "Which horse to bet?" is the wrong question. Remember, racing has little room for neat and tidy, black and white, yes or no.

Want to win at the races? Ask yourself which horse's odds are out of proportion to his chances to win. Do not be afraid to be wrong, as long as the price is right. And remember—an individual horseplayer can never know it all. That's good. It means all of us have a lot left to learn.

Handicapping is a lifelong pursuit. And along the way, there is nothing better than an afternoon of playing—and winning—at the races.